Assessment and Case Formulation in
Cognitive Behavioural Therapy

GW00391787

Assessment and Case Formulation in
Cognitive Behavioural Therapy

Second
Edition

Sarah Corrie
Michael Townend
Adrian Cockx

Los Angeles | London | New Delhi
Singapore | Washington DC

Los Angeles | London | New Delhi
Singapore | Washington DC

SAGE Publications Ltd
1 Oliver's Yard
55 City Road
London EC1Y 1SP

SAGE Publications Inc.
2455 Teller Road
Thousand Oaks, California 91320

SAGE Publications India Pvt Ltd
B 1/I 1 Mohan Cooperative Industrial Area
Mathura Road
New Delhi 110 044

SAGE Publications Asia-Pacific Pte Ltd
3 Church Street
#10-04 Samsung Hub
Singapore 049483

Editor: Susannah Trefgarne
Assistant editor: Laura Walmsley
Production editor: Rachel Burrows
Marketing manager: Camille Richmond
Cover design: Lisa Harper-Wells
Typeset by: C&M Digitals (P) Ltd, Chennai, India
Printed and bound by CPI Group (UK) Ltd,
Croydon, CR0 4YY

First edition published 2008. Reprinted 2008, 2009, 2010,
2011, 2012, 2014

This second edition published 2016

Library of Congress Control Number: 2015939913

British Library Cataloguing in Publication data

A catalogue record for this book is available from
the British Library

ISBN 978-1-4739-0275-6
ISBN 978-1-4739-0276-3 (pbk)

At SAGE we take sustainability seriously. Most of our products are printed in the UK using FSC papers and boards.
When we print overseas we ensure sustainable papers are used as measured by the PREPS grading system.
We undertake an annual audit to monitor our sustainability.

Contents

List of Figures and Tables

Figures

Tables

About the Authors and Contributors

Sarah Corrie is a Consultant Clinical Psychologist and Visiting Professor at Middlesex University. She is currently Programme Director of the Postgraduate Diploma & MSc in Cognitive Behavioural Psychotherapy at Central and North West London NHS Foundation Trust in conjunction with Royal Holloway, University of London, Programme Director of the Certificate in CBT Skills, and Programme Director of the Post-Qualification Certificate in CBT Supervision. A central focus of Sarah's career has been her commitment to, and passion for, supporting the career development and well-being needs of professional practitioners which has been the subject of much of her writing and research. Sarah was Chair of the British Psychological Society's Special Group in Coaching Psychology between 2012 and 2014, and is a faculty member of the Professional Development Foundation, Membership Officer for the International Association for Professional Practice Doctorates and a member of the Course Accreditation Committee of the BABCP.

Michael Townend is a Reader in Cognitive Behavioural Psychotherapy at the University of Derby where he teaches and researches cognitive behavioural psychotherapy. He is a Consultant in Cognitive Behavioural Psychotherapy at the SPIRE Parkway Hospital Solihull. Michael was the founding Editor of the BABCP Journal, *The Cognitive Behavioural Therapist*. He is currently Programme Leader for the Doctorate in Health and Social Care Practice and is passionate about the development of practice-based evidence to underpin therapeutic work that has compassion and the therapeutic relationship at its heart.

Adrian Cockx currently works as a High Intensity CBT Therapist with the Brent IAPT Service in North West London as part of Central and North West London NHS Foundation Trust. He has worked in the field of mental health for over 20 years although his introduction to the field of mental health started as a cleaner working in a psychiatric hospital in 1991. Fascinated by the way individuals perceived reality Adrian trained as a mental health nurse in 1993 and since has worked in forensic services, in-patient services, community mental health and as a senior lecturer, prior to undertaking training to become a cognitive psychotherapist in 2003. Adrian's passions have always been centred around client work and despite having had the opportunity to undertake training with many specialists in the field, he always maintains that his greatest teachers are the clients with whom he works.

Katy Bradbury is a Clinical Psychologist and an accredited cognitive behavioural psychotherapist. She works clinically for the National Health Service in London and has extensive experience working with people who present with a variety of complex mental and physical health difficulties. She has a special interest in working with clients who have long term chronic pain conditions. She is an Associate Assessor on the Central North West London NHS Foundation Trust Postgraduate Diploma in Cognitive Behavioural Therapy and provides training, lectures and supervision in numerous aspects of CBT.

Sandra Bucci is a Senior Lecturer in the School of Psychological Sciences at The University of Manchester, UK, and a Clinical Psychologist at Manchester Mental Health and Social Care Trust. Sandra has been involved in clinical research in psychosis for 15 years. Her research interests include psychological mechanisms involved in voice hearing and psychological treatments for psychosis. Sandra has worked on a number of research council funded CBT trials in both Australia and the UK and in more recent years has focused on developing innovative methods to increase access to psychological therapies for people with serious mental health problems.

Kate Daley is a Clinical Psychologist and Accredited CBT Therapist. Since qualifying she has worked within a number of IAPT Services, specialising in delivering group and individual interventions to those with depression and anxiety disorders. Kate has a particular interest in adult mental health and working within organisational systems.

Simon Darnley is currently Head of Clinical Pathways for a wide range of mental health services in Lambeth, London. Prior to this he was the Principal CBT Therapist and Manager of the residential unit at the Bethlem Hospital that specialises in the national treatment of people with resistant anxiety disorders, especially OCD and BDD. He completed his mental health nurse training in 1985 before training under Professor Marks in CBT for a wide range of anxiety disorders. Simon was lecturer in CBT for many years, providing training and supervision for nurse therapists. He has worked in many services and has a wide range of clinical and research interests, publishing and speaking on many subjects from irritable bowel syndrome to trichotillomania. He is also an award winning magician and member of the Magic Circle.

Kate Davidson is Honorary Professor of Clinical Psychology at the University of Glasgow. She is a Fellow of the British Psychological Society and Honorary Fellow of BABCP. Her previous Health Service post in the NHS in Scotland was Director of the Glasgow Institute of Psychosocial Interventions. She was also Director of the South of Scotland CBT course for over 20 years. She now works as Editor of an academic journal, CBT trainer and as a practitioner.

Alec Grant is currently Reader in Narrative Mental Health in the School of Health Sciences at the University of Brighton. He qualified as a mental health nurse in the mid-1970s and went on to study psychology, social science and psychotherapy. He was until 2009 the course leader for the MSc in Cognitive Psychotherapy at the University of Brighton, and was triple accredited with the British Association of Behavioural and Cognitive Psychotherapies, as practitioner, teacher and supervisor. He is widely published in the fields of ethnography, autoethnography, narrative inquiry, clinical supervision, cognitive behavioural psychotherapy, and communication and interpersonal skills. His current and developing scholarly interests coalesce broadly in the area of narrative research, and postmodern and poststructural developments in qualitative inquiry, in mental health and other health care areas.

Nick Grey is a Consultant Clinical Psychologist and Joint Clinical Director of the Centre for Anxiety Disorders and Trauma (CADAT), South London and Maudsley NHS Foundation Trust, King's Health Partners. He is accredited as a practitioner, supervisor and trainer with the British Association of Behavioural and Cognitive Therapies. He is the editor of *A Casebook of Cognitive Therapy for Traumatic Stress Reactions* (2009, Routledge) and joint editor of *How to Become a More Effective CBT Therapist* (2014, Wiley).

Gillian Haddock is Head of the Clinical and Health Section in the School of Psychological Sciences and Lead for the Centre for New Treatments and Understanding in Mental Health (CeNTrUM) at the University of Manchester and is Honorary Consultant Clinical Psychologist in Manchester Mental Health and Social Care Trust. She has been awarded over £5 million in external research funds with colleagues on trials evaluating psychological therapies for people with psychosis, and has 20 years' experience in conducting clinical trials within the NHS. She has numerous publications in this area and is the editor of two clinical books describing the development of CBT approaches for people with psychosis.

Helen Macdonald is an accredited Cognitive Behavioural Psychotherapist, Supervisor and Trainer, Mental Health Nurse and Health Psychologist. She specialises in treating adults who have persistent pain, long-term health conditions and trauma, teaches internationally on CBT for Pain Management, and is co-author of the self-help book *Overcoming Chronic Pain* (Constable and Robinson, 2005).

Teresa Palmieri is a Cognitive Behavioural therapist currently working in an NHS IAPT service delivering CBT to adults with depression and anxiety disorders. Teresa completed her clinical training in Italy and an MSc in Applied Psychology at the University of East London before specialising in CBT at Royal Holloway. She has extensive experience working with young people and has been involved in a number of projects targeting mental health issues in the homeless population. She has a particular interest in working with individuals with anxiety disorders.

Rita Santos is a clinical psychologist who specialises in CBT, anxiety and anxiety disorders. She finished her clinical training in Lisbon, Portugal (1998) and specialised in CBT for anxiety disorders by completing a two-year MSc (2000). Pursuing her interests further, Rita completed a PhD on cognitive aspects of anxiety and performance at Royal Holloway, University of London (2007), conducting cutting-edge psychology research including functional magnetic resonance imaging (fMRI). Her research provided the main empirical underpinning of a novel theory of anxiety: attentional control theory. Following a period as a post-doctoral researcher and lecturer at Royal Holloway, she pursued further CBT training in the UK by completing a Postgraduate Diploma (2011). During her career she has developed a broad range of skills, including extensive academic experience (conducting research, publishing papers, and delivering undergraduate and postgraduate level teaching) and wide clinical expertise (ranging from working privately to psychiatric hospitals, student support centres, and the NHS). She currently provides CBT training and supervision, and works as a cognitive behavioural psychotherapist.

Dzintra Stalmeisters, PhD, is an Accredited Cognitive Behavioural Psychotherapist and Chartered Psychologist. She teaches on the MSc Cognitive Behavioural Psychotherapy course at the University of Derby and is also in private practice.

Blake Stobie is a Consultant Clinical Psychologist based at the Maudsley Hospital in London, where he manages a service for people with treatment resistant anxiety disorders who have not maintained gains from previous treatments. Blake's research and clinical interests include the psychological factors influencing the treatments which service users are offered, factors which can complicate treatments, and how these can be addressed by modifying standardised treatment approaches.

Rita Woo is a Clinical Psychologist with extensive experience in working with individuals presenting with complex and debilitating mental health difficulties, including psychosis and chronic and recurring mood and anxiety disorders. She has a special interest in the training and supervision of psychologists and other mental health professionals, and currently works as a Senior Tutor and Supervisor for the Central and North West London Mental Health Trust and Royal Holloway University CBT Post Graduate Diplomas.

Kerry Young trained as a Clinical Psychologist in Oxford in the early 1990s. After a brief stint in neuropsychological rehabilitation, she went on to work at the Traumatic Stress Clinic in London for many years. Recently, alongside her role as Clinical Director of the Doctoral Training Programme in Clinical Psychology at UCL, she developed an interest in modifying traditional CBT approaches to work with multiple traumas. She has written and taught about this widely. Currently, she is the Clinical Lead of the Forced Migration Trauma Service, an NHS service in Central and North West London NHS Foundation Trust for refugees and asylum seekers with PTSD. Kerry also works as a Research Clinical Psychologist for EPaCT (Experimental Psychopathology and Cognitive Therapy Lab, Department of Psychiatry, Oxford University, a translational research team developing imagery-based interventions for bipolar disorder, anxiety and depression.

Foreword by Alec Grant

People should not be confused with disorders, diagnostic categories or randomized control trial outcomes. A few years back, James Bennett-Levy used the term 'paradigmatic antipathy' to sum up his perception of the disdain expressed by many in the mainstream cognitive behavioural community towards qualitative inquiry (unless it was positivist-realist in methodological form). He was spot on in my estimation. For 26 years, from when I started my CBT training in 1983, I regularly attended BABCP and EABCP events and read the literature relevant to my practice and, later, teaching. Ever the closet ethnographer waiting to out, I never stopped being surprised by the absence of adequate discussions, at conferences and in journals and books, about the messiness of flesh and blood people, relationships, and CBT practice cultures. Also absent for most of the time were discussions about the politics of practice, and about professional and disciplinary critical reflexivity. It seemed to me that a kind of defensive and insular muscularity prevailed, governing what could and should be talked and written about in the name of 'evidence-based' CBT.

So I tried in a small way to remedy this state of affairs in my teaching and writing. In my final years in CBT, I waved a supportive flag for the postmodern, poststructural and narrative turns as they impacted on theory, therapy and representational practices; for the need for practitioners to embrace paradigmatic pluralism; for more practitioner and disciplinary reflexivity; and for less sanitised and reductionist research and practice agendas. From this broad contextual base, before finally jumping paradigms into narrative inquiry in 2009, I used my position as CBT book editor/writer to bring clients' stories more into the frame, enabling them to talk about their experience of therapy and their therapists. It seemed to me that such detailed accounts and concerns, from experts by lived-experience, needed to be accorded greater respect than was normally the case in formulation development and representational practices in the mainstream CBT world.

People are dialogic, relational, and position themselves, others and the material world in the stories they tell about their lives, and to their great credit this is a central message in Corrie and Lane's (2010) ground-breaking text. This apparently mundane but deeply significant fact is either more or less acknowledged, or appears between the lines as a sometimes troubling spectre, in CBT practice books. This should be a cause for concern; the centrality of the client narrative promises much for sensitive practice of CBT assessment and formulation and squares with a key paradigm shift impacting mental health practice currently.

We live and work in times characterised by the emergence of an increasingly recognised professional need to embrace and develop narrative-based approaches, in order to better understand and respond to human misery (DCP2013). To borrow from the writing of Schon (1987), implicated in this paradigm shift is a related need to destabilise the dominance of the *technical-rational* research and practice agendas characteristic of mainstream mental health generally with approaches that honour the importance of the development of *professional artistry*. Such – broadly speaking – narrative paradigm approaches include an important role for cognitive behavioural formulation. In my view, this demands increasing levels of narrative competence on the part of practitioners and an unrelenting respect paid to the contextual nuances of clients' accounts of their difficulties (Grant 2015). Those involved in CBT formulation need to ensure that their work isn't perceived by people active in the recovery and survivor communities as yet another oppressive tool to pathologize and colonise difference.

Context-rich formulations function as a necessary antidote to narrow, de-contextualised understandings of people-as-disorders. Carefully and collaboratively finessed and crafted formulation stories help people address and deal with the interruptions to their life narratives that come with periods of extreme psychological distress. Good formulations also help people and others in their worlds and beyond as guiding exemplars and as points of reference to help re-story lives, serving as tools for what Arthur Frank (2011) describes as 'narrative healing'. They address and redress the worst excesses and limitations of institutional psychiatric business-as-usual. It's sad that in our mental health systems, '... people can spend years coming in and out of hospital without anyone sitting down and discussing their experiences and their distress in order to make sense of them.' (Johnstone, 2014: 53). Because of this, such people can and do become narratively entrapped in 'official' stories imposed on them, which are often pejorative, confusing, contradictory, lacking in clarity, and ultimately disempowering.

At a philosophy of science level, good stories aim for narrative coherence rather than correspondence with some imagined bottom line of indisputable fact. So 'truth' for all of us always and inevitably comes with a small 't'. To perhaps abuse and over-extend a metaphor, the truth (and proof) of the narratively coherent formulation pudding is in how it satisfies, nourishes and helps people grow strong. In this diet, evidence-based ingredients are necessary but by no means always sufficient, and sometimes may be dispensed with in order to improve social-psychological taste and digestion.

All of the above said, it's pleasing for me to see that people's dialogically developed stories continue to be celebrated in this current volume in several respects, not least by the inclusion of dialogic exchanges between clients and therapists in many of the case studies. It's also good to read the ways in which this second edition builds sensitively on the first in many ways, including in acknowledging markers of difference between people in their communities. Although CBT and I have been more or less divorced from each other for 6 years now, I'm very pleased that we remain on cordial terms, that I still have visiting rights, and that I can still contribute in some small way to the well-being of my old family! Sarah, Mike, Adrian and all contributors have done an excellent job, and I commend this second edition to you. I hope it helps you in your own ongoing, storied development as a practitioner, and benefits all the people you work with along the way.

**Alec Grant, Reader in Narrative Mental Health,
University of Brighton**

References

Corrie, S. and Lane, D. (2010) *Constructing Stories, Telling Tales: A Guide to Formulation in Applied Psychology*. London: Karnac.

Division of Clinical Psychology (DCP) (2013) *Classification of Behaviour and Experience in Relation to Functional Psychiatric Diagnoses: Time for a Paradigm Shift*. Leicester: British Psychological Society. (Available from: http://shop.bps. org.uk/classification-of-behaviour-and-experience-in-relation-to-funtional-psychiatric-diagnoses-time-for-a-paradigm-shift.html).

Frank, A. (2011) 'Foreword', in A. Grant, F. Biley, H. Walker, *Our Encounters with Madness*. Ross-on-Wye: PCCS Books.

Grant, A. (2015) 'Demedicalising misery: Welcoming the human paradigm in mental health nurse education', *Nurse Education Today*, 35: E50-e53.

Johnstone, L. (2014) *A Straight Talking Introduction to Psychiatric Diagnosis*. Ross-on-Wye: PCCS Books.

Schon, D.A. (1987) *Educating the Reflective Practitioner*. San Francisco: Jossey-Bass.

Foreword by David Kingdon

Assessment and case formulation are central to providing coherent, comprehensive and comprehensible interventions in mental health. Formulation is fundamental to CBT as originally conceived by Aaron Beck and subsequently developed by others. Formulation (or conceptualisation as it is sometimes known) differentiates high quality client-focussed CBT from manual-based and technique-driven cognitive and behavioural approaches. If utilised in a careful and thoughtful way it is the cornerstone of effective practice through the provision of a systematic relation-based framework on which to base care planning that is derived from current best evidence.

Effective formulation requires therapists who are flexible and who can work from a variety of theoretical perspectives. It also needs to be based on a collaborative process and a detailed assessment and description of an individual's predisposing, precipitating, perpetuating and protective factors, as well as current concerns and social and physical issues. Both the assessment and formulation need to be revisited and revised as part of a dynamic process that underpins the therapy. This dynamic process ensures the continued involvement of the client and frequently leads to unexpected and important surprises and insights for both the therapist and client. Corrie, Townend, Cockx and colleagues describe and illustrate these processes clearly and cogently, dividing assessment into personal individualised processes complemented by the judicious use of valid and reliable measures in the classical style of the scientist-practitioner. Rich case examples throughout the book demonstrate relationship development processes and in both a strategic and step-by-step way how assessment informs formulation, how theory can inform formulation and how individual differences can also be incorporated from a range of perspectives. These features make this book unique in the field.

This second edition of *Assessment and Case Formulation in Cognitive Behavioural Therapy* addresses how assessment and formulation can provide a useful way of grouping conditions into a transdiagnostic whole which shows promise as a more valid and reliable method for understanding a person than a simplistic biological marker. Interestingly and importantly diagnosis is not dismissed as a prescriptive medicalised approach. Rather, careful consideration is given to how diagnosis can inform and complement formulation by providing nomenclature that can guide individuals to relevant information and self-management tools, and aid communication between professionals and services. Such an enlightened approach can help to avoid mistakes of the past where diagnosis has perhaps at times obscured individuals' needs and their uniqueness.

In addition, the difficult issue of the assessment of readiness for CBT is thoughtfully considered: this is an area that has undergone considerable change as more severe conditions have been demonstrated to be amenable to CBT. Previously the emphasis has been on whether the client has been ready for CBT - now greater consideration is being given to whether the therapist is sufficiently skilled and competent to present their intervention in an acceptable way. Again such issues are considered from a variety of perspectives and contexts. This is especially the case where that person may not think they have a mental illness but may be able to accept that they have problems which are worth at least discussing with a therapist. The authors have managed to incorporate all these ideas and more, such as whether the person is 'psychologically minded' or 'able to access negative thoughts' and especially whether they are able to 'form a therapeutic relationship' through skilled engagement, careful formulation, and guided understandings being demonstrated and then utilised in the development of shared goals and interventions. Another issue that the authors discuss is how formulation can influence the timing of interventions and when interventions might need to be changed or consolidated (such as avoiding CBT until the person is 'stabilised' leading to missed opportunities – crisis intervention as an example has long been advocated as a time when change can occur at a rapid pace).

The field as I understand it, and which is beautifully addressed in this book, is evolving rapidly with core competences being defined and curricula for training agreed and then updated as developments occur. The implementation of CBT has been given a previously almost unimaginably strong boost with its underpinning evidence-based approach and the launch and development of the Improving Access to Psychological Treatment (IAPT) programme for depression and anxiety disorders in England. Again such contexts are fully considered in this text. Key to IAPT success has been the establishment of core standards and outcome measurement which has been able to demonstrate the effectiveness, including cost-effectiveness, of formulation-based interventions. IAPT for severe mental illness (SMI) is now beginning to emulate this with access and waiting standards for psychosis established that have a similar emphasis on competences and outcome measurement. This book is a bridge between all of these developments.

Given all of these factors it is very timely to focus on assessment and formulation. In doing so, Corrie, Townend and Cockx make an important contribution to supporting the training and continuing professional development necessary for practitioners to meet the evolving and complex world of practice for psychological interventions.

**David Kingdon, Professor of Mental Health Care Delivery,
University of Southampton**

Acknowledgements

There are a number of people who have contributed to the development of this book and whose interest, encouragement and support we wish to acknowledge.

First, we would like to thank everyone at Sage who has worked with us to bring this project to completion. Particular thanks go to Susannah Trefgarne and Laura Walmsley, our editorial team, who have been such a solid source of support throughout the process.

Second, we would also like to acknowledge Alec Grant and Jem Mills as editors and contributors to the first edition of this book. Their ideas and work have been a source of inspiration and in writing this second edition, we have attempted to remain true to the vision that made the first edition so popular and influential.

Third, we thank Christine Padesky and Robert Leahy for their contributions and comments to the chapters where their work has been discussed. Having guidance from two such respected and influential contributors in the field of CBT is a great honour.

Beyond those directly connected with this project, we are deeply grateful to all those who, over the years, have shaped our understanding of both cognitive behavioural therapy and of assessment and case formulation using this approach. A particular mention goes to the many teachers and supervisors with whom we have had the good fortune to work and from whom we have learned so much. We also acknowledge our current and former students and colleagues who continue to challenge us and who have in so many ways shaped this edition.

Special thanks go to Ian Lacey for proofreading the manuscript and for his encouragement, critique and support of the project on many different levels. In addition:

Sarah Corrie wishes to acknowledge the talented team of supervisors, trainers and students at The Central London CBT Centre who have provided the inspiration for many of the ideas presented in this book. Her thanks also go to David Lane and colleagues at the Professional Development Foundation, and at the Institute for Work Based Learning at Middlesex University who have shaped her understanding of learning and professional development in profound ways. Finally, her thanks go to the many clients with whom she has had the privilege to work and who teach her how to do better every day.

Michael Townend wishes to acknowledge Jenny, his family and friends for their love, understanding and patience. His thanks also go to all his colleagues at the University of Derby, for their inspirational ideas and helping to create the space to enable work on this book to proceed. Finally he thanks his clients who by their experiences and feedback have contributed to this text. They also act as a reminder that it is a privilege to be in a position to work with them.

Adrian Cockx wishes to acknowledge his loved ones, and family, clients, students, supervisors, supervisees, teachers, colleagues and the researchers in the field for helping him find a way to help others and navigate through the difficulties of life.

Confidentiality

The case studies and all additional case material included in this book have been inspired by dilemmas encountered in the context of delivering CBT in a variety of health care settings. However, care has been taken to ensure anonymity in all cases. In order to preserve confidentiality a number of potentially identifying features have been changed, with some cases representing a composite of several clients.

PART 1

Enhancing Effectiveness in CBT Assessment and Case Formulation

ONE   Introduction and Orientation to the Current Status of CBT

Sarah Corrie, Michael Townend and Adrian Cockx

Learning objectives

After reading this chapter and completing the learning activities provided you should be able to understand:

- The aims of this book.
- How competence is defined and understood in cognitive behavioural therapy.
- The increasingly complex contexts in which CBT is now commissioned and delivered.
- How to use this book to best meet your learning and development needs.

Introduction

The aim of this book is to help you understand the philosophies, principles, methods and techniques that can inform the effective assessment and case formulation of your clients' needs and, in doing so, assist the development of your mastery of cognitive behavioural therapy (CBT).

Assessment and case formulation, within the context of a co-constructed therapeutic relationship, lie at the heart of effective CBT. Conducting a thorough, theoretically and relationally informed assessment and using the information obtained to devise a case formulation that can assist intervention planning are clinical activities that have been consistently identified as forming the backbone of CBT (Grant and Townend, 2008; Corrie and Lane, 2010). However, knowledge of the optimal ways of carrying out these activities remains lacking. Despite some laudable attempts to provide clearer guidance (see for example, Butler, 1998; Kuyken et al., 2009; Corrie and Lane, 2010), the lack of consensus about how to assess and formulate clients' needs disadvantages those practitioners who seek to develop a rigorous and systematic approach that can take account of developments in the field, respond to the demands of different service contexts and remain attentive to the unique characteristics of the individual client.

The lack of definitive guidelines on how best to assess and formulate clients' needs is perhaps not surprising when we consider the terrain that must be navigated. Contemporary CBT is a broad, emerging therapeutic landscape that encompasses a range of concepts, theories, models and styles of working, rather than a single, unified discipline (Gilbert, 2008; Grant et al., 2008; Westbrook et al., 2011). What constitutes effective assessment and case formulation within one 'school' of CBT may, therefore, look somewhat different in another and may also alter with the passage of time as advances in the field occur.

Although certain fundamental assumptions may be shared (for example that cognition plays an important role in distress and is amenable to intervention) the range of problem-specific formulation models and disorder-specific constructs guiding assessment and intervention planning has increased exponentially. As noted by Grant and Townend (2008), the amount of content that needs to be absorbed can feel overwhelming until the theoretical assumptions shared across models become clear.

Experienced practitioners who are confident that their knowledge of models and protocols remains current will also encounter challenges at least some of the time. Indeed, navigating a constantly changing theoretical and empirical landscape whilst holding in mind our clients' self-told stories arguably *should* be a challenge. Clients do not always present with neatly packaged difficulties that can be swiftly or easily categorized according to therapists' preferred classification schemes. Even where clients appear to have relatively uncomplicated needs or clearly do meet diagnostic criteria for a particular disorder, the way in which therapy unfolds will depend on a wide variety of factors including the skillfulness of the therapist in engaging, understanding, conceptualizing and responding to emergent issues on a moment-by-moment and session-by-session basis. As Padesky (1996a) observes, competence requires both knowledge of cognitive and behavioural theory and an ability to apply this knowledge in a systematic fashion to the material encountered in the consulting room. This was echoed more recently by the Improving Access to Psychological Therapies (IAPT) initiative (see www.iapt.nhs.uk/about-iapt/website-archive/competencies-and-national-occupational-standards/cognitive-behavioural-therapy-competences-framework) where it is noted that although a structured therapy, CBT:

...works best if therapists consistently maintain a sense that clients need to understand themselves through a process of 'guided-discovery', so that they find out about themselves for themselves... CBT should help clients learn skills which enable them to cope with future adversity in a more effective way.

Individuals with the same diagnosis or problem of living are not a homogeneous group and when working with clients, therapists face an unending series of choices about which direction to take. Therapy will always need to be tailored to the individual client even where what is being offered is a manualized intervention.

Contextual factors shaping the delivery of CBT

At the same time as having to negotiate an evolving scholastic and clinical terrain, CBT practitioners also need to embrace the shifting demands and expectations of their services. In the past 50 years or so, the ways in which psychological therapies are mandated, organized and practised have changed radically (Lunt, 2006). The development and delivery of CBT is couched within a broader political, social and economic climate characterized by unprecedented levels of unpredictability, complexity and volatility. This evolving and uncertain climate has a number of implications for the knowledge and skills that CBT therapists are expected to acquire, the clinical problems with which they need to be equipped to work and the training routes available to facilitate the development of their competence.

A first implication of this rapidly changing professional climate is that in recent years the professions themselves have come under greater scrutiny and control (see Lo, 2005; Lane and Corrie, 2006, for a review of these debates). This has contributed to the increasing professionalization and regulation of the psychological therapies including CBT, as well as the need for more objective standards to guide policy. Both the demonstrated efficacy of cognitive and behavioural therapies for a diverse range of mental health problems and the commitment to ongoing refinement through the accumulation of a robust evidence-base have enabled CBT to secure an advantageous position with government and other funding bodies who seek evidence of efficacy as a basis for commissioning (McHugh and Barlow, 2010). In the context of a health care climate organized around empirically-supported interventions, CBT is likely to remain a desirable commissioning choice.

A second major, and related, development has been the advent of the UK government's initiative for England, *Improving Access to Psychological Therapies* (IAPT; Department of Health, 2008a), funded and developed to improve the psychological well-being of the population through more rapid and consistent access to evidence-based therapies. IAPT has resulted in the emergence of a new CBT workforce to deliver routine and first-line stepped care interventions – a workforce created to support Primary Care Trusts in implementing National Institute for Health and Clinical Excellence (NICE) guidelines for people suffering from depression and anxiety disorders. The ability of this workforce to deliver on the targets specified requires skill in the implementation of empirically-supported interventions which in turn depend upon well-honed knowledge of how to assess and formulate clients' needs within the context of protocol-guided practice. Thus, through IAPT, CBT has become uniquely placed within the government's mandate to increase the availability of psychological therapies.

A third implication is that there are now in the UK established pathways through which individuals can become formally 'accredited' as CBT practitioners, based on their ability to evidence sufficient levels of clinical experience, knowledge, skill and professionalism. As the lead organization for CBT in the UK, the British Association for Behavioural & Cognitive Psychotherapies (BABCP, 2012) specifies the 'Minimum Training Standards' for eligibility for accreditation. These standards outline the number of CBT cases which must be completed, the number of clinical practice hours to be accrued and the amount and type of supervision that must be received to support this practice. Additionally, written submissions are required demonstrating both theoretical and clinical understanding of a spectrum of client presentations. IAPT therapists in particular are offered employment contracts on the basis of completing a rigorous training that maps on to these requirements and follows a specific curriculum.

As protocols are developed to target the unique cognitive and behavioural profiles of specific disorders, issues of adherence (i.e. whether the therapy is delivered according to the protocol) and competence (whether the therapy is delivered with sufficient skill) become vital to ascertain. However, this gives rise to questions about the nature of competence itself – in particular, what does 'competent' CBT look like, what is the knowledge and skill-base that needs to be acquired and how can competence be reliably and accurately measured?

Muse and McManus (2013: 485) have defined competence in CBT as, '... the degree to which a therapist demonstrates the general therapeutic and treatment-specific knowledge and skills required to appropriately deliver CBT interventions which reflect the current evidence base for treatment of the patient's presenting problem'. In their work aimed at identifying the activities that typify proficient CBT for clients with depression and anxiety disorders, Roth and Pilling (2007) have devised a map of competences which provides important clarification of the knowledge, skills and attitudes required. Through reviewing the efficacy of therapeutic approaches demonstrated in controlled trials, and studying the associated treatment manuals, Roth and Pilling have identified over 50 competences that appear central to the delivery of effective CBT for depression and anxiety disorders. The authors note that given the number and levels of competences outlined, the framework should not be used in a prescriptive way but rather seen as an aid to decision-making, competence development and assessment of therapist skill.

The identified competences have been organized into five domains each of which comprises a range of activities which in turn consist of a set of specific skills. These are as follows (see also www.ucl.ac.uk/CORE):

1. Generic (the so-called 'common factors' of effective therapy such as knowledge of mental health problems and the ability to form positive working alliances with clients).
2. Basic CBT competences (such as a working knowledge of common cognitive distortions, the ability to structure therapy and how to explain to clients the rationale for homework).
3. Specific behavioural and cognitive techniques (e.g. the principal methods and techniques that are employed in most CBT interventions such as exposure and response prevention and guided discovery).
4. Problem-specific competences (those CBT interventions and procedures adapted to specific disorders. The competence framework details these for specific phobias, social phobia, panic disorder, obsessive-compulsive disorder, generalized anxiety disorder, post-traumatic stress disorder and depression).
5. Metacompetences (those 'higher order' skills of thinking and procedural knowledge that enable a therapist to implement and adapt, pace and time specific interventions in response to client need).

Assuming that competence can be defined, described and identified in practice, how do we assess our own and others' progress towards it? In their review of the methods currently available for assessing proficiency in CBT, Muse and McManus (2013) identify examples of both transdiagnostic CBT rating scales (that is, those assessing the general CBT competences demonstrated in a particular session) and disorder-specific measures (i.e. assessing the competences required to deliver a particular treatment protocol for a given disorder). An example of the former would be the Cognitive Therapy Scale – Revised (Blackburn et al., 2001), whereas an example of the latter would be Cognitive Therapy Scale – Psychosis (Haddock et al., 2001). There can be challenges with implementing disorder-specific measures of assessment in routine clinical services (Muse and McManus, 2013). Nonetheless, competence frameworks, generic and disorder-specific measures of therapist competence and the available evidence-base all point to an emerging clarification of what proficient CBT comprises, the knowledge, attitudes and skills to which novice CBT therapists need to aspire, and the abilities that supervisors and trainers should inculcate in their students.

The above factors represent just some of the enabling and constraining factors which CBT therapists must understand and negotiate in order to provide an optimally effective service to their clients. What is also evident is that within these rapidly evolving professional contexts, practitioners are increasingly required to take responsibility for their professional development, to be able to synthesize insights from theory, research and practice to inform their work with clients, and to see themselves as lifelong learners so that their knowledge and skills remain fit for purpose (we address this in more detail in Chapter 17). Indeed, there is an argument that professional 'survival' is tied to our commitment to remain informed and justify our practice (Guest, 2000). This book speaks to this agenda and in the chapters that follow we have attempted to provide information, offer guidance and acquaint you with the necessary skills that can serve to enhance the quality of your CBT practice and aid your endeavours as lifelong learners.

The second edition of this book: the vision behind the content

Knowledge of clinical presentations is never static and since the first edition, scholarly activity, professional expertise and changes in diagnostic classification have taken collective understanding of clients' difficulties and needs in new directions, a process that will undoubtedly continue. In this second edition we have sought to retain the essence of what made the first edition so influential and popular, whilst also remaining abreast of developments in the field as well as standards in professional practice and the diverse contexts in which CBT therapists now deliver their services.

We have sought to capture some of the many ways in which CBT is practised by including a series of case studies describing the adaption of CBT assessment and case formulation for different clinical presentations. As noted previously, there is no single model of therapy that is 'CBT' and it will become evident from reading the different chapters that our contributors (and indeed ourselves as the authors of this text) do not adhere to identical understandings of what precisely CBT is or how it is optimally delivered. This diversity is intentional as we believe that any text seeking to do justice to such a rich discipline needs to reflect at least some of the perspectives that now characterize the field.

As Clark (2014: xv) asserts, the task for therapists is always one of needing to '...tailor CBT methods whilst remaining true to the core principles'. Our contributors have, we believe, achieved this admirably, demonstrating how they have adapted their approach to engage and work effectively with their clients while remaining committed to the core principles that define the field. What our contributors share is (1) a commitment to empirically underpinned and theoretically informed approaches to the therapeutic relationship and to assessment and formulation; (2) an ability to provide a contemporary perspective on their area of expertise; and (3) a first-hand knowledge of how rewarding (but at times challenging and even bewildering) therapeutic practice can be.

The brief we gave our contributors was to hold in mind information and guidance that would support CBT practitioners in working towards mastery of a particular application of CBT assessment and formulation, as well as reflective exercises to support readers' further engagement with the topic. Additionally, we wanted to avoid the 'polished' case studies that can sometimes attract criticism from (especially novice) readers that they are too remote to feel entirely accessible. In practice, there is often a need to balance accuracy and helpfulness. Decisions are always context-dependent and involve an understanding of what is possible in the settings in which we work (Lane and Corrie, 2012). How precisely CBT assessment and case formulation are undertaken will be impacted by a variety of factors. These include case management concerns (e.g. risk assessment) and service constraints (some services may 'cap' the number of CBT sessions provided at a level which falls below that recommended by NICE guidelines for a particular disorder) and will at times incorporate clinical decision-making that involves cross-disciplinary input.

As such, although our contributors have presented their clinical reasoning very clearly, they have focused on what works when attempting to make sense of clinical dilemmas in the messy 'real world' settings in which therapy is often delivered, rather than on how therapeutic outcomes ideally look when confounding factors are removed. We were delighted that our authors supported this vision and are enormously grateful to them for sharing their knowledge and expertise. As is often the case, editing the case studies has enabled us to grow in our knowledge and understanding of how to work effectively in a rapidly changing field.

Who is this book for?

Our aim is to support the learning and development needs of CBT therapists at all stages of their careers so that regardless of their baseline level of competence and service setting, readers can become increasingly skilled in undertaking CBT assessments and developing case formulations. We hope, therefore, that this book will be useful for a wide range of practitioners including:

- CBT therapists at the start of their careers who are grappling with the complexity of clinical material for the first time.
- Newly qualified CBT therapists who are seeking to refine their core skills in key areas.
- More experienced professionals wishing to hone their approach and wanting a helpful CPD text.
- CBT supervisors wanting systematic and effective ways of helping their supervisees make sense of their clients' needs as the clinical picture emerges.
- Trainers who wish to expand their repertoire of approaches for introducing students to the fundamentals of assessment and case formulation in CBT.

We also hope that this book will be a useful source of information for clinical leads, service managers and others involved in the professional development and mentoring of CBT practitioners in a wide variety of training and professional practice contexts.

About the book

The book is divided into three parts. In Part 1, the reader is introduced to the fundamental and more advanced technical and procedural aspects of cognitive behavioural assessment and case formulation. Specifically, Chapter 2 examines both nomothetic and idiographic assessment and offers guidance on how to approach this. The therapist's ability to understand and adapt to the internal world of the client is of critical importance. The meanings attributed to self, others and the world that the client inhabits (including enabling and disabling environments, and personal history) and the contexts in which certain beliefs and behavioural repertoires have developed, are all part of the terrain with which the therapist must become acquainted.

Of central importance to the collaborative nature of the approach, CBT relies upon the relationship between therapist and client, and the ability of the therapist to manage the therapeutic process. In addition to the technical requirements of assessment and formulation attention must, therefore, be paid to the collaboration formed with the client from the earliest stages of engagement. Chapter 3 examines the process and relational aspects of CBT assessment. There is a paucity of research (and indeed training opportunities) in this area relative to other areas of CBT practice. Moreover, given the outcome orientation of many services in which CBT is delivered, and a variety of caseload and other service-related pressures, there can be a tendency towards time-efficient models of service delivery that prize task-focused over process-oriented elements – a criticism which has been levied at the field of CBT historically (see for example, Safran and Muran, 2000). Appreciating how process and relational factors can be understood by the theories and research that inform CBT practice is, therefore, a vital contribution to enhancing therapist effectiveness. This chapter offers the reader an opportunity to broaden their practice and better understand the intricacies of both the opportunities and challenges that can arise in aiming to develop a collaborative working relationship with clients.

Chapter 4 examines the fundamentals of case formulation. Kuyken et al. (2009) have argued that case formulation in CBT requires higher-order skills and propose the need for 'focused training' particularly as therapists use clinical data to move from the descriptive to the more explanatory levels which require more theory-driven inferences. Chapter 4 provides some frameworks that can help you make sense of the data gathered and offers guidance on how to systematically improve your skills in case formulation, building on the ideas presented in Chapters 2 and 3.

Finally, Chapter 5 attends to what has been termed a 'transdiagnostic' approach, considering more integrative models of assessment and case formulation. In recent years, much of the research within CBT has been dominated by a disorder-specific outlook, with approaches to assessment, formulation and intervention adapted for the needs of a particular psychological difficulty or diagnostic classification. However, as noted by Harvey et al. (2004), there are marked similarities in cognitive and behavioural processes across clinical presentations. This has given rise to an interest in those processes that appear to be 'shared' across disorders. As an important development within the field of CBT, Chapter 5 considers the implications of this for our approaches to CBT-focused assessment and formulation so that readers can have a working knowledge of this perspective, even if they choose to work using a disorder-specific approach.

In Part 2 we explore the application of CBT assessment and formulation further through a series of case studies drawn directly from our contributors' clinical work. This enables readers to appreciate how the material of Part 1 can be applied to clients with different needs and presenting concerns.

The case study chapters are divided into two sections. In the first section, the reader can learn how to approach their CBT practice with potentially more straightforward clinical presentations. We have grouped under this category those chapters describing work with clients who are experiencing panic disorder and agoraphobia; depression (using a traditional Beckian approach and then in the following chapter a contemporary behavioural approach); health anxiety; generalized anxiety disorder; and social anxiety. In the second section, we have grouped together those chapters that describe work with clients whose clinical presentations are potentially more complex, namely obsessive-compulsive disorder (OCD); post-traumatic stress disorder (PTSD); physical health problems; borderline personality disorder; and psychosis. It should be noted here that the distinction between 'simple' and 'complex' case studies is somewhat arbitrary and used principally for ease of organizing the material. It is not meant to imply that the case studies in the first section describe 'easy' clinical presentations or indeed that the second section details work with clinical presentations that will be inevitably complex to conceptualize and challenging to work with. Nonetheless, as complexity increases, therapists often find themselves needing to make adaptations that can accommodate the specific difficulties with which clients are grappling, and which take the work beyond the boundary of the existing evidence-base. The direction that these adaptations may take is addressed by our contributors through the recommendations and guidance they provide, based on their extensive experience of the clinical presentation described.

Finally in Part 3, a shorter section, we offer some concluding comments and recommendations for the field as a whole. We reflect on progress in assessment and formulation over the last few years, identify potential trends, opportunities and challenges for the future, and offer some final thoughts on developing competence in CBT assessment and case formulation. We conclude the book with a reflective practice task for you to use for yourselves (or with your supervisees and students if you are in a training role) to inform the ongoing development of your learning and any next steps that you might wish to take in enhancing your CBT-related knowledge and skills.

How to use the book

This book can help you structure your clinical thinking more effectively and systematically and we would encourage you to personalize your reading to your own learning and development needs. It is, therefore, worth spending some time considering what your primary learning needs might be and how you can use the book to best advantage. Are you, for example, at the start of your career and seeking to establish a framework that you can use to support the development of your practice? Or are you seeking to hone your assessment and formulation skills in the context of a specific disorder (you may feel relatively confident working with depression, but somewhat mystified by OCD). Or as an experienced practitioner do you suspect that with the passage of time there has been some 'therapist drift' (Waller, 2009) and that you have slipped into bad habits which you would like to rectify? Alternatively, you may be a supervisor or trainer wanting to find helpful ways of introducing key concepts and approaches that can support your work as a mentor to junior members of the profession. Not all of the contents will be equally relevant to your professional requirements, so feel free to skip over any chapters which do not apply to you at this point in your career.

You will also find it helpful to give some thought to what you might need to support you in your learning. You may, for example, want to try out one or two of the frameworks on offer and make notes of your results in a learning journal. A growing area of interest in the CBT literature is the development of the professional self of the practitioner (see Bennett-Levy et al., 2015; Corrie and Lane, 2015) and we embrace this here, encouraging you to interact with the material, ponder its implications for your work and your effectiveness and where appropriate to experiment with the ideas presented. Although we do our best to signpost key debates within the field as they relate to matters of CBT assessment and formulation, it is beyond the scope of this book to review broader conceptual, professional and political issues in detail. If questions arise, you will find it helpful to refer to the additional reading lists provided as well drawing on the networks of professional development that are available to you.

However you decide to support your learning, we hope that by engaging with the material and the recommended exercises, you are challenged to think about your practice in new ways. This may feel exciting or unsettling and you may find yourself confronting questions that are most suitably followed up in supervision or in a training environment. From our point of view, if you find that the material leads to further dialogue we will be well pleased. Given that there is no single uniform approach called CBT, different approaches within this broad family of therapies *will* assess and conceptualize client material in different ways and this provides much opportunity for reflection, discussion and debate.

A final comment

A variety of theoretical, empirical and professional contributions have greatly advanced our understanding of psychological disorders and emotional difficulty. Alongside these developments, the increasing recognition of what CBT has to offer has resulted in a growing demand for well-trained professionals who can think and practice in ways that are consistent with cognitive and behavioural theory. However, therapeutic practice will never be a precise science and gaining, as well as maintaining and enhancing, competence is neither an easy nor a guaranteed outcome. No matter how long we have been practising, we can never become complacent that our knowledge and skills remain fit for purpose.

Regardless of the contexts in which you deliver CBT and the reasons you are choosing to read this book, we hope that you will enjoy the chapters which follow and benefit from the topics addressed. Although it is important to be aware that this book is not in any way intended to be a substitute for CBT training or supervision, we hope that it will be a useful companion in your attempts to develop your knowledge and skill, and that it might complement other forms of professional learning and development that are available to you. Above all, we hope that this new edition of *Assessment and Case Formulation in Cognitive Behavioural Therapy* might support the development of your clinical skills and prove to be a worthy companion as you undertake this complex task known as CBT. We welcome feedback and look forward to your comments.

TWO Assessment in CBT

Michael Townend, Sarah Corrie, Adrian Cockx and Alec Grant

Learning objectives

After reading this chapter and completing the learning activities provided you should be able to understand:

- The purpose and aims of assessment in CBT.
- The relevance of, and distinction between, nomothetic and idiographic approaches.
- The role of functional analysis.
- The key areas of a client's life and experience which need to be assessed for the purposes of formulation and intervention planning.
- The importance of tailoring your assessment to accommodate issues of diversity and difference.

Introduction

The cognitive behavioural approach to human difficulties provides a means of exploring the personal meanings, emotions and behaviours relevant to the individual. This understanding takes account of the client's history, biological and genetic influences and current environmental factors.

Chapter 2 examines the role of assessment in CBT and provides guidance on how to improve your skills in this area. We begin by considering what, in broad terms, therapists set out to achieve by conducting a CBT-focused assessment. We then consider different ways of approaching the assessment, considering the contribution of both nomothetic and idiographic approaches and the role of functional analysis. We introduce the commonly used 'five areas' approach as a basis for organizing the material obtained and then consider issues of suitability and diversity.

Through examining these areas, the aim is to support you in conducting more thorough, systematic and effective assessments that can form the basis of a useful formulation and realistic intervention plan.

The nature and purpose of assessment in CBT

Beck et al. (1979) used the term 'collaborative empiricism' to signify how therapists' work with clients is based on transparent agendas and partnership-based relationships. CBT therapists are also empiricists in that, along with their clients, they seek to test the validity of predictions, assumptions and beliefs that appear implicated in the client's difficulties and that, once tested, might offer up pathways for change. Through the process of guided discovery, therapist and client develop insight into what has contributed to the client's problems, what is maintaining them and potential ways to achieve recovery (Grant et al., 2010). A first step towards fulfilling this potential is to conduct a comprehensive assessment of the client's difficulties and needs.

In CBT the assessment process is underpinned by a number of aims for both therapist and client. In broad terms these are as follows:

1. Achieving a detailed understanding of the client's problems in terms of environmental triggers, thoughts, behaviours, emotions and physiological responses.
2. Arriving at a thorough understanding of how factors from the client's background and past have contributed to the development of the presenting problems (although sometimes these more distal factors only become apparent over a period of sessions).
3. Achieving a detailed understanding of factors implicated in maintaining the client's problems.
4. Identifying and defining the client's strengths.
5. Identifying and using measures that provide a baseline of problem severity.
6. Providing a reasoned and research-based outline of how therapy might proceed based on the formulation emerging from the assessment.
7. Describing to the client the nature and importance of the therapeutic relationship in supporting the work.
8. Deciding whether, on balance, a CBT approach is best suited to the client's needs.

Realizing these aims will entail attention to the characteristics of any specific disorder that the client is experiencing (the nomothetic approach to assessment) and the client's idiosyncratic presentation in the context of their personal history, current context and self-told story (the idiographic approach). As these approaches are likely to build the foundation upon which any therapy subsequently takes place, they are considered in some detail in the next section.

Nomothetic assessment: diagnostic classification systems

Nomothetic assessment refers to assessment based on the aggregated features of particular disorders. These are gathered from large-scale studies of populations who have been identified as experiencing the symptoms of specific disorders. Thus, this form of assessment pays attention to the classification of a person's problem in the form of diagnosis.

The American Psychiatric Association's *Diagnostic and Statistical Manual* (5th edition) (DSM; APA, 2013) is perhaps the most widely used and is the 'gold standard' for diagnosis of mental illness in the United States. The DSM comprises five different axes on which an individual may be assessed: clinical syndromes, personality disorders, general medical conditions, psychosocial and environmental problems, and global functioning.

An alternative diagnostic framework is the World Health Organization's *International Statistical Classification of Diseases and Related Health Problems* (ICD-10; World Health Organization, 2002). The appearance of ICD-10 is viewed by many as an important publication as the classification of mental health problems is based on a consensus of experts and schools of psychiatry worldwide, under the co-ordinating leadership of the World Health Organization. Unlike the DSM which is produced by a single national professional association, the ICD is produced by a global health agency with a constitutional public health mission. As such, the ICD-10 aims to support the development of an international language, in order to allow global communication about mental health and facilitate research across cultures and countries.

Diagnosis has an important role to play in certain contexts – for example, in medical care when a rapid diagnosis of an underlying disease process is an essential precursor to saving life. However, the issue of diagnosis in mental health care is contentious. Although it is beyond the scope of this book to review the current debates about diagnosis (see Corrie and Lane, 2010, for an introduction) it is important to consider carefully the advantages and disadvantages of organizing CBT practice around classification systems such as DSM-5 and ICD-10. For example, with any such system, there is an inevitable loss of information. As clinicians look for similarities across conditions, so individual differences become averaged out and obscured. An additional concern is the stigma associated with the diagnosis of a mental illness and the potential stereotyping of those affected. Moreover, the terminology associated with the study and treatment of mental illness varies considerably across health professions and cultures.

A further point to note is that diagnostic systems classify disorders and not people. Terminology is very important and it is no longer acceptable for clients to be referred to as 'schizophrenic' or 'bipolar'. Rather, such individuals are referred to as 'persons with schizophrenia' or 'individuals with bipolar disorder'. Thus although diagnostic systems may be helpful in identifying the characteristics of specific problems, their limitations need to be respected in the context of the assessment process and augmented by an approach that focuses on the characteristics unique to the individual client.

Idiographic assessment: the role of functional analysis

In contrast to nomothetic assessment where the client's presenting problems are considered in the context of a diagnosable disorder, idiographic assessment is concerned with understanding the relevant individual contributing factors. Personal rather than disease-focused, the idiographic approach is essential in a psychotherapeutic context, overcoming the categorical limitations of diagnostic classification by accommodating dimensional and contextual factors.

Idiographic assessment is particularly important when working with people with chronic or complex conditions where a wide range of psychological or physical factors will be exerting an influence. This is particularly true for individuals with chronic conditions such as severe and relapsing depression, dysthymia, psychosis, bipolar disorder and personality disorders (Grant et al., 2010), and in physical problems such as heart disease, diabetes and chronic pain where psychological factors play a part in how well the individual conforms to self-management or health education guidance (see Chapter 14 of this book).

The idiographic approach is sometimes referred to as functional analysis. Functional analysis is a crucial component of CBT assessment, preceding and informing the development of an intervention plan (see Hawton et al., 1989, and Grant et al., 2010, for a historical review within behaviour therapy). It is essentially the process of determining the 'function' of unwelcome behaviour and helps define and understand the client's problems. It is only through carrying out detailed functional analyses that hypotheses for the maintenance of client problems can be developed, and an individualized intervention plan be devised. Table 2.1 provides a comprehensive overview of the information needed to conduct a comprehensive functional analysis of a client's needs.

It is important to remember that carrying out an assessment is not about a list of questions, asked in rigid succession. True to the principle of collaborative empiricism, the assessment needs to be a process of joint discovery, albeit led by the therapist. As Sanders and Wills explain, 'The outline of assessment is not intended to be a fixed rota for therapists to stick to.

Table 2.1 Information to gather as part of a CBT assessment

1. **Five Ws:**

   - What is the main problem or problems (as described by the client in their own words)?
   - Where does the problem occur?
   - When does the problem occur?
   - Why (what is the feared consequence or belief)?
   - With whom does the problem occur?

2. **FIND:**

   - What is the FREQUENCY of the problem?
   - How INTENSE are the symptoms (using a scale of 0–10 or 0–100%)?
   - What NUMBER of times does the problem occur?
   - What is the DURATION of the problem or episode?

3. **ABC analysis:**

   - Antecedents: What are the triggers to the problem: internal/external and proximal/distal?
   - Autonomic/physical: What physical sensations are present?
   - Behaviour: What does the person do (e.g. avoidance, checking, reassurance-seeking, rituals, safety behaviours, escape)?
   - Cognitive content, cognitive process and emotions: What goes through the person's mind before, during and after an episode? Are there any images? If so, what is the meaning associated with the images? Identification of processes: self-focused attention, thinking errors, worry, thought suppression; inflated sense of risk or threat. What emotions are evident? What core beliefs and rules are evident?
   - Consequences: What happens afterwards in terms of reduced or increased distress, others' reactions and interactions? Further client behaviours or thoughts?
   - Coping strategies: What does the client do to cope? What coping skills and assets do they possess?
   - Modifiers: What makes the problem better or worse?

4. **Development of the problem:**

   - Onset: When did the problem start? What happened at the time? What was going on at home or work at the time? Were any stressors present at the time? Was there any trauma?
   - Formative: Are any key themes, rules, beliefs or assumptions evident from the individual's background, upbringing, life both past and present? Is there any history of trauma or abuse?
   - Fluctuations: Is the problem lifelong or recurring? Is the problem static or has it changed over time?

5. **Goals and expectations from therapy (questions to ask the client):**

   - Why are you seeking therapy at this point in time?
   - What do you want to achieve from therapy?
   - What are you expecting from therapy?

- What are your hopes and fears about therapy or the therapeutic process?
- If you had a magic wand and you could make the problem disappear, what would be different?

6. **Medication and substance use**

- Medication: What medication is being taken? Are any side effects present?
- Alcohol intake: How many units of alcohol are consumed in a week? Is alcohol used to self-medicate or cope?
- Caffeine intake: What is the client's intake of coffee and/or soft drinks that contain caffeine?
- Smoking: Does the client smoke tobacco?
- Non-prescribed drugs: Does the client take illegal substances, or any so-called 'club drugs' or new psychoactive substances that provide 'legal highs'? If yes, what do they take? Are they taken for recreational or self-medication purposes? Are any long-term effects of drug use present?

7. **Assets and strengths:**

- What coping resources (personal/social/environmental) are available to the client?
- What are the client's strengths?

8. **Impact of the problems on the client's life:**

- What has been the effect of the problems on the client's work, home, leisure and relationships?

9. **Mental status:**

- Appearance: How does the client appear? Are they caring for themselves? Do they appear anxious, agitated or depressed?
- Speech: What is the form and flow of the client's verbal communication?
- Mood: Does the client feel low or depressed? Do they feel anxious? Do they experience any other emotions such as guilt and shame? Is there any diurnal variation in mood?
- Appetite: Have there been any changes in appetite? Has the client lost or gained weight recently?
- Sleep: How many hours is the client sleeping? Are there any difficulties falling asleep? Do they wake during the night? What time do they awake in the morning? Have there been any recent changes? Does the client have nightmares?
- Libido: Have there been any changes in the client's sex drive?
- Anhedonia: Is the client able to enjoy life or activities?
- Irritability: Does the client feel irritable or agitated?
- Self-worth and self-image: How do they view themselves? How do they think others see them? Are there any body image issues?
- Hopelessness: How does the client view the future in terms of optimism or pessimism?
- Risk/self-harm/suicide: Are any indicators of risk present concerning self-neglect, self-harm, self-abuse or suicide? Does the client have suicidal thoughts? Has the client made any plans for suicide? Does the client have access to means for suicide? Is the client a danger to others?

(Continued)

Table 2.1 (Continued)

- Psychosis: Does the client experience hallucinations or delusional beliefs, or have overvalued ideas? Is there any evidence of thought disorder?
- Concentration: What is the client's level of concentration? Have there been any recent changes?
- Orientation: Is the client oriented in time and location?
- Memory: What is the client's memory like? Have there been any recent changes?

10. **Medical history:**

- Has the client previously received therapy for the main problem?
- What is the client's medical and psychiatric history?

11. **Ethico-legal:**

- Does the client have any convictions?
- Are there any legal cases currently in progress?
- Are there any child protection issues?
- Is the client currently seeking compensation for injury or negligence?
- Is there anyone affected by the client's difficulties whose needs or safety might need to be considered and assessed?

12. **Personal circumstances:**

- What type of accommodation does the client have and how secure is this?
- With whom does the client live? Are there any problems at home?
- Is the client employed/unemployed/at college or university/school?
- What does the client do in their leisure time?
- How does the client describe their personality?
- Are there any recent changes to personality?
- Are there any relationship or sexual problems?
- How does the client describe their relationships?
- Do they have any children/step-children? What are their ages? Are there any problems?

13. **Family history:**

- Parents: relationship, changes, work.
- Siblings: relationship, changes, work.
- Is there a family psychiatric history?
- Are there any inherited disorders in the family?

14. **Developmental history:**

- Childhood and adolescence: Did any critical incidents occur? What was the atmosphere like at home? How did they get on with others? Were they abused? Were they happy?
- Schooling and education: What was the client's experience of school? How did they get on with their teachers and peers? How successful were they at school? What further education have they had?
- Work: What have they done in terms of work since leaving school? Any significant future plans?

Rather it is a series of coat hooks on which to hang information as it is assimilated' (2005: 80). Throughout, the therapist needs to keep in mind the aims of both identifying the primary problem and uncovering those factors serving to maintain the problem.

While most assessments will take place in a clinic setting, CBT therapists also need to consider the value of conducting an element of the assessment in the 'real world' context of the client which may include family members. Direct observation or contemporaneous self-monitoring can be helpful because the client may not be aware of their habitual thinking or behaviour. For example the client with OCD may not be able to recall how often they wash their hands or what is a normal hygiene routine. This type of assessment can be particularly helpful when it is unclear why the client does not appear to be improving, despite completing assigned homework. The therapist will, however, need to consider carefully any risks posed by the assessment process and the policy of the organization in which they work.

The three systems and five areas analysis

The three systems approach, originating in the 1960s and later expanded (Lang, 1968; Hugdahl, 1981), proposes that clients' emotional experience can be understood in the context of three interlinked systems:

- Behavioural: what does the person do?
- Cognitive: what thoughts and images are occurring, and how is information processed?
- Physiological: what physical sensations or reactions occur? (See Hawton et al., 1989; Grant et al., 2004.)

Cognitive theories emphasize that environmental triggers – whether external or internal to the individual – will activate an emotional response if they are significantly meaningful for the individual. Once the three systems are activated, how an emotionally distressed person behaves will be influenced by their thinking and physiological reactions, which in turn impact the level of emotional distress. For example, a person who is socially anxious may experience the emotion of shame due to their blushing in public, with related thoughts and images, avoidance and safety behaviours as well as physiological changes such as palpitations and sweating.

The three systems approach can assist therapists and their clients in understanding different response patterns to activating events. One person might appear more 'cognitive' than another in terms of self-reported cognitions or distressing images, while for others the physiological system might be emphasized. For example, people with generalized anxiety will describe worry (typically a verbal process) while people experiencing panic attacks

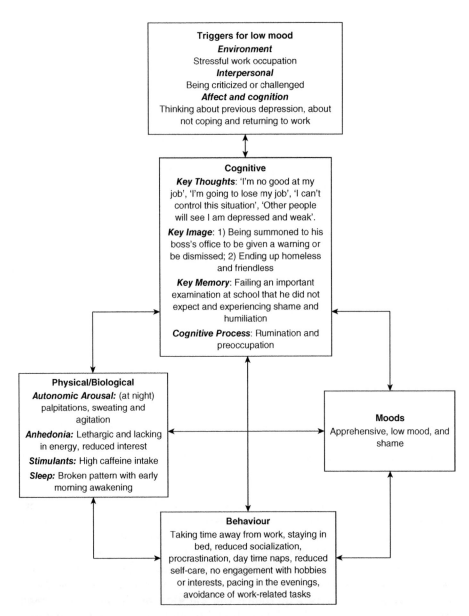

Figure 2.1 The five areas analysis in assessment

focus particularly on the physical sensations that they fear. The three systems model also helps to explain the phenomenon known as synchrony, where all three systems change together, and desynchrony whereby a client might improve in one or more of the systems but more slowly or not at all in the others (Hodgson and Rachman, 1974).

The five areas model is a framework that is useful for both assessment and formulation (Greenberger and Padesky, 1995; Williams and Garland, 2002). It is valuable at the proximal level of assessment with regard to specific episodes of a problem. Consider the example of 'John', who was referred following work-related depression leading to repeated absences from work. The five areas model illustrates for him the situation-specific information and episodic vicious circle formulation (see Figure 2.1) When seen for therapy he was off work again and felt continuously depressed which was worse in the morning with increased anxiety as the day progressed. By assessing a typical day it was possible to assess the environmental, interpersonal, affective and cognitive triggers for low mood and resultant cognitive, emotional, behavioural and physical responses that were maintaining his depression.

An understanding of these areas is crucial for assessment and formulation as this can help illuminate why a client might have improved in one area or system but not another. As therapy proceeds, additional therapeutic strategies can be used to target the unresolved system in order to bring about change.

Measuring outcomes

Measuring therapy outcome is arguably essential with all clients in order to evaluate the effectiveness of the interventions used. It is helpful to approach the issue of outcome assessment with each client from three different perspectives: (1) person-specific (idiosyncratic) measures; (2) standardized symptom measures; and (3) quality of life measures. In each case, measurement should take place (at the very least) at the beginning, mid-point (or where a change in therapeutic strategy is made) and end of therapy and (ideally) at one month, three months and six months after therapy during a follow-up phase. The follow-up phase is important in order to monitor progress over the longer term and provide any assistance with relapse prevention.

Person-specific measures

Person-specific measures include problem and goal ratings. Problem ratings deal with the specific problems the client is expressing. After defining them in a measurable way, the therapist asks the client to rate each one in terms of the amount of discomfort or interference with normal activities that the problem causes. End of therapy goal ratings apply to the goals which the therapist and the client negotiated at the start of therapy. These are usually specific, measurable, attractive, realistic and within a specified time frame (SMART). In both problem and goal statements the scaling system often used is an eleven point scale (0–10).

Other bespoke measures include the frequency of a particular behaviour, such as panic or anger outbursts, and its duration (e.g. the length of time spent hand-washing in someone with an obsessive compulsive disorder). Individualized diaries are usually developed by the therapist for this form of self-monitoring measurement. Personal distress ratings (typically referred to as SUDS (subjective units of discomfort/distress)) or belief ratings using a 0–10 scale (where 0 = no belief and 10 = complete conviction) are also a useful, minimally intrusive and common feature of assessment, formulation and measurement practice (Hawton et al., 1989; Antony and Barlow, 2002).

Standardized symptom and quality of life measures

Standard symptom and quality of life measures have been specifically developed and designed to measure the symptoms of a problem, syndrome or concept, such as depression, self-esteem, hopelessness, shame, panic or anxiety, and the impact of problems on people's quality of life. Quality of life measures are an important part of the outcome measurement process because they evaluate improvements in the overall functioning of the individual. There are now many such measures available for use by CBT therapists, which can be rather overwhelming.[1] A list of some of the most commonly used measures is shown in Table 2.2 below:

Table 2.2   Measures commonly used by CBT therapists[1]

Measure and type	Source of psychometric information
Person Specific:	Information on problems and targets can be found in Marks (1986).
Problems and Targets	
Frequency Counts	
Duration Measurement	
Subjective Units of Discomfort (0–10 scale or 0–100%)	
Strength of Belief Scale (usually 0–100%)	
Standardized Clinical:	
Social Phobia – Social Phobia Inventory (SPIN)	Connor et al. (2000) 'Psychometric properties of the Social Phobia Inventory', *British Journal of Psychiatry,* 176: 379–86.

---

[1]It is an important ethical and legal responsibility to check the copyright status of all measures you use, as these may need to be purchased from the copyright holder.

Measure and type	Source of psychometric information
Social Phobia – Social Phobia and Anxiety Inventory (SPAI)	Beidel, D. C., Turner, S. M., Stanley, M. A. and Dancu, C.V. (1989) 'The social phobia and anxiety inventory: Concurrent and external validity', *Behavior Therapy,* 20(3): 417–27.
Obsessive Compulsive Disorder – Obsessive Compulsive Inventory (OCI)	Foa, E. B., Kozak, M. J., Salkovskis, P. M., Coles, M. E. and Amir, N. (1998) 'The validation of a new obsessive-compulsive disorder scale: The Obsessive-Compulsive Inventory', *Psychological Assessment,* 10(3): 206–14.
Obsessive Compulsive Disorder – The Yale-Brown Obsessive Compulsive Scale (Y-BOCS)	Goodman W.K., Price L.H. and Rasmussen S.A., et al. (1989) 'The Yale-Brown Obsessive Compulsive Scale: I. Development, Use, and Reliability', *Arch Gen Psychiatry,* 46(11): 1006–11.
Post-traumatic Stress Disorder – Impact of Event Scale (IES)	Sundin, E. and Horowitz, M. (2002) 'Impact of Event Scale: Psychometric properties', *British Journal of Psychiatry,* 180: 205–9.
Post-Traumatic Stress Disorder – The Post-traumatic Stress Disorder Diagnostic Scale (PTDS)	Foa, E.B., Cashman, L., Jaycox, L. and Perry, K. (1997) 'The validation of a self-report measure of posttraumatic stress disorder: The Posttraumatic Diagnostic Scale', *Psychological Assessment,* 9(4): 445–51.
Health Anxiety – Health Anxiety Inventory (HAI)	Salkovskis, P.M., Rimes, K.A., Warwick, H.M.C., Clark, D.M. (2002) 'The Health Anxiety Inventory: development and validation of scales for the measurement of health anxiety and hypochondriasis', *Psychological Medicine,* 32: 843–53.
Panic/Agoraphobia – Mobility Inventory	Chambless, D.L., Caputo, G.C., Jasin, S.E., Gracely, E. and Williams, C. (1985) 'The Mobility Inventory for Agoraphobia', *Behaviour Research and Therapy,* 23: 35–44.
Depression – Hospital Anxiety and Depression	Zigmond, A.S. and Snaith R.P. (1983) 'The Hospital Anxiety And Depression Scale', *Acta Psychiatr Scand,* 67: 361–70.

(Continued)

Table 2.2 (Continued)

Measure and type	Source of psychometric information
Depression – Beck Depression Inventory (BDI)	Beck, A.T., Ward, C.H., Mendelson, M., Mock, J. and Erbaugh, J. (1961) 'An inventory for measuring depression', *Archives of General Psychiatry:* 561–71.
Phobia – Fear Questionnaire	Cox, B.J., Parker, J.D. and Swinson R.P. (1996) 'Confirmatory factor analysis of the Fear Questionnaire with social phobia patients', *British Journal of Psychiatry,* 168: 497–99.
Anger – Novaco Anger Inventory	Novaco, R. (1994) 'Anger as a risk factor for violence amongst the mentally disordered', in H. Monahan and H.J. Steadman (eds), *Violence and Mental Disorder: Developments and Mental Disorder.* Chicago. IL: University of Chicago Press.
Generalised Anxiety Disorder – Penn State Worry Questionnaire	Meyer, T.J., Miller, M.L., Metzger, R.L. et al. (1990) 'Development and validation of the Penn State Worry Questionnaire', *Behaviour Research and Therapy,* 28: 487–95.
Anxiety – Beck Anxiety Inventory	Beck, A.T., Epstein, N., Brown, G. and Steer, R.A. (1988) 'An inventory for measuring clinical anxiety: Psychometric properties', *Journal of Consulting and Clinical Psychology,* 56(6): 893–7.
Quality of Life and General Well-being:	
Work and Social Adjustment Scale (WSAS)	Mundt, J.C., Marks, I.M., Greist, J.H. and Shear, K. (2002) 'The Work and Social Adjustment Scale: A simple accurate measure of impairment in functioning', *British Journal of Psychiatry,* 180: 461–4.
Patient Health Questionnaire (PHQ) Family of Measures (including the PHQ-9 for depression and the GAD-7 for anxiety)	Further details can be found at: www. pfizer.com/phq-9
CORE-10	Further information can be found at: http://www.coreims.co.uk/forms_mailer.php

[1]The above table was constructed and updated after consultation with the following sources: Marks (1986); Department of Health (2008a); Robinson et al. (1999); Grant et al (2004); Grant et al. (2008); and Grant et al. (2010).

The use of detailed questionnaires and measures

Using detailed questionnaires and measures is often helpful in the extended assessment process, and is consistent with the role of the CBT therapist as 'scientist-practitioner' (Salkovskis, 2002). However, the extent to which precision is prioritized from the outset may relate in part to the core profession of the therapist gathering the information. For example, according to Sanders and Wills (2005), psychiatrists and psychologists tend to favour structured interviews and standardized measures early in the process, privileging the gathering of precise current data. In contrast, those with a background in counselling or psychotherapy may prioritize the emerging historical and interpersonal story unfolding from the dialogue with clients before using questionnaires (see Corrie and Lane, 2010, for a review of how different professions within applied psychology approach the task of formulation).

Standardized measures may at times be best used after the first session, when a therapeutic bond has been developed between client and therapist. Some therapists and service contexts advocate session-by-session completion of questionnaires, even after the first assessment session, and would encourage any reluctance to complete these as a source of exploration. Beck, for example, advises that, 'If the patient resists filling out forms, the therapist adds this problem to the agenda so that he can help her identify and evaluate her automatic thoughts about completing forms' (1995: 30). Care does, however, have to be taken as client resistance to completing questionnaires could be unhelpfully pathologized. Alternatively, there may be a moral imperative to encouraging clients to complete standardized questionnaires to identify risk or make adjustment to therapy (e.g. a number of questionnaires such as the Beck Depression Inventory have specific items relating to suicidal intent).

The 'demand characteristics' of measurement can also influence clients' responses. Sanders and Wills (2005) argue that long and detailed questionnaires might prove off-putting to some individuals, especially those who have literacy difficulties. Clients may complete measures in such a way as to 'fake good' in order to please their therapists in the spirit of impression management (Goffman, 1969). Clients may also 'fake bad' in order to access a service or extend the duration of therapy. Qualitative measures can be used in response to these issues, such as direct observation of clients in problem- and goal-related scenarios. However, direct observation is not without methodological challenges either, since the presence of the therapist may serve to reassure the client, and thus artificially reduce the client's distress.

Assessment of suitability for CBT

As observed in Chapter 1, the rapid development of CBT has facilitated the adaptation of the approach to a wide range of clinical problems. Nonetheless, in all cases the therapist needs to decide whether CBT is suitable for the client given their current presentation, motivation and situation.

Addressing the question of suitability is important for a number of reasons. First, if the therapy is offered when it is not suitable the chances of a successful outcome for the client are reduced and the therapist might be acting unethically. Second, an inappropriate intervention may have an actively detrimental impact on the client and on the reputation of the therapeutic approach as a whole. Offering therapy to clients in inappropriate circumstances also denies therapy to other clients who might benefit to a greater degree. There are then clinical, ethical and economic reasons for giving careful consideration to the issue of suitability, particularly during the assessment and formulation phases. So what criteria can be used to guide such decisions?

Behaviour therapists have historically used the following set of questions to help guide their decision-making:

1. Are the presenting problems observable?
2. Are the problems current?
3. Are the problems predictable?
4. Can clear behavioural goals be agreed between therapist and client?
5. Does the client understand and are they able to consent to therapy?
6. Are any contra-indications for behaviour therapy present?

These questions, while helpful for assessing a range of observable behaviours, do not work as well when applied to the wider range of clients who can now be helped with cognitive and behavioural approaches. For example, not all problems (such as worry or obsessional thoughts) are observable, yet both are now routinely addressed. The question of the problem being current is also problematic: therapy for trauma using reliving and rescripting focuses on 'recapturing' the original traumatic incident (Ehlers and Clark, 2000). Schema therapy and compassion-focused therapy also use approaches that, while grounded in the 'here and now', draw heavily on past experiences (Young, 1990; Gilbert, 2005).

The third question concerning the predictability of the presenting problem is a challenge if applied to CBT in an inflexible way. Many client problems are predictable if appropriate theory is considered, but not all problems are predictable all of the time. On occasion, working with the client to make the problem more predictable, and developing coping strategies for unpredictability, are useful therapy goals.

The fourth question of clear behavioural goals is partially relevant, as goals are important. Nonetheless, goals might not necessarily be behavioural, but relate more to cognitive-affective components such as reducing the distress from delusional beliefs.

The fifth question of consent and agreement is still of critical importance while the sixth – absence of contra-indications – has changed in light of how the field has developed over the last 20 or 30 years. In the past, individuals with psychosis, personality disorders, learning disabilities, substance misuse or severe depression would have been routinely excluded from therapy. Now specific approaches have been developed to support clients with these types of circumstances and needs (Jones et al., 2012).

Given these criticisms of behavioural criteria, further frameworks have been developed to help the CBT therapist with suitability decisions. Safran et al. (1993) produced suitability criteria that identify how clients are more likely to benefit from time-limited CBT if they can:

- Access negative automatic thoughts (with a little prompting from the therapist).
- Identify and differentiate emotions.
- Accept responsibility for change.
- Relate to the cognitive rationale and approach to change.
- Form an effective therapeutic relationship (predicted from current in-session behaviour and relationship history).
- Present with acute problems that have a recent onset.
- Draw upon psychological processes and coping behaviours in order to restore a sense of psychological security when this is threatened.
- Demonstrate an ability to work in a problem-focused way.
- Be reasonably optimistic about therapy.

Along similar lines, it has been suggested (Sanders and Wills, 2005) that the criteria outlined below (which we have adapted and developed further) are particularly useful for inexperienced therapists. We would always recommend that decisions about suitability are considered in the context of service setting and discussed in supervision.

Acceptability of the approach to therapy

The client

- Can recognize automatic thoughts or images.
- Can recognize and distinguish changes in affect or emotions.
- Can recognize helpful and unhelpful behaviour in self or in others.
- Resonates with the approach and formulation.

Therapeutic relationship

The client

- Can, or has the potential to, form a therapeutic relationship.
- Is able to tolerate the therapeutic process.
- Has coping strategies that are not so extreme or excessive that they impede engagement in therapy.

Individual and attitudinal factors

The client

- Has some optimism regarding therapy.
- Accepts both responsibility and the need for change.
- Is willing to carry out homework assignments.
- Is able to make the time for therapy sessions and homework assignments.
- Is able to concentrate and focus on an agreed agenda.
- Has problems which are not too severe or chronic.
- Is able to contribute to establishing a problem and goal list.

Physical

The client

- Has no medical contra-indications to therapy.

Ethical

- Therapy won't result in harm to the client or to another person.
- The client is able to give informed consent (or others are able to do so legally for the client).

Economic

- Therapy is justified on clinical grounds so that others are not denied a service.
- The private client is able to afford the fees.
- The client can afford the sundry costs of therapy such as exposure materials or travel.

Contextual

- The client is not in the middle of an unrelated crisis.
- The problem can be contained or worked with within the specific setting proposed.

It should be noted that relative to other areas of CBT there remains a lack of substantive evidence on how best to 'align' therapies and clients, and the above represent guidelines rather than clear-cut criteria that should be stringently applied. If it is unclear whether an individual can benefit from the approach, it is often useful to negotiate a 'trial period' of sessions to establish whether CBT might offer the client a helpful means of addressing their problems.

Physical problems

An important issue with regard to decisions about suitability is to ensure that the problem is not due to underlying physical problems or being maintained at least in part by such problems. Certain physical and psychological conditions inhibit psychotherapeutic approaches and some physical problems present as psychological difficulties. In such circumstances, not only would the psychotherapeutic approach be unhelpful, but critical underlying physical problems requiring medical intervention would be overlooked. For example, hyperthyroidism (an overactive thyroid gland) can be mistaken for anxiety, whilst hypothyroidism (underactive thyroid) can be mistaken for depression.

Certain medications can also inhibit the effects of the therapy. For example, benzodiazepines such as diazepam can prevent anxiety reduction when exposure approaches are being used in phobic or obsessive compulsive problems, thus preventing progress. In the case of sedative drugs (benzodiazepines), a commitment to gradual withdrawal, under medical supervision, is often needed before psychotherapeutic work can commence (Marks, 1986). Therapists should also assess for the effects of stimulants such as caffeine, particularly in people who are seeking help with an anxiety problem.

Table 2.3 identifies some of the physical conditions that can mimic anxiety or depression and will, therefore, need further discussion with an appropriately qualified medical practitioner to aid differential diagnosis.

Table 2.3   Physical conditions that mimic anxiety and depression

Physical problem	Mimicked psychological problem	Symptoms	Differentiating characteristics
Hyperthyroidism	Anxiety	Tachycardia, diarrhoea, sweating, weight loss, irritability	Preferences for cold weather; weight loss despite increased appetite; bulging eyes (some cases)
Hypothyroidism	Depression	Lethargy with reduced energy levels	Difficult to identify through observation or interview. Blood test needed before therapy for depression should commence; little daily variability in mood or energy levels
Excessive caffeine	Anxiety and/or panic	Irritability, headaches, tachycardia, tremor, palpitations, insomnia	Symptoms reduce or are eliminated on caffeine reduction

(Continued)

Table 2.3 (Continued)

Physical problem	Mimicked psychological problem	Symptoms	Differentiating characteristics
Hypoglycaemia	Anxiety	Disturbed out of character behaviour, tremor, periods of unexplained fatigue	Specific periodic anxiety, especially when having not eaten
Hyperventilation	Anxiety and/or panic	Most anxiety symptoms but with tingling and dizziness particularly prominent	Dizziness; ringing in the ears

Attending to diversity

Cognitive behavioural approaches have been criticized for adopting and promoting culturally insensitive, Eurocentric, white and middle-class positions in both research and practice (see Okazaki and Tanaka-Matsumi, 2006). Understanding diversity and being able to work respectfully with this are essential prerequisites to effective therapy (Martell et al., 2004; LaTaillade, 2006; Okazaki and Tanaka-Matsumi, 2006).

In order to be collaborative in a way that is sensitive to difference, CBT therapists need to have some familiarity with the major religions and other societal or community level beliefs and take every opportunity to learn from their clients who have backgrounds different from their own (Newman, 2007). In consequence, it is essential to consult with clients, colleagues, community and spiritual leaders and to undertake relevant reading in order to know how to adapt therapeutic work with particular clients or client groups. Some of the main issues for consideration include:

1. The importance of traditional family systems, hierarchical social structures and family roles, for example for Asian clients. Respect for parents or the head of the household (if not the parent) and the strong influence of shame with consequent reticence in revealing information or engaging in behaviours that might be seen as shaming for the family. In assessment this is more helpfully understood as being dutiful to the family rather than as resistance.
2. Black clients may be concerned about receiving prejudicial treatment from white therapists. This may be usefully incorporated into the formulation with particular attention to the therapeutic relationship. A further issue that can also arise in therapy in our experience is that some clients of mixed race, or in some cases black clients brought up by white parents following adoption, have difficulty identifying with either 'black' or

'white' cultures and report feeling lost, isolated and unsure of their own identities. These issues, if present, need to be identified and addressed within the formulation.

3. Religion and its associated beliefs and rituals need to be understood by the CBT therapist if any subsequent formulation is to fully reflect the individual and their needs. It can also be helpful to build religious beliefs into the formulation when there is agreement that it is relevant to do so.

4. Poverty has the greatest and most directly measurable effect on rates of psychological need. People in lower income brackets, lower educational status, and certain occupations have a two to threefold increase in their likelihood of developing psychological problems. Racism, discrimination and bullying in the workplace are also associated with disorders such as chronic anxiety and depression (LaTaillade, 2006). These issues need to be raised and assessed and incorporated into the formulation when therapist and client agree that it is relevant to do so.

It is also important to assess for protective factors and coping strategies (for example, positive core beliefs, and assertive challenging of discrimination). Such strengths, even in the face of continued stress, can promote positive therapeutic outcomes. Other important protective factors might include forms of family, community or other social support, spiritual or religious beliefs and a strong sense of identity commitment to a particular sexual orientation, such as being gay or lesbian (Padesky, 1989). These all provide an individual with resources for challenging negative stereotypes (LaTaillade, 2006).

A number of specific culture-bound conditions have been identified and described in the international psychiatric literature. An awareness of these can be important for CBT therapists when assessing clients from particular populations. Some of these culture-bound syndromes have been listed in DSM-5 and ICD-10. Among the terms listed are a number of low mood and anxiety-based reactions which present as physically or psychologically focused problems and reactions. A list of these, adapted from Wolfgang (2001) and Wen-Shing (2006) is shown in Table 2.4 below.

In relational terms, by demonstrating that they understand or are taking the opportunity to learn about the person's heritage or religious beliefs, therapists strengthen the therapeutic relationship and help build trust (LaTaillade, 2006). In order to work respectfully and effectively with difference, we also recommend a willingness to reflect upon and challenge our own discriminatory beliefs.

The current climate of 'political correctness' may make it difficult for therapists, experienced or otherwise, to admit to some form of bias through a fear of criticism or professional censure. Nonetheless, evidence from work on social cognition suggests that to be human is to be biased and therefore prejudiced in one way or another (Augoustinos et al., 2006). This point is made not in the spirit of condoning sexism, ageism or racism

Table 2.4 Culture-bound syndromes

Culture-bound syndrome	Language or Region	Name given to the 'syndrome'
Fear of genital shrinking	Malay-Indonesian Mandarin Chinese Languages	Koro Suo-yang
Fear of semen leakage	India	Chat or Jiryan
Dissociative reactions to a specific startle stimulus	Malay-Indonesian languages Thailand Phillippines Siberia Rural populations of French-Canadian background in the Northeast of the US	Latah Bah-tschi Mali-mali Miryachit Jumping
Fear that one's external appearance is offending to others	Japan	Taijin-kyofu
Acute stress depression symptoms	North American indigenous population	Anomie
Vision disturbance when reading	African students	Brain fag

but simply highlighting that therapists are not discrimination-immune. It is preferable to acknowledge and work with therapist biases (either in clinical supervision or through other developmental processes) rather than to simply ignore them or pretend that they do not exist. Indeed, we would maintain that this is an essential professional obligation.

For this reason, we recommend that therapists continually revisit this issue by asking themselves the following questions:

1. Do I manifest an ideology that promotes a biased attitude on the grounds of age, culture, race, religion or sexuality?
2. How have or might I have internalized or developed an attitude or behaviours that reflect bias or prejudice in some way?
3. What past or recent experiences or events including media portrayals might have biased me?

Summary

✓ Assessment and measurement of client problems includes both idiographic and nomothetic approaches.
✓ Idiographic assessment based on a functional analysis is the core of CBT assessment.
✓ Key areas of assessment include cross-sectional and longitudinal elements.

✓ Three systems and five areas analyses are useful frameworks for developing a cross-sectional understanding of clients' problems.
✓ Throughout the assessment process it is essential to remain attentive to matters of diversity and difference and to accommodate these within the emerging understanding of clients' needs.

Activities

- Consider the way that you utilize diagnosis in therapy and its usefulness.
- Examine the balance between idiographic and nomothetic approaches in your own practice.
- Consider how you might make the best use of five areas analysis within the assessment process.

Further reading

Antony, M. and Barlow, D.H. (2002) *Handbook of Assessment and Treatment Planning for Psychological Disorders*. New York: Guilford Press.
This edited text provides an authoritative review of assessment strategies and tools.

Grant, A., Townend, M., Mulhern, R. and Short, N. (2010) *Cognitive Behavioural Therapy in Mental Health Care*. 2nd edn. London: Sage.
An excellent introductory text that covers basic processes and procedures within CBT and a range of problem areas.

THREE Process and Relational Factors in CBT Assessment and Case Formulation

Adrian Cockx, Sarah Corrie and Michael Townend

Learning objectives

After reading this chapter and completing the learning activities provided you should be able to:

- Appreciate the rationalist and constructivist approaches that have shaped understanding of the therapeutic relationship.
- Identify how knowledge of cognitive distortions and the use of guided discovery and Socratic dialogue can support collaborative understanding of the cognitive model.
- Describe how CBT understands ruptures and resistance in the therapy relationship.
- Understand the value of self-practice and self-reflection in CBT.
- Describe how therapist beliefs and schema mismatches can impact the therapy relationship, and appreciate ways in which this can be addressed.

Introduction

The chapter on process and relational issues in the first edition of this book (Grant et al., 2008) provided the reader with a thorough overview of the relational aspects of the assessment process. In the intervening years, it would appear that relatively little has changed. There remains a paucity of research in this area and opportunities for CBT training on process and relational issues continue to be limited relative to the training devoted to disorder-specific models.

The aim of this chapter is to look at how process and relational factors are influenced by the theories and research that inform CBT practice, and how attention to these factors is vital to the client's experience of the usefulness of therapy. Through gaining an understanding of process and relational issues the reader will be able to broaden their practice, understand any obstacles that arise and find ways to balance the technique-oriented and process-related elements of which good therapy comprises.

Elaborating understanding of CBT assessment: rationalist and constructivist approaches

As described in Chapter 2, CBT approaches to assessment and case formulation seek to understand clients' presenting problems through gathering information that can explain the relationship between the activated emotions, thoughts and behaviours that serve to maintain the problem. Through this process of information-gathering, past and present issues are considered alongside the impact of predisposing biological and genetic factors. Once these factors have been identified and collated, new understanding can be achieved – often illustrated by a diagrammatic cycle demonstrating how the problem is maintained in light of significant critical incidents. This enables the client and therapist to establish a shared view of the problem and thus work towards changing the patterns identified (Freeman et al., 2004).

Although owing much of its current popularity to levels of efficacy established through randomized controlled trials, it is important to remember that CBT is never as simple as a three-step process of: (1) problem identification; (2) protocol-based intervention; and (3) goal attainment. Such a singular view can minimize the role of many micro-factors inherent in the delivery of therapy. Protocol-driven interventions are important. However, a parsimonious approach that combines the most effective elements of this rationalist view with a constructivist perspective can offer therapists a wider, more complete approach to the assessment and formulation of their clients' needs.

Rationalist perspectives are based on the assumption, 'as you think, so you shall feel'. Problems, therefore, are conceptualized as dysfunctions that take the form of 'symptomological' thoughts, feelings and behaviours in the context of internal and external cues. A constructivist perspective, in contrast, attempts to view clients' difficulties as a process of developmental and historical experience emerging in a specific context, thus identifying the tensions between environmental challenges and the individual's present capacities (Mahoney and Gabriel, 2002).

Mahoney (1988) identified an explicit difference between rationalist and constructivist approaches to CBT which is evident in the view of reality adopted by each. A rationalist perspective views reality as external and stable and subject to confirmation and validation, whereas a constructivist view understands reality as entirely subjective and idiosyncratic. A rationalist perspective will seek to validate knowledge through logic and reasoning, with priority given to thought or behaviour over emotion. Through a constructivist perspective knowledge is seen as an integrated cognitive-behavioural-affective experience. Table 3.1 below highlights the implications of some of these differences for the assessment and case formulation process.

Table 3.1 Differences between rationalist and constructivist approaches (Mahoney and Gabriel, 2002)

Issue/theme	Rationalist view	Constructivist view
Intervention/ emphasis	A. Historical B. Problem-focused C. Control-focused.	A. Historical B. Process-focused C. Development-focused.
Conceptualization of problem	Problems are dysfunctions or deficits, they should be controlled, eliminated or redressed.	Problems are discrepancies between environmental stressors and current capacities; they reflect limits in abilities and should not be mistaken for their abstract ordering processes.
Conceptualization of emotion	Emotion, especially when intense and negative, is a problem; irrational thinking is the cause.	Emotions are primitive, powerful ways of knowing: affective experience and exploration should be encouraged.
Resistance	Resistance reflects lack of motivation, ambivalence, or avoidance. Resistance is an impediment to therapeutic change and must be 'overcome'.	Resistance reflects self-protective processes that guard systemic integrity and protect against rapid 'core' change. Resistance should be worked *with* rather than *against*.
Insight	Insight into irrational beliefs is necessary and (almost) sufficient for therapeutic change.	Insight may help to transform personal meanings and facilitate change, but emotional and behavioural enactments are also important.

Issue/theme	Rationalist view	Constructivist view
Therapeutic relationship	The therapeutic relationship entails technical instruction and guidance.	The therapeutic relationship provides a safe, caring and intense context in which the client can explore and develop relationships with self, others and world.
Relapse and regression	Relapse and regression reflect failures in maintenance and generalization that should be avoided and minimized.	Relapse and regression reflect limits in current capacity and/or cycles in psychological development; they involve important learning opportunities.

© Mahoney and Gabriel (2002)

Most approaches emphasize the therapist-client relationship as central in effecting change (Schaap et al., 1993). While not going as far as person-centred approaches where it is argued that a good therapeutic relationship is all that is required to promote change, CBT therapists do embrace the idea that the better the relationship, the more likely clients are to share their experiences openly and honestly and to listen carefully to any challenges that their therapists offer to pre-existing thoughts and beliefs (Townend and Grant, 2008). As such, the relationship underpins both CBT technique and strategy and this is the foundation on which the CBT approach is based.

Questions and questioning in CBT

It is through the client's narrative that the therapist can start to identify how maintenance of the presenting problem occurs. Questioning styles provide a vehicle of exploration that enables greater clarity and understanding of the cognitive processes implicated in the client's distress (Burns, 1980).

Questions serve a variety of functions that span gathering information, developing interest and encouraging critical thought or evaluation. The current CBT literature focuses predominantly on Socratic questioning (Overholser, 1993; Carey and Mullan, 2004). Identified by Padesky (1993) as a 'cornerstone' of CBT, Socratic dialogue is a process of enquiry devised by the classical Greek philosopher Socrates, aimed at encouraging the individual to question their existing perspectives and, where appropriate, develop new understandings. The process is one of enabling the person to identify information that is potentially available to them but which falls outside of their current awareness. As such, the client is supported in arriving at their own conclusion about some aspect of their life or experience, rather than being 'instructed' by the therapist on what to think.

Westbrook et al. (2011) describe the Socratic method of questioning as an 'ideal tool' for facilitating the search for novel possibilities. They highlight three broad categories of question that form an important part of the CBT therapist's armoury. These are:

1. Questions aimed at uncovering evidence (e.g. evidence for and against a specific cognition).
2. Questions aimed at identifying alternative perspectives (e.g. other ways of viewing the event or situation; how the client thinks another person might view the situation).
3. Questions relating to consequences (e.g. the implications, emotionally, behaviourally and interpersonally, of having a particular thought or belief, including what is helpful and unhelpful about holding a particular view).

Westbrook et al. (2011) highlight how the use of questions drawn from these categories can facilitate a fuller and more balanced perspective while also enabling greater self-understanding that can minimize any tendencies towards self-criticism (i.e. 'Given that I have been viewing the situation this way, it is not surprising that I have been so low').

Socratic questions are not the only method of questioning that is useful in CBT. Indeed, sometimes it can be counter-productive (for example, if the aim is to gain information in as efficient a manner as possible, or if a client does not have the knowledge of the topic in hand to engage in this type of exploration). James et al. (2010) argue that there is limited literature and training available for CBT therapists on the use of more general questions in therapy and that further training in this area may help support the development of therapist skill. However, there is a burgeoning literature on the facilitative power of questioning styles in the fields of both education and coaching which can augment the CBT therapist's tool-kit (the interested reader is referred to de Bono, 1995 and Kline, 1999, for a good introduction to this field).

In selecting your approach to questioning, it is critical that you are clear about what you are aiming to achieve with your line of enquiry. For example, are you seeking to gather information that can inform judgements about whether a client is exhibiting the signs of a particular disorder? Aiming to clarify your own understanding of the main issues as a basis for formulation? Wishing to communicate an empathic understanding, or hoping to draw the client's attention to contradictory aspects of their narrative? Each objective will require a different approach and every questioning style needs to be considered for its potential impact. As Beck et al. warn,

> Questions constitute an important and powerful tool for identifying, considering, and correcting cognitions and beliefs. As with other powerful tools, they can be misused or artlessly applied. The patient may feel he is being cross-examined or that he is being attacked if questions are used to 'trap' him into contradicting himself. (1979: 71)

Using cognitive distortions and Socratic dialogue in guiding discovery

During the client's unfolding narrative, and via the process of questioning, the therapist will become aware of certain expressed thoughts and activated behaviours that are associated with high levels of emotion. Goleman (1996) refers to this as 'emotional hijacking' whereby the brain seemingly switches between modes and styles of thinking. Automatic attention processes scan the environment for various types of information that will either support or disconfirm an individual's initial thoughts or beliefs. These cognitions can also be verified by past experiences, physical sensations and those around us. It is these emotional hotspots that provide the therapist with an opportunity to pursue a line of enquiry and explore the role and nature of these cognitions. Table 3.2 identifies some of the common and well-documented cognitive distortions along with brief examples to illustrate how emotional hijacking can present.

Any incongruence within the client's narrative provides the therapist with a means of exploring the presenting conflicts and any associated cognitive distortions. When goals are in conflict with beliefs and behaviours the therapist is presented with a golden opportunity to see what is maintaining

Table 3.2   Common cognitive distortions

Distortion	Example
Dichotomous thinking: Seeing things in 'all-or-nothing' categories.	Nadia thought she was a failure as she was unable to get a new job.
Overgeneralization: Seeing a single negative event as a never-ending pattern of defeat.	Nick thought he would spend the rest of his life being single after a relationship ended.
Mental filter: Picking out a single negative detail and dwelling on it to the exclusion of others.	Felix thought he would never get anywhere in his life because he had been unwell and unable to do any work that week.
Disqualifying the positive: Rejecting positive experiences by insisting they don't count.	Despite her friends saying how beautiful her dress was, Jennifer was upset as one person had said they didn't like what she was wearing.
Jumping to conclusions; mind reading: Arbitrarily making conclusions about what others are thinking. (See also fortune telling: predicting that things will turn out badly.)	Caroline assumed that her boyfriend didn't love her because he didn't tell her every day. Jo thought her day was going to be terrible because she walked under a ladder.

(Continued)

Table 3.2   (Continued)

Distortion	Example
Magnification (catastrophizing)/ minimization: Exaggerating or shrinking the importance of events inappropriately.	Despite visiting the doctor and having tests, Amboj believed he had cancer as there was a rash on his stomach.
Emotional reasoning: Thinking that negative emotions reflect the way that things really are, thus basing decisions on emotions alone.	Following a bad day at work George decided not to go out with his friends as he sensed they were just asking him to be polite.
Should statements: Criticizing oneself and others using unfair rules and standards.	Adrian thought he should have a stable job and be married by the time he was 35 years old.
Labelling: Calling oneself names in response to events.	Kamaleeka thought she was stupid because she failed her driving test at first attempt.
Personalization: Blaming oneself or others for something without accounting for other factors that were involved.	Sam thought he was unpopular because fewer people came to his party than he had expected.

these competing factors. The use of Socratic dialogue enables a stance of curiosity to be utilized to help the client identify these factors for themselves. As therapists we are aware that research has been able to provide us with techniques and approaches that are known to be effective. However, clients are living with behaviours and beliefs that they have often maintained for a substantial period of time. If beliefs are held strongly it is going to be more difficult for the therapist to question and find alternatives. This is where Socratic dialogue can be helpful.

Padesky's (1993) keynote address to the European Congress of Behavioural and Cognitive Therapies identified the Socratic approach as instrumental in the effective delivery of therapy. Specifically she proposed that Socratic dialogue enables therapists to understand how using an exploratory questioning style can help clients recognize the impact and influence of their current beliefs, values and behaviours on their presenting problems. Padesky also points out that therapists often need to 'not know' where they are going when asking Socratic questions. This presents therapists with an interesting dilemma; if practice is informed by research which demonstrates that certain types of cognition and behaviour are integral to specific disorders, the therapist is likely to follow a line of questioning that fits the specific theory. Nelson (1997) described this approach as being a process of 'logical reasoning' in as much as the therapist will ask a series of questions that will eventually confirm their hypothesis. Therefore, as noted previously, it is important to hold in mind what you are attempting to achieve through the questions asked.

Padesky (1996b) has devised a method in which the therapist utilizes the client's narrative to help guide their own discovery and identify alternatives, thus providing some structure to the process. Her approach comprises four main elements:

1. Informational questions: aimed at helping the client describe their problem, looking at functional aspects in relation to how the problem was formed and how it is being maintained.
2. Empathic listening: the therapist acknowledges the struggle the client has with the identified problem. This can be demonstrated non-verbally (e.g. through facial expressions) and verbally (with acknowledging statements).
3. Summarizing: once the client has described the problem the therapist will summarize their understanding in their own words, acknowledging the emotional context and establishing with the client that their understanding is correct.
4. Analytical/Synthesizing questions: which ask the client to review the written summary and compare the information gathered with their original beliefs or conclusions they have drawn.

An example of this can be found in the following dialogue:

Informational Question

Therapist: Can you tell me about a time when you experienced your problem and how that made you feel?

Client: Well, when I am at work I am always being judged by others. No matter what I do people are looking at me, talking about me and thinking that I am a failure which makes me feel like not doing anything.

Empathic Listening

Therapist: [Non-verbal: Therapist nods head, shows an expression of discomfort acknowledging the difficulty of the emotion.]

Therapist: [Verbal:] That must be very difficult for you and I can understand that thinking in such a way would not motivate you into wanting to do anything.

Summarizing

Therapist: If I understand you correctly, what you are telling me is that when you are at work you think that your colleagues are

> judging you and talking about you, which makes you unable to get on with your work.

Client: Yes, that's right.

Synthesizing

Therapist: How do these ideas fit with your original thought? How do you fit these experiences together with the thought 'Others think I'm a failure'?

Client: There are times when I feel like I am being judged but it is most difficult when it happens at work. When I am at home with my family or with my friends I feel accepted and I am able to do the things I need and want to.

Therapist: It's good to hear that there are times when you feel able to get on well with others. Is being accepted at work something you would like to achieve from therapy?

Client: Yes that seems like a good goal.

Making use of guided discovery, therapist and client are able to acknowledge the emotional context and develop a goal for therapy. The next step would be to place the problem within a formulation. The efficacy of CBT first relies on the client being able to understand how their thoughts have an impact on the maintenance of the problem and it is through the cognitive model that an understanding can be developed (Townend and Grant, 2008).

The cognitive model

The cognitive model allows the therapist and client to develop a shared understanding of how the client's difficulties are impacted by the inter-relationship between different 'layers' of cognition. These are best presented by Padesky (1997) in the form of the Levels of Thought diagram shown in Figure 3.1.

The outer ring of the model points to the level known as 'automatic thoughts'. This is the most accessible level of cognition, representing the stream of consciousness that enters our minds in response to everyday events. This level of cognition includes negative automatic thoughts and images that may subsequently become the focus of a number of cognitive and behavioural interventions.

The middle ring represents a set of typically less accessible and more general beliefs, often referred to as underlying assumptions. These beliefs are tacitly held, apply across situations, and can be conveniently understood as 'rules for living'. They are associated with patterns of response in how people act towards themselves, other people and the world around them. For instance a person who holds the assumption 'Unless I do things 100% right then I am a failure' may exhibit perfectionist behaviour or avoid challenges.

In the central ring of the model are core beliefs, also sometimes known as schemas. As the least accessible level of thinking, core beliefs represent the fundamental views we hold about other people, the world and ourselves in general. These beliefs typically arise from our early life experiences and can be seen as emerging from the first and enduring lessons that life has

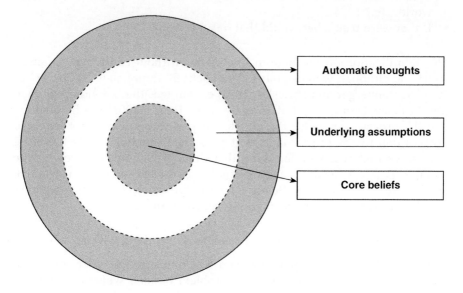

Figure 3.1   Padesky's Levels of Thought diagram

© 1987 Christine A. Padesky

Source: Padesky, C.A. and Mooney, K.A. (2005) *Winter Workshop in Cognitive Therapy* (workshop handouts). Palm Desert, CA.

taught us. Core beliefs are strongly related to self-esteem, self-confidence, prejudice and world views and are evident in the way in which we view ourselves, others and the world when we are exposed to emotional distress.

Eliciting rules, underlying assumptions and core beliefs

The themes in a client's automatic thoughts and the cognitive distortions in their information processing are often indicative of patterns in their underlying assumptions and core beliefs. In order to establish their relationship to any presenting problems and to support socialization to the model, a process known as the 'vertical downward arrow technique' can be utilized. Downward arrowing is a specific type of questioning that enables clients to elaborate upon and identify any deeper meanings underlying their surface level cognitions, emotions and reactions (sometimes termed 'getting to the bottom line'). These questions can take a variety of forms but often include the following:

- What was the absolute worst thing about that situation for you?
- If that were true, what would it say about you (other people, life, the world, etc.)?
- If that were true what would that mean to you?

The identification of 'the bottom line' is not without controversy (James, 2001) and although well-established self-help literature such as *Mind Over Mood* (Greenberger and Padesky, 1995) encourages the individual to identify these levels of thought at an early stage, James (2001) has highlighted that the process can cause the client to experience unnecessary levels of distress due to the often unpleasant associated emotions. It is therefore imperative that when undertaking this element of guided discovery the therapist is able to ensure that the client leaves the session in a constructive and hopeful frame of mind. Below is a narrative example of how to address the identification of core beliefs in a sensitive manner.

Client:	It's just terrible. I can't seem to do anything with myself.
Therapist:	I'm sorry to hear that you feel that way. In order for me to try and understand your problem better I wonder if you can describe a recent situation when this happened.
Client:	Well, I was at home the other day and thought I would make myself a cup of tea. When I went to the fridge I realized I had run out of milk and then just couldn't face going to the shop to get some milk.
Therapist:	And what did you think would happen if you did go out and get some milk?
Client:	I thought what a mess I am and that everyone I met would see me looking so down and awful.
Therapist:	And how would this make you think about yourself?
Client:	It would make me think I am a failure.
Therapist:	As you say those words 'I am a failure' what feelings do you experience?
Client:	I feel depressed and down.

Here, the therapist uses a behavioural example to elicit the automatic thoughts the client experiences with regard to a feared consequence. It is also worth noting that this is done compassionately and with understanding. The emotions associated with the core belief 'I am a failure' also need to be explored to ensure that what is being identified relates to the client's initial presentation. It is at this point that the therapist can elicit any related core beliefs in relation to others and the world in general. This process can be facilitated by asking the following questions:

Therapist: You have described seeing yourself as a failure. When you feel this way what do you think about others?

Client: I think others are better than me.

Therapist: And when you think you are a failure and others are better than you how do you see the world around you?

Client: I think the world is a judgemental place.

As mentioned earlier, James (2001) has identified that the process of eliciting core beliefs can potentially cause a client unnecessary distress. In order to alleviate any potential distress and instil hope the following questions can be asked:

Therapist: From what you have told me, at present the way that you are thinking is seemingly contributing to your problem. However, can you tell me about a time when things were going well for you?

Client: Oh yes. Last year I was working on a construction job and supervising ten other workers.

Therapist: And how would you have described yourself at that time?

Client: I would say I was capable.

Again the same process as above can be used to elicit the more helpful schematic patterns:

Therapist: And when you felt capable, how did you think about others?

Client: I thought others were no better or worse than me.

Therapist: So when you were feeling capable and that others were no better or worse than you how did you see the world in general?

Client: I thought the world was full of opportunity.

Figure 3.2 Continuum example

Once helpful and unhelpful core beliefs have been identified an opportunity arises for therapist and client to construct a continuum that illustrates how the way in which we think about ourselves differs as a function of context. In many cases, by drawing on past experience, the therapist has an opportunity to instil hope by communicating that change is possible. Figure 3.2 illustrates this aspect of empiricism, using a cross and a percentage to show how it is possible to move along the continuum dependent on the situation. Through establishing a continuum and percentage ratings the therapist is able to provide an opportunity to question the evidence that the client has for their beliefs respective of internal and external environmental cues.

Prior to developing methods through which to test the evidence supporting the client's automatic thoughts, underlying assumptions and core beliefs, it is necessary to utilize a structured framework that shows how their problems are maintained within a vicious cycle. However, this process does not always go according to plan. Clients are often uncertain about therapy and unable to see how it will help them. It is at these times that therapists need to look at interpersonal factors that are potentially inhibiting a collaborative understanding. This includes themselves.

Therapeutic ruptures

In a study examining what works in therapy, Lambert and Barley (2002) found that although it is difficult to conceptually differentiate the therapist variables of individual style, warmth, empathy and positive regard, the greatest predictor of change was the therapeutic relationship at 40 per cent. Technique on the other hand accounted for only 15 percent of the variance, which was the same as client therapy expectancy (that is, knowing that they were addressing the presenting problems). This must make us question our style of practice within a heavily technique-driven approach such as CBT. Anecdotally, for one of us (Cockx) it is not uncommon to come across students reporting that they have tried every technique that has been validated by a randomized controlled trial but that the client still seems unable to grasp the concept or achieve behavioural change – an observation that can all too easily be interpreted as 'resistance to change'. However, it is precisely at these times that we can explore what is happening within the therapeutic relationship and what is happening for the client that is preventing progress.

Understanding resistance

In his book, *Overcoming Resistance in Cognitive Therapy*, Leahy (2001) provides an in-depth exploration of the concept of resistance from a CBT perspective. He proposes that when relying on structured nomothetic protocol-driven interventions, CBT therapists can often neglect the client's individuality. This lack of attention to developing a shared, validated understanding of the presenting problems can lead the therapist to blame the client and the client to feel that they are not being understood. Leahy (2001) makes reference to the role of 'counter transference', as it is often the self-preservation strategies of our clients that are being activated.

Leahy identified the following dimensions of resistance:

- **Validation:** The client 'gets stuck' in needing validation for their distress and their perspective.
- **Self-consistency:** The client may have 'sunk costs' and believe that changing their situation will only make them feel worse about themselves.
- **Schematic resistance:** Unhelpful beliefs that the client holds about themselves are activated through the process of change, and the associated affect may be too challenging to experience.
- **Moral resistance:** A client's world view is questioned through the process of therapy and due to moral reasons they feel that they are not worthy of change or change is unjust.
- **Victim:** The client may see themselves as a victim and entitled to their suffering or are unable to see another's perspective.
- **Risk-aversion:** The risks associated with change may feel too much for the client. Challenges to the view of self and status quo engender too much fear.
- **Self-handicapping strategy:** Too much focus on the presenting problem could shadow other factors that are inherent in the maintenance of the problem.

Developing a shared understanding through both the initial case formulation and a conceptualization of the perceived resistance are key elements to ensuring a good outcome. Gaining an understanding not only of factors present in the client's resistance but of those activated in the therapist is also important in identifying how resistance might best be approached. This highlights the invaluable role not only of supervision, but also the therapist's own self-practice and self-reflection.

Self-practice and self-reflection for CBT therapists

Traditional behavioural therapy rejected the role of self-practice and personal therapy during training, but this view has been challenged within the CBT community over the past 10–20 years. Leaders in the field (e.g. Beck 1995; Padesky, 1996a) have proposed that therapists are well-advised to use those techniques they introduce to their clients on their own material first. This allows therapists to gain a personal understanding of how specific techniques work and how they can be experienced, thus enabling a shared experiential perspective with their clients. Research undertaken by Bennett-Levy et al. (2001; see also Bennett-Levy et al., 2015) found that CBT trainees were more effective in the delivery of therapy if they had first tried the techniques they used with their clients on themselves. This research further suggested that where long-standing personality difficulties were present in their clients, the therapist's knowledge of their own thoughts, feelings and schemas helped in the prevention of these becoming enmeshed with their clients'.

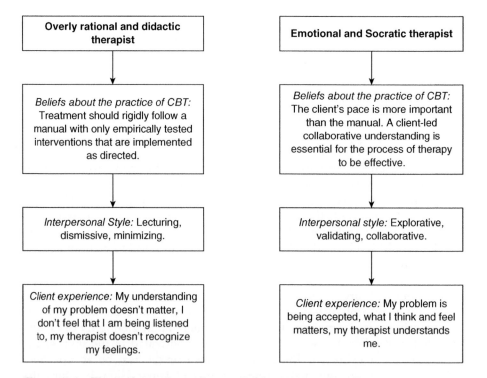

Figure 3.3 Therapist style and potential impact on the client

Developing a personal understanding of the techniques used in therapy alongside our own beliefs, values and schemas can be of potential benefit in resolving any ruptures we may face within the therapeutic relationship. Through the use of a self-focused case formulation and utilizing identified problematic areas, a therapist illustration can be developed. This combined with the client's formulation will allow competing beliefs and values to become apparent.

Schema mismatch and therapist beliefs

Leahy (2001) recognizes the impact of the therapist's own view of self within the therapeutic relationship. He examines how the schemas a therapist holds can influence the progress of therapy in the context of the previously identified dimensions of resistance, making reference to the fact that all therapists have different interpersonal styles and emotional philosophies. For example, if a therapist is keen to keep to a strict agenda when a client is expressing high levels of emotion, the likelihood is that an unsympathetic message of 'emotions are not relevant' is conveyed and the client may experience thoughts such as, 'My emotions are embarrassing to others' and 'I am stupid to show my emotions'. Equally, if a therapist is quick to rescue the client from their feelings through reassurance, an implicit message may be given to the client that there is a need to eradicate painful emotions rather than explore them. This could lead to an increase in client avoidance and affirm avoidance as a coping strategy.

Figure 3.3 has been adapted from Leahy (2007) to illustrate the differences in therapist style based on the beliefs about the practice of CBT, and their potential impact on the client.

Identifying therapist beliefs

Padesky (1999) makes reference to how CBT's apparent success has been built on the development of specific protocols that give the therapist a structure. This in turn provides the client with a framework of understanding and specific interventions that relate to their presenting problems.

Protocols provide a standardized method through which the efficacy of therapy for specific disorders can be measured. This in turn gives the therapist confidence in knowing that there are tried and tested methods that have worked for others with similar problems. However, outcome studies tend to overlook therapist factors inherent in the therapeutic process. Through the identification of cognitive distortions and client emotion an opportunity presents itself to explore what is happening for not only the client but also the therapist. This may first take the form of feeling emotionally hijacked (Goleman, 1996) where emotions become overwhelming and clarity of thought and an ability to follow the client are difficult to sustain. Negative automatic thoughts and physiological sensations become more apparent triggering feelings of hopelessness and helplessness. Padesky (1999) draws on the work of Epstein (1994) who identified rational and emotive processing systems termed experiential and analytical. Both these systems have their strengths and weaknesses; the experiential system can quickly and efficiently direct behaviour since this is primarily influenced by emotion, whereas the rational system directs behaviour through logical principles. Although the rational system can correct the experiential system it is slower and requires more cognitive processes to function effectively. The rational system can influence the experiential system through repetition once a problem has been identified and new adaptive responses have been tested. However, it may be helpful to identify some examples of the potential factors that provide a therapist with the opportunity to reflect on themselves, their practice and the relationship with their client. The following emotions, thoughts, sensations and behaviours are those which a therapist may experience when their beliefs are mismatched with a client in therapy:

Emotions: Feeling overwhelmed, tired, nonchalant, anxious, fearful, sad, angry, irritable, cynical, hopeless, helpless.

Thoughts: 'I don't seem to be getting anywhere'; 'This client doesn't want to get better'; 'I'm wasting my time'; 'I cannot focus on what the client is saying'; 'Why doesn't the client see how obvious this problem is?'; 'I must get this right'.

Physical: Tightening of the stomach, increased heart rate, feeling sleepy, phasing in and out, stifling yawns, muscle tension, shallow breathing, experiencing a sinking feeling.

Behaviours: Becoming more didactic, clock watching, going over the agreed time, terminating the session prematurely, interrupting the client, emotional avoidance, indulging too much in eliciting emotions.

Once the inter-relation of the above aspects has been identified there is enough information for the therapist to begin formulating what is occurring. Time to reflect on key cognitions, emotions, beliefs, assumptions and behaviours gives the therapist an opportunity to identify how the pattern is being maintained and to develop new strategies which complement both client and therapist goals. This can be seen diagrammatically if both the client formulation and therapist formulation are placed side by side (see Chapter 15 for an example of how therapist material that had the potential to unhelpfully impact therapy was identified and explored).

Summary

✓ CBT has gained great popularity based on rigorous research that has been aligned to diagnostic categories and studies that have been designed to test theoretical principles.
✓ Tried and tested interventions that address the various disorders provide therapists with an understanding of potentially effective strategies.
✓ However, it is essential to attend to the more subtle aspects inherent in the therapeutic relationship as an over-dependence on technique may come at the cost of achieving a mutually agreed result.
✓ It is the role of the therapist to understand not simply the treatment protocols that might underpin their practice but also the intricacies of the developing therapeutic relationship.
✓ Cognitive and behavioural interventions should not only be there to help our clients but also to help us understand ourselves.

Activities

Develop your own formulation of a problem you are having with a client:

1. Identify your own behaviours, assumptions and core beliefs, paying attention to the emotions and physical sensations you experience.
2. Formulate the problem using the five areas model (© 1986 Christine A. Padesky, www.padesky.com) to diagrammatically illustrate the vicious cycles (see Chapter 2).
3. Noting the goals of the client and your own goals for therapy, become aware of any incongruent factors that could impede therapy. Consider what adjustments might need to be made.
4. Consider what action, based on the above, you can now take to address this problem. (This may include use of supervision, completing a thought diary for yourself, or constructing a behavioural experiment.)

Further reading and resources

Gilbert, P. and Leahy, R.L. (2007) *The Therapeutic Relationship in the Cognitive Behavioural Psychotherapies*. Hove, East Sussex: Routledge.
This book provides an excellent overview of the therapeutic relationship in CBT.

(Continued)

(Continued)

Leahy, R.L. (2001) *Overcoming Resistance in Cognitive Therapy*. New York: Guilford Press.
This seminal book explores aspects of resistance, helping the therapist become more aware of how ruptures are formed and maintained.

Padesky, C.A. (1999) *Therapist Beliefs: Protocols, Personalities and Guided Exercises* [Audio recording]. Huntingdon Beach, CA: Center for Cognitive Therapy.
The above is available from http://store.padesky.com and is an invaluable aid to identifying therapist beliefs.

FOUR The Fundamentals of CBT Case Formulation

Sarah Corrie, Michael Townend and Adrian Cockx

Learning objectives

After reading this chapter and completing the learning activities provided you should be able to:

- Understand and explain the rationale for, and function of, formulation in CBT.
- Describe and distinguish generic, problem-specific and idiosyncratic models of formulation.
- Describe and distinguish different levels of formulation.
- Consider the importance of client strengths within formulation development.
- Be able to construct formulations of your clients' presenting difficulties and needs.

Introduction

Case formulation has been identified as a defining competence in the skilled delivery of psychological therapies (Lane and Corrie, 2006; Corrie and Lane, 2010) and as lying at the heart of effective CBT (Beck, 1995; Roth and Pilling, 2007). Indeed, some would argue that it is the act of formulation that distinguishes the delivery of psychological interventions from the kinds of support offered by lay helpers (see Butler, 1998). But what is case formulation, how specifically does it support clinical practice, and how can practitioners approach the task of improving their CBT formulations for the benefit of their clients?

Having considered how to approach CBT assessment (Chapter 2) and the need to attend to process and relational issues (Chapter 3) this chapter examines the role of case formulation (also known as case conceptualization) in CBT and offers some approaches for developing your skills in this area. First, consideration is given to how case formulation supports the delivery of effective CBT and the functions that formulation can serve. Some of the challenges that therapists face when undertaking what is widely recognized as a complex task are then considered. Following this we offer some approaches that can support you in developing a more effective and systematic approach, drawing on current theory and research in the field, and distinguishing the different types and levels of formulation through which an understanding of clients' needs can be achieved. Through examining these areas, the aim is to ensure that you are able to collaboratively construct accounts of your clients' needs that can have a substantive, positive impact on the work that follows.

What is case formulation and why does it matter?

Emerging from the scientist-practitioner perspective (see Lane and Corrie, 2006, for a contemporary definition), case formulation arose in part as an alternative to traditional psychiatric diagnoses (Bruch and Bond, 1998). In general terms, a formulation is a psychologically-informed explanation of the client's dilemmas or problems which can provide the basis for deciding how to approach the task of bringing about positive change (Corrie and Lane, 2010). For CBT therapists, the aim of developing a case formulation is to arrive at an individualized theory of a client's difficulties that is derived from cognitive and/or behavioural theory (Persons and Davidson, 2010). In conjunction with a comprehensive assessment, a case formulation synthesizes knowledge of a client's concerns, difficulties and resources with knowledge of the cognitive model of emotional disorder, and any theoretical and research literatures relevant to the challenges that the client is facing. As such, a formulation provides a bridge between theory, research and practice (Kuyken et al., 2005) that can inform understanding of a client's needs and make use of this understanding to devise an intervention plan.

Although its primary purpose is to aid therapists in developing a therapeutic strategy (including the selection, planning and sequencing of interventions), there are a number of additional purposes that case formulation can serve. Drawing on earlier work by Butler (1998), Corrie and Lane (2010) have highlighted how case formulation has been identified as supporting therapists and their clients with achieving the following:

- Clarifying key hypotheses and relevant questions.
- Developing a broad understanding of the client's context, circumstances and needs.
- Prioritizing client issues and concerns.
- Normalizing the client's experiences in the context of their life story.

- Helping therapist and client make links between thoughts, emotions, behaviours and environmental factors.
- Making sense of the 'vicious cycles' that maintain the presenting problems.
- Determining criteria for a successful outcome, including organizing therapist and client around the same goals.
- Predicting client reactions to specific situations or events.
- Predicting obstacles to progress.
- Thinking systematically and productively about lack of progress.
- Identifying patterns in a client's actions and responses that can be examined impartially and collaboratively.
- Identifying missing information and gaps in understanding.
- Helping refine the search for relevant theoretical constructs or processes.
- Deriving a coherent understanding of the links between past and present.
- Forming judgements about the extent to which a case is typical (and how any intervention plan may need to be adjusted in the light of atypical features).

When constructed carefully and shared effectively, a case formulation can also instil hope in a client, demonstrating that their difficulties can be understood and that steps can be taken to bring about change. Consider for example a client who experiences seemingly random episodes of powerful physical sensations that include dizziness, light-headedness, palpitations and intense fear, and whose physician has eliminated a medical explanation for these difficulties. In the absence of any obvious trigger, the client concludes that such sensations are indicative of an inability to cope with life and signal impending madness. Working with a therapist who is able to offer an alternative explanation that combines knowledge of how the body and brain respond in conditions of perceived threat with the cognitive theory of panic disorder and the client's self-told story is likely to reassure the client that there is a credible, non-catastrophic explanation for their experiences. Shared with the client and elaborated through discussion, establishing goals and intervention planning can follow as the previously inexplicable becomes both understandable and amenable to change. In this way, the formulation enables the therapist to understand the client and communicate that a solution to the client's difficulties can be found (Beck, 1995; Needleman, 1999).

The challenges of constructing effective case formulations

Despite serving a number of critical functions for us as therapists, it is not always the case that clients find our theoretically-informed explanations helpful. Whilst some clients receiving CBT appear to find the formulation process beneficial, others report the experience as unhelpful and distressing (Chadwick et al., 2003). Although there are a number of possible explanations for this (see Corrie and Lane, 2010), one credible explanation is the complexity of the task itself. Case formulation has been noted as being one of the most sophisticated activities undertaken by the CBT therapist (Roth and Pilling, 2007; Kuyken et al., 2009). In addition to the judicious application of technical knowledge, the capacity to produce case formulations depends on the effective use of more generic skills including the interpretation of ambiguous data, and decision-making in the context of incomplete information. As noted by Corrie and Lane,

> The information provided by clients and gleaned from various assessment tools is typically complex and ambiguous. Understanding the client's needs is, therefore, a process of constructing a sense of meaning out of the mass of data obtained. (2010: 6–7)

Perhaps for these reasons, undertaking the task of formulation can be beset by challenges and pitfalls. In reflecting on their experience as supervisors and trainers (which would echo our own), Kuyken et al. (2009) identify common challenges as including those occasions where:

- Case formulations simply 'copy and paste' CBT theory over the client's details.
- Case formulations describe the current situation but lack the inclusion of relevant theory such that no adequate explanatory inferences are made.
- (Particularly in the context of complex or co-morbid presentations) the therapist produces new conceptualizations for each area of difficulty creating overwhelming amounts of material that are hard to make sense of in any practical way.
- The case formulation is elaborated to such an extent that, as Kuyken et al. describe, 'it looks like an electrical circuit board' (2009: 26).
- The amount of detail is inconsistent with the phase of therapy (for example, too many inferences are made before adequate information has been gathered).
- The formulation seems to have been developed unilaterally by the therapist and imposed on the client, rather than developed conjointly.
- The content of the therapy sessions bears no relation to the formulation.
- The therapist assumes a shared understanding with the client without establishing whether this is the case.
- Therapist and client appear to be organized around different understandings of the client's problems.

Not surprisingly then, ensuring that a case formulation is fit for purpose gives rise to many questions, and therapists need to be able to decide the following:

- How many elements need to feature in the formulation:

  o Is a maintenance cycle sufficient or is a full longitudinal formulation necessary to do justice to the clinical material?
  o How 'widely' (taking account of multiple areas of a client's life and circumstances) or 'narrowly' (focusing on the client's overt 'symptoms') do I focus the formulation?

- How much of the formulation is useful to share with the client at different stages of the process:

  o How much will prove useful to share and when?

- How is it best to share any emerging hypotheses:

  o Will it be most helpful to begin the process together? Or will it be more helpful to begin by sharing my ideas and then seeking feedback?

- What is the likely impact:

  o Is this information likely to be well-received and reassuring to the client, or could it be uncomfortable or distressing?
  o Are working hypotheses emerging that it is perhaps best not to share with the client because they might leave the client feeling intruded upon or exposed? (Padesky, 2003, notes how in CBT it is good practice for case formulation to be shared with the client at all stages of its development. However, there may be times when the therapist chooses to exercise caution. For example, if a client appears to fear interpersonal intimacy and the therapist suspects that the client was sexually abused by a primary caregiver during childhood, this hypothesis may not be shared initially for fear of this being experienced as a further intrusion on the client's person).
  o If I suspect that the formulation might make the client feel uncomfortable, what steps do I need to take to address this?

- Based on this emerging understanding, and in light of the above, which areas of a client's experience or behaviour need to be prioritized in any intervention offered:

  o On what criteria do I base my choice?

Given some of the challenges of co-constructing case formulations, how can you go about developing a systematic approach that will increase the likelihood of your achieving consistently effective results? Here, there are a number of aspects to hold in mind. These include: (1) some core elements that need to underpin your approach; (2) being clear about the type of formulation you seek to construct; and (3) managing the process aspects effectively. These different elements are examined in turn.

Core elements to underpin your approach

When co-constructing a case formulation, your initial thinking will be usefully supported by attending to the following: (1) make sure that you develop a problem list; (2) consider the role of diagnosis and whether your formulation will be drawing on diagnostic criteria; (3) identify and incorporate relevant measures; and (4) construct a working hypothesis.

1. Developing a problem list

According to Persons and Tompkins (1997), it is important to begin the task of formulation by compiling a problem list. The problem list alerts the therapist and client to specific areas of difficulty as well as themes and possible relationships between diverse aspects of the client's distress.

The process of making a problem list can be containing for both client and therapist, allowing them to work collaboratively in several problem domains. Additionally, a comprehensive list minimizes the risk of issues being overlooked, while simultaneously ensuring that both client and therapist feel less overwhelmed by the client's difficulties.

While opinions about this vary, Persons and Tompkins argue that the problem list should be an exhaustive list of the client's difficulties, stated in concrete, behavioural terms. Rather than incorporating a diagnostic category (e.g. 'depression') it should contain reference to behaviours, emotions and cognitions since these are the fundamental building blocks of a CBT formulation:

> ...we suggest that problems be described in these terms whenever possible. For example, through careful questioning the problem 'My job performance is slipping' can become any of the following: 'I'm not returning phone calls' (behaviour); 'I don't enjoy my job so at times I don't show up for work at all' (mood and behaviour); or 'I feel guilty because I know my co-workers think I'm a real flake' (mood and cognition). (1997: 323)

2. Consider the role of diagnosis and whether your formulation will be drawing on diagnostic criteria

Will you be organizing your understanding of the client's needs around a specific disorder, derived from diagnostic criteria, or not? Formulation organized around a particular diagnosis is an approach that has a long history in medicine and psychology. Strictly speaking, psychiatric diagnosis is not part of CBT formulation although Persons and Davidson (2010) argue that it can support its development, particularly if therapists are seeking to offer a protocol-driven intervention. Nonetheless, as described in Chapter 2, the use of diagnosis in psychological interventions is contentious.

The challenges to diagnostic classification have included questions about reliability, as well as the legitimacy of medicalizing human experience (see Double, 2002, for a review). As a result, we have to ensure that diagnostic criteria are complemented by an understanding of those features that are distinctive to the client and the client's context, including biological features, psychological mechanisms and the client's strengths and resources.

A further source of debate has been the oft-cited gap between those diagnosed and treated in randomized controlled trials and the more varied disorders of clients in practice-based contexts. A number of studies have pointed to the difference in outcome measures between trial and practice data (e.g. McGowan and Hill, 2009). In part this is because in clinical trials, clients are typically selected on the basis of how closely they resemble a standard diagnosis whereas in practice, clients do not fit as 'neatly' (Barkham et al., 2008). Thus, not all CBT therapists would acknowledge diagnostic classification as a legitimate basis for case formulation. In positioning yourself in relation to these debates, it will be important to understand the context of your service and any expectations of you in this regard.

3. Identify and incorporate relevant measures

Standardized and idiosyncratic measures are a helpful component of case formulation (Persons, 1989; Beck, 1995; Persons and Davidson, 2010). Chapter 2 reviewed the rationale for and use of these, differentiated standardized and person-specific measures and introduced you to some of the tools currently available. To recap, although measurement is an important part of CBT there are different views on the frequency with which measures should be used. It is important to be aware, therefore, of the expectations operating in your service. Additionally, as we discussed, it is important to remain aware of how clients make sense of this aspect of your work together and to ensure that they appreciate your understanding of how the use of such tools can support your work together. Measures, used both at the start of the therapy process and administered at regular intervals subsequently, provide an important adjunct to the unfolding narrative of the client's self-told story and offer additional data to inform the developing and testing of key hypotheses. (The case studies in Part 2 of this book provide illustrations of disorder-specific measures that can be helpful.)

4. Constructing a working hypothesis

Persons and Davidson (2010) argue that the working hypothesis lies at the heart of the formulation. It is essentially a mini-theory of the person and their difficulties that describes the relationship between problems on the problem list, and which can be linked to cognitions, emotions, behaviours, environmental and any biological events that may be implicated. According to Persons and Davidson (2010) the working hypothesis should address the core beliefs which are causing or serving to maintain the problem via underlying assumptions and automatic thoughts.

Maintaining an awareness of these core elements will support you in developing a more consistent and robust approach. However, there is no single correct way of constructing case formulations. Authors such as Persons (1989), Kuyken et al. (2009), Corrie and Lane (2010) and Bruch (2015) offer different approaches based on differing emphases on both content and process. It is important, therefore, to give some thought to the type of formulation that you need to work effectively with the client in front of you.

Developing a systematic approach to case formulation: types and levels

There are a number of ways to approach the task of developing case formulations. For example, it is possible to construct different types (generic, disorder-specific, and idiosyncratic), to focus on different levels (the individual 'case', the problem/disorder, or the situation), and to organize understanding around specific areas of focus (at the level of overt problems and underlying psychological mechanisms). Each of these options – used singly or in combination – offers a specific and potentially helpful 'lens' through which to view a client's needs.

1. Types of formulation

Formulations can be generic, problem- (or disorder-) specific or idiosyncratic. Generic models, such as the five areas model that was introduced in Chapter 2 (Greenberger and Padesky, 1995), the SETB (situation-emotion-thought-behaviour) model (Bieling and Kuyken, 2003) and the more traditional Beckian linear formulation (Beck, 1995) can be particularly helpful when clients present with diffuse life difficulties rather than clinically significant problems. It is helpful to use one or more of these to help socialize the client to the CBT approach. Padesky and Mooney (1990), for example, use the five areas model in the early stages of therapy to introduce clients to the notion that there is a relationship between their feelings, thoughts, physical sensations, behaviour and environment.

In contrast to these generic approaches, problem-specific models aim to provide a theoretically-informed understanding of the particular problem or disorder with which a client is presenting. Thus, the literature has supplied formulations of panic disorder, social anxiety, GAD, depression and

PTSD, amongst others. Disorder-specific models often provide a gateway to the latest theories and research in the field as they have typically undergone rigorous empirical scrutiny in research trials.

Recent decades have witnessed a proliferation of disorder-specific models, and as the field advances, understanding of the unique features of different clinical presentations is likely to be refined. Although it is beyond the scope of this book to examine the range of validated models of case formulation currently available, examples of their application can be found in Part 2. From these chapters it can be seen that disorder-specific models coalesce around a conceptual understanding that there is a connection between a client's cognitions, emotions, physiology, behaviour, their environment and interpersonal context, and situations or occurrences that represent precipitating events. Where the models differ is the emphasis they place on the nature of those connections and the psychological processes that are involved.

A particular benefit of disorder-specific models is that they can guide the therapist swiftly to theoretical constructs that are likely to be relevant to understanding the client's difficulties. Thus, returning to the case example described previously, knowledge of the cognitive theory of panic disorder can enable the therapist to identify, and readily test, hypotheses about the client having formed catastrophic misinterpretations concerning the presence of specific physical sensations. However, a tendency to guard against (particularly for novice therapists and indeed more experienced therapists who are facing stringent service targets that can drive a 'throughput' mentality) is to focus too specifically on the model at the expense of a more complete understanding of the 'client in context'. Where misunderstood or misapplied, disorder-specific models offer a clarity that can be more illusory than real, which can have the unintended outcome of fitting clients to models, creating confusion when data emerge that do not appear consistent with what the model suggests, or when a client displays the features of more than one disorder. This can result in therapists selectively attending to information that appears to 'fit' the model, ignoring information that does not, and feeling flummoxed by an emerging clinical picture that suggests the client has multiple problems. The question, 'Which model should I use?' is a good example of the type of confusion that can arise from an overly rigid adherence to disorder-specific models.

Moreover, in many service settings individuals present with multiple problems or with problems for which no empirically supported disorder-specific model exists. Because of this, it is often necessary to work collaboratively with clients to co-construct either idiosyncratic formulations or formulations which combine disorder-specific and idiosyncratic elements. Idiosyncratic models offer particular advantages for clients with complex circumstances or needs, where those difficulties appear to be atypical of what is described in the literature and where the client's personal history appears to be strongly implicated in current challenges.

Idiosyncratic models afford considerable flexibility allowing the construction of an explanatory account that is tailored to the unique needs of the client. This can aid understanding of the links between present and distal factors and can accommodate an extensive variety of factors pertinent to the individual. However, although intuitively appealing, they run the risk of being overly inclusive, incorporating material that is not necessary to the resolution of a particular clinical issue. They may also increase the likelihood of therapist and client arriving at false causal assumptions.

As Bieling and Kuyken (2003) observe, while practitioners can agree at the descriptive level about key features of a case, their interpretations of the more explanatory components vary widely. As a result, the more idiosyncratic the formulation, the more potential there is for inaccuracy. Eells (1997) also warns that therapists do their clients a disservice when they 'over-individualize' their formulations at the expense of empirically derived knowledge of psychopathology. This concern is echoed by Lane and Corrie (2012) who, in identifying some of the barriers to effective decision-making (including the limitations of our own cognitive processing), make the case that it is not easy to have confidence in the formulations we generate. Perhaps for these reasons, Persons and Davidson (2010) argue that clinicians have an ethical duty to use validated, disorder-specific models of case formulation where these exist. Reconciliation between idiosyncratic and protocol-driven formulations is possible in their view because therapists always have to personalize nomothetic formulations to take account of individual variations and to effectively manage the therapeutic process.

2. Levels of formulation

The notion that there are different levels of case formulation can also be a helpful way of understanding the emerging clinical picture. Persons and Davidson (2010) have specified three possible levels around which therapists can focus their efforts. These are:

1. The level of the case: that is, a formulation of the person's problems in their entirety. This seeks to explain the relationship between the specific difficulties the client is experiencing.
2. The level of the problem: that is, a formulation of the particular problem or disorder with which the client is presenting. (Ehlers and Clark's, 2000, formulation of PTSD would be an example of this.)
3. The level of the situation; that is, a micro-formulation of a client's responses in a particular situation. (The SETB model outlined earlier would be an example of this.)

Formulating at each of these levels will direct the therapist and client towards specific forms of data-gathering. For example, at the level of the situation, the therapist may select a thought record or activity diary as a tool for providing critical information about the relationship between situation, emotion, thought and behaviour.

At a case level, Persons (1989) argues that problems manifest as *overt difficulties* and *underlying psychological mechanisms*. Overt difficulties constitute problems which the client experiences on a regular basis, and which could relatively easily be described using a triggering situation, event, automatic thoughts and behaviours (SETB) formulation. However, the therapist will also find it helpful to hypothesize about the influence of underlying psychological mechanisms such as core beliefs and underlying assumptions (see Chapter 3; Beck, 1995; Needleman, 1999). In considering relevant psychological mechanisms, a therapist might also consider a range of cognitive processes such as selection attention, rumination, thought suppression or the functioning of working memory (see Chapter 5 for a discussion of trans-diagnostic assessment and case formulation).

In undertaking formulation there is often a tension between the need to obtain a sufficiently detailed understanding and getting underway with the work of change. In addressing this issue, it can be helpful to draw upon the work of Kuyken et al. (2009: 27) who, in their 'case conceptualization crucible', emphasize evolving levels of conceptualization along with collaborative empiricism and client strengths. The metaphor of a crucible is used to highlight three defining features in which:

1. Heat drives chemical reactions in a crucible (collaborative empiricism between therapist and client provides the heat).
2. Like the chemical reaction in a crucible, the formulation develops over time, starting with more descriptive elements and then being elaborated to include a consideration of predisposing and protective factors.
3. The new substances formed in a crucible are dependent on the characteristics of the chemical compounds put into it.

Kuyken et al. (2009) make the point that case formulation always begins by describing presenting problems in cognitive and behavioural language. The therapist initially brings to the client's story an account that is expressed in terms of thoughts, emotions, physiological reactions and behaviours. The next stage involves making theoretically informed explanatory inferences about factors that are involved in triggering and maintaining difficulties. This is defined as the second 'product' of the crucible. Finally, the therapist develops explanatory inferences about what contributed to the development of the problems, and encompasses distal vulnerabilities and areas of resilience that can be understood as predisposing the client to, or protecting them from, current difficulties now and in the longer-term. Kuyken et al. (2009) note that the stages of formulation required are those that will enable the goals of therapy to be realized. The third, most inferential level will, for example, often be included when working with clients with complex and long-term problems, whereas for more recent or straightforward difficulties a focus on stages 1 and 2 may be sufficient.

Managing the process of co-construction: general principles to guide your approach

Having considered the types and levels of formulation that can inform the content of your formulations, we turn now to some general principles that can enable you to manage the process effectively and which, if held in mind, will increase the likelihood of your case formulations fulfilling the functions described at the start of this chapter.

1. Begin the task of formulation from the earliest stages of working with the client

A common question for CBT therapists who are at the start of their careers is when to begin the task of formulation. When do they have enough information to be confident that they can begin devising an explanatory account that can provide the basis for a treatment plan? Often (as indeed is the case in this book) the tasks of assessment and formulation are presented as separate aspects of practice. This is so that authors can draw attention to the unique features and different emphases of each task. However, in practice these activities often take the form of overlapping phases of thinking, information-gathering and hypothesis-testing. Indeed, in the case of more complex clinical presentations revisions to the original formulation are often ongoing as the process of therapy unfolds and new information emerges.

Thus, because the relationship between assessment and formulation is a reciprocal one, the development of hypotheses will be central to the earliest stages of the clinical interview and will continue until the end of therapy (Beck, 1995). As a general principle then, we would recommend beginning formulation from the first session with the information you have available to you (even though this is likely to be an incomplete clinical picture). While the initial focus is likely to be on the more descriptive aspects of the client's needs with increasing levels of inferential understandings added over time, seeing formulation as an integral aspect of the earliest stages of engagement enables the therapist to begin the tasks of mapping the broad terrain, identifying relevant hypotheses and prioritizing client concerns.

2. Consider pacing and timing

As noted previously, the skill of formulation involves not just knowing what content to include but also how to share this information in ways that the client can hear and will find helpful. This entails careful attention to matters of pacing and timing in line with the client's capacity to absorb information (in depression, for example, information processing capability is known to be compromised), their style of learning, the extent to which the therapist's formulation concurs or conflicts with the client's own (e.g. if the client adopts a medicalized interpretation of their difficulties a psychological understanding may be experienced as challenging), and a variety of additional needs and resources that the client brings to therapy. As highlighted previously, clients do not always find our efforts at constructing an understanding of their needs to be helpful. It is important always to hold in mind the potential impact of hypotheses co-constructed and shared and to recognize that clients may need time to reflect upon any emerging explanation of their needs, as well as opportunity to test out its implications (Bennett-Levy et al., 2004). Kuyken (2006) uses the helpful analogy of the navigator and driver, and how the driver can be hindered by the overly conscientious navigator who insists on sharing the entire road map, rather than just the information that is central to navigating the current location. 'Shoulder to shoulder' collaboration is essential.

3. Ensure that your formulation is helpful

If a formulation is fulfilling its function, it will help you understand your client and track their progress, guide you in selecting and pacing interventions, and support you in addressing any obstacles encountered. Once you have an initial formulation, it is always useful to ask yourself the 'So what?' question. If you have an effective formulation, you will be able to answer this question in terms of specific hypotheses to test and interventions to incorporate. If your formulation looks detailed and robust but leaves you mystified as to what to do next, this is a sign that it is not fit for purpose.

Additionally, as therapy progresses new information will arise which paves the way for an elaborated understanding of the client's needs. This may require adjustment to an intervention plan or even a change in direction. Do not, therefore, get too attached to any formulation developed early on in the work, but revisit it regularly and keep asking yourself if it is working for the benefit of the therapy.

4. Ensure that your formulations convey a positive message

Padesky (2008b; cited in Grant et al., 2008) proposes that problems are described using *deconstructive* language, or in the past tense. In contrast, goals are stated *constructively*. This means that the clients' goals should represent their vision of how they would like things to be different. By engaging in this kind of future-oriented exploration, the therapist strives to encourage a sense of hope in the client.

As we saw earlier, instilling hope can be an important function of formulation, especially for those clients whose difficulties appear to them to be incomprehensible or without solution. This recommendation reflects a growing awareness in CBT of the importance of incorporating client strengths into our formulations.

Kuyken et al. (2009) note that seeking to build on successes and enhancing client resilience have always been central to the principles and methods of CBT, and that the commonly cited intention of enabling clients to become their own therapists through acquiring knowledge, experience and skill, speaks directly to this agenda. In the context of case formulation specifically, they argue cogently that the inclusion of client strengths can:

- Build on existing resources and promote client resilience.
- Help clients identify areas of strength and existing resources in their armoury that can be generalized to current challenges.
- Broaden the range of possible interventions.
- Reduce any tendency for the client to feel overwhelmed, summed up or 'pathologized' (incorporating strengths provides a holistic account which can be more engaging and consistent with a focus on instilling hope).

Approaches outside of CBT such as design-based, systemic and solution-focused models have also adopted 'forward looking' perspectives where, rather than focusing on identifying problems and analyzing the influencing process (the focus of disorder-specific models), emphasis has been placed on looking to the future and the strengths people bring to achieve desired states. Formulating from this perspective highlights the central role of creative thinking in identifying desirable outcomes and exploring how these might be achieved (George et al., 1990). With the challenge to psychological approaches from the emerging discipline of positive psychology (e.g. Snyder and Lopez, 2005), the importance of incorporating client strengths has been an increasing focus of the CBT literature (e.g. Bannink, 2012), including the integration of client strengths with mainstream CBT practice (Mooney and Padesky, 2002). More is said about this development in Chapter 17.

Case formulation as a work in progress: some concluding thoughts

When a formulation is truly 'doing its job' for therapists and their clients, it becomes a therapeutic intervention in its own right. By creating a shared understanding of problems that perhaps at the outset seemed incomprehensible and intractable, the therapist has at their disposal a powerful vehicle for enhancing motivation, encouraging curiosity and instilling hope. Kuyken et al. (2005) have described case formulation as the cornerstone of evidence-based CBT, and for good reason. It is where theoretical knowledge, research findings and clinical expertise come together to offer the client a personalized route to meaningful change.

As we have seen in this chapter, developing a case formulation is a complex skill requiring of therapists the ability to make effective decisions about how to assess, gather information and interpret data in ways that are meaningful for both parties and palatable for the client. Clients do not always experience our best endeavours to 'formulate' their concerns as helpful. Moreover, despite assertions that formulation is a critically important task, there are actually limited data that verify its relationship to therapeutic outcome (Zivor et al., 2013).

There are different ways of approaching formulation, with different types and levels of formulation offering different 'lenses' through which to view a client's needs. The question of which approach to take with a particular client is, therefore, one that needs constant revisiting as the work unfolds and therapist and client seek to accommodate new levels of understanding. A critical decision is how to help the client while avoiding areas that may be intriguing but which have little direct relevance to the client's presenting problems (Eells, 1997). This is not always easy to discern, particularly at the start of the therapeutic engagement.

Of course, finding ways to bridge the tension between what the science tells us and what practice requires is an ongoing issue. Professional practice demands of us the capacity to think at multiple levels, hold in mind diverse sources of data, and aim for understanding about what contributes to particular concerns whilst simultaneously being able to devise novel solutions (Lane and Corrie, 2012). A formulation is always incomplete and always an approximation as therapists attempt to bring together the rapidly accumulating knowledge of the field of CBT whilst honouring the unique story of the client in front of them.

It is perhaps comforting, then, to note Butler's (1998: 8) view that formulations do not have to be '100% accurate or complete'. For her, case formulations are not concerned with providing answers but rather with generating questions and ideas that can add value to the work. Thus, the benchmark criterion may be one of usefulness rather than accuracy, as determined by the client's response to the intervention.

In distinguishing the different types and levels of case formulation, it is important to understand that these are not presented as mutually exclusive or indeed competing approaches. Indeed the most helpful approach is often to combine them. For example, it might be very helpful to combine a validated model of social phobia with an idiosyncratic formulation that takes account of unhelpful core beliefs formed in an invalidating environment early in the client's life. The different approaches described in this chapter are offered as a means of helping you devise a framework for making sense of the client's self-told story, information from baseline questionnaires and the theories and models of practice that reflect a CBT approach to meaningful change.

Summary

✓ Case formulation is a complex task that involves synthesizing general knowledge of CBT theory and research with the idiosyncratic features and needs of the client.
✓ Formulations can take different forms and occur at different levels of understanding.
✓ Effective formulations require attention to both content and process issues.
✓ Increasingly, it is considered good practice to incorporate client strengths and resources within therapist formulations.

Activities

1. Identify a current client and attempt to formulate this individual's difficulties using generic, disorder-specific and idiosyncratic approaches. What do you gain and lose through adopting each approach?
2. Identify a different client and develop a formulation of this individual's needs. First build your formulation focusing only on problem areas (i.e. those areas that you and/or the client wish to change). Second, build your formulation in a way that takes account of both problem areas and client strengths. What are the strengths and limits of each approach in the context of your understanding of this particular client?
3. Keep a record of your case formulation decision-making over a period of three months. Notice the approaches that you tend to favour and those you tend not to use. If it feels appropriate to do so, discuss your findings in supervision.

Further reading

Corrie, S. and Lane, D.A. (2010) *Constructing Stories, Telling Tales: A Guide to Formulation in Applied Psychology*. London: Karnac.
This text provides an authoritative review of approaches to and debates around case formulation including the issue of diagnosis.

Kuyken, W., Padesky, C.A. and Dudley, R. (2009) *Collaborative Case Conceptualization: Working Effectively with Clients in Cognitive-Behavioral Therapy*. New York: Guilford Press.
An excellent text providing a summary of the current state of knowledge in CBT formulation as well as introducing the reader to their approach.

FIVE   Generic, Disorder-specific, Transdiagnostic and Multi-level Approaches to Formulation

Michael Townend, Sarah Corrie and Adrian Cockx

Learning objectives

After reading this chapter and completing the learning activities provided you should be able to:

- Understand the theoretical underpinnings of multi-level and transdiagnostic approaches to formulation.
- Recognize the strengths and limitations of single dimensional and multi-level models of theory and formulation.
- Describe the similarities and differences between generic, disorder-specific and multi-level approaches to formulation.
- Recognize the advantages and disadvantages of generic, disorder-specific and multi-level approaches to formulation.
- Understand how formulations can incorporate diversity.

Introduction

The last 40 years has seen the rapid development of the field of CBT (Grant et al., 2008). The research underpinning this expansion has followed a scientific approach of testing interventions in defined groups. This 'disorder-focused' approach has led to the development of a body of evidence that demonstrates the efficacy and effectiveness of CBT across a considerable number of disorders (Roth and Fonagy, 1996; Hofmann et al., 2012). It has also resulted in the development of a variety of models, usually based on appraisal theories that have subsequently been used by clinicians to underpin formulation in their practice (Tarrier et al., 1998).

In Chapter 4, we examined the numerous functions of developing a case formulation. We also considered how, in order to utilize formulation in practice the therapist needs to have a good theoretical knowledge and importantly the ability to adapt that knowledge to the presentation of the client, without trying to fit the client into a model. In order for formulations to be optimally helpful, the therapist needs to be skilled in a variety of psycho-education strategies and techniques. These include didactic explanations, the construction of vicious circle diagrams, the completion of formulation worksheets, the use of analogies and metaphors to assist understanding, and the judicious and planned use of behavioural experiments to test out the validity of the formulation.

The previous chapters, this current chapter and the case studies within this text all demonstrate that formulations can be based on a number of frameworks or theories, which can broadly be categorized as generic, disorder-specific, transdiagnostic and multi-level. In this chapter each of these approaches will be critically considered. In addition, the fictitious case study of 'Aarti' will be used to illustrate the approaches and emphasize the strengths of each approach. In this chapter there will be a particular focus on the transdiagnostic and multi-level approaches.

Case study: Aarti

Aarti was a 26-year-old third generation British Asian Hindu woman with a seven-year history of OCD involving contamination fears and rituals alongside co-morbid major depression. The major depression was recurrent with a first episode when she was 18 years of age, when she had been referred to the local mental health service. Despite her psychological difficulties she had completed university, subsequently trained as a teacher and was holding down a full-time job. Six months prior to referral she had also set up her own business alongside her full-time job. She had been brought up in a traditional close-knit family. The family had a strong work ethic and worked hard to maintain status within the Indian community. Three generations of the family had lived together. She had recently moved out of the family home and lived alone. There was considerable pressure to get married although at the time of referral she was single. Aarti was the eldest of four children. She believed that her parents favoured her younger brother who was the eldest son. She described a confused upbringing of Eastern and Western influences. She attended the Hindu temple regularly. She was referred for CBT when her OCD and depression had worsened but she was still able to work even while complaining of heightened stress and generalized anxiety.

Generic models

Generic models such as the five areas model (Greenberger and Padesky, 1995), the SETB (situation-emotion-thought-behaviour) model (Bieling and Kuyken, 2003) and the more traditional Beckian linear formulation are widely used in practice (Townend et al., 2002). They are generic in that they are simply a framework that is used to guide the construction of a description of a client's difficulties and maintenance factors. The generic model – in this case the five areas model – is shown in Figure 5.1 using Aarti's presenting problems as a case illustration.

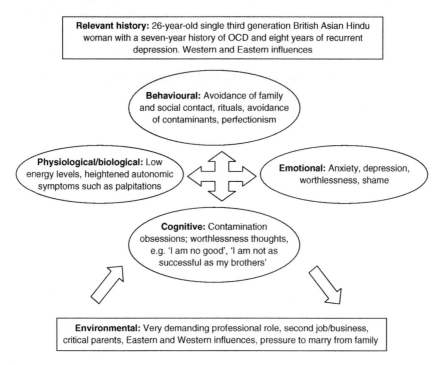

Figure 5.1 Example of the five areas model applied to Aarti

Evaluating generic models

Below are some of the advantages and disadvantages of using generic models to guide your formulations.

Advantages

- Generic formulations can be successful in capturing and describing many of the features of the client's problems.
- They are relatively easily understood by both clients and therapists and are thus clinically very useful and important.
- They are personal to the client and can be easily updated as new information emerges.

Disadvantages

- Generic formulations do not offer the clinician an opportunity to develop more holistic explanations that take into account interactions between different disorders or emotional states within the client.
- They are relatively weak at explaining the origins and development of problems over time (these factors may vary greatly between individual clients).
- They do not account well for psychological processes without some modification.
- They do not account for emotions that are produced automatically or in the absence of appraisal processes.
- They are not based on explanatory or predictive accounts and thus cannot be tested.

Disorder-specific approaches to formulation

Cognitive behavioural disorder-specific theories and models have now been developed for a wide range of disorders including depression, generalized anxiety, PTSD, phobias, panic, personality disorders, OCD, conduct disorders in children, symptoms of psychosis, morbid grief, marital and relationship problems, health anxiety, chronic pain, chronic fatigue and irritable bowel syndrome (Tarrier et al., 1998; Clark and Fairburn, 2005; Grant et al., 2008).

Disorder-specific formulations can usually be traced back to the original clinical model of Beck and his co-workers (Beck et al., 1979) but are adapted to take account of the specifics of a particular disorder and, most importantly, the content and form of the cognitions associated with that particular problem. In other words, they follow the premise of the cognitive content specificity hypothesis which states that disorders can be separated

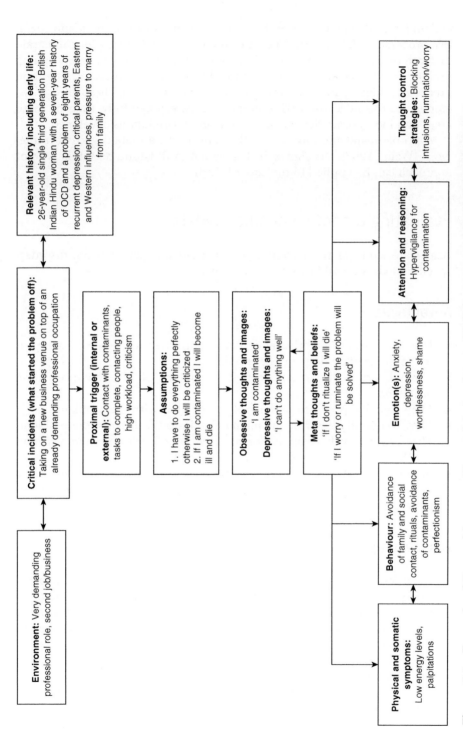

Figure 5.2 Example of the problem-specific model, drawing on Wells' meta-cognitive framework (1997) applied to Aarti

and understood on the basis of the differences in thought content and cognitive processes (Wells, 1997). The case studies in Part 2 of this book illustrate in depth the important and sometimes subtle variations between presenting problems in terms of the types of thoughts, cognitive processes, attention processes, memory forms and types of behaviours at play. These differences emphasize the need for CBT therapists to assess carefully each of these areas and incorporate the 'specifics' into any formulations developed.

A problem-specific model – in this case using a meta-cognitive framework (Wells, 1997) – is shown in Figure 5.2 to illustrate how this type of approach can be applied to the case of Aarti.

Evaluating disorder-specific models

Below are some of the advantages and disadvantages of using disorder-specific models to guide your formulations:

Advantages

- Disorder-specific theories and related formulations describe many of the features of anxiety and depression.
- They describe the specific cognitive content of different presenting problems.
- They describe processes commonly associated with the problem.
- They frequently describe the main behavioural features of the problem.
- They are relatively easily understood by both clients and therapists and are thus clinically very useful and important.
- Based on the above, disorder-specific formulations offer the possibility of the most appropriate intervention being selected and targeted at key maintaining variables.

Disadvantages

- Disorder-specific formulations do not always offer the clinician an opportunity to consider transdiagnostic processes, or cultural or environmental influences, and therefore may potentially hamper the development of holistic formulations that take into account interactions between different disorders or emotional states within the individual.
- They do not account well for physiological processes without some modification.
- They do not provide full details of the development of the problem, which may vary greatly between individuals.
- They do not account for emotions that are produced automatically or in the absence of appraisal processes.

The case for transdiagnostic and multi-level approaches to formulation

Despite the considerable value of problem-specific approaches to theory, research and practice there is a growing interest in multidimensional models which propose an interaction of risk factors in the aetiology, development and maintenance of psychological problems (Harvey et al., 2004). For example, a linear, single dimensional explanation of a particular disorder such as depression might propose that the origins of unhelpful thinking or behaviour can be traced to a single or relatively straightforward cause (e.g. a chemical imbalance, conditioning or early experiences of family conflict, trauma or adverse life events).

In contrast, a systemic, multidimensional approach to formulation would propose that many factors could influence the production of unhelpful thinking, feelings and behaviour in later life. For example, frameworks for schema, defined as an individual's 'construction and understanding of the world', are in a constant state of change and evolution (Freeman and Martin, 2004: 225). Schemas change through an active and evolutionary process when perceptions and existing cognitive structures are applied to novel situations, while new cognitive structures are developed to serve old functions in new situations (Freeman and Martin, 2004).

From this perspective, if individuals are unable to develop new structures or continue to fit old structures to new situations, their construction and understanding of themselves and the world around them may be incongruent and lead to psychological problems. Similarly, other influences on unhelpful thinking, feelings and behaviour can occur through traumatization or biological influences such as the ease of conditioning ability of an individual. Schema development can also be influenced by a broad range of experiences, including those of culture and social learning.

Cultural and social learning factors in any formulation cannot, therefore, be analysed out of context of the individual's unique interpretation of their environment. The relationship between behaviour, cognition and the environment has been emphasized in the social learning theory of triadic reciprocal determinism (Bandura, 2004). This theory proposes that behaviour, cognition and the environment all act as interlocking determinants which can affect each other in a bidirectional way, illustrated in Figure 5.3.

The context of the individual is defined as their biological state, genetic make-up and behaviour, in conjunction with cognitive and emotional responses. The environment is defined in terms of social, cultural, physical environmental and economic factors (Gilbert, 2006). Any one component of these systems may affect the other components. From this perspective, depression cannot be understood simply as a product of either biochemistry or social environment. Rather, it is viewed as a complex, evolving and in part genetically influenced problem, which is expressed when the

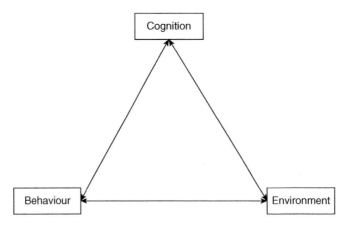

Figure 5.3 Schematic representation of triadic reciprocal determinism between cognition, behaviour and the environment

individual is exposed to a variety of 'risk' variables. Such variables may be environmental, social, metabolic or psychological, depending upon the type of depression or the form that it takes.

These ideas pose a significant challenge for CBT therapists attempting to keep abreast of the research on the factors influencing the onset, development and maintenance of even relatively straightforward clinical problems. The advantage of using multidimensional models, as demonstrated in the health anxiety chapter of this book (see Chapter 9), is that it can prove possible to develop a better explanatory account than might be achieved through adhering exclusively to a single factor model.

The transdiagnostic approach to research and practice

The notion that there may be utility in shifting the perspective away from a pure 'disorder-specific' focus to a more 'across disorders' or transdiagnostic approach has created considerable interest in the field of CBT. What transdiagnostic theoreticians are attempting to develop is a unifying framework that provides a coherent explanation for all disorders in all situations. This area of research is guided implicitly by the philosophical principle of parsimony (Occam's razor); that is, if two (or more) theories explain a phenomenon equally well, the theory that provides a simpler explanation is to be preferred until such time that the simpler theory is refuted and superseded.

The term 'transdiagnostic' was first coined by Fairburn and his colleagues to describe their cognitive behavioural approach with eating disorders (Fairburn et al., 2003). Their work was seeking to test if models developed for bulimia would work equally well for other eating disorders. Similarly in the US, Barlow and colleagues have developed what they refer to as a unified protocol for the emotional disorders of anxiety and depression (Barlow et al., 2011).

What is different about these approaches to theory and formulation is that the underpinning formulation is transdiagnostic with interventions targeted at cognitive or behavioural maintenance processes that are prevalent in each of the disorders. In the UK Harvey and colleagues have developed a comprehensive approach to transdiagnostic practice, the essence of which considers parsimoniously the reasoning, behavioural, attentional, memory and thought processes that are common across emotional disorders. They also draw our attention to the factors that might predispose individuals to develop and maintain problems, or promote remission and recovery (Harvey et al., 2004). This form of transdiagnostic thinking is illustrated in the case study of Aarti below and in Figure 5.4.

Case study of Aarti using a transdiagnostic formulation

The case study for Aarti and the formulation shown illustrate the series of processes associated with the maintenance of her OCD and depression. They demonstrate the relationship between her mood disturbance and anxiety as she was depressed about her OCD symptoms and her depression served to increase her anxiety. There was also a relationship to her job role changes. Specifically, her perfectionism and intolerance of uncertainty added to her stress levels and further primed her to ruminate which impacted negatively on her mood. This approach to formulation also gives the therapist an opportunity to consider interactions between the processes associated with each problem. These processes include the ease of recall of negative categorical memories, in turn influencing memories related to ritualistic behaviour. They also include the reduction in activity levels leading to reduced exposure to contamination fears and either the prevention of habituation or a reduction in experiences that might disconfirm her OCD-related beliefs.

There is now a growing body of research evidence to support the utilization of transdiagnostic approaches. Within the context of randomized controlled trials for example, transdiagnostic CBT for adults with anxiety and/ or depression and eating disorders can be effective (Fairburn et al., 2009; Norton, 2012; Titov et al., 2013). The potential to improve the outcomes not only for the identified problem but also in co-morbid presentations

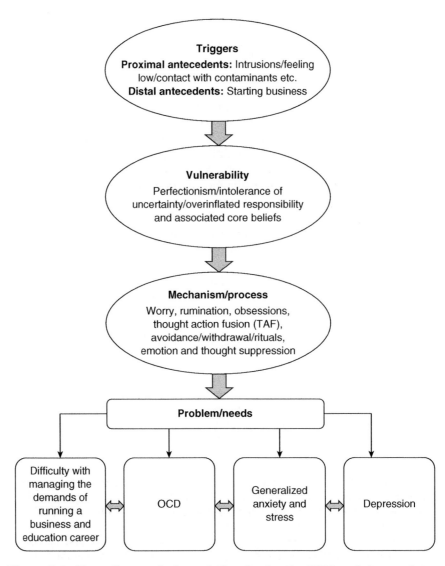

Figure 5.4 Transdiagnostic formulation for Aarti – OCD and depression

is being observed; indeed it has been tentatively proposed that targeting common processes may help with relapse prevention and thus improve the longer term outlook for clients (Weiss, 2014).

Evaluating the transdiagnostic model

Below are some of the advantages and disadvantages of using transdiagnostic models to guide your formulations:

Advantages

- Transdiagnostic models can help understand and explain why many psychological problems are co-morbid.
- They support the continued evolution of the field through the generalization of knowledge from existing validated models of psychological disorders to disorders that are yet to be fully understood.
- They potentially improve access to psychological therapies through an integrated therapy protocol that is effective for a variety of problems and co-morbidities.
- They can potentially improve long-term outcome through relapse prevention.

Disadvantages

- Some of the elements within transdiagnostic models may need more specific definition (for example, attention and emotions are very broad concepts).
- The transdiagnostic model is yet to fully explain why, given the similar behavioural and cognitive processes, problems present so differently.
- Like many other approaches, transdiagnostic models have relatively little to say about the environment and context of the individual.

Multi-level formulations

A further transdiagnostic approach to formulation is what can be termed multi-level theories. Research indicates that emotion is probably influenced by several cognitive and conditioning (associative) processes (Dalgleish, 2004; Power and Dalgleish, 2008). In order to understand these processes, cognitive scientists have developed a number of what are referred to as multi-level or multi-representational theories. Two of the most influential multi-level theories are the Schematic Propositional Associative and Analogical Representational System (SPAARS) (Power and Dalgleish, 2008) and the Interacting Cognitive Subsystems (ICS) (Teasdale, 1997; Teasdale and Barnard, 1993). Both these theories were originally developed to help understand everyday human experiences but have since been applied to understanding psychopathology.

An underlying assumption of ICS is that there are several types of information code executed by the individual in the process of everyday functioning and meaning-making. This takes place within a comprehensive overall system or framework. The ICS framework includes seven input subsystems into the 'central engine' of the model. These subsystems are proprioceptive (feeling sense), imagery (visual images), visual (what the person can see in the environment), acoustic (what the person can hear), peripheral, articulatory (movement) and morphonolexical (what is said to the person). These subsystems feed into the two main systems that are responsible for the management of meaning – the propositional system (moment-by-moment verbal meaning) and the schematic or implicational system. The central engine of the theory is thus the interplay between the propositional and implicational levels of meaning. The diagrams below provide an overview of the architecture of ICS framework.

According to ICS, the propositional system is not directly linked to the generation of emotion but is characterized by a memory system of verbal, non-emotional representations of meaning. The propositional codes represent specific meanings that can be expressed verbally and can be subject to rational appraisal. In other models these are referred to as negative automatic thoughts. In ICS formulations, emotion is generated through the activation of a generic affect-related implicational belief system, again stored within its own memory structure. The implicational system stores holistic meanings, patterns of direct sensory inputs, detail of environmental events and responses derived from a wide variety of inputs (Gumley and Power, 2000). Thus it is the implicational part of the system that is centrally important in emotion. The system is self-regulating in everyday situations with problems or psychopathology occurring when the system becomes interlocked or there is a delay in processing somewhere within the system. Examples of propositional and implicational meanings are given below.

The explanatory capacity of the ICS framework is that it enables both targets for intervention and particular types of intervention to be specified. For example, in clients who are depressed a state of 'depressive interlock' is believed to be operating through cognitive, attentional processes, somatic and behavioural feedback loops which lead to the maintenance of low mood. In the case of depression an interlock is thus hypothesized as occurring when the implicational schematic modes are continually being processed without being updated. This suggests that for therapy to be effective, both the content and processing found in depression need to be addressed. Interventions for depression might therefore include distraction to reduce the negative propositional processing, and cognitive restructuring or behavioural activation to remodel implicational negative models of the self (Barnard, 2004).

Example of ICS propositional and implicational codes

When teaching postgraduate students we frequently use an exercise to illustrate propositional and implicational meanings. The students are given a flashcard with just the single word FISH written on it. They are then asked what the first thing is that they notice. These initial responses vary – as would be predicted by the ICS framework. Some students report simply noticing words such as 'creature' or 'swim' without any physical reactions, imagery or other responses. This is a propositional response. However, others report experiencing strong emotions, indicating an implicational response. One such example is, 'Fish is Friday, images of being sat at a table feeling alone, feeling tense with a parental voice saying to stay at the table until they have finished their meal, experiencing the smell of fish, feeling a sense of disgust with nausea and sweating.' Figure 5.5 gives a simplified overview of the ICS Framework.

An additional multi-level theory has been developed specifically for PTSD – dual representational theory (Brewin et al., 1996). This can be used as the basis for formulation in PTSD, and as an alternative to the Ehlers and Clark (2000) framework particularly when it is important for clients to understand why some aspects of their trauma memories cause them more

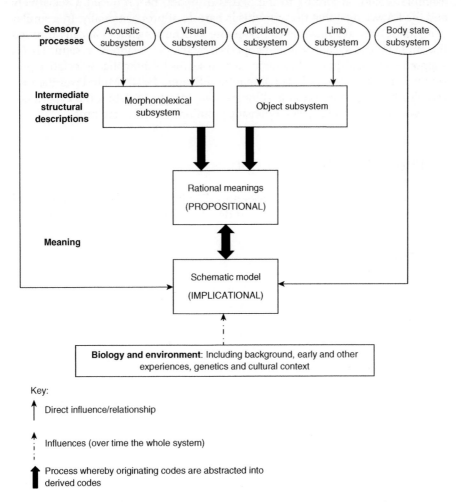

Key:

↑ Direct influence/relationship

↑ Influences (over time the whole system)

↑ Process whereby originating codes are abstracted into derived codes

Figure 5.5   Simplified interacting subsystems framework showing the relationship between the seven subsystems and the propositional and implicational (meaning) system (adapted from © Teasdale and Barnard, 1993)

distress than others, and why they keep re-experiencing their trauma in the form of flashbacks, images and nightmares.

The main advantage of multi-level theories over other models is their capacity to explain that emotions can be created in two ways using different processes. There is an accumulating body of research that supports both clinical observations and theoretical supposition that processing can occur at one cognitive level, in the absence of processing at another level. A good example of this can be found in specific phobias. Exposure to the phobic stimuli for people with phobias results in intense fear when seeing the feared animal, insect or object despite knowing that it is harmless. The fear in this example would, according to the SPAARS model, be produced associatively and the knowledge (that the stimulus is harmless) propositionally. In a similar vein, the ICS would view the fear response as occurring automatically through the implicational system without appraisal by the propositional system. This is supported by experimental evidence which seems to show that associative processing can be non-conscious (Ohman and Soares, 1994). Multi-level theories can also help us understand and incorporate into formulation the experience of having two emotions (even opposing emotions) at the same time.

Evaluating multi-level theories

Below are some of the advantages and disadvantages of using multi-level theories in the context of the overall development of your formulations:

Advantages

- There is good evidence that emotions can be produced automatically and by pre-attentive processes for which other models frequently fail to account.
- Multi-level theories offer clinicians an opportunity to incorporate transdiagnostic processes and therefore develop holistic formulations which take into account interactions between different 'disorders' or emotional states.
- The frameworks help us to understand different levels of meaning (hot and cold cognition).
- The ICS framework helps us to understand the relationship between physical and meaning processes.

Disadvantages

- Multi-level theories are complex and need simplification for client use.
- The multi-level theories and frameworks currently available are all very different from each other.
- They are frameworks rather than testable theories.

Application of ICS to formulation practice

In addition to the health anxiety example of the clinical application of ICS in this book (see Chapter 9), ICS can underpin formulation where rational approaches such as thought records (working at the propositional level) do not seem to be helping. In the case example of Aarti it can also help explain how, at one level (propositional), she knows that her fears are groundless yet still experiences fear and disgust on contact with a contaminant (implicational level meaning) leading to ritualizing. This is illustrated in Figure 5.6 below.

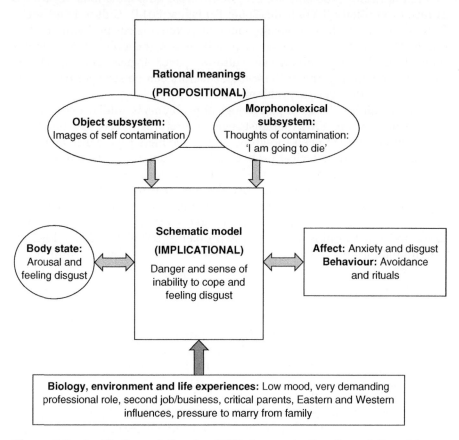

Figure 5.6   Aarti's formulation for OCD demonstrating the relationship between the rational (propositional) and schematic (implicational) level meanings

Cultural and social factors in formulation

Cultural and social factors are important determinants of psychological problems in a number of ways, and need to be accounted for in CBT case formulation (Hays and Iwamasa, 2006). The frameworks discussed earlier need some adaptation to incorporate these determinants. This is important so that the therapist and client can fully understand the experience of distress and how the problems have formed over time. For example, culture impacts through social learning on how clients express and manifest their difficulties, the style of coping adopted, the family and community supports employed, the willingness of clients to seek therapy and how they might present their problems to their family doctor and, ultimately, their therapist. Similarly, the culture of psychological therapy services and mental health services in general influence diagnosis, treatment and the delivery of services.

Mental health problems are prevalent across all populations, regardless of race or ethnicity (LaTaillade, 2006; Paniagua, 2014). Cultural and social factors contribute to the development of psychological problems and as outlined previously, psychological problems are the product of complex interactions between biological, cultural, psychological and social factors. The role of any one of these major factors can be stronger or weaker, depending on the specific problem.

The overall incidence of psychological problems is similar between the larger ethnic groups. CBT therapists need, therefore, to recognize that there are a number of high-need sub-groups that have higher incidence and prevalence rates of psychological problems. These sub-groups have often been obscured in larger community surveys (LaTaillade, 2006).

Poverty has the greatest and most directly measurable effect on rates of psychological need. People in lower income brackets, of lower educational status, and in certain occupations have a two to threefold increase in their likelihood of developing psychological problems (LaTaillade, 2006). Racism, discrimination and bullying in the workplace are associated with disorders such as chronic anxiety and depression (LaTaillade, 2006). Beyond the working environment, individuals and groups may be confronted with racism and discrimination which, together with frequent exposure to violence and poverty, can exert a potentially toxic effect on psychological well-being in susceptible individuals. There is also evidence that some minority groups have a distrust of mental health services, citing clinical bias and stereotyping as significant factors in their mistrust (Paniagua, 2014). These issues can and should be incorporated into the formulation when the therapist and client agree that it is relevant to do so.

In Chapter 2, and drawing on the work of Newman (2007), we emphasized that in order to be relationally-focused and collaborative in a way that respects difference, it is important for CBT therapists to be familiar with the main tenets of the major religions as well as relevant community or societal beliefs and expectations that help contextualize a client's distress. In support of this principle, Kumar (2007) argues that within Indian cultures standard CBT approaches need to be adapted to incorporate a spiritual dimension as a matter of routine. Thus SETB (situation-emotion-thought-behaviour) becomes SETBS (situation-emotion-thought-behaviour-spiritual) and the five areas model becomes six with the specific addition of the spiritual dimension. Hebblethwaite (2002), in his therapeutic work with people with strong Christian beliefs, argued for adapting standard cognitive models of therapy and formulation by incorporating the influence of the Holy Ghost or Will of God into therapy. These approaches demonstrate innovative thinking in relation to the structure and content of formulation in particular religious contexts that may facilitate connectedness with the client.

Drawing together formulation approaches

As recommended previously (see Chapter 4), when developing formulations it is important to ensure that they are neither so simple that key factors are missed nor so complex that they are overwhelming for both client and therapist. In other words, the formulation must be parsimonious. The formulation needs to be able to account for all the factors at play in maintaining a client's psychological difficulties. What this means in practice is that CBT therapists need to be comfortable using a range of different approaches.

Elaborating on the material covered in Chapter 4, we have found it helpful to consider formulation at three levels (which are not hierarchically arranged). The levels in the framework include multi-level, transdiagnostic, disorder-specific and generic formulations. We are not proposing that CBT therapists develop these different levels of formulation with each and every client, but rather that the different levels may offer new and potentially helpful perspectives at different points in time. What is important is that the most appropriate level for explaining the maintenance (and/or onset and development) of the distress being experienced by the client is selected.

The version that the formulation takes may also change as therapy progresses, either through the use of different models or through additions to existing models. For example, simpler levels of formulations may be sufficient for use with clients while multi-level formulations can enable therapists to reflect on more complex ideas such as propositional and implicational forms of knowing. We have also found it helpful to use multi-level formulations later in therapy to help the client to understand why they have or have not improved with certain interventions, why they may be experiencing particular types of imagery, how their schemas have been formed and maintained and processes of non-cognitive conditioning and automatic experiences of emotion.

In bringing this chapter to a close, and before we illustrate many of these issues through the case studies produced by our contributors, we wish to stress that the range of approaches to formulation now available to CBT therapists is a major strength of the field. Collectively, they enable a flexible approach to understanding our clients' distress. We hope that the concluding diagram (Figure 5.7) will help you further reflect on the complex and interacting factors operating in psychological problems and the different approaches that can be taken within a collaborative approach to practice.

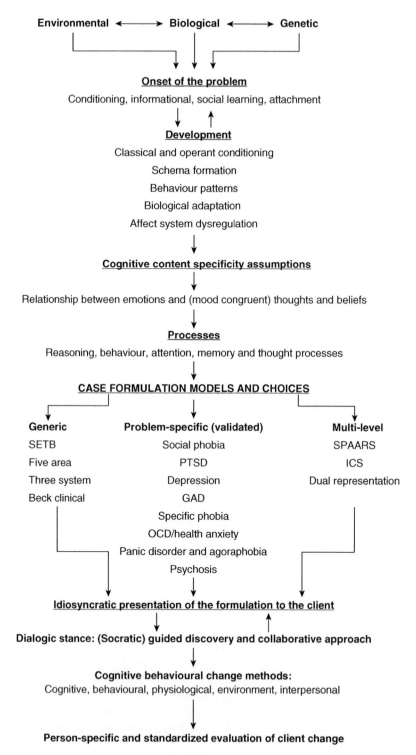

Figure 5.7 Framework of formulation in CBT

Summary

✓ Recently transdiagnostic approaches have been developed that consider psychological processes across disorders.
✓ Formulation can be developed at generic, transdiagnostic, disorder-specific and multi-level perspectives. Each approach has strengths and limitations.
✓ The cognitive content specificity hypothesis underpins disorder-specific models with many models having been subject to empirical validation.
✓ The cultural context of the individual influences psychological problems and is critically important to include in any formulation developed.
✓ Formulations should be developed in collaboration with the client within a relational context.

Activities

1. Think of two people whom you are currently trying to help. Formulate their difficulties using a range of different approaches, and do a cost-benefit analysis of each approach for you and the client.
2. Identify one suitable individual with whom you are working. Consider in detail the influence that cultural or socioeconomic factors have played in either the onset and/or development of the presenting problems.

Further reading

Harvey, A., Watkins, E., Mansell, W. and Shafran, R. (2004) *Cognitive Behavioural Processes across Psychological Disorders, a Transdiagnostic Approach to Research and Treatment*. Oxford: Oxford University Press.
This book signals a whole new approach to formulation and research in the field of CBT through the exploration of processes across disorders.

Paniagua, F.A. (2014) *Assessing and Treating Culturally Diverse Clients: A Practical Guide*. 4th edn. London: Sage.
This book addresses in an accessible way the important competences involved in working therapeutically with culturally diverse clients. A well-established text that gives some theory but which is also very practical.

Power, M. and Dalgleish, T. (2008) *Cognition and Emotion: From Order to Disorder*. 2nd edn. New York: Psychology Press.
This book is a superb theoretical account of cognition and emotion and essential reading on multi-level theories.

PART 2.1

Case Studies: Straightforward Clinical Presentations

SIX   Anna: A Case Study of Panic Disorder and Agoraphobia

Rita Santos

Learning objectives

After reading this chapter and completing the activities provided you should be able to:

- Conceptualize panic and agoraphobia based on an understanding of theoretical literature and current evidence-based practice.
- Understand and develop an idiosyncratic cognitive conceptualization for panic and agoraphobia that can inform an individualized approach to therapy.

Theoretical and research basis for therapy

There is substantial evidence supporting the conceptualization of panic disorder (PD) and agoraphobia; the former as a learned response to fear of particular body sensations and the latter as a behavioural response to such sensations and their escalation into panic attacks. Panic attacks are defined in the DSM-5 as,

> ...an abrupt surge of intense fear or intense discomfort that reaches a peak within minutes, and during which time (four) or more of the following symptoms occur: ... palpitations, sweating, trembling or shaking, sensations of shortness of breath or smothering, feelings of choking, chest pain or discomfort, derealisation, fear of losing control, fear of dying. (APA, 2013: 214)

According to Craske and Barlow (2008), panic attacks are characterized by strong autonomic arousal that is associated with perceptions of imminent threat or danger (e.g. death or loss of control). The efficacy of CBT for PD and agoraphobia is also well-established (Clark, 1996; Otto and

Deveney, 2005) with several randomized control trials establishing its effectiveness and superiority to other treatments (Clark et al., 1994; Arntz and van den Hout, 1996).

The diagnosis of PD (WHO, 1993; APA, 2013) is relevant to those individuals who experience recurrent panic attacks, and the anticipation of panic and its consequences. Individuals with panic disorder and agoraphobia (PDA) identify situations with an increased likelihood of occurrence of panic attacks and tend to avoid them. It is the fear of recurrent panic attacks combined with the perceived imminent threat or interpretation of symptoms that differentiates PD from other disorders, and the most influential research focuses on the cognitive understanding of PD (e.g. Beck et al., 1985; Clark, 1986, 1988, 1996; Salkovskis, 1988).

The cognitive model for PD proposes that panic attacks result from an enduring tendency to interpret bodily sensations as indicative of impending physical or mental catastrophe (Clark, 1988). The initial state of apprehension results from the perception of the trigger stimulus (internal or external) as threatening. Autonomic arousal, when also interpreted as threatening, further increases the initial apprehension which in turn escalates the symptoms resulting in a positive feedback loop that culminates in a panic attack. Occasional panic attacks are common in the non-clinical population (Brown and Cash, 1990). However, the cognitive theory proposes that individuals will only develop PD if the catastrophic interpretation of the autonomic arousal becomes a common response (Clark, 1996). PD can be accompanied by agoraphobia, and the cognitive model suggests that agoraphobic avoidance mostly occurs when individuals experienced their initial panic attacks away from home, when help was not readily available (Clark and Salkovskis, 2009). Several variables seem to be responsible for the maintenance of the problem, and enhanced interoception and safety-seeking behaviours are two of them (Clark and Salkovskis, 2009). The client hypothesizes that performing safety behaviours prevents the anticipated catastrophe (e.g. having a heart attack, fainting, or losing control), thus reinforcing the belief that such behaviours are the only thing that stand between them and the anticipated danger when the catastrophe does not actually occur (Salkovskis, 1991). These factors prevent the disconfirmation of the consequences of the bodily sensations, and may also contribute to the exacerbation of the autonomic arousal (Salkovskis et al., 1999).

This is a case study that describes a cognitive behavioural intervention developed for a client who presented with panic disorder and agoraphobia.

Case summary and main presenting problem

Anna was referred to her local IAPT service by her GP because of complaints of panic and severe anxiety for the past two years. At the time of assessment Anna was housebound, experienced several panic attacks each week and had considerable apprehension about having panic attacks. She avoided routine activities such as travelling inside or outside well-known areas, travelling by train or bus, theatres, crowded places, lifts, flying, escalators, restaurants and open spaces. Such situations were avoided both alone and accompanied.

Case assessment

Anna was a 20-year-old unemployed woman living with her parents and siblings. She described a stable and normal family life, being particularly close to her mother, having good friends and a healthy social life. Anna was a Christian and frequently attended events at the local church with her family. She described having a normal development without major problems or difficulties.

The identified onset of panic occurred at age 18. Anna was attending a lecture on abnormal psychology at university, which was about anxiety and stress. This triggered the thought, 'If this is what stress feels like, then that is how I should be feeling', and physical sensations such as palpitations, dizziness, difficulties breathing, shaking, sweating, a lump in the throat and 'jelly legs' followed. After such sensations and thoughts Anna also believed that unless she left the room, she would faint or stop breathing and suffocate. Anna described how she continued going to university but began feeling anxious during lectures in both lecture theatres and smaller tutorial rooms.

The frequency of panic episodes started to increase while at university. Anna's main misinterpretations of threat concerned fainting, having a heart attack and eventually dying. She developed over several months a marked fear of the panic attacks themselves.

At the age of 19, Anna felt that it was difficult to continue enduring the anxiety and panic, and started worrying about her academic performance during exams, and if she would even manage to sit the exams (misinterpretations of threat and anticipatory anxiety). To cope, she requested that her exams took place in a small room, close to an open window, and achieved borderline pass marks.

During this time her family also experienced difficulties after the death of a family member and her mother became depressed after an unsuccessful operation. Anna felt increasingly anxious and started experiencing panic attacks every time she left her home and went anywhere on her own. Her difficulties coping with university, worrying about her mother's health, and anxiety about her family and the loss of her loved ones all contributed to an increase in anxiety and panic attacks. Anna started to overestimate danger and underestimate her ability to cope.

In consequence, Anna decided to take a year off university and stay at home for several months to take care of her mother. A few months later, after recovering from a second and more successful operation, her mother

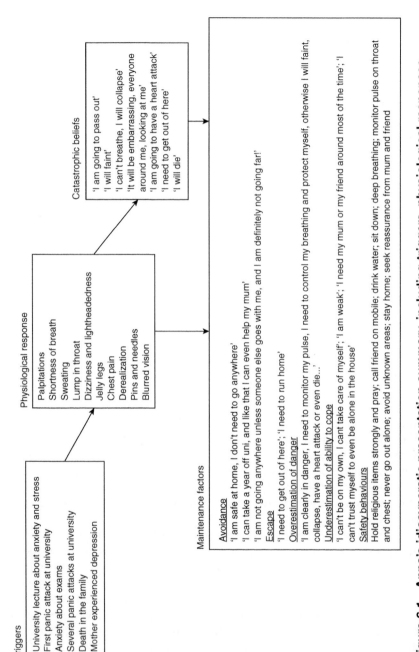

Triggers

University lecture about anxiety and stress
First panic attack at university
Anxiety about exams
Several panic attacks at university
Death in the family
Mother experienced depression

Physiological response

Palpitations
Shortness of breath
Sweating
Lump in throat
Dizziness and lightheadedness
Jelly legs
Chest pain
Derealization
Pins and needles
Blurred vision

Catastrophic beliefs

'I am going to pass out'
'I will faint'
'I can't breathe, I will collapse'
'It will be embarrassing, everyone around me, looking at me'
'I am going to have a heart attack'
'I need to get out of here'
'I will die'

Maintenance factors

<u>Avoidance</u>
'I am safe at home, I don't need to go anywhere'
'I can take a year off uni, and like that I can even help my mum'
'I am not going anywhere unless someone else goes with me, and I am definitely not going far!'
<u>Escape</u>
'I need to get out of here'; 'I need to run home'
<u>Overestimation of danger</u>
'I am clearly in danger, I need to monitor my pulse, I need to control my breathing and protect myself, otherwise I will faint, collapse, have a heart attack or even die...'
<u>Underestimation of ability to cope</u>
'I can't be on my own, I cant take care of myself'; 'I am weak'; 'I need my mum or my friend around most of the time'; 'I can't trust myself to even be alone in the house'
<u>Safety behaviours</u>
Hold religious items strongly and pray; call friend on mobile; drink water; sit down; deep breathing; monitor pulse on throat and chest; never go out alone; avoid unknown areas; stay home; seek reassurance from mum and friend

Figure 6.1 Anna's idiosyncratic presentation summary, including triggers, physiological responses, anxious cognitions and maintenance factors

decided to visit family in America before returning to work. Anna refused to go as she thought she could not cope with flying. While at home with her father (who was unaware of her difficulties, as Anna had only told her mother) she had a panic attack, fell on the floor and thought she was going to faint and not wake up. Although the feared consequence did not occur, Anna developed severe anxiety about fainting and asked her mother to return early from her holiday, which she did. Her mother then delayed returning to work for another month to care for Anna, and took Anna to her GP who prescribed beta-blockers (which Anna took only once).

Following this period, Anna avoided getting out of the house and experienced panic attacks on the rare occasions she attempted to do so (e.g. when going to church). She became mostly housebound and, because of that, decided to try to manage her anxiety by asking for help so that she could return to university the following year.

Anna described how she relied extensively on safety behaviours that included rarely leaving the house, carrying religious items, water, a phone and beta-blockers, seeking reassurance from her mother and engaging in deep breathing. Avoidance behaviours and self-monitoring of physical symptoms were her other principal coping strategies.

Figure 6.1 is a graphical representation of Anna's presentation with further descriptions of her cognitions, physiological response and maintenance factors.

Self-report measures and questionnaires

To inform the conceptualization and formulation, Anna completed several questionnaires. A summary of these and the clinical significance of her scores are provided in Table 6.1.

Table 6.1   Questionnaires completed at assessment stage, end of treatment and overall clinical significance

Questionnaire		Score
PHQ-9	Patient Health Questionnaire – Depression Severity (Kroenke and Spitzer, 2002)	0–27
GAD-7	Patient Health Questionnaire – Anxiety Severity (Spitzer et al., 2006)	0–21
PS	Phobia Scales (Department of Health, 2008a)	0–8
MI	Mobility Inventory (Chambless et al., 1985)	1–5
ACQ	Agoraphobic Cognitions Questionnaire (Chambless et al., 1984)	14–70
BSQ	Body Sensations Questionnaire (Chambless et al., 1984)	16–80

(Continued)

Table 6.1 (Continued)

Questionnaire	Assessment	End of treatment	Clinical significance
PHQ-9	8	5	
GAD-7	17	6	At assessment stage Anna presented
PS			with mild depression and severe
Social phobia	3	1	anxiety affect accompanied by strong
Panic and			agoraphobic avoidance.
agoraphobia	7	1	
Specific phobia	8	4	
MI			
Alone	5	1.8	At the end of treatment the scores
Accompanied	4.5	1.5	indicated only residual depressed
ACQ	52	21	and anxiety affect, and non-clinically
BSQ	69	20	significant agoraphobic avoidance.

Case conceptualization

Anna's case (see Figure 6.1) illustrates a young adult characterized by a number of anxiety-provoking situations. She described feeling distressed and anxious at university, experiencing her first panic episode during a lecture, and losing a member of her family. Her mother (who provided her with most support) underwent surgery and experienced depression. Such events seemed to have happened over a short period of time, were overwhelming and appeared to have contributed to the development of Anna's difficulties. Anna became anxious during her exams, started to experience frequent panic attacks, developed catastrophic misinterpretations about her physical sensations and started avoiding situations, gradually becoming housebound. The assessment showed that Anna left home only occasionally to go to church with her mother, and that her history of panic preceded the avoidance behaviours.

The maintenance of panic attacks has been attributed to several factors including interoceptive hypersensitivity and the misinterpretation of bodily sensations (Clark, 1996), and avoidance and safety-seeking behaviours (Clark, 1996; Craske and Barlow, 2008; Clark and Beck, 2010). Anna's history was consistent with the cognitive model of panic, which suggests that the escalation of bodily symptoms is associated with the misinterpretation of the feared consequence of such sensations (Clark, 1996) which are, in turn, exacerbated. The constant reassurance from Anna's mother also seemed to be a maintenance factor.

Anna presented both external (e.g. supermarkets, trains, buses) and internal (e.g. palpitations, lump in throat, shortness of breath) triggers for panic attacks. Her misinterpretations about physical and mental sensations included beliefs that she was going to have a heart attack, suffocate or faint. Her reactions to panic attacks were mostly escape behaviours in which she tried to leave the situation as soon as possible and call for help. The anticipation of the attacks typically led to avoidance. Her safety-seeking behaviours included constantly carrying water, religious items, beta-blockers, phone, taking deep breaths, praying, seeking reassurance, as well as leaving the situation as noted earlier.

The idiosyncratic model of panic for Anna is shown in Figure 6.2 below. The formulation refers to one panic attack, including the emotions, physical sensations, misinterpretations of threat, and safety-seeking behaviours adopted by Anna for the specific situation.

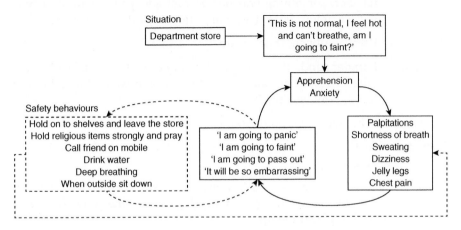

Figure 6.2   Anna's individual version of the panic cognitive model (Clark and Salkovskis, 2009) for one particular panic attack

The formulation was developed collaboratively with Anna at the end of assessment and a recent panic attack was reviewed, as illustrated in the following dialogue between the therapist and Anna:

Therapist: So how about we both try to make sense of what's happening during a panic attack?

Anna: Yes, I'd really like that.

Therapist: Ok, let's think about your most recent panic attack. Can you describe where you were, with whom and what you were doing when the panic started?

Anna: My friend had her graduation and wanted a dress, and begged me to go to a department store with her. It was close to my home and I thought, 'I'll make sure it's fast', so I went.

Sorry... Yes, I was at a department store with my friend in the morning, when it was empty.

Therapist: So you were trying to do something nice for your friend. What were you doing when the panic started?

Anna: I was looking around and then when I looked back, my friend wasn't there...

Therapist: What physical sensations did you notice at that moment?

Anna: I felt hot, and that just felt like it wasn't normal. I thought, 'Am I going to faint?'

Therapist: Let me see if I understood you correctly. At that moment you felt hot, something was not normal and you wondered if you were going to faint. Did you notice any other sensations?

Anna: I was really short of breath.

Therapist: I understand. It sounds really unpleasant and difficult. And when you felt hot and out of breath, you wanted to get out of there, why was that?

Anna: I thought I was going to panic badly.

Therapist: At that stage did you notice any other physical sensations in your body?

Anna: Yes, my heart was racing, my chest was hurting, I was sweating, felt really dizzy and my legs were like jelly, like they couldn't hold me up.

Therapist: And how were you feeling?

Anna: I was really anxious and apprehensive.

Therapist: And at that point what was going through your mind?

Anna: I thought I was going to faint or something...

Therapist: And if you did what would be the worst that could happen?

Anna: Oh... I don't know... I guess just having everyone around me, looking at me. It would be so embarrassing.

Therapist: So if I was to summarize what you have just shared with me, you thought that you could panic badly, faint, and that people would gather around you which you would find really embarrassing. Did I understand that correctly?

Anna: Yes, you did, it's exactly that.

Therapist: When you were thinking like that did you notice any other physical sensations?

Anna: Yes, I guess my legs were like jelly, really weak and I was more dizzy.

Therapist: And what happened to your thoughts at that point, when you were feeling your heart racing, chest pain, sweating, more dizziness and now also jelly legs?

Anna: They got worse and worse, the more I felt, and the more I thought I was going to pass out.

Therapist: From 0 to 100 per cent how much did you believe that that would happen at that point in time?

Anna: 100 per cent.

Therapist: So it looks to me like your thoughts, your feelings and your body sensations influence each other and make each other worse. As you can see I have been writing what you've been telling me and made some arrows as we went along. What does this tell you? (Showing client the diagram.)

Anna: It is a vicious circle.

Therapist: Hm. There is one last thing that I want to ask you about. What did you do to cope, make it better, or to try and control the sensations?

Anna: I held on to the shelves for a few seconds while I called my friend to say I wanted to get out of there.

Therapist: So you tried to escape at that point. Did you do anything else?

Anna: Um... yes, the usual stuff, I held my rosary strongly and prayed in my head, drank some water, took some deep breaths and then my friend arrived. After all she was really close by.

Therapist: What happened when your friend arrived?

Anna: We went outside fast, and then I sat down and did more deep breathing.

Therapist: So we could add those behaviours to the graph here and we can draw an arrow from those to your thoughts here. They may be keeping your thoughts going as if you keep doing these things you will never really see what would happen if you didn't. Does that make sense to you?

Anna: Yes, it makes a lot of sense. I'm in the middle of a full vicious circle. I have to stop this!

Therapist: I can see that you're motivated to do so. Let's look at the diagram and summarize what we just did together.

Course of therapy

Cognitive therapy for panic relies heavily on the correction of misinterpretation of symptoms of anxiety as indicating an impending catastrophic consequence. Therapy has three main goals: (1) the identification of catastrophic misinterpretations; (2) promoting the ability to generate alternative appraisals; and (3) testing the validity of both catastrophic and non-catastrophic interpretations (Clark and Salkovskis, 2009) by dropping safety behaviours and systematic testing through behavioural experiments. If avoidance is extensive then graded exposure is also indicated.

Goals

After the assessment, Anna's idiosyncratic model was developed collaboratively and discussed in session (see Figure 6.2).

PDA can be very debilitating and in severe cases leave people housebound (as in the example presented here). The therapeutic relationship can play a role in the effectiveness of psychological therapy for PDA. Anna benefited from a therapist who was respectful, empathic, caring, and collaborative and who conveyed understanding. She also benefited from the therapist conveying confidence, offering explanations and providing instructions at later stages in therapy. Although limited, research on PD and PDA has suggested that a more directive and explanatory style in the early stages is associated with poorer outcomes, whereas a relationship characterized by empathy, understanding and warmth at the initial stages is associated with better outcomes (Williams and Chambless, 1990; Keijsers et al., 1995).

Anna agreed with the formulation and realized through guided discovery that she needed to perform behavioural experiments targeting the feared situations, and challenge her anxiety rather than avoid it. A description of CBT and its processes was provided and Anna agreed to undergo a course of CBT for PDA. She described her goals as, 'To reduce my anxiety levels, be able to get out of the house so that I can go to university and manage my anxiety better in general'.

Content of therapy

The specific cognitive behavioural techniques shown to be effective during the treatment of PD and agoraphobia were used and are summarized in Table 6.2.

Table 6.2 Summary of performed interventions during Anna's therapy sessions and respective outcome

Interventions	Outcome
Psycho-education: 1) Prevalence, false-alarm or fight/flight responses, hypervigilance, attentional biases, evolutionary perspectives, and neurobiological underpinnings were discussed. 2) The anxiety curve, anxiety levels, escape and avoidance behaviours, and consequent dissipation of anxiety were discussed.	Anna described that she now realized that her reaction and fear actually made sense considering that she was fearful of passing out or even dying, and also said: 'This is pretty crazy, this actually means that my body is working just fine, but I am having far too many alarm responses because I see panic everywhere!'
An idiosyncratic formulation was collaboratively developed (see Figure 6.1). The CBT treatment was explained and discussed.	Anna found the formulation very helpful and through guided discovery realized that she was not only misinterpreting her body sensations as threatening but also that her safety behaviours and avoidance were counterproductive and maintaining her difficulties.
Discussion techniques: 1) Effects of naturally occurring distraction. 2) Word pair associates exercise. 3) Cardiac study discussion.	1) Anna described having been distracted from panic attacks a few times when receiving phone calls. 2) Anna reported feeling breathless and having palpitations while focusing on the meaning of the words she was reading. 3) Anna identified herself with the image representing PD patients. Summary of learning: 'Catastrophic thinking is related with the physical sensations experienced during a panic attack, basically I understand now that I am focusing on my body a lot and that I am scared of what I feel, even here in the room reading a piece of paper....'. Anna found the techniques helpful and reported they increased her motivation to understand and challenge her anxiety.
Interoceptive exposure to shortness of breath and palpitations.	Anna realized that some of her safety behaviours during a panic attack (i.e. deep breathing) were actually having a paradoxical effect. She also realized that the sensations triggered in session were very similar to the ones she experienced during a panic attack, that her body went back to normal very fast by doing nothing about it and that the exposure to such sensations could potentially increase her tolerance to anxiety.
Behavioural experiments: a set of BEs were developed and performed. Anxious cognitions were identified, alternatives were developed and belief ratings obtained. For the BEs, predictions were obtained and when anxiety levels decreased they were re-evaluated.	At the beginning of treatment, Anna was housebound, and therapy took place at her home. Therefore the initial BEs were collaboratively developed to test her beliefs about being outside while dropping her safety behaviours. See an example in Table 6.3. As the sessions progressed Anna started attending sessions at the clinic, enrolled in driving lessons, passed her driving test, informed the university she was coming back to resume her studies, and travelled to central London several times accompanied and alone.

Table 6.3 Example of Anna's behavioural experiments record

SITUATION	PREDICTION (belief 0–100%)	EXPERIMENT	OUTCOME	WHAT I HAVE LEARNT (belief 0–100%)
Go for a walk outside with the therapist for 10 minutes.	I will start to panic, my legs will fail me and I will faint. (80%)	Go for the walk, think about what anxiety means and that if my blood pressure is high I can't faint. Also I know that I don't need to have safety behaviours, therefore I will not take my religious items or the beta-blockers with me.	As we were just starting to walk I felt palpitations and shortness of breath and wanted to go back inside. But I stopped and thought about what I've learned and continued walking. It was really hard but I didn't faint although I felt very dizzy.	I can go for walks without safety behaviours and if I stay in the situation when panicking the anxiety actually goes down and I don't faint. (10%)
Go for a walk alone for 10 minutes while the therapist is waiting at my home.	I will really panic on my own, lose control, and will have a heart attack and nobody will be there and I could die. (70%)	Going for a walk without safety behaviours, staying there walking, and reminding myself of what I know about anxiety and fight or flight responses. The problem is my anxiety not the street or the walk and I need to experience this differently!	I felt very intense palpitations and chest pain, thought I was going to have a heart attack but I tried really hard to stay and think about the therapy sessions. After a while my anxiety went down and nothing else happened.	Although it is really hard and I am still scared, I have learned that my anxiety goes down as soon as I challenge it. I can go for walks! (20%)

Therapy outcome

Therapy outcome was measured using the questionnaires and clinical observation during therapy. Belief change and a shift in the misinterpretation of threat and body sensations were achieved successfully and were reported within the treatment sessions. The questionnaire data suggested that substantial change occurred during treatment (see Table 6.1).

Obstacles and reflections

In general the case proceeded satisfactorily. Anna's goals were achieved and the original conceptualization was shown to be a robust and useful description of the case and well-supported by theory (Clark and Salkovskis, 2009).

Anna was initially housebound and so treatment started from her home. Her avoidance was severe and her escape strategies rigid. It was difficult to promote belief change during the initial sessions and psycho-education was a vital step. Without psycho-education it would have been difficult to provide a rationale that would have satisfied Anna's need for understanding. Persistency and consistency of the message delivered, a therapeutic relationship characterized by an understanding, caring and empathic stance, and availability to answer her questions were fundamental factors in Anna's engagement. This understanding was crucial for her subsequent participation in behavioural experiments.

The use of discussion techniques was very effective, especially the introduction to interoceptive exposure after which positive change was observed on a weekly basis. This emphasizes the relevance of engaging in guided discovery and reflection while experiencing body sensations and understanding their non-threatening nature. Behavioural experiments were also crucial and had a substantial impact on Anna's experience. They facilitated belief change and promoted helpful discussions with the client about acquired learning, as Anna progressively accumulated evidence that she could cope, that anxiety was not dangerous, and that safety behaviours were counterproductive.

The case formulation process was vital. It allowed a good understanding of the presentation, triggers, key cognitions, the associated physiological response, and the safety behaviours Anna had developed to keep herself as safe as possible. Sharing a formulation allowed Anna to feel understood, and a common goal and understanding, once established, drove the teamwork carried out during the intervention. The formulation was also crucial to the development of an effective therapeutic relationship that allowed Anna to feel safe enough to relinquish some control and experience her feared body sensations.

Although Anna had a supportive family environment, this was at times also an obstacle. Her mother constantly 'interfered' with therapy and engaged in frequent reassurance. This was explicitly formulated as a safety behaviour and behavioural experiments were designed to target this. Her mother was also invited to one session, during which Anna shared her formulation and emphasized maintenance factors. Her mother was then supportive and facilitated therapy.

Anna's account of her experience of therapy was as follows:

> I have achieved so much more than my initial therapy goals, I love that I worked towards becoming my own therapist and that I can think of experiments to challenge my anxiety on my own. I have even learned to reflect which hopefully will help me with university and my life in general. Anxiety is indeed scary but so important, and I feel that I now understand it much better and manage it fine. I am doing everything I want to do really, so I really enjoyed CBT and thank you for everything!

Recommendations

When working with clients with PDA, severe avoidance and a plethora of escape strategies are common and can prove difficult to address. Some advice on how to overcome these is presented next.

1. The client asks numerous questions and has difficulty understanding and/or accepting the CBT model for PDA

Prepare for sessions thoroughly. Make sure that your understanding of anxiety goes beyond general psycho-education, that you can explain not only the fear response in psychological terms but also the role of attentional biases, hypervigilance, relevant neurobiological aspects of anxiety, and the emotional processing theory.

2. The client demonstrates high levels of 'fear of fear' and you have difficulty initiating behavioural experiments, even if the client understands and engages with the model

Spend as many sessions as necessary doing interoceptive exposure and experimenting with the physical sensations. This creates an opportunity to induce the feared sensations several times which in turn allows the disconfirmation of the catastrophic misinterpretations. This is fundamental work and promotes the effectiveness of behavioural experiments at a later stage. When clients experience derealization and depersonalization, it is important to emphasize rational explanations for these experiences, provide links to psycho-education and develop behavioural experiments to test them.

3. The client seems to be improving but only in their own home or in the therapy room. It is proving difficult to generalize beyond these settings or to achieve further goals

Several stages of therapy will promote change if performed either at the client's home or therapy room, such as psycho-education, discussion techniques and interoceptive exposure. Nonetheless, those specific therapy settings can limit the generalization of acquired learning and can become safety behaviours themselves. It is fundamental that, when working with PDA, behavioural experiments are also performed in the natural environment. Experiments undertaken in the natural environment that also benefit from the guidance of the therapist (e.g. through feedback, suggestions for safety behaviour reduction and development of alternative experiments to test specific predictions that occur at that specific point in time) can be particularly effective. The use of behavioural experiments in the natural environment without the therapist can also be effective allowing the client to practice new skills, become more independent and generalize their learning.

4. The client seems to perform behavioural experiments easily and quickly

The client may be performing subtle safety behaviours such as telling themselves that they are home, safe watching TV, that this will be quick or even that everything will be fine because the therapist is close at hand. It is important to ask the client 'What is going through your mind right now?' and 'What are you feeling in your body?' while performing the experiment, or to ask the client to guide you through what they are doing and why, what their predictions are and what they have learned so far. This will help the client focus on the task at hand and will give the therapist information about what is actually happening.

5. The client expresses concerns about possible relapse or not making enough progress as a result of experiencing anxiety and distress during a behavioural experiment

Emphasize that the goal of the experiments is not the absence of anxiety. In fact, without experiencing anxiety there will be very little opportunity to gather evidence that the client is overestimating danger and underestimating the ability to cope, as well as learning to manage anxiety in a more helpful manner.

Summary

✓ There is good evidence to support the efficacy of CBT for panic disorder and agoraphobia.
✓ The CBT model of panic disorder offers a relevant and useful basis for formulating the client's idiosyncratic presentation.
✓ Ensure that your understanding of anxiety and how it manifests goes beyond general psycho-education so that you can provide a thorough explanation of the fear response should this be needed.
✓ Be attentive to subtle safety-seeking behaviours that the client may not initially report.

Activities

1. Think of a client that you are working with or have worked with who presented with panic and agoraphobia. Conceptualize the difficulties as suggested in this chapter making links to the literature and model.
2. For the same client develop two or three different formulations for specific situations, making clear links between the relevant physical sensations, misinterpretations and safety behaviours.
3. Reflect on the contribution that this chapter may make to your future practice and consider what changes you may introduce in future assessments and model-specific formulations.

Further reading

Clark, D.M. (1996) 'Panic disorder: from theory to therapy', in P.M. Salkovskis (ed.), *Frontiers of Cognitive Therapy*. New York: Guilford Press. pp. 318–44.

Clark, D.M. and Salkovskis, P.M. (2009) 'Panic disorder', Unpublished cognitive therapy manual for IAPT high intensity therapists. Oxford: Department of Experimental Psychology, University of Oxford (available on request from first author).

Craske, M.G. and Barlow, D.H. (2008) 'Panic disorder and agoraphobia', in D.H. Barlow (ed.), *Clinical Handbook of Psychological Disorders*. 4th edn. New York: Guilford Press.pp. 1–64.

Salkovskis, P.M., Clark, P.M., Hackmann, A., Wells, A. and Gelder, M. (1999) 'An experimental investigation of the role of safety-seeking behaviours in the maintenance of panic disorder with agoraphobia', *Behaviour Research and Therapy*, 37: 559–74.

SEVEN   Farid: A Case Study of Depression using Traditional, Beckian CBT

Rita Woo

Learning objectives

After reading this chapter and completing the activities provided you should be able to:

- Understand the importance of a client's history, cultural background, gender, and the role of the family in the development and maintenance of depression and include these in the conceptualization of the client's difficulties.
- Use 'standard' Beckian CBT to address the cognitive and behavioural maintenance factors associated with depression.
- Adapt the therapy approach and therapeutic style to working with depression.
- Understand the impact of hopelessness and helplessness commonly associated with depression on the client's family and mental health professionals involved in their care.

Theory and research base

Depression is a common mental health problem with lifetime prevalence rates between 4–10 per cent (NICE, 2009) and in its severe form, can be a disabling condition that is often difficult to treat. The helplessness and hopelessness associated with this state can affect both client and clinician.

Cognitive therapy was originally developed for the treatment of depression (Beck et al., 1979) and cognitive mediation lies at the heart of Beck's model.

He suggested that the content and process of negative thinking and cognitive vulnerability are important in understanding the development and maintenance of depression.

A pattern of negative thoughts about the self, the world/others and the future, known as the 'cognitive triad', is a central feature of Beck et al.'s (1979) model of depression. These cognitions activated by external events are thought to play a crucial role in both vulnerability to and maintenance of depression via a reciprocal feedback loop where negative thoughts intensify the low mood and reduce motivation, energy, and engagement in activities. These in turn seem to confirm the negative thoughts giving rise to a vicious cycle.

Thinking in depression is characterized by a specific attributional style (Abramson et al., 2002) which renders the recall of information mood state dependent (Teasdale and Cox, 2001; Kuyken et al., 2003). A depressed individual is more likely to recall and process information in a negative way, particularly when beliefs associated with the cognitive triad are activated. This results in an apparent absence of positive experiences past or present. Furthermore, negative events are attributed to stable, global internal factors (e.g. 'This means I'm useless') which has implications for self-worth and the future. In contrast, positive events are discounted and attributed to external factors without lasting consequences (e.g. 'That was just lucky'). Other cognitive processes also present in depression include thinking biases such as all-or-nothing thinking, jumping to conclusions etc. (Beck et al., 1979); over general memory (i.e. an inability to recall memories of positive events) (Williams et al., 2000); a ruminative thinking style (Nolen-Hoeksema, 1991); and interpreting thoughts as accurate reflections of reality rather than internal events (Teasdale et al., 2002).

Treatment of depression typically involves the following (Westbrook et al., 2011):

- Identifying specific problems for treatment (e.g. reduced activity, difficulties in close relationships, rumination, etc).
- Socialization to the cognitive model and developing a conceptualization of the presenting concerns with the client.
- Reducing depressive symptoms using behavioural and cognitive strategies.
- Identifying and evaluating negative automatic thoughts (NATs) associated with the cognitive triad via verbal reattribution techniques and behavioural experiments.
- Addressing and modifying conditional assumptions and/or core beliefs if necessary towards the end of therapy to reduce the risk of relapse.

There is a range of evidence supporting the effectiveness of CBT for depression (Paykel et al., 1999; Hollon et al., 2002; DeRubeis et al., 2005; Hollon et al., 2006). This evidence has contributed to the development of the IAPT initiative in which depression is one of the many mental health problems targeted. However, despite evidence to support the effectiveness of CBT for depression, for many individuals depression remains a chronic and relapsing condition, with the risk of recurrence increasing with each depressive episode (Solomon et al., 2000). This raises many clinical challenges for effective and longer lasting treatments.

Case introduction

Farid, a 48-year-old Arabic man, had been in contact with mental health services for over a year following an attempt at suicide which was precipitated by repeated unsuccessful attempts to re-establish his business. Farid was diagnosed with depression and prescribed anti-depressants, and was regularly reviewed by a psychiatrist within a mental health team. He had been allocated a care co-ordinator, who had helped to partially resolve the family's financial and accommodation issues, as well as monitored his mood and suicide ideation. He had also been referred to the occupational therapist within the team to help increase his level of occupational and social activities. Despite persistent efforts from Farid and the professionals involved in his care there had not been significant improvement in his mood. Instead there seemed to be an increasing sense of hopelessness and helplessness in all involved. This was especially noticeable in Farid who had changed from an active man into one disabled by somatic pain. There was no previous psychiatric history. This was the context that led to a multidisciplinary team discussion and a request for a psychological assessment and possible therapy from the author, as the team clinical psychologist.

Presenting concerns

Farid's descriptions of his difficulties were consistent with depression. He stated that he felt sad, constantly tired, and reported difficulties with concentration, disturbed sleep, and poor appetite. Since he lost the business he spent most of the day at home. Previously he had been involved in the community, attended the mosque on a regular basis, socialized with friends, and spent time with his 11-year-old son.

During the sessions, Farid appeared withdrawn and hopeless, and constantly stated 'I'm useless and a total failure' and 'I've made a mess of my family's life'. Since his overdose, his daughters, aged 17 and 15 years, looked after his medication and shared responsibility for accompanying him everywhere. Consequently Farid was rarely alone as his family feared that he would attempt suicide again. There had also been a notable deterioration in his son's behaviour at school. Farid believed that he was a useless father who could not even look after his children. Furthermore his wife, who had not worked during their 22 year marriage, was currently working and Farid believed that this together with his depression had contributed to a deterioration in their relationship culminating in decreased sexual intimacy and increased arguments. All these factors were exacerbating his thoughts of being useless and a failure. Moreover he spent a large part of the day thinking about the loss of his business and felt that he should have been able to 'sort things out'.

During the initial sessions, Farid presented as flat in affect, avoided eye contact, and was softly spoken, often to the point of whispering. His speech was extremely slow and laborious. He described being in constant pain due to arthritis and walked with the aid of a walking stick. He attended the assessment appointments accompanied by his wife but added that they left the house two hours earlier to get to the appointment on time to allow for frequent stops along the way due to his pain. Farid's sense of hopelessness and helplessness was palpable and he often stated, 'What's the point of trying, it won't work, my business didn't. There's nothing I can do'; 'There's no point to my life' and 'What's the point of living?'

Farid's history

Farid, the eldest son in his family, is of Middle Eastern origin. He described his father as a role model who was frequently away on business trips. Each time before going, he recalled his father telling him, 'Son look after your mother and your sisters whilst I'm gone, you're the man'. When his father was at home his conversations with his children were focused on their academic achievements.

At nineteen, Farid left home to study at an English university. He then set up a business that was successful until the recession. Recently, Farid's mother had been ill and whilst she recovered, she was looked after by a carer. Farid stated that he felt 'guilty and useless' as he could neither provide for her nor visit her due to his financial situation.

Assessment

There were several aspects of the assessment. First, a cognitive behavioural analysis of the presenting concern was conducted to develop an understanding of the interaction between the cognitive, behavioural, emotional, attentional, physical, environmental, and interpersonal factors contributing to the maintenance of Farid's depression. This aided the development of a cross-sectional conceptualization of his current difficulties. Attention was also paid to identifying the most urgent and accessible problem that might contribute to the goals of therapy and the sequencing of interventions (e.g. suicidal thoughts, hopelessness, a deterioration in functioning, social withdrawal).

Second, his level of motivation, suicidal intent, and attitudes towards therapy were explored. This helped to elicit potential obstacles to engagement in therapy, and therapy-interfering behaviours. Whilst he felt hopeless and helpless with fleeting suicidal thoughts, no apparent suicidal intent was elicited and there were protective factors.

Third, a developmental and personal history was gathered to identify key events and social and learning processes that might have contributed to the development of core beliefs and assumptions which were increasing his vulnerability to depression. Of interest were the early learning experiences about achievement, self-worth, and gender roles and expectations within the family and wider community. Particular attention was paid to the beliefs he developed about himself, the world, and others associated with these experiences, which helped with differential diagnosis and the subsequent overall formulation of Farid's difficulties. In this respect, it was useful to determine whether Farid's current presentation could be understood in the context of depression or low self-esteem given his beliefs about being 'useless and a failure'. Farid's strengths, coping resources and how he responded to challenges in the past were also explored. All this contributed to the development of the longitudinal aspect of the formulation as well as clarification about the most appropriate way of understanding his presentation.

Fourth, the suitability of CBT for Farid was explored. Factors such as his ability to identify cognitions and emotions, recognize helpful and unhelpful behaviours, optimism about therapy, acceptance for responsibility for change, and his capacity to reflect on his experiences were considered (Safran and Segal, 1990; Butler et al., 2008; Townend and Grant, 2008).

With Farid's consent, the family were invited to the assessment sessions and his wife, daughters and son attended. This helped explore the impact of Farid's depression on the family and how they were coping. It also highlighted their sense of helplessness and hopelessness about the current situation.

The final aspect of the assessment involved identifying and defining Farid's goals for therapy. The agreed goals were:

- To do the things that he had previously enjoyed such as spending time with his son, going to the mosque and cooking.
- To stop judging himself as being 'useless and a failure'.
- To have hope for the future.

Measures

A combination of nomothetic and idiographic measures was used throughout therapy to monitor progress. Nomothetic measures included the Beck

Depression Inventory (BDI-II) (Beck et al., 1996) the Beck Hopelessness Scale (BHS) (Beck and Steer 1993), and the Work and Social Adjustment Scale (WSAS) (Mundt et al., 2002). The idiographic measures devised were based on his goals. These included monitoring the occasions he was engaged in activities he previously enjoyed and the level of conviction (0–100) of his beliefs 'I'm a failure' and 'I'm useless'. He also noted how motivated he felt in planning and participating (0–100) in activities he had always wanted to do but for which there had previously seemed little time (e.g. day trips with his wife, learning Italian) as an indication of hope for the future.

Case formulation

From the information gathered at assessment, it appeared that Farid's 'useless and failure' cognitions were activated following the loss of his business rather than throughout his life across different contexts. Prior to the collapse of his business he seemed to have had a sense of self-efficacy. Moreover, the 'useless and failure' cognitions were accompanied by hopelessness about the future and learned helplessness that led to attempted suicide. These themes may be considered more commonly associated with depression rather than a pervasive sense of failure both in the past and for the future (as is more often the case for low self-esteem). Accordingly, a formulation based on Beck's (1995) model of depression was used to encapsulate the overall picture of Farid's difficulties. The use of the most appropriate formulation to guide treatment planning is one of the CBT competences (Roth and Pilling, 2007) and increases the validity and effectiveness of the interventions used.

The formulation in Figure 7.1 was developed jointly with Farid in two stages. The first stage helped him understand the factors contributing to the maintenance of the depression. The second stage focused on the assumptions and core beliefs developed from his childhood experiences that increased his vulnerability to developing depression following the loss of his business, thereby shattering his perceptions of what it means to be a man.

Farid most easily described a sense of hopelessness, helplessness, and a 'life without purpose'. He seemed to be preoccupied with thoughts about loss and failure, and his responses were slow and succinct. The dialogue below helped to explore one factor that contributed to Farid's depression, namely handing over the responsibility of his medication to his daughters.

Therapist: What kind of situations on a day-to-day basis do you think keep these feelings (helplessness and hopelessness) going?

Farid: [*silence*] Everything.

Therapist: No wonder those feelings are so strong if it's everything. Shall we see whether we can break down 'everything' into smaller things?

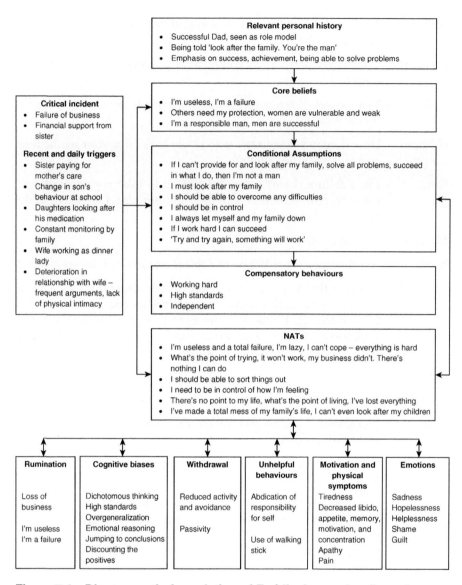

Figure 7.1   Diagrammatic formulation of Farid's depression (based on Beck, 1995, and Moorey, 2010)

Farid: [*silence*] You can try.

Therapist: OK, I'll try but you'll have to help me out to solve this. Are these feelings around when you're with your daughters?

Farid: Yes.

Therapist: What brings these feelings on when you're with them?

Farid: They look after my medication and give me the tablets I need to take.

Therapist: When they do that, do you have any thoughts about how they see you?

Farid: Yes [*pause*], I'm a useless father. I can't be trusted to take my medication.

Therapist: How do you see yourself when they look after your medication and give you the tablets?

Farid: I'm a failure, I can't even be trusted to take my medication... take the right tablets... take the right amount, take them at the right time [*long pause*].

Therapist: Anything else?

Farid: Another man wouldn't be like this [*Farid's voice is barely audible*].

Therapist: It seems that when your daughters look after your medication, it makes you think that you're a failure as you can't be trusted to take the right tablets at the right time. This makes you feel hopeless and helpless, and that another man would have coped better. Have I got that right so far?

Farid: Yes.

Therapist: When that happens, how do you respond?

Farid: [*Farid makes eye contact for the first time in our conversation*] I just let them do it.

Therapist: How does that make you feel when you're already thinking that you're a failure and feeling hopeless and helpless?

Farid: It makes me feel more helpless and a failure [*pause*]. It makes me feel stuck and I keep blaming myself. It makes me more depressed and tired. My family can see that and I know it makes them worry [*pause*], worry that I'll try to take my life again.

Therapist: If you were like your daughters and knew that their father was depressed and were concerned that he might take his life again, what would you do?

Farid: I would definitely be in charge of his tablets and watch him and be with him all the time [*said with more energy and in a louder voice*].

Therapist: From that, how do you think the depression makes you think and feel, and how you and your daughters cope with it?

Farid: The depression makes me think I'm useless and a failure constantly, it makes me give up any responsibility I have for myself making my daughters do it for me; it makes everything at home worse. It makes me feel less of a man for not being able to look after my daughters, instead of the other way round, and not solving this.

Therapist: Are there other situations on a day-to-day basis that follow a similar pattern?

The above dialogue helped socialize Farid to the cognitive behavioural model, and began the process of helping Farid develop a greater understanding of the nature and consequences of the depression and how general withdrawal from activities and daily responsibilities, cognitive biases and rumination contributed to its maintenance. Developing the formulation of Farid's difficulties beginning with maintenance factors helped to emphasize that the depression and its consequences were not his fault. His understanding of the factors contributing to his judgement of being useless and a failure also helped determine some of the steps he could take to help reduce this (for example, gradually taking more responsibility for his medication). This helped instil some optimism and reduce the hopelessness associated with depression for Farid and his family, as well as the team involved in his care.

Course of therapy

After introducing the cognitive model of depression and developing a shared formulation of Farid's current difficulties, the next stage of therapy involved the use of behavioural strategies, namely activity scheduling to help reduce Farid's symptoms of depression. In standard CBT for depression, this is considered a core therapeutic technique (Beck et al., 1979) and is associated with the idea that reduced activity and its accompanying cognitions and emotions is one of the 'vicious cycles' contributing to the maintenance of depression. This also fitted with Farid's goals of therapy and the conceptualization of his current difficulties.

Farid used the weekly activity schedule (WAS) to self-monitor the activities he was engaged in on an hourly basis and to record the amount of enjoyment from 0 (none at all) to 10 (the most possible) as well as the degree of 'usefulness' he derived from it. Given Farid's current level of depression and the overwhelming feelings of helplessness, to maximize the likelihood of him completing the WAS and to minimize his thoughts around failure, he was initially asked to complete the WAS for the morning (i.e. on an hourly basis from 8am to 12 noon) before this was built up to include

Table 7.1 Key interventions used in the treatment of Farid's depression

Aim/Presenting issue	Intervention	Outcome
Socialization to the cognitive behavioural model of depression and its cognitive, emotional and behavioural consequences	Psycho-education about the nature and consequences of depression	Increased awareness of the contribution of rumination, cognitive biases, withdrawal, unhelpful behaviours, motivation, and emotions to the maintenance of depression
	Joint development of maintenance cycles	Minimizing self-blame associated with the consequences of depression
	Development of the longitudinal aspect of the formulation	Instilled hope
		Clarified treatment goals
Decreasing the symptoms of depression by addressing the vicious cycle of withdrawal and reduced activity	WAS – recording the amount of enjoyment and degree of 'usefulness' when engaged in activity	Identified activities contributing to shift in mood as well as those Farid no longer engaged in since becoming depressed
	Graded activity to improve mood	Increased engagement in activities providing enjoyment and a sense of 'usefulness' (e.g. walking his son to school and gradually taking charge of his medication).
	Identify unhelpful cognitions interfering with engagement in activities	Developing alternative cognitions that encourage engagement in activities (e.g. 'I can try to see if it works'; 'If I keep trying something will work. It has in the past')
	Behavioural experiments putting unhelpful thoughts (e.g. 'What's the point, it won't work', 'There's nothing I can do', 'Everything is hard') 'on ice' to test out the effect of these on activity	Decentering from thoughts and seeing them as just thoughts rather than inherent truths (e.g. 'The depression is making me think and act this way. I know that I can do it, I've done it many times before'; 70% conviction)
		Reduced sense of hopelessness and helplessness.

Aim/Presenting issue	Intervention	Outcome
Identifying and evaluating NATs associated with the cognitive triad of depression	Three column thought record (situation, emotions, NATs) and information about thinking biases	Farid identified his NATs and labelled his cognitive biases which helped him to understand how they affected his behaviour
	Seven column thought record (situation, emotions, NATs, evidence for, evidence against, alternative thought, behaviour/action plan)	Further distancing from thoughts, 'The depression makes me tired and lazy. When I take small steps, I can do things and I don't feel so useless. I can enjoy doing things even though I'm still depressed' (65% conviction). This cognition was strengthened by continued activity scheduling
Evaluating negative thoughts about the self: 'I'm useless, lazy and a total failure'	In a discovery behavioural experiment, Farid was encouraged on alternate days for a week to respond to these thoughts in the same way that he would respond to his son when his son told him about the detentions and getting into trouble at school	Farid realized that when he responded kindly to the negative thoughts about himself, his mood would improve and he was more likely to continue with his activity scheduling. This contributed to a further improvement in his mood. However, at times he had to remind himself to be kind as the negative thoughts could easily return. This encouraged him to continue being kinder to himself when his mood was low
Evaluating negative thoughts about the future: 'What's the point of trying, it won't work. There's nothing I can do to change things' (95% conviction)	A series of behavioural experiments where Farid would gradually self-administer his medication, beginning with one day a week, to three days a week, to the whole week	Farid was surprised that his daughters agreed to the plan and he noticed how he felt more motivated to try the more days he was in charge of his medication. This led to an improvement in mood which was further increased by his daughters spending time

(Continued)

Table 7.1 (Continued)

Aim/Presenting issue	Intervention	Outcome
		watching TV with him. His alternative thought was 'Things are worth a try. It might be difficult at first but if it works, things can change' (65% conviction)
		The alternative was reinforced by Farid continuing to self-administer and to include other activities into his WAS
Evaluating assumptions: 'I should be able to overcome any difficulty, and be in control' (85% conviction)	Exploration of the short- and long-term consequences of holding onto the rule himself and if he were to pass the rule onto his son	An alternative rule was developed: 'As long as I've tried, that's what matters. There are many things that I can't control, the best I can do is to accept it, and then I won't be beating myself up for nothing' (50% conviction)
	Farid agreed to try to resolve a housing issue with the support of his key worker. This involved visiting a housing organization to explain the family's overcrowded situation and to gather the necessary paperwork for future rehousing. Farid agreed to inform his wife and children about the progress he was making	Farid stated that although he knew that it would be a long time before the family could be re-housed he felt satisfied that he had tried. When he explained the situation to his family and the actions he had taken, the family were very understanding and told him they knew of families who had been waiting a long time to move. His wife praised him for trying. 'As long as I've tried, that's what matters. There are many things that I can't control, the best I can do is to accept it, and then I won't be beating myself up for nothing' (90% conviction)

Aim/Presenting issue	Intervention	Outcome
'If I can't provide for and look after my family and succeed in what I do, then I'm not a man' (95% conviction)	Farid agreed to talk to his wife about her job as a dinner lady	He learnt that his wife wanted to have her own interests as their children had grown up and she no longer had to be at home all the time. Farid became aware that his wife was introduced to this job by the Imam's wife, who was also a dinner lady at the same school. 'If I can't provide for and look after my family, succeed in what I do, then I'm not a man' (90% conviction)
	A survey was designed for Farid to ask the Imam and his friends from the mosque	Farid learned that 'being able to provide for the family was part of being a man, but there were other things like accepting weakness in ourselves and others, being true to our faith, being humble, being kind to others and giving to the community (75% conviction)
		This was strengthened by exploring with Farid what it would mean to 'be a man in different contexts' and the different behaviours that would be evident (e.g. with friends, within his community, at the mosque, with family). Farid kept a record of the times he demonstrated these behaviours
Addressing rumination	Guided discovery to explore the nature and controllability of rumination and its effect on mood	Farid learnt the following about the ruminative process: – Once it starts, it is difficult to stop but can be interrupted if his children talk to him – Makes his mood low – Loses motivation to do things – Focuses on the loss of his business, something he can't do anything about now

(Continued)

Table 7.1 (Continued)

Aim/Presenting issue	Intervention	Outcome
	Rumination diary to monitor triggers (internal and/or external), time engaged in rumination, and the consequences of engaging in rumination	He recognized the triggers to the rumination were feeling tired, being in pain, lying in bed first thing in the morning. He reported 55% of his time ruminating, the consequences of which were low mood, loss of motivation to engage with people and activities
	Changing contextual factors associated with rumination	Farid altered his morning routine. Instead of lying in bed ruminating, he got up to make breakfast for his children. This also had an impact on his NATs 'I can't even look after my children' and 'I'm lazy'
	Shift in thinking style using imagery to recall playing football with his son. Farid practised recalling this image when he recognized some of the triggers to rumination (e.g. feeling tired and being in pain)	He was able to spend much less time ruminating (20%), and more time with his family and friends

the afternoon, and eventually the evening. It was also emphasized that the activities he might find enjoyable (e.g. eating) might not contribute to feelings of 'usefulness' and vice versa.

From the WAS, Farid gained a better picture of the overall activity level and the types of activities he was engaged in that gave him pleasure and/ or a sense of 'usefulness', and thus contributed to some improvement in his mood. This awareness formed the platform for graded activity planning and included restarting some of the activities he used to enjoy, as well as those that had given him a sense of usefulness (e.g. walking his son to school and going to the mosque).

The WAS was also useful in identifying the range of NATs ('What's the point, it won't work'; 'There's nothing I can do'; 'Everything is hard') that were interfering with Farid's engagement in some of the activities. Empathizing that these thoughts might be an obstacle to engaging in specific tasks and exploring with him the helpfulness of these thoughts by asking, 'How do the thoughts, "What's the point" and "It won't work", impact your ability to spend more time with your son?' was useful in differentiating cognitions that interfered with his engagement in different activities from those that helped him to engage. This led to a behavioural experiment to test out the effect of putting unhelpful thoughts about the activity 'on ice' (Moore and Garland, 2003). This also helped Farid recognize that these were just thoughts rather than inherent truths.

After Farid and his family had noticed an improvement in his mood and a decrease in his sense of hopelessness, he was encouraged to manage his medication gradually supported by a series of behavioural experiments. This not only lessened his 'useless' thoughts but also improved his relationship with his daughters, contributing to further improvement in mood and a decreased sense of 'failure'.

Other interventions used in the treatment of Farid's depression included using thought records to identify NATs associated with the cognitive triad, thinking biases, reappraising the validity of NATs and conditional assumptions through the combination of verbal reattribution strategies and behavioural experiments, addressing rumination using strategies from rumination-focused CBT for depression (Watkins, 2011) and relapse prevention (see Table 7.1).

Process and engagement in therapy

A curious stance during the assessment was adopted with the aim of developing a therapeutic alliance with Farid. As a way of helping to increase his motivation and hope, the negative cognitions associated with the cognitive triad, his sense of hopelessness, and the biological symptoms of depression were normalized. This was also useful to help Farid understand that his thoughts about being 'useless and a failure' were not inherent attributes and later on in therapy provided opportunities for behavioural experiments. It is considered helpful to adjust the level of activity, direction and structure in the session throughout the course of therapy in response to the client's depressive symptomatology and needs (Beck et al., 1979; Moore and Garland, 2003). Consequently, a more active and directive stance was initially adopted by using short and simple questions and eliciting concrete and specific responses. This aimed to decrease apathy and increase motivation. Moreover, sessions were shortened to 30 minutes but session frequency was increased to twice weekly for the first four weeks of therapy during activity scheduling. Thereafter, Farid was seen for 50 minutes on a once weekly basis for 12 sessions.

To counteract the cognitive deficits associated with depression (e.g. memory and negative biases), emphasis was placed on frequent repetition of information and eliciting summaries of key learning points from Farid, clear and specific plans for homework, and written recordings of predictions and results of behavioural experiments (see Table 7.2).

Based on the interaction between gender role socialization and social psychological processes, Addis and Mahalik (2003) have proposed a variety of factors for understanding men's help-seeking behaviours and this has been applied to depression (Sierra Hernandez et al., 2014). Of interest was the impact of depression on Farid's definition of masculinity, being strong, retaining control, and actively managing problems. Consideration of these factors placed additional emphasis on collaboration, ensuring that Farid had a clear rationale for engaging in therapy and the strategies used. This may perhaps be considered contrary to the idea that individuals of Farid's

Table 7.2 Strategies used to manage features of depression (based on Moore and Garland, 2003, and Padesky, 2003)

Features of depression	CBT strategies
Client passivity and withdrawal	Therapist activity and preparation
Hopelessness	Problem solving, gradual CBT skill acquisition, clear structure and focus in session
Pessimism	Thought testing via verbal reattribution and behavioural experiments
Low motivation	Behavioural experiments, SMART goals
Global description of difficulties	Clear goal setting, focus on specific situations
Self-criticism	Empowerment through collaboration and guided discovery
Poor treatment adherence	Address therapy interfering beliefs, emphasize or develop beliefs that help therapy engagement
Relapse	Therapy blueprints, addressing assumptions

cultural origin enter therapy with the expectation that the therapist will adopt an authoritative position and offer specific suggestions to problems (Abudabbeh and Hayes, 2006).

Constant exposure to the negativity associated with depression can leave the therapist demoralized. Being mindful of the model of depression, the client's formulation, and supervision to discuss practical techniques to manage the client's pessimism (as well as the opportunity for therapists to explore their thoughts about the progress of therapy) may be beneficial (Moore and Garland, 2003; Kennerley et al., 2010). Playing therapy recordings during supervision may also help the therapist maintain a collaborative stance, especially when the therapist has been more proactive and directive during the earlier stages of therapy in response to the client's depression-related passivity and avoidance.

Outcome and follow-up

Farid made good use of the 20 sessions offered to him (see Table 7.3 for Farid's scores on outcome measures). A follow-up at two months was arranged to see whether his gains were being maintained.

Table 7.3 Farid's scores on measures of outcome

Measures	Pre therapy	Mid therapy	Post therapy	2 mth Follow-up
Beck Depression Inventory (BDI-II)	44 (Severe depression)	21 (Moderate depression)	13 (Minimal Depression)	12 (Minimal depression)
Beck Hopelessness Scale (BHS)	12 (Moderate)	7 (Mild)	0 (Minimal)	0 (Minimal)
Work and Social Adjustment Scale (WSAS)	40 (Severe functional impairment)	27 (Severe functional impairment)	10 (Significant functional impairment)	8 (Normal)
Conviction in beliefs (0–100%)				
'I'm a failure'	100	85	60	55
'I'm useless'	100	75	45	40
Motivation in planning and participating in future activities e.g. learning Italian, day-trip to Bath with his wife (0–100)	0	45	80	80

At the end of therapy Farid was no longer clinically depressed or feeling hopeless about the future. Whilst his score on the WSAS fell just within the 'significant functional impairment' range, there were changes in his activity levels. Most notably, he was not using a walking stick and no longer reported being debilitated by pain. He stated that his goals for therapy had been met and that he felt 'more like a man'. He also described a much improved relationship with his wife and that there was now physical intimacy between them. Although the level of conviction in his beliefs 'I'm useless' and 'I'm a failure' was considerably lower post-therapy, he still considered himself to be 'a failure'. He attributed this to receiving benefits and not working, and believed that he needed to work to look after his family. In the meantime, he was volunteering at the mosque. These gains were sustained at the two-month follow-up.

Summary

✓ It is useful to include longitudinal factors as well as maintenance cycles in the conceptualization of depression to help think about potential adaptations to therapy and the therapeutic style.

✓ Adaptions to therapy and the therapeutic style combined with small achievable goals and activities throughout therapy may help to counteract the hopelessness and helplessness commonly associated with depression.

✓ In this case study, a good outcome was achieved by 'standard' Beckian CBT for depression targeting the cognitive and behavioural factors maintaining the depression. These gains were maintained at two-month follow-up.

Activities

1. Consider your work with clients presenting with depression as an aspect of their current difficulties. Think about how you would combine the information gained from the assessment of their history and background as well as the cognitions, emotions and behaviours that help you decide on (a) the main presenting problem and (b) how you would conceptualize it.
2. From the above, think about any adaptations you might make when delivering CBT.
3. Reflect on how the helplessness and hopelessness commonly associated with clients presenting with depression have affected you and your responses, and how you have managed these.

Further reading

Garland, A. and Scott, J. (2007) 'The obstacle is the path: Overcoming blocks to homework assignments in a complex presentation of depression', *Cognitive and Behavioural Practice*, 14: 278–88.

A useful paper highlighting the difficulties with increasing activity in clients presenting with persistent depression. Helpful clinical suggestions with links to a case study are included.

Moore, R. and Garland, A. (2003) *Cognitive Therapy for Chronic and Persistent Depression*. Chichester, West Sussex: Wiley.
A practical guide for adapting 'standard' Beckian CBT for depression to working with clients presenting with chronic and persistent depression.

Moorey, S. (2014) '"Is it them or is it me?" Transference and Countertransference in CBT', in A. Whittington and N. Grey (ed.), *How to Become a More Effective CBT Therapist: Mastering Metacompetence in Clinical Practice*. Chichester, West Sussex: Wiley. pp. 132–45.
An interesting chapter discussing the theory and clinical implications of the role of interpersonal schemas in therapy. Useful suggestions on how to manage the interaction of client and therapist's interpersonal schemas are included.

EIGHT Mohammad: A Case Study of Depression using Behavioural Activation

Katy Bradbury

Learning objectives

After reading this chapter and completing the activities provided you should be able to:

- Recognize the similarities and differences between a behavioural activation formulation for depression and a Beckian CBT formulation for depression.
- Understand the importance of coping strategies and reward and punishment in the maintenance of depression.
- Understand and appreciate the key elements of assessment and formulation as applied to behavioural activation for depression.
- Recognize the importance of linking formulation to empirically validated interventions.

Theoretical and research base

Depression is an often chronic and debilitating condition. Diagnostically, it is characterized by a depressed mood and/or a loss of interest or pleasure for at least two weeks. Other symptoms can include difficulties sleeping or sleeping too much, agitation, or feeling slowed down, loss of energy and motivation, and feelings of worthlessness or guilt (APA, 2013). CBT has been shown to be effective in managing depression in randomized controlled trials (e.g. Wiles et al., 2013) and accordingly the National Institute for Health and Clinical Excellence (NICE) recommend that a cognitive behavioural approach to treatment be taken with people who have depression. Recommended CBT approaches include computerized CBT, group CBT and individual CBT (including behavioural activation; BA).

Continued research in the field of CBT has led to developments in clinical practice. From an initial first wave of therapies focusing on how people's behaviour impacted on how they felt (behaviour theory, e.g. Lewinsohn, 1974), CBT evolved to incorporate cognitions and how they affect behaviour and emotions. Central to this more 'traditional' second wave of CBT is the idea that unhelpful thinking patterns will influence a person's mood and behaviour. Helping people to re-evaluate their thoughts and modify them to represent more realistic ways of thinking can lead to improvements in mood and behaviour (see Beck, 1995).

Traditional CBT treatments for depression are based on this model. However, some additional current trends appear to have moved away from a focus on specific thoughts and beliefs and back towards more behavioural interventions. Questions are being asked about whether challenging thoughts is necessary within CBT (e.g. Longmore and Worrell, 2007). BA is part of this 'third wave' of therapies, paying less attention to the content of specific thoughts, and giving more weight to changing behaviour. Unlike the first wave of behaviour therapy, cognitions are still seen as important, but rather than challenging specific thoughts (as in more traditional CBT) clients are encouraged to react differently to them, with more acceptance (see Martell et al., 2013).

There have been several randomized control trials and meta-analyses which suggest that BA can be helpful in depression (e.g. Cuijpers et al., 2007; Mazzucchelli et al., 2009). The well-known study by Jacobson et al., (1996) did not show any evidence to suggest that the cognitive therapy treatment package produced better results than BA at termination of treatment or at six month follow-up. At the two year follow-up (Gortner et al., 1998) there was still no evidence that the cognitive therapy condition had any advantage over BA in preventing relapse.

Martell et al. (2013) have described 10 core principles of BA which can helpfully guide sessions (see Table 8.1).

BA formulations are based on the principle that the short-term coping strategies that people choose to cope with their depression (such as avoiding others, not going to work etc.) will ultimately lead to maintaining their depression. These behaviours maintain depression by leading to low levels of positive reinforcement (e.g. reducing the opportunity for pleasure or a sense of achievement) and/or high levels of punishment (e.g. leading to arguments with family members, reduced finances or increasing feelings of guilt or worthlessness). As such, what the actual behaviour is, its form, is less important than the function it serves (e.g. whether it is reinforcing or punishing, if it provides escape or avoidance) in maintaining depression.

Table 8.1   10 core principles of BA (adapted from Martell et al., 2013)

Principle 1	Changing what people do can change how they feel.
Principle 2	The way that people try to cope with difficulties encountered in life in the short-term can lead to further difficulties and depression over time.
Principle 3	What happens before and after certain behaviours can help to determine what will make a client feel better or worse.
Principle 4	Making decisions about what activities to engage in based on mood can lead to continued depression. Instead schedule in activities based on a plan of what to do regardless of mood.
Principle 5	Start with small changes.
Principle 6	Naturally reinforcing activities are an important part of an activity schedule.
Principle 7	The therapist needs to function as a coach.
Principle 8	View the introduction of new activities as an experiment, to be learnt from, even if the results are not what was expected.
Principle 9	Although talking about what changes to make is an important step, actually making the changes is what will make a difference.
Principle 10	Discuss and problem-solve any difficulties that could be encountered when introducing new activities.

Within a BA formulation thoughts are viewed as important, but more as a private behaviour that can be rewarding or punishing, with less attention paid to their content. For example, rumination is considered a helpful target of sessions. However, the content of the rumination is seen as less important than its consequence. If by spending a lot of time ruminating a client was avoiding processing negative emotions, or was not engaging with family or friends, it is this that would be examined rather than the content of the thoughts. In BA, rumination might be tackled through discussion about the consequences of rumination, encouragement of high engagement tasks, and practising exercises that help clients pay attention to their current experiences (noticing smells, sights, colours etc.). BA formulations also take into account life events and the impact these have had on the development of depression. Again the focus is generally on the impact these have on access to rewards or punishments, rather than how they influence the development of beliefs and assumptions (as in more traditional forms of CBT).

Many therapists meet depressed clients who present with social histories of displacement and loss and who are living in challenging social conditions. It is often all too apparent that these clients have few rewarding activities in their life which could maintain their depression, making BA, with its emphasis on life events and context a particularly valuable approach. Addressing this lack of reward and the presence of punishing conditions can often feel like a practical first step (and sometimes only step) in treatment. This chapter describes a case study of a client who presented with a difficult history of displacement and loss. BA's emphasis on context appeared to offer a helpful approach to formulation of this client's circumstances and needs.

Mohammad

Mohammad was a 49-year-old Iranian Muslim male with an eight-year history of depression. He was referred for psychological therapy by his general practitioner (GP). His GP also mentioned that Mohammad experienced ongoing persistent pain, following a shoulder injury eight years ago.

Presenting problem

Mohammad's main presenting complaint was low mood, which he had experienced since coming to the UK from Iran about 8 years ago. Mohammad was unemployed and not studying and spent most of his day sat in a chair in his flat. He felt unmotivated to go out, with low energy and poor sleep. He only slept for four or five hours a night, and woke early in the morning. He would then sleep in the afternoon for a couple of hours. He obtained little pleasure in activities he used to enjoy.

He lived at home with his wife and two sons (15 and 17 years old). He did not feel able to work, help with the house work or care for their children because of his symptoms of depression and chronic pain. The family received benefits. This made Mohammad feel useless and guilty and contributed further to his low mood. Mohammad met and married his wife in his early 20s. They had a generally loving relationship but more recently had started to have arguments. These were often triggered when his wife suggested that he did things to keep himself active and get him out of the flat (such as going for a short walk) which would result in him becoming angry and shouting at her. He also found himself getting irritated at his children, for example for making noise when he was trying to sleep during the day.

Mohammad felt low in mood throughout the day, and described how his mood would often worsen after a confrontation with his wife or children. He also described feeling sad and angry at what he had lost since coming to the UK (a career, his extended family, a familiar way of life) and disappointed at how his life had turned out. He described many negative thoughts about his life in the UK, his family and his future, such as, 'what's the point in trying' and 'my family are disappointed with me'.

Previous treatments

Mohammad had not received any psychological treatments for depression. He had recently met with a clinical psychologist and physiotherapist to discuss managing the pain in his shoulder, and they had recommended a referral for psychological therapy. Due to his low mood and reduced energy and motivation, he found it difficult to engage in the sessions. His GP had prescribed anti-depressant medication, which he had been taking for about two years, with limited effectiveness.

Personal, social history, medical and mental status and diagnosis

Mohammad worked as a history teacher in Iran. He came to the UK with his family for fear of persecution for his political beliefs. He had indefinite leave to remain. Whilst making his journey to the UK he injured his shoulder and continued to feel pain in his shoulder and arm. He explained that his pain often felt worse when he was feeling particularly low in mood, but that having a bad pain day would also lead him to feel low in mood. Mohammad described no other health problems and did not smoke or drink.

Mohammad described no significant incidents that occurred to him as a child, and felt his childhood had been 'normal', and 'stable'. He progressed well at school and university, having a large circle of friends. He described having a 'normal' relationship with his brothers and sister (one older brother, one younger brother and sister), reporting that they all got on well as children, although grew apart as adults. He described growing up in Iran as 'unpredictable' but felt that he had been well-protected and supported by his parents. He went to university in Iran. His family continued to live in Iran and Mohammad described this as a worry for him.

Mohammad was a well-presented 49-year-old man, dressed in smart clothes. He spoke English well and made good eye contact. Objectively he appeared low in mood, becoming tearful at points, particularly when discussing his former life in Iran.

Measures

Mohammad obtained a score of 28 on the Beck Depression Inventory (BDI II; Beck et al., 1996) indicating a moderate depression, and met DSM-5 (APA, 2013) criteria for a diagnosis of depression. Given his physical symptoms of chronic pain Mohammad also completed the Hospital Anxiety and Depression Scale (HADS; Zigmond and Snaith, 1983) which places less emphasis on the physical symptoms of depression that can be confounded with physical health symptoms. He obtained a score of 6 on the anxiety scale (normal range) and 14 on the depression scale (moderate range).

Assessment

Value and goals

Within BA, as with other forms of CBT, an important part of the assessment is investigating the client's goals. Identifying values can be key in helping clients to think about their long-term goals. Unlike a goal, a value is not something that can ever be achieved, but can provide a direction towards things that are considered important in life and help clients think about goals that are important to them. Mohammad and I spent some time in sessions discussing what his values were. It became apparent that two very important values were family (being a good husband and father, spending quality time with his children and wife) and also employment (to be able to contribute positively to society, to be able to earn money to provide for his family, to be hardworking). Mohammad initially found it difficult to think about his long-term goals but over the course of our sessions was able to come up with: to find paid employment; to spend quality time with his wife and children and to attend a pain management programme.

Activity levels

A second important part of the assessment was to gain an accurate sense of how Mohammad was spending his days. Carrying out a functional analysis enabled us to identify antecedents, behaviours and consequences as a way of identifying which behaviours might bring rewards (in the long-term and short-term) through feelings of achievement or pleasure, or by working towards a valued goal. We also wanted to identify which activities might lead to negative consequences (in the long-term or short-term) through reducing access to positively reinforcing activities, or producing negative feelings. Mohammad completed an activity chart. Initially he filled in his chart very briefly, for example, writing 'sat on chair' for a three-hour block (see Figure 8.1). Following discussions in our sessions, Mohammad was gradually able to fill out more information, and we were able to identify other behaviours such as rumination (see Figure 8.2).

	Morning	Afternoon	Evening
Monday	Sit in chair	Sit in chair Meeting at job centre	Eat dinner with family Watch tv
Tuesday	Make breakfast Sit in chair	Sleep	Eat dinner with family Watch tv

Figure 8.1   **Example of one of Mohammad's initial activity charts**

	Monday	Mood 1 (not at all depressed) – 10 (very depressed)
5-7am	Awake, lying in bed, thinking about how much I don't want to get up.	5
7am	Awake, lying in bed, thinking about the past.	7
8am	Get up, don't shower, sit downstairs in a different room to wife and children.	4
9am	Son brings me coffee and toast, sit in a chair thinking about how life is different now.	6
10am	Sit in a chair in the living room after wife and children go out, thinking about home.	6
11am	Sit in a chair in the living room after wife and children go out, thinking about home.	6
12pm	Eat lunch that wife has prepared. Have a conversation with my wife about going for a walk, tell her I'm tired and so don't want to go. I can tell she's disappointed in me.	7
1pm	Go upstairs to the bedroom, try to sleep, but thinking about the conversation with my wife.	6
2pm	Sleep	3
3pm	Sleep	3
4pm	Sleep	3
5pm	Get woken by my sons, get angry at them for making a noise, then feel bad.	7
6pm	Eat dinner that wife prepared.	5
7pm	Sit in the living room with wife and children but get fed up of the noise from the tv. Go and sit in the bedroom.	5
8pm	Try and read a magazine, can't concentrate, lie on the bed.	5
9pm	Lie on the bed thinking	6
10pm	Lie on the bed thinking	6
11pm–5am	Restless night's sleep, maybe sleep for 4 hours on and off.	6

Figure 8.2 Example of a later activity chart

Some important aspects of Mohammad's behaviour were identified from the charts. He appeared to spend a lot of time ruminating about his past life, and how unhappy he was currently, triggered by reminders of how different his life was now and how dissatisfied he felt. We focused less on the content of this rumination and more on the consequences of it. As anticipated, it appeared to increase the intensity of Mohammad's low mood. Mohammad rated that sleeping during the day improved his mood. However, after discussion it became clear that this was a short-term improvement due to avoiding arguments with his wife and children and that in the long term, it lowered his mood. It meant that he slept poorly during the night and also meant he wasn't able to engage in any activities consistent with his values and goals during this time. A further issue that became apparent from Mohammad's chart was that he engaged in very little activity that he found rewarding.

Formulation

Mohammad's depression started after he moved to the UK from Iran eight years ago. Life had been difficult when he lived in Iran but he had engaged in several 'anti-depressant behaviours' (such as working in a job he found meaningful and spending time with family and friends) which meant he had not become depressed. He felt that his behaviour had a useful purpose and he could look after and support his family. He had been hopeful that a move to the UK would provide a better life for him and his family. He described how the culture of his family growing up had encouraged independent thought and working hard to achieve something that was meaningful. This felt to him to be at odds with the culture encouraged by the Iranian government. He described himself as an educated and cultured man, and had hoped that he and his family would fit well with what he identified as the values and cultural norms of the UK (such as personal freedom and equality of treatment).

On moving to the UK, Mohammad realized that his life was not as he had expected. He was unable to work while he was applying for indefinite leave to remain, and found it humiliating to receive 'hand-outs' from the government. He found it difficult to navigate the UK legal system and reported that the pain in his shoulder and arm prevented him from helping out around the house or doing activities he used to enjoy, such as reading or writing. In Iran, Mohammad felt he was contributing to society through his work, and providing for his family. In the UK he had none of these reinforcements. His individual culture and value system contributed to this feeling of failure at not being able to do these things. He started to feel low in mood, with little energy and low motivation.

Once Mohammad started to feel low in mood and unmotivated, he started to withdraw. He began sleeping during the day as a way to avoid his family and their requests for him to go out and do things. He resisted efforts made by his wife to mix socially with friends she had made and avoided leaving the flat. This often led to arguments with his wife. He spent much of his time when he wasn't sleeping ruminating about his past life, and how unhappy he was in his current life. It was hypothesized that this rumination was, in part, an attempt to avoid his sadness and anger over how much his life had changed, and prevented him from engaging with his current life and future. He experienced short-term relief at these coping behaviours, but over time, they contributed to his low mood by reducing his access to positive reinforcements (see Figure 8.3).

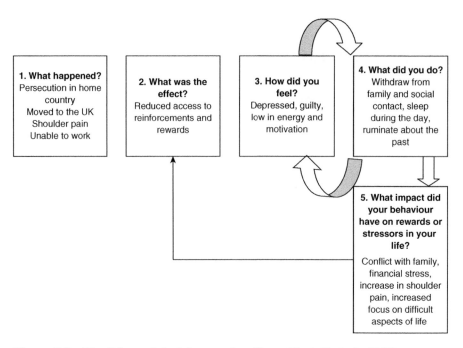

1. What happened?
Persecution in home country
Moved to the UK
Shoulder pain
Unable to work

2. What was the effect?
Reduced access to reinforcements and rewards

3. How did you feel?
Depressed, guilty, low in energy and motivation

4. What did you do?
Withdraw from family and social contact, sleep during the day, ruminate about the past

5. What impact did your behaviour have on rewards or stressors in your life?
Conflict with family, financial stress, increase in shoulder pain, increased focus on difficult aspects of life

Figure 8.3   The BA model of depression (from Martell et al., 2013)

Treatment

In line with NICE guidelines and consistent with the formulation of his needs, Mohammad was offered 16 treatment sessions of BA. He responded well to the idea of BA sessions and was able to enter into a collaborative therapeutic relationship which allowed us to explore his activity levels and the effect this had on his mood. The assessment and formulation highlighted several potential avenues for BA treatment, including experimenting with new behaviours that might act as anti-depressants (in line with his values and goals) and helping to reduce Mohammad's avoidant behaviours, such as rumination and sleep during the day.

Sleep: Having completed the activity log, Mohammad was able to see that sleep would be a useful focus of intervention. We reviewed helpful sleeping habits in the session. Initially Mohammad scheduled in shorter nap times earlier in the day, but over time was able to eliminate them completely. This initially resulted in a drop in mood as it increased the time he spent with his family. This led to him feeling under pressure to do things and often contributed to arguments. We were able to problem-solve this in our sessions and come up with ways that Mohammad could manage these situations, including talking to his family about how he felt and gradually increasing the activities he engaged in with his family.

Rumination: Mohammad appeared to spend much of his time ruminating about his past life, and how unhappy he was with his current life. We discussed how this could be a way to avoid the sad and angry feelings he had when he thought about missing his home country and losing his extended family, way of life and career. It felt important to tackle this avoidance and allow time in sessions for Mohammad to start to process his difficult journey. Initially his conversations appeared to be ruminating aloud. It was helpful to try to move Mohammad past this ruminating and start to process some of the feelings he was experiencing. This enabled him to take part in discussions about moving forward with his life so he could become more active again *despite* his sadness and feelings of loss. We discussed how helpful it was for Mohammad to spend such an extensive amount of time thinking about his past. Over several sessions, Mohammad came to understand that his persistent rumination about the past prevented him from engaging with his current life and future.

Increasing anti-depressant behaviour: Mohammad's activity log demonstrated that he engaged in very little activity that gave him a sense of pleasure or achievement. We initially chose some small behaviours that Mohammad could try, which we hypothesized might act as an anti-depressant. These behaviours were sometimes linked with his values (to take a walk with his wife) and were sometimes related to things that he had enjoyed in the past (to read a chapter of a fiction novel), which had the potential to lift his mood and make working towards his goals more manageable. We agreed that it was important to start with small adjustments in behaviour to ensure that any changes remained manageable. Additionally, we were unsure about what would help lift Mohammad's mood and so were experimenting with different activities in order to discover what might exert a positive effect.

One barrier that was constantly encountered was Mohammad's experience of chronic shoulder pain. Discussing Mohammad's chronic pain did present somewhat of a dilemma, in that Mohammad was not able to engage with pain management sessions due to his depression, but his pain was making it difficult for him to engage with anti-depressant activities. It was important to liaise with the musculoskeletal service (with Mohammad's consent) where he had been a patient in order to understand what activities it was and was not possible for Mohammad to undertake. I had a useful conversation with his physiotherapist to help me understand that Mohammad's injury had healed despite his pain persisting, and movement and activity was encouraged. He also described how they had discussed the idea of Mohammad gradually increasing his activities and movement of his arm.

Mohammad and I discussed this conversation and how we might be able to use this information in our sessions.

Relapse prevention and follow-up: Towards the end of our sessions we developed a relapse prevention blueprint to help Mohammad identify what behaviours acted as an anti-depressant, which behaviours increased his levels of depression, how he could take what he has learnt to progress further, and to prepare for setbacks and high risk situations in the future. Mohammad also had a follow-up session three months after the completion of treatment to check his progress and to see whether the relapse prevention plan needed amending.

Outcome

Gradually, Mohammad was able to increase his rewarding activities and gain more pleasure and meaning in his life. He described how he thought his mood had improved. His BDI score had dropped from 28 to 14 (from moderate to mild depression). His HADS anxiety score remained fairly constant (dropping from 6 to 5, in the normal range) and his HADS depression score dropped from 15 to 8 (from moderate depression to mild). Mohammad was not yet in paid employment, but had generated a hierarchy of activities, of varying levels of difficulty, which would help him to work towards this goal. He was regularly scheduling in these activities to his weekly diary sheet. One of these steps was volunteering at a local community centre, which he was doing once a week. He was spending time with his children when they came home from school and was leaving the house with his wife for a walk once a day. His future planned activities involved attending a pain management programme.

Therapy implications and recommendations to therapists

1. Mohammad initially struggled to fill out the activity chart, filling it in very briefly. It was helpful to ensure that Mohammad understood the purpose of the activity chart and that we took a graded approach to completing it – initially completing the chart for the morning, afternoon and evening, and gradually working towards completing it for every hour. It was also important to ensure adequate time was given in the session to discuss the chart and Mohammad's activities so it was possible to review the kinds of things that would be helpful to include.
2. Although the principles of BA appear simple and straightforward, applying them to individual cases is far less simple and straightforward and requires sensitivity and careful exploration of an individual's difficulties.

3. BA is not simply about increasing a client's activity levels. It is important to understand the function of the activities in order to ascertain if that activity is helpful or not.
4. BA is not about escaping negative feelings, and when avoidance of experiencing certain negative feelings is identified (e.g. through rumination), tackling this avoidance is a helpful target of sessions.
5. BA can be a helpful way to formulate clients who have depression alongside health problems. Close liaison with relevant health care professionals is important.
6. NICE guidelines suggest that there is little evidence in relation to personal characteristics to guide choice of treatment for depression. However, after assessment and formulation it sometimes becomes obvious that a lack of reward and reinforcement in a client's life is playing a key role in maintaining their depression, or a client appears to struggle to access the content of their cognitions. BA may be a particularly useful first line treatment in these cases.

Activities

1. Select a client whom you previously saw for depression, using a Beckian CBT approach. Try reformulating this client using a BA approach. What do you gain and lose by conceptualizing the client's needs in this way?
2. Reflect on the role of rumination in depression as understood in BA. What is your usual way of intervening with rumination and consider what, if anything, a BA approach to rumination might add to your practice.

Further reading

Martell, C.R., Addis, M.E. and Jacobson, N.S. (2001) *Depression in Context: Strategies for Guided Action*. New York, NY: Norton.
Martell, C.R., Dimidjian, S. and Herman-Dunn, R. (2013) *Behavioural Activation for Depression: A Clinician's Guide*. New York: Guilford Press.

NINE Wendy: A Case Study of Health Anxiety

Michael Townend

Learning objectives

After reading this chapter and completing the activities at the end of it you should be able to:

- Appreciate the epidemiological significance of health anxiety in primary and secondary care populations.
- Recognize the important advantages of an underpinning formulation from a variety of perspectives.
- Understand the importance of a client's history and background in the onset and subsequent maintenance of health anxiety.
- Understand and appreciate the key elements of assessment and formulation as it applies to health anxiety.

Theoretical and research base

It is very common for people to seek medical consultation on a recurrent basis for problems which, in spite of considerable investigation, do not appear to have any organic basis. These problems are referred to either as medically unexplained symptoms or functional somatic symptoms (Brown, 2006). People with functional symptoms are a heterogeneous group of clients with problems such as chronic fatigue syndrome, somatization disorders, hypochondriasis or health anxiety and body dysmorphic disorder (APA, 2000; APA, 2013; WHO, 2006). It has been estimated that as many as 15–50 per cent of all consultations in primary care or new out-patients might fall within this group (Bass, 1990; Kroenke, 2007). People with these problems are significantly distressed by their symptoms, have high rates of co-existing psychiatric problems and tend to utilize significant health care resources. They, and frequently the health care professionals who work with them, remain frustrated by a medical system that only tells clients what they *don't* have while failing to provide a satisfactory account for their very real symptoms and consequent distress. For health care professionals few options exist for offering effective help.

Summary of the CBT evidence-base

Over the last 20 years significant strides have been made with understanding the problem of functional somatic symptoms at both the individual and systems level. Despite this progress, the macro organization of flexible and responsive services has been much slower than the development of effective CBT interventions for health anxiety and other related difficulties where a moderate to good outcome can now be regarded as the norm for individuals who can access and be engaged with therapy (Kroenke, 2007; Buwalda and Bouman, 2009).

CBT is appropriate for hypochondriasis as it can be understood as a cognitive problem, defined as a morbid preoccupation with illness based on the person's misinterpretation of bodily sensations and other bodily variations (APA, 2013). A particular challenge is that health anxious clients are frequently reluctant to accept psychological therapies because they believe themselves to be physically ill. This has made CBT a potentially useful approach for engaging clients on the grounds that a model can be developed that both accounts for the reality of their symptoms and offers an alternative, benign and credible explanation for them (Salkovskis and Warwick, 1986). This strategy has led to well-defined cognitive behavioural interventions that seem effective in 40–60 per cent of cases when tested within uncontrolled and randomized therapy trials (Warwick and Marks, 1988; Warwick et al., 1996; Clark et al., 1998; Salkovskis et al., 2003; Greeven et al., 2007).

A case study of health anxiety with an evolving formulation

This chapter describes a case study of a 36-year-old woman with health anxiety, diagnostically referred to as 'hypochondriasis' (APA, 2000; 2013). The client was seen in the context of a secondary care specialist cancer and psychological therapies service.

Initial pioneering conceptualizations of health anxiety were based on conditioning theories alongside exposure and response prevention with a particular emphasis on reductions in reassurance seeking (Warwick and Marks 1988). More sophisticated cognitive behavioural theories were subsequently developed, based on an integration of the earlier behavioural theories of panic disorder which placed the catastrophic misinterpretation of bodily symptoms and process at the heart of the maintenance process of health anxiety (Warwick and Salkovskis 1990). These ideas have recently been incorporated into the National Curriculum for the Improving Access to Psychological Therapies Programme (IAPT 2011).

The formulation model that underpinned the approach to therapy in this case study was based on an evolving approach. An evolving approach is where hypotheses for the onset, development and maintenance of the problem are formulated in the mind of the therapist who uses their knowledge of theory and experience of previous clients with similar problems, along with the summary factors below, to underpin the assessment process:

- Behavioural

    o Avoidance, self-inspection and checking, manipulation of affected area, consultation, reassurance, scanning for information, prevention measures

- Affective

    o Anxiety, depression, anger

- Cognitive

    o Misinterpretation of bodily reactions, focus on body, monitoring of bodily changes, attention to negative information, helplessness, preoccupation, rumination, discounting positive information

- Physiological

    o Increased arousal, changes in bodily function, sleep disturbance, physical reactions due to excessive behaviours

In this case, the initial formulation (see Figure 9.1) was based on an adapted Warwick and Salkovskis (1990) model of hypochondriasis. This model offers a comprehensive framework and approach to formulation that is relatively straightforward and at the personal idiosyncratic level can be developed 'shoulder to shoulder' with the client. The model is also parsimonious in that it accounts for most of the onset, development and maintenance factors for initial therapy planning purposes.

The above formulation whilst a useful basis for therapy did have a number of limitations. First, the client's health anxiety worsened considerably and rapidly in response to low mood. This occurred even in the absence of obvious triggering factors for health anxiety. The second problem was that even after the behavioural factors were addressed her belief that she might die from cancer continued. The client found this both

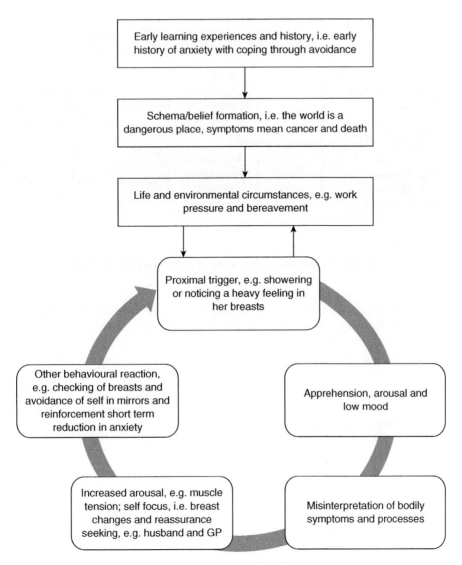

Figure 9.1 Hypothesized vicious circle for health anxiety used as the basis for formulation

puzzling and upsetting. As therapy progressed, the formulation evolved to using a multi-level theory to underpin the formulation ICS (interacting cognitive subsystems) (Teasdale and Barnard 1993). ICS offers a framework that can provide an integrated explanation of the interaction of automatic and conscious thoughts, emotions and behaviours, and also the disjuncture of thought, emotions and physiological responses found in some psychological problems.

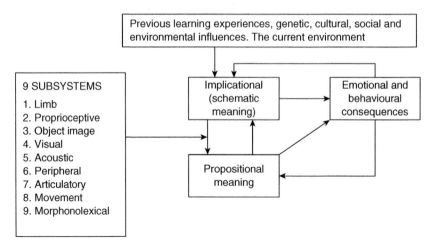

Figure 9.2   Simplified model of the interacting subsystems theory

The ICS framework differs in an important way from Beck's model of emotional disorders (Beck et al., 1979), in that it specifies two qualitatively different levels of meaning. These levels of meaning play distinct roles in the production, maintenance and modification of emotion, clarifying the

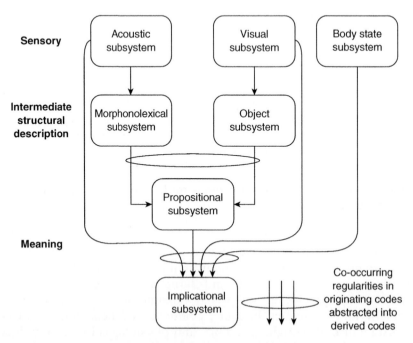

Figure 9.3   The Interacting Cognitive Subsystems Framework (reproduced from the ICS Framework; © Teasdale and Barnard, 1993)

distinction between 'cold' or intellectual beliefs (propositional meaning) and 'hot' or emotional beliefs (implicational meaning). The ICS framework is further discussed in Chapter 5 of this text with Figures 9.2 and 9.3 providing an overviewing of the architecture of ICS theory.

In health anxiety, maintenance of the problems is hypothesized to have occurred as a perpetuation of idiosyncratic models, where the self or others are viewed as diseased, and naturally occurring physical symptoms and physical arousal have become encoded as threatening (Teasdale and Barnard, 1993; Barnard, 2004). In the case of health anxiety, physical arousal, physical symptoms or bodily changes, mood, attention processes, and behavioural configurations have all become encoded together.

Case introduction

Wendy was a 36-year-old white female client who was seen at a specialist cancer service. Prior to referral, a cancer specialist had assessed and investigated her symptoms. The assessment and investigations had not detected any cancer-related reasons for her symptoms. She had also been given supportive counselling and psycho-education from a specialist breast cancer care nurse about the relationship between anxiety and physical symptoms. This had produced a minimal effect in reducing her anxiety and she continued to seek regular reassurance regarding her symptoms. Wendy was therefore referred to a CBT service for people with health anxiety.

Her psychological assessment indicated that Wendy was an appropriate candidate for CBT. This decision was made on the grounds that she had a distressing problem that could be conceptualized in psychological terms (Brown, 2006).

Presenting complaint

Wendy's presenting problem was preoccupation and fear that she had breast cancer. Five days a week she would spend up to 80 per cent of her day thinking about the possibility that she might have cancer or that she had the symptoms of breast cancer. On the other two days she would have fleeting ideas that she might have cancer, but was able to dismiss them and continue with her normal activities. She sought reassurance from her husband at least ten times a day and visited her general practitioner, again for reassurance, at least once a fortnight. She was unable to look at herself in the mirror as this evoked images of herself with cancer, and was also unable to examine her own breasts as this would evoke an automatic fear response. She consequently avoided all forms of appropriate self-examination for months at a time. However, every three to four months she would become so overwhelmed and self-focused on the possibility that she had cancer that she would spend several hours examining her breasts and armpits. This would lead to tenderness in these areas which she interpreted as a sign of cancer. Every six months she would ask for a referral for a private consultation with a cancer specialist.

Wendy's history

Wendy had no problems with health anxiety until the age of 33. She did however have a history of generalized anxiety symptoms at times of prolonged stress. For example, she reported high levels of anxiety during examinations at school, college and university. Despite this, she did well at university leaving with a first class honours degree in business studies. She had one young child and had been married for 17 years. She had worked full-time and then changed to part-time work with the same company after her child was born.

Her problems with health anxiety started several months after her mother died from breast cancer. Wendy had been the main carer for her mother as her father had been unable to cope with his wife's illness. She coped through this difficult and distressing time by throwing herself headlong into caring for her mother, making her death as comfortable as she could by reassuring her and comforting her and other family members. She also provided support for her father and was the point of contact for all health care staff involved. Finally, she provided some of the physical care for her mother in the later stages of the disease and made all the funeral arrangements following her death.

Following her mother's death, Wendy was unable to grieve due to feeling isolated, detached and depressed. Her mother had died three years prior to Wendy's initial assessment. When seen for assessment she was tearful and talked about her guilt for being unable to cry for her mother. Her health anxiety had started during routine breast self-examination. Around this time she had been feeling low in mood due to work pressures and looking after her daughter. She recalled thinking 'I have cancer' and 'I am going to die like my mum'. She subsequently experienced an image of herself lying on a hospital bed with cancer.

Wendy made an immediate appointment with her general practitioner who did not detect any abnormality but referred her to a breast cancer specialist in order to reassure her that everything was normal. Wendy then waited a few weeks for the appointment, during which time she carried out daily examinations and felt very low and anxious. She became increasingly worried that she might have cancer and she spent most of the day preoccupied with this possibility. She also began to think that 'something must be wrong' because the general practitioner referred her to a specialist. Subsequent investigation by the cancer specialist did not indicate any problems and she was referred to the breast care nurse for follow-up and reassurance.

Assessment

The assessment process took place over four interlinked and overlapping stages. The first stage consisted of a cognitive behavioural analysis of the main presenting problem (guidelines for cognitive behavioural analysis can be found in Chapter 2 of this book). A cognitive behavioural analysis was carried out in order to develop an idiographic understanding of cognitive, attentional, emotional, behavioural and physical factors and their interplay maintaining Wendy's health anxiety. Both motivational and mental status assessment was also carried out – the former to identify any potential problems around engagement with psychological therapy and the latter to help rule out any contraindications to therapy. It was also important to assess the role of any depression that may have predated the health anxiety, examine its possible maintenance role, and to rule out psychosis and identify any other co-morbid problems.

The final stage of the assessment process consisted of taking a psychiatric, developmental and personal history. This process, while similar to general psychiatric practice, differs in one important way. The information is collected in order to identify key events or life stages that might have influenced or predisposed the person to develop health anxiety through learning processes and any associated meaning. In particular, early learning about illness and illness experiences as a child or adolescent were assessed and her experience of her mother's death later in life was particularly important. Assessment measures were also administered to the client, the details of which are outlined below.

Measures

Idiographic and nomothetic screening and outcome measurement were important features of working with Wendy and were used throughout the therapeutic process.

A useful screening tool was the Somatoform Symptom-7 Scale (Rief and Hiller, 2003). This is a self-report instrument that provided information about the presence and severity of 53 commonly found somatic symptoms. Idiographic measures included Problem and Target statements (Marks, 1986) and a specific two item strength of belief (SB) scale and subjective units of discomfort scale (SUDs). The SB scale utilized 0–100 per cent quantitative measurement, where 0 per cent implied that over the last week she had not believed that she had cancer, and 100 per cent that she believed without doubt she had cancer. The SUDs were also rated using a 0–100 per cent scale, where 0 per cent implied that she had not been distressed in the last week and 100 per cent that her distress was as bad as it could possibly have been.

Nomothetic measures included the Fear Questionnaire (Marks, 1986) which was used to assess both phobic avoidance and dysphoria and the

Work and Social Adjustment Scale (WSAS) (Marks, 1986) to assess and measure the effect of the health anxiety on the client's wider life. Further measures and assessment tools for consideration are fully reviewed in Taylor and Asmundson (2004).

Case conceptualization

Wendy's preoccupation with breast cancer, or the belief that she had breast cancer, was reported as being triggered by a number of internal (felt) and external triggers. A speculative hypothesis was formed during the assessment that her physical symptoms, emotional responses, avoidance, checking and reassurance seeking behaviours had occurred due to the development of an implicational system related to the danger posed by the physical symptoms. This can be predicted by ICS theory (Barnard and Teasdale, 1991; Barnard, 2004) where a number of subsystems (proprioceptive – feeling tense; imagery – images of cancer; visual – observation of self in a mirror; acoustic – hearing or saying the word cancer; peripheral; articulatory – repeated checking; and morphonolexical – what was said to her about cancer) were all feeding into the two main subsystems of moment-by-moment meaning and higher order implicational meaning.

The ICS interaction hypothesis was supported by the case conceptualization, as Wendy would often experience immediate negative automatic thoughts such as 'I have cancer'. These thoughts were underpinned by implicational beliefs that any physical symptoms were a sign of serious illness which would lead to her inevitable death. Once her implicational level of meaning had been triggered, her global sense of being in danger would elicit the emotional response of fear. This was accompanied by a physiological response of increased palpitations, muscle tension and hyperventilation. She would then become preoccupied and ruminate about her symptoms, with an internal self-focused attention on how her breasts felt.

The unhelpful cycles relating to her health beliefs and anxiety therefore included:

- Preoccupation with her health, increasing the conviction that she was in fact seriously ill; the more time she spent thinking about this the stronger the beliefs became.
- Attentional patterns of both automatic and purposeful scanning for evidence that her health beliefs were true.
- A biased view of her symptoms and autonomic arousal.
- Behavioural reactions of checking, reassurance seeking and avoidance, which further maintained her problem through negative reinforcement and prevented her from recognizing that her beliefs were false.

These processes in ICS terms are shown in Figure 9.4.

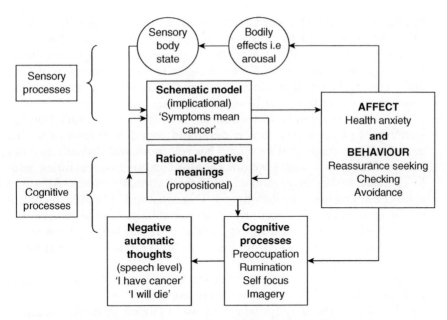

Figure 9.4   Idiosyncratic formulation of Wendy's health anxiety based on Interacting Cognitive Subsystems Theory (adapted from © Teasdale, 1996, p. 33)

Structure of therapy and assessment of progress

The model of therapy used to work with Wendy was based on the theoretical premises of ICS. The framework of the therapy followed a weekly structure of:

1. Pre-therapy assessment including intrinsic motivation, risks posed, decision about suitability for CBT and outcome measures.
2. Weeks 1–2: A full cognitive behavioural assessment, mental status assessment, measures, individual conceptualization and socialization to CBT.
3. Weeks 3–4: Further assessment of Wendy's medical and psychiatric history and personal and developmental history. While this is similar to a psychiatric history, its purpose is to understand the formation of her unhelpful beliefs and behaviour within a developmental context. Work also took place to identify internal and external triggers for health beliefs and behaviours through functional analysis, with homework using self-monitoring diaries. During these sessions, psycho-education, the developing conceptualization and the idea of 'interlock' from ICS were also introduced to help explain her belief systems, hot and cold cognitions and her now almost constant preoccupation with her health.

4. Weeks 5–6: Thought records were used in order to identify unhelp-ful thinking and aid the early recognition of physical tension, auto-nomic arousal and bodily states. Therapy during this stage was linked to behavioural experiments aimed at reducing her reassurance seeking and checking behaviours and monitoring the effects of these behaviour changes on her anxiety and belief conviction.

5. Weeks 7–10: The emphasis was on developing a more detailed under-standing of physiological, behavioural and cognitive responses during periods of low mood that increased her self-focus and strengthened her beliefs. This phase was a continuation of cognitive restructuring with links made to her propositional and implicational systems. Attention control training was also introduced. This consisted of breathing control whilst focusing on the word 'relax' on the exhale. This technique was not framed as a relaxation strategy but as a way of helping train her to switch her attention away from her physical symptoms and thus break the 'interlock' cycle.

6. Week 11: The focus during this session was on consolidating therapy, with problem-solving and further homework.

7. Weeks 12–15: The conceptualization was updated as to the structure and content of the implicational system and its lifeline formation through prior learning experiences. Her experience of caring for her mother and her family's responses were particularly important. Positive data logging, and challenging unhelpful beliefs and rules were used to strengthen her new implicational systems through continuation and recording of behavioural experiments and flashcards. The development of a relapse prevention blueprint, to consolidate the new implicational system and prevent future reoccurrences of health anxiety, was also developed.

Process and engagement in therapy

Wendy responded well to CBT. This was probably because she engaged fully and worked hard to overcome her difficulties. Regular reviews with Wendy indicated that she found therapy helpful. She also fed back that having a formulation helped her begin to recognize what the problem was rather than what it was not, and indicated that the cognitive interventions, behavioural experiments and exposure enabled her to develop more help-ful beliefs and behaviours.

In some cases of health anxiety, and related problems within the cate-gory of medically unexplained symptoms, engagement in therapy can be a problem. This occurs simply because the client believes so strongly that their problem is physical and therefore can see no reason to engage in psy-chological therapy (Sayer and Townend, 1992). This form of resistance can helpfully be managed by the following:

1. NEVER arguing with the client about their beliefs. Instead, engage in discussion with the client as to the reasons for their very real concerns.
2. Gently probing for any doubts that they might have about their illness beliefs.
3. The therapist feeding back acceptance of the real symptoms that the client is experiencing, being careful not to link those with the disease the client believes is the cause of the symptoms. Again, it can be helpful to ask if they think that other normal processes could have produced the symptoms.
4. Using behavioural experiments in the session to illustrate or demonstrate the effects of preoccupation, self-focused attention, repeated checking or reassurance seeking, or manipulation or repeated contact with areas of the body that the person believes are diseased.
5. Asking the client if they would be willing just to engage with psychological therapy for a short trial – of say 6 sessions – to consider alternative, anxiety-based, explanations of their problem to rule them out.

Case management considerations

In this case study, as in all cases of functional symptoms, it is imperative that physical explanations for the symptoms are ruled out (Bass, 1990). In this case, close liaison with the cancer team was essential, and all necessary investigations had been concluded and a short period of supportive psychotherapy had been provided by the referring team. Following referral, it was agreed with both the team and the client's general practitioner that no further investigations would be carried out for the presenting symptoms until the psychological therapy had been concluded (Brown, 2006). Relapse and setbacks are not uncommon in people with functional symptoms (Bass, 1990), so a relapse plan was put in place to help Wendy manage future problems.

Follow up

After completion of therapy, a follow-up period was initiated as part of her relapse plan. This consisted of the client being seen at one, three, six and nine months after discharge. At each of these sessions the outcome measures were completed to check progress against baseline measures, and reviews and problem-solving of any difficulties were carried out.

Therapy and formulation implications of the case

Wendy's presentation was typical of cases of health anxiety seen by CBT therapists. The multi-level approach to formulation used here was helpful in explaining to Wendy why her belief conviction ratings fluctuated, and the relationship of these with mood changes. It also helped to explain the internal or introspective cues for anxious thoughts or images as well as situational cues.

Implications for clinicians

The ICS theory of the cognitive behavioural approach underpinning this case study specifically targets meanings, sensory elements and cognitive processes of health beliefs and behaviours. The distinction between propositional and implicational meanings subsystems is important in conceptualizing two important and sometimes puzzling elements for both the clinician and the client. These are the tendency for the health preoccupation behaviour to occur immediately following an internal or external trigger (directly via the implicational route) or after a delay following a period of dysphoria and preoccupation (indirectly via the propositional route). It can also help clinicians understand beliefs held by clients which are clearly unhelpful but which go without question by the person with medically unexplained symptoms.

Conceptualization is at the heart of the therapeutic process; when a comprehensive conceptualization is developed in a way that seems to fit the presentation and responses of the client, alternative implicational models can be built through cognitive restructuring, behavioural changes and the development of more adaptive coping strategies.

Summary

✓ Health anxiety (also variously referred to as hypochondriasis, functional somatic symptoms, and medically unexplained symptoms) is a common and disabling problem in both primary and secondary care services.
✓ Interacting cognitive subsystems is a framework that can help to understand, assess and formulate health anxiety.
✓ A good outcome was achieved by targeting key cognitions and behaviours with empirically validated approaches.
✓ Follow up indicated maintenance of progress, after therapy was completed.

Activities

1. Consider your own practice with health anxious individuals, and how you engage with clients who believe their problem is physical and dismiss psychological factors.
2. Review your approach to formulation and consider if using the ICS as a framework can help you to understand health anxiety and its maintenance further.

Further reading

Barnard, P. (2004) 'Bridging between basic theory and clinical practice', *Behaviour Research and Therapy*, 42: 977–1000.
This article, part of a tribute to John Teasdale, lays out the value of interacting cognitive subsystems as both a cognitive and clinical framework.

Brown, R.J. (2006) 'Medically unexplained symptoms', in N. Tarrier (ed.), *Case Formulation in Cognitive Behaviour Therapy: The Treatment of Challenging and Complex Cases*. Hove, East Sussex: Routledge. pp. 263–92.
This chapter applies the principles of case formulation to medically unexplained symptoms using a cognitive behavioural approach.

Taylor, S. and Asmundson, G.J.G. (2004) *Treating Health Anxiety: A Cognitive Behavioural Approach*. New York: Guilford.
This is a comprehensive text that focuses on CBT for health anxiety.

TEN Sally: A Case Study of Generalized Anxiety Disorder

Teresa Palmieri and Adrian Cockx

Learning objectives

After reading this chapter and completing the activities at the end of it you should be able to:

- Understand how GAD can present in primary care through the presentation of a case study.
- Understand key elements of assessment and be able to conceptualize factors in a coherent manner.
- Describe some of the strategies adopted in the cognitive behavioural treatment of GAD based on an individualized case formulation.

Introduction

Worry is a common human experience that can cause significant disruption to an individual's life. Excessive and uncontrollable worry is the central defining feature of generalized anxiety disorder (GAD). This chapter describes the assessment and treatment of a client who was referred to a primary care mental health service with symptoms of GAD. We begin by considering the diagnostic criteria for the disorder and follow this with an overview of the theoretical models for GAD. Key issues implicated in the assessment and conceptualization of GAD are discussed within a CBT framework. The chapter also explores some of the challenges clinicians encounter when assessing and working with individuals with GAD and concludes by discussing some of the clinical implications.

Theoretical and research base

GAD is an anxiety disorder characterized by 'excessive worry and preoccupation about a number of events and activities' (APA, 2013: 222). To attain a diagnosis of GAD (see Table 10.1) worry must occur on more days than not for a period of at least six months and should not be explained within the context of another psychological, physiological or medical condition. GAD is conceptualized as chronic and pervasive worry that is difficult to control and generally associated with three (or more) symptoms of anxiety. The worry must cause significant distress or impairment in important areas of functioning.

Table 10.1   A summary of the diagnostic criteria for GAD

A. Excessive anxiety and worry (apprehensive expectations), occurring more days than not for a period of at least six months, about a number of events and activities
B. The person finds it difficult to control the worry
C. The anxiety and worry are associated with three (or more) of the following six symptoms:

    (1) restlessness (or feeling keyed up or on edge)
    (2) being easily fatigued
    (3) difficulty concentrating or mind going blank
    (4) irritability
    (5) muscle tension
    (6) disturbed sleep

D. The anxiety, worry or physical symptoms cause clinically significant distress or impairment in social, occupation or other important areas of functioning

Adapted from APA (2013)

GAD first appeared as a diagnostic category in the DSM in 1980. The disorder is prevalent in the primary care clinical population with an estimated 8 per cent of individuals seeking psychological help and 25 per cent of them receiving a diagnosis (Maier et al., 2000). It is often chronic and unremitting in nature, more common among women than men, and co-morbid with mood disorders such as depression and dysthymia as well as other anxiety disorders.

Despite the development of theoretical models and psychological treatments tested through randomized controlled trials over three decades, GAD remains an anxiety disorder with a low diagnostic reliability (Brown et al., 2001). This is mainly due to the observation that although a number of individuals experience symptoms of GAD and report significant distress, they do not meet diagnostic criteria. Given the high co-morbidity characterizing this disorder, discriminant evidence has also been questioned. It is acknowledged that clinicians find it difficult to agree on the presence of GAD more than any other anxiety disorder (Brown et al., 2001) even if disagreement seems to originate from the difficulty in applying the categorical cut-off to phenomena which are intrinsically dimensional.

Cognitive models of GAD

Both cognitive and behavioural theories have been suggested as useful for informing therapy for GAD. Research evidence suggests that CBT is the most empirically supported approach (Fisher, 2006; Covin et al., 2008) and it is therefore recommended as the treatment of choice (NICE, 2011). The NICE guidelines for the treatment of GAD include psychological treatments and medication, both provided by GP or other health care professionals in primary care within a stepped care model, summarized in Table 10.2.

Table 10.2   Summary of NICE guidelines recommendations (2011)

Step 1: For all known and suspected presentations of GAD offer identification, assessment, education about symptoms of GAD and active monitoring.

Step 2: For people with GAD whose symptoms do not improve with education and active monitoring, offer one or more of the following as a first-line intervention, guided by the person's preference: individual non-facilitated self-help, individual guided self-help or psycho-educational groups.

Step 3: For people with GAD and marked functional impairment or that has not improved after Step 2 intervention, offer either an individual high-intensity psychological intervention or drug treatment. If a person with GAD chooses a high-intensity intervention offer either CBT (usually 12–15 weekly sessions) or applied relaxation. Both treatments should be based on the treatment manuals used in the clinical trials and be delivered by a trained and competent practitioner.

Beck et al. (1985) theorized that worry and anxiety occurs in individuals who have developed a danger schema and who, as a result, make enduring appraisals whereby they consistently overestimate the level of danger and underestimate their ability to cope with the perceived threat. This idea, while at times clinically useful, lacks specificity when applied to individuals with GAD. Leading researchers in the field have developed subsequent theories which have identified different constructs of the disorder. These are outlined below.

- GAD is seen as a form of cognitive avoidance by Borkovec (1994). Worry is understood as a verbal thought-based activity that inhibits somatic and emotional processing, including the emotional processing of fear which is necessary for the successful habituation to, and extinction of, anxiety.
- According to Wells (1997) the activation of negative meta-cognitive beliefs about worry plays a more central role than the actual worries themselves, and it is this that distinguishes GAD from high levels of normal worry. In consequence, therapy should address the individual's beliefs about worry, both positive and negative.
- Dugas et al. (1998) postulated a model of GAD where the intolerance of uncertainty is the defining feature (this will be described in more detail later in this chapter).
- A deficit in the regulation of emotional experience is central to the approach developed by Mennin et al. (2002) which theorizes that individuals suffering from GAD become overwhelmed when strong emotions occur due to the inability to regulate emotional experience. Worry is consequently used as a strategy to cope.
- The acceptance-based model developed by Roemer and Orsillo (2005) emphasizes how an individual's problematic relationship with their internal experiences (thoughts, feeling and bodily sensations) contributes to the onset and maintenance of GAD.
- Clark and Beck (2010) tried to integrate the advances made by previous researchers in their cognitive model. They identify three main phases in the process of worry (evocative, automatic processing and elaborative processing phases) emphasizing the activation of maladaptive schemas about general threat and the individual's behavioural responses.

Padesky (2012) introduced the difference between 'danger' and 'coping' disorders. She proposed a model which reintegrates Beck's basic anxiety model (Beck et al., 1985) through the use of the anxiety equation which describes anxiety as deriving from the interaction between the individual's overestimation of danger and the underestimation of their ability to cope. The main components of intervention entail increasing clients' perceptions of their ability to cope by assisting them in shifting from their 'what if' cognitions to 'then what' behavioural responses. Helping them explore ways to deal with their worst case scenarios in behavioural terms both lessens the anxiety and enhances sense of coping.

A brief overview of the main cognitive approaches and their key aspects of intervention are provided in Table 10.3.

Table 10.3 Theoretical models of GAD (adapted from Behar et al., 2009)

Model of GAD	Main components	Key intervention elements
Avoidance model of worry (Borkovec, e.g. 1994)	Cognitive avoidance; positive beliefs about worry; ineffective problem-solving; ineffective emotional processing; dysfunctional attachment styles	Self-monitoring; stimulus-control program; present-moment focus; response-prevention; worry outcome monitoring; self-control desensitization techniques
Meta-cognitive model of worry (Wells, 2006)	Positive and negative beliefs about worry; type 1 and 2 worry; ineffective coping strategies	Modification of negative beliefs and appraisal about uncontrollability of worry; modification of meta-worry and beliefs about danger of worry; identification and challenging of positive beliefs
Emotion dysregulation model (Mennin et al., 2002)	Emotional hyper-arousal; poor understanding of emotions and ineffective reaction to the negative ones; ineffective emotion regulation	Emotion education; emotional skills training; relaxation training; experiential exposure exercise
Acceptance-based model (ABM; Roemer and Orsillo, 2005)	Internal experiences; problematic relationship with internal experiences; experiential avoidance; behavioural restriction	Psycho-education about ABM; mindfulness and acceptance; behavioural changes and valued actions
Padesky (2012)	GAD as a coping disorder; basic anxiety model; anxiety equation	Non-GAD thinking vs GAD-thinking; shift from 'what if' to 'then what'; 'from avoid to approach' principle
Cognitive model (Clark and Beck, 2010)	Evocative phase and schematic activation; attentional threat and interpretation bias; automatic processing phase; maladaptive beliefs about threat; elaborative processing phase; meta-worry; intolerance of uncertainty	Education: cognitive restructuring and decatastrophizing; worry control strategies; identification of maladaptive GAD; Schemas: risk and uncertainty inoculation; elaborative processing of the present

Reference to alternative approaches used in combination with standard CBT will be made throughout this chapter. However, the main focus will be on the model developed by Dugas et al. (1998) because of its emphasis on the 'intolerance of uncertainty' – a feature which has been identified as relevant across theoretical models. More specifically, it was identified as playing a central role in maintaining our clients' difficulties. According to Dugas' model, individuals with GAD find it difficult to accept uncertainties and the process of worry involves the exploration of all possible outcomes in the attempt to achieve a certainty. As a result the individual will focus on the feared outcome rather than initiate a process of problem-solving. Despite possessing effective problem solving skills, individuals with GAD seem to have a negative problem orientation; that is they perceive themselves as unable to solve problems. In addition, somatic and cognitive symptoms occur as a consequence of excessive worry making it harder to focus on identifying solutions. Individuals with GAD will avoid approaching or thinking about the problem due to the distressing nature of uncertain outcomes and heightened anxiety. Such avoidance will then feed the maintenance cycle while reinforcing individuals' positive beliefs about worry and the intolerance of uncertainty.

Cognitive themes found in GAD

Clients are often preoccupied with 'what if...' cognitions which they apply to situations that could happen. The predictive anxiety about these events is generally high and often leads to negative automatic thoughts (NATs) and through avoidance the thoughts and fears are confirmed.

During the assessment and formulation process it is important for the therapist to ascertain levels of anxiety through use of an idiographic Likert scale (usually 0 being the lowest and 10 being the highest the client has ever experienced). Other dominant NATs that are evident usually start with 'I can't...' again leading to avoidant behaviours and confirmation of the NATs. When the client reports these dominant cognitive themes the therapist can use the opportunity to explore how they contradict with the goals of therapy. The use of gentle Socratic questioning around these narratives can help with the developing formulation and demonstrate vicious maintenance cycles.

Physiology in GAD

GAD is accompanied by a number of distressing physiological sensations. There has been a long debate in the literature regarding the inclusion of autonomic arousal symptoms as distinguishing features of the disorder. Previous research (Brown et al., 1995) led to the exclusion of most bodily sensations from the DSM, although this decision raised concerns about increased difficulties in distinguishing GAD from other disorders (Clark and Watson, 1991). Clinical observations and recent research (Roth et al., 2008) have demonstrated that even though individuals may present with chronic anxiety and hyperarousal they will not necessarily meet the diagnostic criteria for GAD. This is an important issue to take into account when establishing the components of therapy to offer to individuals with highly distressing bodily symptoms. When clients present with heightened physiological responses behavioural interventions such as relaxation techniques may be considered, as recommended by the NICE guidelines. However, we recommend first identifying the maintaining factors of distress by formulating the client's idiosyncratic difficulties. This is particularly relevant for individuals who have experienced several setbacks as it is shown that, even though relaxation techniques contribute to changes in the GAD symptoms, individuals will continue to experience residual sensations (Öst and Breitholtz, 2000).

Case introduction

Sally is a 32-year-old white female who was referred by her GP to her local IAPT service for 'anxiety and stress'. The IAPT service offers evidence-based psychological therapy to individuals suffering from mild to moderate levels of depression and/or anxiety. A preliminary assessment is aimed at establishing suitability for the service including both the nature of the client's problems and their ability to work within a CBT model of therapy. Excluding criteria refer to presence of psychotic symptoms, high level of risk to self and/or others and substance misuse. The assessment indicated that Sally was an appropriate candidate for CBT.

Sally worked as a receptionist for an editorial services company. She lived at home with her husband and their two children aged five years and six months. She was on maternity leave at time of referral and was planning to return to work in the near future.

Assessment

The assessment aimed to identify the cognitive, behavioural, physical and emotional factors contributing to and maintaining Sally's distress. As there are no anxiety characteristics unique to GAD, it is important to assess the features in full. It is particularly important to focus on:

- Chronicity, severity and pervasiveness of worry.
- Content of the worry.
- The client's understanding of the worry process.
- The client's life circumstances and any stressors at the time of assessment and in the past.

GAD is a disorder characterized by high co-morbidity and it is therefore important to be able to differentiate this from other disorders. An overlap of somatic symptoms has been observed particularly with respect to major depressive disorder (fatigue, poor concentration, sleep difficulties). One of the main features of depression is the individual's tendency to ruminate which can easily resemble the 'dwelling' thought process present in GAD. To help with differentiation, clinicians are encouraged to obtain a detailed account of the content of the client's thoughts and examine the temporal focus of the worry; individuals with GAD show a tendency to focus on potential future events whereas depressed clients tend to concentrate on past events. Where the content of worry relates to past events, a discriminant feature will be their fear about possible repercussions as opposed to thinking of the same event as further evidence of their failing.

Questions and observations in the assessment of GAD

In the absence of consistent monitoring it is important to attain a picture of how the client functions on a day-to-day basis, establishing situations when the problem is activated and the subsequent cognitions, physiology, emotions and behavioural responses. Table 10.4 gives examples of areas to consider and questions to ask a client during the assessment process.

Table 10.4 Useful indicators of GAD and helpful questions to ask

Non-verbal signals to remain alert to include:

- poor eye contact (e.g. unable to look at the therapist whilst talking);
- startled response to sudden noise;
- fidgeting (e.g. wringing hands, playing with jewellery);
- easily distracted (e.g. keeps checking their phone).

Past history:

- When did you first notice you had a problem and that you needed psychological help?
- Would you describe yourself as always being a worrier?
- When did you first start to worry? What were the circumstances?
- How has the worry changed or developed over time?
- Would you describe any members of your family as being worriers?
- Have there been times in your life when things have gone really well for you? (What, when, where, with whom?) How did you cope with difficulties at that time?
- Is it important to you to be aware of what is going on all the time?

(Continued)

Table 10.4 (Continued)

Present:

- How often have you been worried over the last two weeks? How long does it last?
- Can you rate the intensity of the anxiety on a scale of 0–10, with 10 being the worst anxiety you have ever experienced in your life and 0 no anxiety at all?
- Can you give me an example of the last time you were worried and felt out of control? How did you feel? What physical sensations did you experience? What thoughts and images went through your mind? What did you do?

Long- and short-term impact:

- How has your problem impacted your relationships?
- Do you find yourself more dependent on significant others? Has this happened in the past?
- Have you lost relationships due to your problem?

Sally's assessment

Sally arrived at our first meeting well-dressed. She engaged well, although appeared noticeably anxious, tapping her foot and fidgeting on her chair. She became tearful during the consultation and found it difficult to stay focused.

Presenting problem

Sally initially described worrying about 'everything and anything'. However, the assessment identified that in reality her worry was more focused on her children and her own role as a mother. Her anxiety intensified after the birth of her second child and the distressing feelings were accompanied by several physiological sensations including tense muscles, chest pain, twitching and restlessness. She felt overly irritable and fatigued at the end of each day but was unable to fall asleep.

Sally's NATs and critical underlying assumptions were elicited by asking her to recall a recent episode of anxiety. Her worries were expressed through a number of 'what ifs...' and the underlying core belief that drove Sally's anxiety concerned doubts about her own competence as a mother ('I'm incompetent'). This belief appeared to have developed as a young child when she felt unable to please her father academically and was further reinforced by his growing absence from the family. Her belief about being incompetent was reactivated by the transition to motherhood when she felt unable to meet the expectations she placed on herself. She was fearful that others could see her struggle looking after the children and that this would reveal her vulnerability.

To manage her worry, Sally would try to suppress her distressing thoughts, avoid dealing with anxiety-provoking situations and procrastinate. She would seek reassurance from others, particularly her mother or her husband. In addition to feelings of anxiety, Sally described symptoms of low mood. She was often tearful and had thoughts that she had let herself and her family down. During this time her motivation to engage in pleasurable activities also reduced. She had lost previous relationships due to her anxiety and acknowledged that her worry was now putting a strain on her marriage which she described as being at 'breaking point'.

Sally had received a brief course of supportive counselling soon after the birth of her first child. She described benefiting from therapy which assisted her in adjusting to the changes in her life following the arrival of her son as well as better coping with stress. However, she felt she was now 'back to square one'. Her second pregnancy had been unplanned and it was hypothesized that her increased sense of responsibility and intolerance of uncertainty re-activated her core belief of being 'incompetent' to which she responded by worrying. This led to the setback. It was observed that unplanned and uncertain events were perceived as threatening and hence likely to trigger another episode of anxiety.

Sally was not taking medication and did not use alcohol or drugs.

Sally's history

Sally described herself as always having been a worrier and as overly concerned about her family. Her mother was also portrayed as a chronic worrier. Over the years, Sally had managed to cope with her excessive worrying by repeatedly seeking reassurance and relying on others which in turn had enhanced her sense of vulnerability and undermined her confidence and self-esteem. Her difficulties worsened when her father left her mother. Sally was 16 years old when this unexpected event occurred and as the elder of two children, she believed that she had to take responsibility for her mother's well-being. She recalled becoming preoccupied with her mother and the future and started to believe that worrying about the future made her more 'in control' and 'prepared for further nasty surprises'.

Measures

The protocol for the treatment of anxiety and depression-based disorders within IAPT services requires therapists to use empirically-substantiated measures of change. For GAD the Penn State Worry Questionnaire (PSWQ; Meyer et al., 1990) can provide particularly useful information. The PSWQ is a 16-item scale widely used to distinguish GAD in a treatment-seeking population. It has a cut-off score of 45. Sally obtained a score of 68 indicating 'High Worry'.

Idiographic measures in the form of a Likert scale were also used in relation to cognitions with high emotional content. As standard IAPT self-report measures of depression and anxiety the Patient Health Questionnaire (PHQ-9; Kroenke et al., 2010) and Generalized Anxiety Disorder (GAD-7) were used and administered at each therapeutic contact to monitor Sally's progress. Her scores indicated moderate depression and severe anxiety. Given Sally's symptoms of low mood, she was also asked to complete the Beck Depression Inventory (BDI II; Beck et al., 1996) which indicated moderate depression. Other relevant measures of worry that can be useful in assessing GAD are reported in Table 10.5.

Table 10.5 Measures of worry

Worry Domains Questionnaire (WDQ; Tallis et al., 1991) is a 25-item measure that assesses extent of worry in five domains: relationships, lack of confidence, aimless future, work and financial matters.

The Why-Worry II (WW-II) (Holowka et al., 2000) is a 25-item tool intended to assess positive beliefs about the function of worry.

The Intolerance of Uncertainty Scale (IUS; Buhr and Dugas, 2002) comprises 27 items that relate to the idea that uncertainty is unacceptable and leads to frustration, stress and inability to take action. Items are rated on a 5-point Likert scale ranging from 'not at all characteristic of me' to 'entirely characteristic of me'.

The Negative Problem Orientation Questionnaire (NPOQ; Robichaud and Dugas, 2005a, 2005b) is a 12-item measure that assesses the dysfunctional cognitive set of negative problem orientation.

The Cognitive Avoidance Questionnaire (CAQ; Sexton and Dugas, 2008) contains 25 items assessing the tendency to use five types of cognitive avoidance strategies.

Development of a collaborative case formulation: moving from 'generic to specific'

In order to help Sally understand how her difficulties were formed and maintained we used a generic formulation in the first instance; in this case Padesky's five areas (Padesky and Mooney, 1990; see Figure 10.1) which illustrates in diagrammatic form how each level of thought impacted on her decision-making process in the context of her emotional responses and subsequent behaviours.

A longitudinal formulation suggested that Sally's early experiences, including the absence of her father during key developmental stages in her life, her mother's worry and the subsequent sense of responsibility following her parents' divorce, modelled a way in which she responded to stressful life events. This contributed to the subsequent development of unhelpful assumptions that included, 'if something happens, I will be seen as a bad mother' and 'only I can look after my children'.

Environment
Distal: mother always been a worrier, developed positive beliefs about worry
Proximal: returning to work, leaving her child in the care of childminder

Thoughts

**Rules and Assumptions (RA), Negative Automatic Thoughts (NATs)
and Core Beliefs (CB)**

'I won't be able to cope when I am at work'	NAT
'What if something happens to my child?'	NAT
'The more I think about the problem,	
the more likely I am to find a perfect solution'	RA
'Only I know how to look after my child'	RA
'If something happens I will be seen as a bad mother'	RA
'I'm incompetent/bad mother'	CB

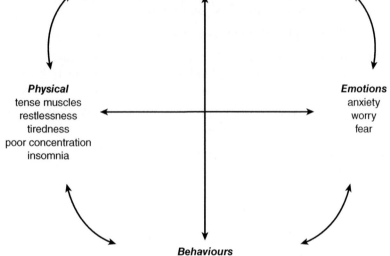

Physical
tense muscles
restlessness
tiredness
poor concentration
insomnia

Emotions
anxiety
worry
fear

Behaviours
procrastinate when having to make a decision
excessive cleaning for fear of being negatively judged (creating a perfect environment)
reassurance seeking from husband and mother

Figure 10.1   Sally's five areas model

Together, we identified how her core belief of being incompetent (and, by extension, a bad mother) was associated with the driving rule, 'the more I worry, the more likely I am to find the perfect solution'. This enabled us to move from the generic to the specific formulation (Figure 10.2), focusing on how the rule contributed to the maintenance cycle and how this related to her intolerance of uncertainty. Through the formulation Sally was able to understand how the rule about 'finding the perfect solution' was implicated in both her problematic behaviours and emotional responses. Because no solution was 'good enough', she relentlessly reviewed her decisions and procrastinated on tasks. The problem remained unsolved as the outcome could not be tested, hence her anxiety heightened. As a result she perceived herself as being consistently unable to problem-solve, leading to further anxiety and demoralization. In order to reduce the unpleasant emotional experience, she would engage in further avoidance strategies including suppressing her thoughts and procrastinating, thus maintaining the vicious cycle of anxiety.

The following dialogue illustrates the conceptualization of Sally's thoughts and behaviours and elicitation of their idiosyncratic function:

Therapist: So Sally I noted that you have been having this thought of being incompetent and a bad mother.

Sally: Yes and I know others will see it if I don't get this childcare right.

Therapist: Right. It seems you believe this quite strongly and I noticed you were emotional as you said it.

Sally: That's right [*looking down and avoiding eye contact*].

Therapist: It sounds very scary. I'm sorry you're feeling that way. I was wondering if you could tell me on a scale of 0 to 10 how much you believe the idea (that you are incompetent) to be true?

Sally: Yes, it is very scary to think that others will think that of me. I would say I believe it about 80 per cent.

Therapist: I can imagine that can be quite distressing. How did you deal with that thought, Sally?

Sally: Well, I started worrying about the problem. I could not stop thinking about it no matter how hard I tried.

Therapist: You found it difficult to stop worrying?

Sally: Yes. But I also tried to do something about it. I made a list of all the child-minders we had already contacted and I went through it again. Then I asked my husband what he thought of them. You know, just to have another opinion.

Therapist: Did doing these things make you feel less worried about arranging childcare?

Sally: Well, not really. I was pretty exhausted by then and could not deal with it anymore.

Therapist: This process must have been really tiring for you. What do you mean by 'you could not deal with it anymore'?

Sally: I didn't think I was going to find a solution. I have been thinking about this for so long and no option felt right. I thought that there was no way I would be able to sort this out.

Therapist: It sounds as if despite reviewing all the options and seeking reassurance from your husband you have been feeling unable to make a decision about childcare. I wonder if your anxiety over making this decision is related to your belief about being incompetent. Is it illustrated in the diagram that we have formulated?

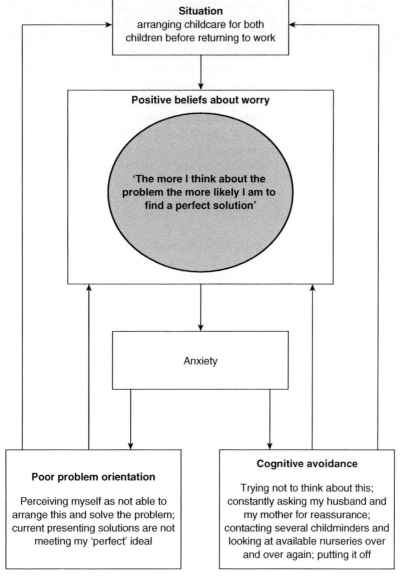

Figure 10.2 Sally's specific case formulation

When thoughts of finding the perfect solution dominate the client procrastination often follows, as the risk – be it physical or psychological – can never be wholly eradicated. Leahy (2005) states that the desire to find a perfect solution often leads to feelings of regret. Through the process of problem-solving all potential solutions are continuously rejected, therefore no potential outcomes are tested, no risk is ever taken and the fear is maintained. Taking these factors into account it is important to ascertain the level of activity the client is engaged in as they can often appear exhausted despite reporting doing very little. Listening for the word 'perfect' in a client's narrative and exploring what it means to them is often useful in this context.

From a cross-sectional perspective, it was hypothesized that Sally's return to work operated as the activating situation and this was used as an opportunity to illustrate some of her unhelpful thoughts and beliefs. She felt preoccupied because she believed that 'if she did not choose the right child-minder something bad would happen to her child'. She was therefore engaging in avoidant and compensatory behaviours. The elicited core beliefs ('I am incompetent' and 'I am a bad mother') and underlying assumptions ('if something happens, I will be seen as a bad mother') drove her thoughts and behaviours contributing to the persistence of GAD.

Goals and treatment plan

It was agreed that Sally's main difficulties were likely to be caused by her excessive worry. She was offered 16 sessions of CBT with a review after six sessions, as per the service guidelines. The focus of therapy was targeting her excessive worry.

Initially, it proved difficult for Sally to establish specific goals due to her belief that 'everything should be perfect'. To overcome this obstacle, Sally was encouraged to create a 'possibility list' as suggested by Mooney and Padesky (2000), that is activities she would like to be capable of doing and what she envisaged it would be like to 'cope'. This approach is particularly helpful when working with clients with GAD as it sustains the therapeutic process of reinforcing new adaptive beliefs about being a capable agent of change. Below are the specific goals that were established:

Short-term goals (within three weeks):

1. To spend 20 per cent less time occupied by worry.
2. To choose a nursery.
3. To improve sleep by one hour extra a night.

Medium-term goals (within six weeks):

1. To make a decision independent of her husband.
2. To spend 50 per cent less time occupied by the worry.
3. To improve sleep by two hours extra a night.

Long-term goals (within three months):

1. To spend 80 per cent of the time less occupied by worry.
2. To make most decisions on her own without seeking reassurance.
3. Sleeping pattern to return to acceptable amounts given her circumstances.

Structure of therapy and treatment

The individualized formulation developed in collaboration with Sally was used to guide the therapy which consisted of four major cognitive behavioural interventions linked to her goals. These were:

1 Psycho-education and worry awareness training

Early sessions were focused on providing Sally with psycho-education on anxiety and specific information about GAD, highlighting the central role of worry. Sally was assisted in thinking of her worries as a process rather than focusing on their content. This is particularly important as it enables clients to identify the function that worry serves in maintaining their distress, and how cognitively avoiding the feared outcome reinforces intolerance of uncertainty. Through the use of guided discovery, Sally was able to see that her worry persisted due to her negative appraisal and beliefs in conjunction with ineffective control strategies. She was therefore assisted in identifying the distinguishing characteristics of pathological and productive worries.

2 Developing new, helpful rules and re-evaluating beliefs about worry

Sally was assisted in determining the helpfulness of worry as a strategy for solving problems. By using verbal re-attribution techniques she was encouraged to question the evidence supporting the value of worry and explored times in the past when she made decisions leading to positive outcomes without worrying. Sally's poor decision-making was determined and maintained by beliefs organized around perfection. Her narrative was strongly characterized by the construct of 'being incompetent' which was explored and re-evaluated. She was further asked to provide examples of situations that she rated as being 'good enough' in order to form a hierarchy from which behavioural experiments could be formulated.

3 Enhancing sense of coping

In a discussion on anxiety disorders, Padesky (2012) argued that GAD can be considered a 'coping disorder' as opposed to other anxiety disorders (such as panic or health anxiety) which she describes as 'danger disorders'. Padesky suggests that disputing unhelpful beliefs may not be enough; instead the focus should be on increasing the client's perceptions of their ability to cope as well as their current coping strategies. Sally's problem-solving skills were identified and reinforced and she was encouraged to deal with current problems by devoting attention to actual problem-solving rather than worrying. For worries about hypothetical situations she was encouraged to move forward despite the inherent uncertainty of the situation and to see problems as a normal part of life rather than threats (D'Zurilla and Nezu, 1999).

4 Intolerance of uncertainty

The link between intolerance of uncertainty and excessive worry was highlighted and the situations in which intolerance of uncertainty manifested also investigated. Sally began to notice that uncertain situations are unavoidable and agreed to seek out uncertainty-inducing situations. Finally she began to refrain from engaging in behaviours that she would normally use to reduce or control uncertainty including reassurance seeking. The focus of the last part of treatment was *in vivo* exposure. Sally was assisted in seeking out uncertainty-inducing situations in a graded way so that she could experience some anxiety while tolerating uncertainty without feeling overwhelmed.

Outcome and follow-up

Sally engaged well in therapy and worked hard to overcome her difficulties. She particularly valued the formulation as it highlighted the factors that were maintaining her problem. Adopting a resilience model that emphasized her coping strategies and resources also proved helpful.

By the end of treatment Sally had achieved both her short- and medium-term goals. She reported worrying less (by 60 per cent) and was no longer relying on her husband to make important decisions. She felt less tense and her sleep had noticeably improved. Behavioural experiments carried out both within and outside the sessions had weakened Sally's unhelpful cognitions and she had significantly reduced her former avoidance and compensatory strategies. In developing a relapse prevention plan, situations likely to reactivate her former core belief about being incompetent were considered and an action plan developed for how she might manage this.

The follow-up session arranged a month after completion of therapy indicated a reduction in her scores for both depression and anxiety on all measures. Sally described feeling more confident and willing to take risks, and both her husband and her mother had observed a positive change in the way that Sally dealt with stressful situations.

Conclusion and implications for clinicians

Sally's presentation is typical of individuals presenting with GAD in primary care mental health settings in as much as worry is the primary feature of their complaint. A number of issues have been highlighted and below are some of the implications that clinicians may want to consider when working with GAD clients:

1. It is common that individuals with GAD focus on the content of their worries rather than examining the process of worry (Wells, 1997). The client's ability to engage in a CBT model of therapy primarily focused on the process of their worry rather than engaging in its content is more likely to make the intervention successful.
2. It is important to assess GAD carefully given the subjectivity of 'excessiveness of worry'. A contextualized analysis of the client's problems is fundamental as life circumstances and current stressors can greatly contribute to an increase in worry.
3. A tendency to seek reassurance from the therapist is common, especially in the early sessions. This obstacle can be managed by: (1) discussing this openly and agreeing with the client to call attention to it when occurring in the interaction; (2) acknowledging the unpleasant autonomic response and emotional distress that the client experiences when resisting the urge to engage in reassurance seeking while at the same time encouraging reflection on the pros and cons; and (3) referring back to the formulation, highlighting the need to change the behaviour in order to change emotional experience, and agreeing behavioural experiments to establish what does and does not occur through relinquishing this strategy.
4. It is essential to keep a stance of gentle curiosity throughout assessment and treatment of GAD due to the nature of worry and the associated catastrophic NATs. It is important not to be afraid of asking detailed questions. This will not only generate affect to work on in the session but will also enable the client to feel more at ease with the therapy process.
5. It is important to assist clients in identifying the link between their NATs and unchallenged assumptions within the context of their behavioural responses. The client's narrative will provide helpful elements for guiding the formulation and intervention planning.
6. It is helpful to highlight the client's skills. Providing solutions will only reinforce their negative problem orientation and they will continue seeing themselves as poor problem-solving agents, thus feeding the vicious cycle of worry.

7. Given the number of psychotherapeutic models developed for the treatment of GAD, it is important to ensure that all the techniques are used in a coherent way. Formulating the client's difficulty using a generic model such as the five areas model can provide the foundation for co-constructing a specific conceptualization of the presenting issues.

Activities

1. Familiarize yourself with the different cognitive models of GAD.
2. Think about an existing case and consider how you could help your client move from the generic to a specific formulation by identifying key core beliefs.
3. Role-play eliciting beliefs related to intolerance of uncertainty, perfectionism and procrastination and formulate these within a maintenance cycle.

Further reading

Borkovec, T.D. and Sharpless, B. (2004) 'Generalized anxiety disorder: bringing cognitive behavioral therapy into the valued present', in S. Hayes, V. Follette, and M. Linehan (eds), *New Directions in Behavioral Therapy*. New York: Guilford Press. pp. 209–42.

Clark, D.A. and Beck, A.T. (2010) *Cognitive Therapy of Anxiety Disorders: Science and Practice*. New York: Guilford Press.

Dugas, M.J. and Robichaud, M. (2007) *Cognitive Behavioural Treatment for Generalized Anxiety Disorder: From Science to Practice*. New York: Routledge.

Portman, M.E. (2009) *Generalized Anxiety Disorder across the Lifespan: An Integrative Approach*. New York: Springer.

ELEVEN Vicky: A Case Study of Social Anxiety

Kate Daley and Adrian Cockx

Learning objectives

After reading this chapter and completing the activities at the end you should be able to:

- Recognize the symptoms of social anxiety and distinguish this from other disorders.
- Be aware of the theoretical base for using CBT in the assessment and treatment of social anxiety.
- Understand key elements of assessment and formulation as it applies to social anxiety.
- Plan an evidence-based cognitive behavioural intervention.

Introduction

Social anxiety disorder (previously known as social phobia) is considered one of the most common of all the anxiety disorders, causing significant distress. It can impair relationships, quality of life and work performance, and has a high degree of co-morbidity with depression, substance misuse and low self-esteem (Dalrymple and Zimmerman, 2011; NICE, 2013). Despite its prevalence, social anxiety is often overlooked and undiagnosed, with many only seeking treatment after 15–20 years of symptoms and others never seeking help at all. Effective treatment has been developed but there is still a need for improved recognition and assessment to allow improved access (NICE, 2013).

This chapter describes a case study of a client who presented to a primary care mental health service with symptoms of social anxiety. It begins with a definition and diagnostic criteria, before providing an overview of the theoretical basis for using a CBT approach in the treatment of this disorder. The chapter discusses key issues involved in the assessment and formulation of social anxiety, and informs the reader on how this formulation can be used to guide treatment. The chapter also explores issues around engagement specific to social anxiety and discusses additional techniques which could be used to increase effectiveness of CBT treatment.

Theoretical and research basis for therapy

Social anxiety disorder has been defined as, 'A persistent fear of one or more social or performance situations in which the person is exposed to unfamiliar people or to possible scrutiny by others. The individual fears that he or she will act in a way that will be embarrassing and humiliating' (APA, 2013: 202).

The fear is recognized as out of proportion to any real threat, and exposure to the feared situation causes significant distress and anxiety (APA, 2013). Anxiety levels can vary in severity and may be generalized or situation specific (Clark and Wells, 1995). The fear or avoidance is considered persistent, typically lasting over six months and is not due to physiological effects of substances or a general medical condition (APA, 2013).

Meeting new people, being in groups, meetings, presentations, or around authority figures are typical triggering situations that evoke anxiety for these individuals (NICE, 2013). In these situations, symptoms such as sweating, trembling or blushing are commonly cited. The individual believes that others will see they are anxious and judge them as incompetent, weak or stupid, fearing they will do or say something embarrassing. As a result, they will try to avoid situations where possible, and if unable to avoid, the situation will be endured with distress (APA, 2013).

For treatment of social anxiety, exposure therapy, applied relaxation and social skills training have all been cited in the literature, with CBT recommended as the treatment of choice (NICE, 2013). NICE guidelines stipulate that CBT for social anxiety should be delivered by qualified therapists over 14, individual 90-minute sessions, delivered across the course of a four-month period (NICE, 2013). The treatment should be based on a cognitive model of social anxiety; this chapter will focus on one such model (Clark and Wells, 1995) and will illustrate how this can be used to understand and guide this course of treatment.

In addition, the Assertive Defence of the Self™ model (Padesky, 1997) will be introduced to demonstrate an alternative CBT approach that can be used in combination with the Clark and Wells protocol.

Cognitive model for social anxiety

Clark and Wells (1995) propose cognition to be crucial in the development and maintenance of social anxiety, using this to explain why continued exposure to social situations does not serve to reduce anxiety. They identify that a shift to an internal focus of attention, implementation of safety behaviours and pre-/post-event processing are all key maintaining factors.

The model postulates that when the individual is exposed to a social situation, their rules and assumptions are activated. Clark (2001) breaks these rules into three categories, these being excessively high standards for social performance ('my performance must be perfect'; 'I must not show weakness'), conditional beliefs about the consequences of particular aspects of performance ('if I shake they will think I'm incompetent') and unconditional negative beliefs about the self ('I am not good enough'). These assumptions lead the individual to perceive a threat in the form of negative evaluation from others ('he looks anxious, he must be incompetent') and as a result they will shift their attention inwards. This self-observation is then used to evaluate how others perceive them ('I feel anxious so they must see I am') which further increases their anxiety symptoms (Clark, 2001).

Individuals typically employ a range of safety behaviours in an attempt to reduce the chance of any negative evaluation, and so their anxiety. For example, an individual who fears others will see them blush and judge them as incompetent may cover their face, evade eye contact to minimize the chance of any interaction, or simply avoid the situation all together (Veale, 2003).

Whilst this reduces anxiety in the short-term, it also prevents beliefs from being dis-confirmed, maintaining the anxiety. Safety behaviours may also inadvertently have the converse effect. For example someone who is covering their face may be more likely noticed or the muscle tension elicited by holding onto something tightly may lead to more shaking. Finally, the anxiety may be further amplified by negative post-event processing and harsh self-criticism (Clark and Wells, 1995).

The treatment of social anxiety should aim to address each of the aspects identified above, and a range of cognitive behavioural interventions can be used for this endeavour; disconfirming negative beliefs and breaking the negative maintenance cycles.

Case history

Vicky is a 32-year-old white British woman who lives with her partner in London and works within the financial sector. She was referred to her local IAPT service by her GP who described Vicky as experiencing low mood and increasing levels of anxiety in her workplace. At screening Vicky explained that she had felt this way for as long as she could remember but was seeking help now as it was beginning to impact significantly on her life. She had recently turned down a promotion opportunity due to her anxiety, and had become withdrawn and isolated as a result.

Assessment

At assessment, Vicky presented as a highly functioning individual. She was dressed appropriately and was able to give a detailed, coherent description of her difficulties. She gave limited eye contact during the assessment but this increased as the session progressed and she became noticeably more relaxed.

Clinical interview

A detailed cognitive behavioural assessment was carried out in the form of a clinical interview guided by the Clark and Wells (1995) model and standardized psychometrics. The purpose of the assessment was to determine suitability of CBT and to establish the main presenting problem. An individualized formulation was then used to guide the treatment protocols.
Two key questions to address within the assessment were:

- What are Vicky's fears?
- What is she avoiding?

Specific questions were asked to find out more information with regard to the situations Vicky was avoiding, what she feared would happen if she did not avoid them, and the level of distress or functional impairment experienced. Recent examples were used to elicit this information where the emotional context was highest. Vicky was asked specifically about key components of the model, namely physiological symptoms, self-image and safety-seeking behaviours. Her attentional focus and anticipatory/post-event processing were also examined. With social anxiety it is particularly important to ask about images in addition to thoughts as images can be a powerful maintaining factor and require clinical intervention in their own right.
As recommended within the NICE guidance (2013), questions were also asked to ascertain if there were any co-morbid disorders present, and to gain details on Vicky's occupational, educational and social circumstances. Vicky was able to clarify that her anxiety preceded her low mood, and so we agreed to treat this in the first instance.

Presenting problem

At assessment, Vicky described her difficulties to be most prominent in group settings, particularly those where she was required to interact with senior staff and those she did not know. Vicky noted that her anxiety peaked when she was required to present to colleagues or felt put on the spot, describing this as her 'worst case scenario'. When in these situations, Vicky would experience physiological symptoms of anxiety including her heart racing, palms sweating and butterflies in her stomach. She reported that her hands would shake and she would feel her face flush. She noted that in these situations she would feel overwhelmed and her mind would go blank. She worried that she would make a fool of herself as a result, and believed others would see she was anxious and judge her to be incompetent.

She feared that this would impact on her progression at work as people would see she that was 'not up to the job'.

To manage her symptoms, Vicky would often avoid situations or leave them as quickly as possible. Whenever she was unable to avoid the situation she would spend a lot of time preparing beforehand, and would sit in a corner at the back of the room avoiding eye contact. Outside of work when she experienced anxiety, she would use her phone to look busy and alcohol to 'calm her nerves'. She explained that after an event she would spend hours replaying what had happened, dwelling on aspects of her performance and speculating about what others may have thought of her.

In addition to her anxiety, Vicky also described symptoms of low mood. She was experiencing a lack of motivation, variable concentration and was often tearful. She noticed that she was finding work stressful and that her symptoms had increased since a company restructure which had changed the nature of her role. Her new role involved more contact with senior members of the team, and had a larger training component that was increasing her anxiety and reluctance to go into work.

Vicky's history

Vicky was initially unable to identify any specific critical events that could have triggered her anxiety and described her childhood as relatively uneventful. However, on closer examination it became apparent she had disliked reading aloud in class and vividly recalls being shouted at by her teacher for not pronouncing words correctly.

Socially she described herself as having always been a shy person with a few close friends. She had been bullied for a time at secondary school but was academically very successful. She had achieved a first class honours degree and good job, but often felt like a 'fraud' and as if she was waiting to be 'found out'.

Vicky was a youngest child, with two older siblings. She was close to her parents and described them as supportive although recalls them being strict and having high expectations of their children, as they themselves had been high achievers. She explained her family didn't often talk about their emotions, taking a 'stiff upper lip' approach and trying to 'just get on with things'.

Vicky did not use drugs and used alcohol only in moderation. She reported no significant physical health difficulties and no risk issues. She had received no previous psychological treatment and was keen to try this as an alternative to medication.

Measures

A validated measure for social anxiety, the Social Phobia Inventory (SPIN; Connor et al., 2000) was used as is standard within an IAPT Service.

The SPIN has 17 items and a cut-off score of 19 or above. It is recommended where there is a provisional diagnosis of social anxiety. Vicky scored 36 on this measure, corroborating the hypothesis that she was experiencing social anxiety. More idiographic measures using a Likert scale were devised on the basis of cognitions that had a high emotional context.

Vicky expressed some relief that there was a name for the difficulties she was experiencing and so welcomed this diagnosis. She had been unsure whether this was something in her personality or something that could be treated. Vicky appeared very psychologically-minded and was pleased to learn that CBT would be a suitable approach for her.

Given the nature of Vicky's difficulties it was important to allow time for a strong rapport to be developed with the therapist, ensuring that Vicky felt able to openly discuss her difficulties without fear of judgement. As by its very nature the therapeutic relationship is a social interaction, difficulties can be replicated in therapy and so caution is required. Safran and Segal (1996) reference the role of emotion and how activated schemas outside of therapy can be triggered within the therapeutic relationship, which is something to be mindful of in this work. Techniques to enable reduced eye contact such as use of a whiteboard were helpful in initial sessions to allow Vicky to feel more comfortable. Regular 'check-ins' were also built in to the therapy to allow Vicky to express how she was finding the therapy, rather than presuming she would volunteer this information freely. As therapy progressed, the relationship was used to test out some of the ideas within the therapy room, for example increasing eye contact as part of the treatment protocol.

Formulation

Cross-sectional view of current cognitions and behaviours

The cognitive model for the maintenance of social anxiety (Clark and Wells, 1995) was used to guide the formulation. Vicky was able to identify a number of recent situations where she had experienced this anxiety which were used to sketch out a cross-sectional formulation as described below.

When Vicky was asked to present to her lead team, she worried that she would shake and that they would perceive her to be incompetent. The fear of rejection or ridicule led her to experience physiological symptoms of anxiety; her heart would race and she would feel hot and shaky resulting in trembling hands. By focusing on her shaking, her perception of threat increased ('they will see and will judge me') and so the physiological symptoms intensified. She then used a range of safety behaviours in an attempt to reduce her anxiety; over-rehearsing beforehand, holding notes tightly, and avoiding eye contact during the presentation. These behaviours provided short-term relief but also prevented her disconfirming her anxious predictions ('if I didn't rehearse and hold my notes tight, I would have shaken and they would have seen how incompetent I am'), thus maintaining her anxiety.

Conversely, some of Vicky's behaviour may have drawn more attention to her and so her thoughts became somewhat of a self-fulfilling prophecy.

Vicky's post-event processing was also likely to have compounded her anxiety; she would analyse only the aspects she perceived as having not gone well, reinforcing her negative beliefs. In avoiding some situations, she was also unable to learn that her anxiety would reduce over time and that her predictions might not come true, again maintaining her vicious cycle.

Longitudinal view of cognitions and behaviours

As a result of Vicky's early experience, it was likely that she developed specific beliefs ('I'm not good enough') and assumptions ('if my performance isn't perfect, then I'm not good enough'; 'if I show emotion, I'm weak') which were driving her thoughts and behaviour. Being shouted at when

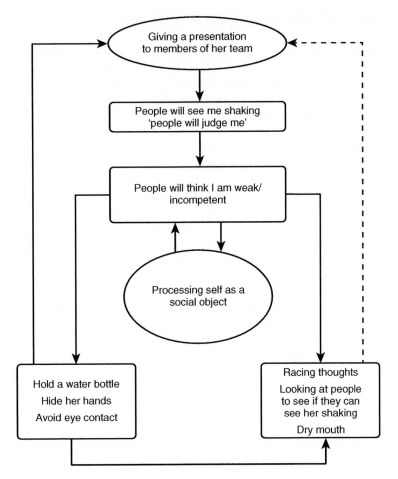

Figure 11.1 Vicky's case formulation

reading aloud in class may have been Vicky's first experience of intense anxiety, forming a connection between being the focus of attention, physical anxiety and feelings of incompetence. The high standards set by her parents were also likely to have had an impact in terms of what she interpreted as the 'norm' of what is expected.

Vicky had not been aware that others suffered from similar problems or that her difficulties were indicative of an anxiety disorder (rather than just 'shyness'). This had increased her feelings of isolation, and alongside her frustration had perhaps led to her low mood. Moreover, her upcoming promotion appeared to have reawakened some of her fears in that she believed that if her presentation skills were not perfect or if she appeared anxious, others would view her as incompetent and therefore a fraud.

Figure 11.1 provides a diagrammatic representation of Vicky's formulation, based on the Clark and Wells (1995) model.

Problem list, goals and treatment plan

It was agreed that Vicky's low mood was likely to stem from her anxiety and so we agreed to target her social anxiety in the first instance. She was using alcohol but we agreed that this was at a relatively low level, should not preclude treatment and would be addressed in therapy as a safety behaviour. She also noted work and relationships to be problematic, again due to her anxiety.

Vicky's short-term, medium-term and long-term goals were to be able to manage her anxiety, to feel confident to apply for her promotion and to become more sociable.

Vicky was offered a course of CBT based on Clark and Wells' model to address symptoms of social anxiety (as per NICE guidelines, 2013). The plan was to review progress after six sessions, evaluating how helpful she was finding it and how effective we were at working towards her goals, extending sessions as appropriate. The primary features of this were:

- Psycho-education and socializing to the CBT model.
- Experiential exercises to illustrate the adverse effect of self-focused attention and safety seeking behaviours on anxiety symptoms.
- Training in shifting and re-focusing attention.
- Within-session experiments to test a range of negative beliefs.
- Increasing awareness of and modifying of pre-/post-event processing.
- Addressing core beliefs and rules.
- Relapse prevention.

A method devised by Padesky (1997; 2008a; 2008b) known as Assertive Defence of the Self™ was also used with Vicky towards the end of treatment, which will be discussed later.

Vicky was able to form a strong rapport with the therapist, although her shyness and reluctance to disclose personal information initially made this difficult. A whiteboard and email communication (rather than eye contact and telephone calls) were used to overcome some of these barriers in earlier sessions, in addition to giving Vicky time to trust that the therapist would not judge her.

Interventions/procedures

As discussed earlier the assessment and early sessions were used to develop an individualized formulation with Vicky. This served as the basis for the intervention that followed, with four particular interventions proving most crucial, as discussed below.

1. Video feedback and survey

Vicky was encouraged to give a presentation to a group of 'stooges', which was recorded by the therapist. Before the presentation Vicky was asked to demonstrate on camera what her shaking would look like and to predict how others would view her. Vicky predicted that they would see she was anxious and think she was incompetent. Following the presentation, the stooges were asked to give written feedback which we used to test these predictions. They were asked to comment on their impression of Vicky, whether they noticed her shake (0–100 per cent) and whether shaking would mean someone was incompetent. Feedback from the stooges indicated that only 1 out of 9 had noticed Vicky shaking, and none of them linked shaking with incompetence. Two noted that they also had this experience when anxious. Most of the stooges reported that Vicky appeared confident and that her presentation had been very interesting.

Vicky was also asked to view the video. It was important to do this as if she were watching a stranger and only infer from information she could see rather than how she felt. On watching the video Vicky noted that she came across better than she thought and that her shaking was barely visible. The combination of survey and video allowed Vicky to identify the discrepancy between her perceived self-image and reality, shifting her beliefs around how noticeable the shaking was and about the judgement of others.

2. Dropping safety behaviours and testing predictions using behavioural experiments

Vicky was able to drop a range of safety behaviours in and outside of the session. For example, she was able to enter a social situation without alcohol, she increased eye contact and spoke out in meetings where she would previously have been silent. She compared these situations to ones where she used safety behaviours and noted that not only was she less anxious but that her performance improved. This was nicely backed up by a compliment received from a colleague.

During these experiments Vicky had rated her anxiety throughout, reporting it to reduce as she remained in the situation, matching the psychoeducation given in earlier sessions. This demonstrated to Vicky the transient nature of anxiety and allowed practice of implicational and experiential knowledge (Teasdale, 1996; see also Chapter 5), reiterating the need for continued exposure to challenge her beliefs.

3. Self-consciousness and anxiety using behavioural experiments

A simple in-session test to show how what we tell ourselves impacts physiologically was undertaken with the therapist. This was achieved by Vicky holding out her arms and saying out loud 'I'm weak, I'm weak' as the therapist applied gentle pressure. The exercise was then repeated with her saying 'I'm strong, I'm strong' with the therapist again applying gentle pressure. There was a distinct difference in resistance, helping Vicky make a connection between what she thinks and how she responds. Once this was applied to her anxiety in social situations Vicky could see how telling herself that she was unable to cope was maintaining the anxiety cycle. Identifying this pattern allowed Vicky to increase awareness, and potentially act differently in order to break the cycle.

Imagery can also be a very powerful tool in the treatment of social anxiety. Often clients will be able to identify vivid images of how they appear to others or of a specific situation that occurred historically. Imagery techniques can be used to restructure or update these images in order to take a more realistic or less anxiety-provoking form. It can sometimes be helpful to revisit earlier memories and update any which may be acting as a maintenance factor.

Obstacles and resistance

4. Assertive defence of the self and dealing with assumptions

In a discussion of social anxiety, Padesky (1997) focuses on the assumptions the individual has in given social situations. These assumptions may be related to how others perceive them, how others respond to them or how they will subsequently act given that perception. Rather than disputing the perceived observations as previously discussed (i.e. testing whether Vicky shakes and others notice and judge), the model works in the same way as any other phobia treatment; this is, by exposure to the feared stimulus, increasing coping resources and subsequently reducing fear.

Padesky (1997) introduces this idea through the Assertive Defence of the Self™ model. The intention of this approach is to help the client provide responses to potentially feared social observations from others and in some cases to directly test their assumptions. This provides them with a defence and an alternative to engaging in their current avoidance or safety behaviours. In doing this they are able to break the maintenance cycle and thereby reduce their anxiety.

Although the Clark and Wells model (1995) helped Vicky to effectively reduce some of her social anxiety, Padesky's Assertive Defence of the Self™ model (1997) was also used to provide Vicky with alternative responses to her most feared judgements. This gave us the option of not only challenging beliefs and assumptions, but also of providing Vicky with an assertive response to the judgement should it be required.

Within the Assertive Defence of the Self™ model, Padesky (2008b) outlines seven stages of the therapeutic process in the treatment of social anxiety:

1. Predict others' reactions.
2. Develop assertive responses.
3. In-session practice.
4. Debrief and coach.
5. Increase difficulty.
6. Outside practice.
7. Debrief and coach.

1. Predict others reactions and create hierarchy

From the initial sessions, Vicky had identified beliefs and assumptions that were activated in social situations. Her main assumption was that others would notice that she was anxious, that this was a sign of weakness and that she would be judged incompetent, confirming her belief that she was 'not good enough'. She identified that when she was in certain social situations others would notice her anxiety by her shaking, having sweaty palms and a wavering voice. Therefore she avoided eye contact, held tightly to her notes and would sit at the back of the room, avoiding contributions to the group. After the assumptions were identified Vicky was asked to rate each in terms of the level of affect and situational avoidance. This formed the basis of her hierarchy. For Vicky, work situations with senior staff members posed the most threat and led to greater levels of anxiety so this would feature at the top. The assumptions identified were as follows (in order of least to most anxiety provoking):

1. If someone notices I am shaking they will know I am anxious.
2. If I speak up I will say the wrong thing and then others will think I am stupid.
3. If I shake, everyone will see and they will think I'm weak and incompetent.

In practice, each of these was examined but for the purpose of this chapter we will focus on just the third assumption.

2. Develop assertive responses

In focusing on a response to the assumption that Vicky would shake and be seen as incompetent, Socratic dialogue was used to devise a response. Vicky devised the response, 'I know I sometimes shake when I'm anxious but that doesn't mean I'm incompetent'.

3–4. In-session practice, debriefing and coaching

The next step was to practice the feared consequence and assertive response in session. The therapist adopted the critical role initially, starting at the bottom of the hierarchy and swapping roles as appropriate. Following the first practice, the therapist completed debriefing and coaching. Given Vicky's fear of incompetence, it was important to handle this sensitively so she could see this as an opportunity for learning rather than highlighting failure (Padesky, 1997).

Throughout the practice, Vicky's assumptions were activated and subsequent behaviours and emotions emerged. The intensity of these emotions was measured, and Vicky noted how they varied in the context of the time she was exposed to this 'feared consequence'. Vicky was able to provide an answer to her feared consequences and the therapist-assisted exposure helped lead to increased confidence in applying the assertive responses once outside the therapeutic environment. During this task, Vicky also noted that it seemed strange to think anyone would actually say that to her, and reflected that if they did she wouldn't think much of them at all.

In cases where clients have some difficulty with the task, associated imagery can be explored to help them access memories, emotions and physical sensations.

5. Increasing difficulty

The therapist then increased the difficulty by saying that Vicky's question was not worth responding to and that it was stupid. To this, Vicky developed the further response of, 'it is exactly that, I do not want to appear stupid by not understanding you, so can you please summarize what you have just said so that I don't end up making a mistake in the future which could be a cost the company'. Vicky noted that the symptoms of anxiety could get worse but used this as a method to assertively respond.

Vicky and the therapist repeated the task with the therapist playing a more critical role to increase levels of difficulty, incorporating debriefing and coaching throughout. The difficulty of the experiment is related to the level of affect the client experiences in relation to their assumptions. For Vicky this was work colleagues being critical and persistent. In this approach it can be helpful to explore more extremely held assumptions that would place the client in greater perceived social danger than they had initially expressed. This allows the hierarchy to go beyond what was originally identified.

The process of increasing difficulty of behavioural experiments and de-briefing in relation to the hierarchy continued until Vicky reached above and beyond her initial goals.

6–7. Outside practice, debrief and coaching

Vicky then practised the above in a team meeting and noted that others nodded and agreed with her, thus disputing her predictions concerning how they would respond. Although no one told her she was stupid for asking the question she found that having a response prepared, should she need it, gave her more confidence to ask.

Assertive responses were consistently practised outside of sessions in order to generalize her skills beyond the therapy room. For example, Vicky decided that she was going to try this within a work context, and deliberately comment on the shaking. The aim of this was for Vicky to become able to recognize the variant nature of anxiety and manage the relationship she had with intrusive thoughts in social situations. It was at this point that her learning was summarized, relapse prevention was completed, and the end of therapy considered.

Creating collaborative behavioural experiments

It is often easy to use a tried and tested method on the basis that because it has worked with one client it is likely to be applicable to another. Although research has firmly established that in the treatment of anxiety disorders exposure to the feared consequence is vital, tailoring experiments to the client based on the information they provide in session is going to be more specific and effective. The formulation will help identify maintenance of the problem, activated beliefs, physical symptoms and associated emotions and the hierarchy will enable a goal gradient. Before entering any socially feared situations it is important that the client understands that the emotion they are experiencing is anxiety and, as previously stated, all emotions are transient in nature.

The assumptions associated with social anxiety disorder often refer to perceptions the client has about themselves and how others perceive them. The experience of intrusive thoughts can often play a part in the maintenance of the problem along with a confirmation bias and selective attention. This is to say that the client will be confirming their assumptions and feared consequences through the observation of how others respond to them. Assertive responses can provide an individual with a mechanism to defend themselves through either sharing or checking out if their assumptions are correct.

Outcome and follow-up

By the end of therapy Vicky was able to manage effectively her anxiety in social situations. She recognized that she often had to prepare for her worst case scenarios but this gave her strength and impetus to interact both professionally and socially, whereas in the past she would have avoided doing so.

Both models and subsequent behavioural experiments enabled her to weaken strongly held beliefs that she had developed over time and helped her understand how they were being maintained. Behavioural experiments in and out of sessions were essential in making implicational knowledge experiential, thus challenging past patterns of thoughts and behaviours.

After completion of therapy, a follow-up session was arranged. Outcome measures were completed and compared to the baseline taken at assessment. Discussion ensued about whether gains were being maintained and what aspects of therapy contributed to the change. The level of conviction in her assumption that people would notice her shaking had fallen to 5 per cent and she reported less anxiety in work situations (falling from 10/10 to 2/10), demonstrating a weakening in her old belief system but maintaining a manageable level of healthy anxiety. The relapse prevention plan was also reviewed.

Case management considerations and recommendations

Ensuring the client is able to grasp the CBT model is essential to the effectiveness of treatment. The speed at which the client understands will impact on the ability to move from conceptualization to the development of behavioural experiments and the outcome is more likely to be favourable.

In Vicky's case her identified core beliefs were, 'I'm weak/incompetent'. A key underlying assumption was, 'if I do a presentation I will shake and then others will see and judge me' and her automatic thoughts in social situations included, 'I need to get out of here'. Formulating these levels of thought allowed Vicky to see the inter-relationship between them.

Although Clark and Wells' model of social anxiety (1995) provides a structured nomothetic approach to treatment, the cognitive model of thought and emphasis placed on problem-activated assumptions provides the therapist with more scope to help a client reach their goals. The basis of standardized CBT assessment and treatment can often be over-shadowed by a need to follow a protocol to the letter. Therefore a therapist must be flexible to change as well as not forgetting the fundamental principles that informed the protocol.

Innovations in therapy

Social anxiety is conceptualized by Padesky (1997) as having coping as a key component. In her approach termed Assertive Defence of the Self™, she noted that it is crucial to learn and practice coping skills. This involved graded exposure beyond the initial goals of therapy and using this approach enabled Vicky to identify her worst case scenario, providing her with a coping strategy should it ever occur.

Summary

Social anxiety is a common and disabling problem which often goes undiagnosed and untreated. The use of a cognitive model to assess, formulate and treat social anxiety can facilitate a good outcome. The need for an individualized approach is paramount to the effectiveness of treatment and assessment should be ongoing throughout the course of treatment. Flexibility to the discovery of distal influences and affect-laden assumptions are often key to the process of recovery. Therefore it is advisable to explore new and existing models not only prior to treatment but throughout the process of intervention via supervision.

Activities

1. Familiarize yourself with physiological aspects of anxiety.
2. Role-play delivering clear psycho-education regarding social anxiety, particularly in discussing maintenance cycles.
3. Formulate a case using the Clark and Wells Model (1995).
4. Read about Assertive Defence of the Self™ and watch the video on social anxiety by Christine Padesky.
5. Consider how you could apply this model to an existing case.

Further reading and resources

Clark, D.M. and Wells, A. (1995) 'A cognitive model of social phobia', in R.G. Heimberg, M.R. Liebowitz, D.A. Hope and F.R. Schneier (eds), *Social Phobia: Diagnosis, Assessment and Treatment*. New York: Guilford Press. pp. 63–93.
This chapter provides a detailed description of the cognitive model of social anxiety, providing a useful overview of social anxiety and treatment strategies.

Padesky, C.A. (1997) 'A more effective treatment focus for social phobia', *International Cognitive Therapy Newsletter*, 11(1): 1–3.
This article provides details of the Assertive Defence of the Self™ model and its application to social anxiety.

Padesky, C.A. (2008a) *CBT for Social Anxiety* [DVD]. Huntington Beach, CA: Center for Cognitive Therapy. (Available from http://store.padesky.com/vsa.htm.)

(Continued)

(Continued)

This is the link to buy the DVD that provides a one-hour demonstration of the Assertive Defence of the Self™ approach from formulation to behavioural experiments.

Padesky, C.A. (2008b). *CBT for Social Anxiety* [Audio CD]. Huntington Beach, CA: Center for Cognitive Therapy. (Available from http://store.padesky.com/sanx.htm.)

This is a 130-minute audio recording of a workshop Padesky taught on her method with clinical demonstrations and Q & A.

PART 2.2

Case Studies: Complex Clinical Presentations

TWELVE Gail: A Case Study of Obsessive Compulsive Disorder

Blake Stobie and Simon Darnley

Learning objectives

After reading this chapter, and reflecting on and practising the key points listed at the end of it, you should be able to:

- Recognize the symptoms of OCD and differentiate this disorder from other diagnoses.
- Describe the key issues to consider when assessing and formulating clients with OCD.
- Describe some of the strategies typically adopted in CBT for OCD.
- Recognize some of the challenges commonly encountered when working with OCD and know how to respond to them.

Obsessive compulsive disorder

Obsessive compulsive disorder (OCD) is characterized by obsessions (repetitive thoughts), compulsions (repetitive mental or physical acts such as checking, washing, ruminating, etc.) or both, which are time-consuming and/or distressing. Obsessions have been defined as repetitive and intrusive thoughts, urges, impulses or doubts, which usually cause distress to the person having them. Compulsions are the ritualistic, deliberate behaviours that people with OCD engage in as a response to their beliefs about the content or presence of the obsessional thoughts.

OCD now sits within its own chapter in the *Diagnostic and Statistical Manual of Mental Disorders* (APA, 2013). This includes obsessive-compulsive along with other disorders which have been hypothesized to be related to OCD, including hoarding, excoriation, substance or medication-induced OCD, OCD due to a medical condition, and trichotillomania. The level of insight of people with OCD can now be specified by clinicians as good/fair, poor, or absent/delusional, in place of the 'with poor insight' specifier in earlier editions of the DSM. A 'tic related' specifier may now also be included for people who have current or past co-morbid tic disorders.

Summary of OCD theory

According to contemporary cognitive models of OCD, everyone experiences intrusive thoughts from time to time. Formulation models of OCD emphasize the importance of the idiosyncratic appraisals of these intrusions and their links to behaviour and emotion. Salkovskis (1999), for example, points to the role of beliefs about responsibility, suggesting that some OCD sufferers believe that unless they take action to avoid a negative intrusive thought coming true they will be responsible, causing great distress. The repeated misinterpretation of the significance of the intrusive thoughts is maintained by individuals engaging in compulsive behaviours to try to resist, block, or neutralize the obsessive thoughts (Wilhelm and Steketee, 2006).

Case example

Gail is a 53-year-old widowed white British woman who lives on her own and works as an administrator. Gail was referred by her GP for a set of CBT sessions to treat her long-standing OCD (centring on contamination and washing compulsions), which had not responded to previous psychological or pharmacological treatments.

Personal and medical history

Formative experiences

Gail had experienced several traumatic events during her childhood. As the eldest of five children she assumed a parental role with some of her younger siblings. Her father was an alcoholic who would sometimes hit her mother. Gail went through a phase of experiencing transient illnesses which prevented her from attending school regularly. She was bullied by her classmates for being studious.

Gail left school at the age of 17 and went straight into clerical work. She married Eugene, a Ukranian who had settled in the United Kingdom, when they were both aged 20. She remained married to her husband until his death aged 47 from cancer. The couple enjoyed a supportive marriage but were unable to have children. Gail's employment history was stable and continuous until six months prior to her referral to our clinic, when her OCD worsened to the point that she was no longer able to work.

Onset and development of OCD

Gail stated that she first became aware of the fact that she was engaging in excessive compulsions when she was 22. Shortly before this she had experienced a miscarriage. The OCD started with constant intrusive thoughts that she might have inadvertently done something which could have caused the miscarriage. Although she stated that she had always been somewhat of a perfectionist and 'house proud', she began to worry more and more about germs, fearing they may cause her to become ill, and began cleaning compulsively for several hours each day. This left her frequently feeling exhausted.

The Chernobyl disaster occurred when she was 25, affecting Eugene's family in Ukraine. Gail started to worry that she or Eugene would become contaminated by atmospheric radiation. These concerns led her to engage in lengthy de-contamination rituals. On returning from work she would strip off all her clothes in the hallway of her home and place them in a bin liner. She would then put fresh plastic covers over her feet, walk straight to the shower and spend hours showering. This was followed by a further hour spent cleaning the shower, bathroom and taps. She insisted that Eugene perform the same rituals and this often led to arguments between the couple. However, he would generally comply with Gail's requests, unless she went away visiting her family. Later Gail began to worry that she could pass radiation poisoning on to other people.

Eugene became ill with cancer aged 43, and died four years later. Despite her close relationship with her husband, Gail's fear of radiation poisoning prevented her from touching or physically comforting her husband whilst he was undergoing radiotherapy. She managed to overcome these fears shortly before his death and was able to touch him and help make him more comfortable in bed. However, her cleaning compulsions increased further.

Past issues and treatments

Gail reported that she had experienced a brief episode of anorexia between the ages of 16 and 17. She had experienced past episodes of health anxiety (predominantly worrying that she might have cancer) in her 20s and 30s which had largely abated. In terms of past psychological treatments, she had received a set of counselling sessions through her GP surgery when she was 44, but this was principally focused on helping her deal with Eugene's cancer diagnosis. Her counsellor admitted that she did not know much about OCD, but advised her to snap an elastic band on her wrist every time she experienced a distressing thought (we do not advise this!). Gail paid for four private hypnotherapy sessions when she was 51. She found the sessions relaxing and was encouraged by the therapist to label her thoughts as OCD when she got them, and to imagine putting them in a box and throwing the box in the sea.

Medical history and medication

Gail had been prescribed propranolol and a benzodiazepine by her GP, which she took as required whenever her obsessions flared up. When she was 28 she was referred to a psychiatrist who had (mis-)diagnosed her with bipolar disorder with psychotic features, possibly because she was staying awake for most of the night cleaning, in response to unusual beliefs held with high conviction ('Radiation is everywhere and is going to contaminate me'). He prescribed antipsychotic medication which she found helpful in reducing her anxiety but not the obsessional thoughts or compulsions. She discontinued this medication because of side-effects.

Gail's physical health had always been excellent, despite her going through phases of worrying compulsively that she might have cancer. Her mother's aunt had had cancer and had come to live with the family for a year before dying. Gail stated that she was not traumatized by this, but it had obviously made an impression on her.

Review of Gail's past psychological and medication treatments

Although Gail's referral stated that she had not responded to previous pharmacological or psychological treatments, reviewing these in the assessment suggested that she may not have been offered optimal treatments, which can unfortunately occur in OCD (Stobie et al., 2007). We would have liked Gail to have had CBT in the past, involving the regular setting of homework, therapist-assisted exposure or behavioural experiments, and a focus on the OCD. We would not encourage the use of elastic bands due to the ineffectiveness of this technique (Foa, 2010), and the difficulty with labelling thoughts as OCD is that this can easily become a ritual in its own right. Randomized controlled trials have not been published on the use of hypnosis in OCD (Foa, 2010), and hypnosis is not recommended in the NICE guidelines (NICE, 2005). The medications which Gail had been offered were also inconsistent with best treatment. NICE (2005) guidelines suggest a selective serotonin reuptake inhibitor (SSRI), starting on a low dose and building up, then switching to a different SSRI if insufficient response, and augmenting with antipsychotic medication if still no response (although the side-effects and relapse rates on discontinuation mean that these medications are problematic). Diazepam and other benzodiazepines are addictive, can interfere with the process of therapy, and do not address the problem.

Gail's diagnosis

At assessment, Gail was diagnosed with OCD. It was also noted that she presented with panic attacks and some features of obsessional personality, as well as hoarding behaviours, and was grieving over the death of her husband. Panic disorder was ruled out as a diagnosis as the panic attacks were occurring in response to obsessional triggers (e.g. passing a hospital), rather than unexpectedly in situations not connected to her obsessional concerns.

Questionnaires and Gail's pre-treatment scores

The Yale Brown Obsessive Compulsive Scale (YBOCS; Goodman et al., 1989) is conventionally cited in research papers on OCD. However, clinicians are expected to have amassed a great deal of experience in assessing people with OCD to use this measure. The Padua Inventory (Sanovio, 1988) and Obsessive Compulsive Inventory (OCI; Foa et al., 1998) are quicker and easier to administer than the YBOCS, and are client rather than therapist administered questionnaires. Gail's YBOCS score at assessment was 32/40 (Extreme), and her OCI total score was 116.

Case formulation

Once confident that a diagnosis of OCD is warranted, a clinician can work collaboratively with the client to dissect a recent example of the OCD, in order to identify the specific beliefs and behaviours which maintain and reinforce it. The cognitive model of OCD developed by Salkovskis (1999) was used to formulate Gail's OCD with her. Figure 12.1, later in this chapter, outlines the formulation which was derived with Gail, and specific elements of the formulation are discussed below.

Early life events, underlying assumptions and critical incidents

The assessment revealed a number of factors from Gail's childhood which may have contributed to the development of her OCD, including her father's violence and bullying at school. Many of the clients seen at our clinic describe backgrounds involving parental violence and school bullying, but not all children who have experienced parental violence or bullying go on to develop OCD. The main focus of this model is on helping clients to understand the elements that are maintaining the problem in the present, rather than what might have caused it in the past. In Gail's case, we included this information because it was helpful in explaining: (1) why she has a tendency to take on responsibility for herself and people around her; and (2) why she believes herself to be more vulnerable than other people.

Specific situation

Wherever possible, it is preferable to base a formulation on an actual incident rather than what generally happens when the client gets caught up in the problem. Although Gail initially found it hard to think of a specific incident, with some prompting she was able to recall a recent flight that she had had to take, which was both memorable but also representative of her concerns. The funnelling question style, starting with open questions and moving to specific questions with regular recaps, helped to elicit this information.

Intrusive thoughts

Discussion of intrusions during a formulation should highlight the idea of intrusions being unplanned/uncontrollable thoughts, images, urges or doubts rather than unwanted mental events. Intrusions can be negative but also positive or neutral and it can be helpful to ask clients to think of examples of each (e.g. 'remembering holiday'; 'must remember to post that letter'). Framing intrusions as part of having an imagination, noting that 100 per cent of people get intrusions (including really unpleasant 'negative' intrusions) because they are part of the imagination and cannot be censored, is a really helpful way of starting the work of normalizing intrusions and helping clients to see that the thoughts are: (1) not the problem; and (2) do not need to be acted on.

The meaning attached to the intrusions

Therapists sometimes struggle to differentiate the intrusions from their meaning. We would suggest that prefacing the meaning with, 'Now I've had this intrusive thought it means...' can help. We also suggest that a meaning may contain three components which differentiate it from the thought itself: firstly, the belief that the thought is real and the terrible outcome implicit in the thought will happen; secondly, that once the thought has occurred to the person it is their responsibility to react to it (or similarly, that it would be irresponsible to not react to it); and thirdly, that the person therefore needs to act in some way. This last component may not be necessary and is an implicit part of the first component, but can be helpful to include as it then explains the link to the subsequent safety-seeking behaviours.

Overt and covert safety-seeking behaviours and linking these back to the meaning

A good formulation should both unfold as a narrative (this causes that, for understandable reasons you then did that, which was intended to do x, but had the consequence of y), and should also answer the question 'So what?' In Gail's formulation (see Figure 12.1), the main point was that her safety-seeking behaviours, whilst intended to keep her and other people safe from harm, were actually exacerbating her unhelpful beliefs that she would die a painful death from radiation, and that she was able to and should take actions to prevent this from occurring.

One way that therapists can help their clients to see the impact of their safety-seeking behaviours on the meanings they attach to their intrusions is by asking them, 'What would happen if you were to have these intrusive thoughts and attach 0 per cent significance to these meanings?' (aiming for 'Life would be much better!'), and then 'Why do you continue to believe these meanings at (e.g.) 70 to 95 per cent?'. The answer which clients usually provide is that it is due to their childhoods, or personalities. Therapists can acknowledge that this is probably true, but may not be the whole answer. Asking clients, 'If you knew beyond the shadow of a doubt that you aren't at risk of radiation poisoning, would you need to avoid metal objects?', followed by 'So what does the fact that you are avoiding metal objects *seem* to imply about the possibility that they are dangerous and contaminated? (or that you are able to prevent yourself being contaminated) – does doing this make this seem more or less real?', can be helpful here.

Problems with formulation which are sometimes encountered by therapists when working with clients with OCD

Other problems which therapists sometimes encounter when formulating OCD include: finding it difficult to know what information to include and

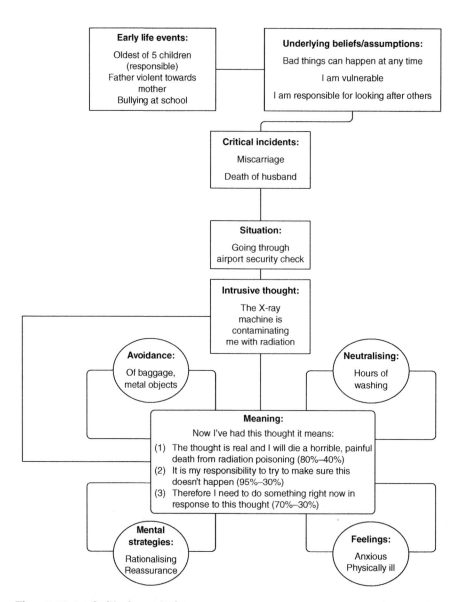

Figure 12.1   Gail's formulation

exclude (here a quick 'test run' though the example before writing it down can help); drawing up a formulation which makes perfect sense to the therapist but not the client (ask the client to explain the formulation back to test understanding); not asking the client to write down the formulation and keep it in their notes (clients sometimes ask to photograph the formulation using their phones; we prefer them to write it down to consolidate it); constantly revising the formulation or doing many formulations (one good formulation with homework to relate it to other examples is usually sufficient).

Other approaches to formulation

Where a therapist has been unable to access a client's cognitions despite significant attempts to do so (perhaps because they have had the OCD for so long that they have forgotten the original reasons for performing the rituals), or where responsibility for harm to self or others is not a feature of their OCD, and where the client is motivated very strongly to reduce their anxiety levels or would find it difficult to understand the vicious flower formulation described above, clinicians may want to consider using an exposure therapy rationale for tackling the problem. Here three graphs to illustrate the effect of avoidance/checking, exposure without response prevention, and exposure with response prevention can help clients to understand how to do effective exposure (and perhaps why it might not have worked in the past). Where a cognitive model is appropriate but clinicians would prefer not to use the Salkovskis (1999) vicious flower model described above, Wilhelm and Steketee (2006) outline a different cognitive model. The advantage of this model is that it highlights how mood can impact across different levels (e.g. on intrusions). A limitation (in our opinion) is the failure to place interpretations centrally in the model as the main area which clinicians should be aiming to help their clients change.

Problem list and goals

We always encourage our clients to bring as many goals as possible. This makes homework setting much easier and gives a clearer idea of how the problem is affecting that particular individual. One way of approaching this task is to ask clients to group their goals into problem areas (e.g. eating, travelling on public transport, going to the dentist, etc). The client can then list the difficulties which they experience in each area before then turning these problems into goals which they would like to achieve. It is better to frame goals positively (e.g. 'go out once a day') than negatively (e.g. 'stop checking'). We ask clients to construct SMART goals (specific, measurable, achievable, realistic goals, with a time scale). It can also be helpful to ask clients to frame things in terms of behaviours/doing. For example, if their goal was to be less anxious, we would ask 'what would you be doing differently if you were less anxious?'

Gail brought four sheets of typed goals to the therapy session. An example of one of her goals is listed in Table 12.1 for illustration.

Course of therapy

The formulation which we derived with Gail contained several implications for treatment. Moving down through the formulation, we wanted

Table 12.1 An example from Gail's goal sheets

Main problem area	Specific example of where this fear interferes with my life	Goals	Difficulty rating (0 = no problem, 10 = extremely difficult)
Radiation contamination concerns	Avoiding wearing different clothes and throwing clothes away because I think that they might have been contaminated	Short: Bring some clothes to the therapy sessions	4
		Medium: To mix clothes and wear different clothes for a whole day without rituals	6
		To keep my clothes in the wardrobe indefinitely (not throwing them away)	
		To buy new clothes if needed (a minimum of one item per month) from anywhere including 'contaminated' shops	
		Long: To treat and wear all clothes the same at all times	7

Gail to put herself in more situations which would trigger intrusions, to become more comfortable with intrusive thoughts, and to shift the meanings which she attached to these thoughts (i.e. to not overestimate the likelihood that awful things would happen because she had thought about them, to believe that it was not her responsibility to act even if she had had the thoughts or been in a difficult situation, and to become less reactive on having the thoughts).

Once we had established a clear and comprehensive goal list, we began an intermediate phase of therapist-assisted work. We went with Gail and stood outside the scanning department next to our clinic. We also went and sat in the dental department opposite our clinic, next to a door with a 'Danger: Radiation' sign on it. We always fed back the results from these experiments into what Gail had learnt about the meaning she was attaching to her thoughts (not whether her anxiety went up or down!). We built on the success of this work by encouraging Gail to devise and carry out behavioural experiments on her own, to test out her unhelpful beliefs, and to discover new information concerning her responsibility to act following thoughts of harm. Regular homework setting and review, review of experiments, therapist modelling, discussion techniques including responsibility pie charts and 'Theory A/B', and construction of a blueprint were all carried out as routine parts of treatment.

Outcome

Gail made excellent progress over the course of the therapy sessions, largely due to the exceptional effort which she put into between-session work. By the end of the therapy sessions her YBOCS had reduced from 32/40 (Extreme) to 12/40 (Mild), and her OCI total had dropped from 116 to 28. She had managed to transform her home, and was using every room. She was travelling on public transport, had gone to the dentist, taken her cat to the vet, and was managing almost all of the goals which she had set for herself.

Obstacles and reflections

Home visits are a part of our therapy sessions for people whose OCD affects their domestic environment. These visits with Gail were useful in identifying and working on several aspects of her home life which were being affected by the OCD. Many of these related to areas which she perceived to be contaminated. For example, she had stopped going into the room where she stored her suitcases as these felt contaminated by X-ray radiation from a flight she had taken. Awareness of this enabled us (with Gail's consent) to help her 'cross-contaminate' her home with the intention of reducing all areas to the same level of contamination (e.g. putting 'contaminated' suitcases on her bed).

During our first home visit, we noticed a number of bottles scattered throughout Gail's home, all of which were filled with a yellow liquid. We asked Gail about the bottles and she informed us that they were bottles of Ukranian brandy from her in-laws. Gail was blushing furiously when she said this though, which made us curious. Gently asking her about this at the next session led to an important discovery: the 'Ukranian brandy' was actually urine which Gail had been hoarding in order to prevent it causing harm to other people. Gail obviously felt embarrassed. However, if we had not done the home visit (and asked her directly about the bottles) we would never have known about this compulsion, and it is possible that it would have continued to interfere with her life. Fortunately Gail was able to see that this behaviour was more compatible with the view of the problem as a 'harm by radiation' problem, than a 'worrying excessively' problem, and this helped her to throw out the contents of all of the bottles and stop hoarding her urine.

Just as we were nearing the end of the therapy sessions disaster struck – or so we thought! Alexander Litvinenko was allegedly murdered by radiation poisoning in London, with several newspaper reports highlighting areas of London in which a trail of radiation had been left by his killers. We were very concerned that Gail's progress would be impeded by this news. However, this turned out not to be the case: Gail had managed to reach a point where even this test did not change her new approach of getting on with her life despite occasional thoughts or reports of radiation and the harm it causes.

Commonly encountered problems in assessing clients with OCD

As a motivated and articulate client Gail was quite straightforward to assess. Nonetheless, in providing supervision to colleagues we have noticed difficulties which can sometimes arise, and so have listed these below along with some suggestions of how to address them. Waller's (2009) excellent article on therapist drift is recommended reading here.

Relational aspects of working with OCD: structure

Some clients believe that unless they tell their therapist in detail about every ritual and the thoughts underpinning it their therapy will be ineffective. Therapists sometimes share similar beliefs, or may believe that it is disrespectful to interrupt clients. This can lead to overly long, unstructured assessments which fail to identify important issues: therapist and client can end up being overwhelmed by detail at the cost of starting the therapy sessions and lose focus on what needs to be worked on.

In the assessment with Gail, giving her a clear time parameter for the assessments, pre-empting the issue of interruptions by stating that we might do this to keep the assessment focused, and following a structured set of questions helped to avoid this problem.

Relational aspects of working with OCD: providing assurance versus reassurance, provision of subtle reassurance

Getting the right balance between providing useful information/psycho-education to clients (some of whom may genuinely have lost sight of what a 'normal' amount of washing is, or may not know about intrusive thoughts) and getting tangled up in reassurance is a common difficulty faced by therapists. Skilful therapists will provide assurance (i.e. useful and needed information to their clients for the first time) but not reassurance (repeating the same information in response to the client's doubts). Clients sometimes gain indirect reassurance from a therapist's body language or facial expressions. If a therapist hypothesizes that a client is seeking reassurance, a good way of addressing this can be to ask the client directly and to discuss how this behaviour might fit into the formulation. Identifying reassurance seeking early on can make it easier to tackle.

Relational aspects of working with OCD: avoiding emotion (clients and therapists) or specific thoughts

Clients are sometimes reluctant to disclose the content of their thoughts (often because of shame or fear of repercussions such as being jailed). In an attempt to be kind, therapists sometimes agree not to discuss the specifics of particular fears, but to formulate them in general terms (e.g. 'worrying scary thoughts'). Unfortunately, in our experience, where the content of thoughts is not disclosed, prognosis is generally poor.

Differentiating assessment from treatment sessions

Whilst the assessment may mirror the treatment process in several ways it is important to inform the person that it is not therapy; specifically, therapy will be a more active process than the therapist just asking questions and the client providing information. With Gail, setting an agenda for the assessment, outlining its purpose and explaining how it differs from therapy was helpful in managing her expectations for the assessment and future sessions. This was particularly important given Gail's previous experience of less structured counselling.

Note-taking

Some therapists are reluctant to take notes during assessment and therapy sessions due to the belief that it prevents them from concentrating or is disrespectful. We would argue that note-taking throughout sessions is respectful of the other person's information and likely to lead to more accurate retention and less misinterpretation.

Normalizing

Therapists sometimes become so overwhelmed by the conflicting tasks of structuring the assessment and deciding which information to pursue and which to set to one side, that they struggle to normalize and empathize during the assessment (or go in the other direction and empathize excessively at the cost of structuring the session and finding out information).

Throughout the assessment with Gail we conveyed that OCD makes sense, and given her beliefs her behaviour was logical and understandable. In order to do this we first had to understand her chain of thinking and her beliefs.

Assessing and managing risk

The NICE (2005) guidelines provide clear recommendations for assessing risk associated with OCD. NICE (2005) suggests that if the health care professional is uncertain about the risks associated with intrusive sexual, aggressive or death-related thoughts that they should consult a professional with specific expertise on the assessment and management of OCD. They then go on to report that 'these themes are common in people with OCD at any age, and are often misinterpreted as indicating risk'. It is of course also important to remember that all of us have intrusive thoughts and that the content of these is frequently sexual, violent or taboo.

Veale et al.'s (2009) paper on the subject should be referenced for more specific details on how to distinguish between obsessional fears of harm versus actual harm (sexual or violent) or when assessing young people. Veale et al. (2009) differentiate primary risk (the risk arising directly from an obsession; that is, that a person will act on their obsessions) and secondary risk (the unintended consequences of acting on compulsions and urges to avoid anxiety-provoking situations). In true OCD, primary risk should not be the focus of risk assessment, as people are fearful of their thoughts and would not act on them. However, secondary risks are often associated with OCD. In Gail's case, her eating was disordered as a consequence of her contamination concerns (she was avoiding eating certain foods in case these were contaminated). Her self-care was also affected by the OCD.

Using disorder-specific questionnaires

General measures of mood are not suited to detecting OCD symptoms and clinicians are advised to use at least one disorder-specific measure. The Padua Inventory and Obsessive Compulsive Inventory are self-rated measures which are relatively easy to score and interpret.

Diagnosis and differential diagnosis

The problems with the reliability and validity of diagnoses, all-or-nothing thinking underpinning diagnoses rather than a continuum-based conceptualization, medicalization and pathologizing, and the failure of diagnoses to consider contextual and environmental factors, are often listed as reasons for avoidance of diagnostic labelling by psychological therapists. Yet for all of the (not insignificant) problems surrounding diagnosis, it underpins cognitive behavioural treatments as well as clinicians' understanding of the key cognitive factors which maintain a problem, and selection of appropriate treatments. The wrong diagnosis will result in inappropriate treatment. We encourage clinicians to make provisional diagnoses based on thorough assessments, disorder-relevant questionnaires, and careful consideration of differential diagnoses. Checking whether and which diagnostic criteria a person with OCD meets (and being explicit about differential diagnoses) can help clinicians be confident that they are offering the right treatment for the right issue, before moving on to a comprehensive psychological formulation.

Summary and key points that can form the basis of therapist practice tasks

✓ It is worth checking exactly what clients have done in previous treatments, in order to assess whether these treatments have been appropriate and if so what prevented gains from being made or maintained.
✓ Wherever possible, base a formulation on a specific incident rather than a composite of incidents.
✓ Knowing about intrusive thoughts and being able to educate clients about them is a vital step in laying a solid foundation for therapy.
✓ In the Salkovskis (1999) cognitive formulation of OCD, the meaning which clients attach to thoughts is what treatment aims to change, and this meaning can often be differentiated from the thoughts by three strands: (1) the fact I have had these thoughts means that they are real and harm will occur; (2) it is down to me to do something about it (responsibility); and therefore (3) I have to do something.
✓ Good formulations unfold as narratives and also have clear implications attached to them as to how the problem can and should be overcome.
✓ Helping clients derive a long list of clear and specific goals can make the process of therapy much easier for client and clinician.
✓ Structuring and directing the flow of sessions, being mindful of explicit and subtle reassurance-seeking in sessions, helping clients disclose the specific content of thoughts, normalizing, note-taking, differentiating assessment from treatment, considering diagnostic and differential diagnostic issues, reading further on risk assessment in OCD and therapist drift, and using disorder-specific questionnaires are all helpful strategies which can help clinicians to assess and treat clients with OCD.

We are grateful to Gail for helping us outline the key issues in engagement, assessment, formulation and goal setting which we believe should occur when working with people with OCD, and to Paul Salkovskis for developing such a clinically useful roadmap in the form of his formulation. Marrying it to the experiences and beliefs of the people we work with builds a strong foundation for effective, robust CBT with well-engaged clients.

Further reading

Clinicians seeking to read more about the Salkovskis 'vicious flower' model of OCD treatment are directed to Salkovskis (1999) and Salkovskis et al. (1998). Wilhelm and Steketee (2006) provide an overview of treatment for OCD for clinicians interested in a slightly different cognitive model. Veale et al. (2009) provide a comprehensive guide to assessing risk in OCD. Clinicians working with children and young people with OCD are referred to Waite and Williams (2009). For relatives of people with OCD, a good book to recommend is 'Loving someone with OCD' by Landsman, Rupertus and Pedrick (2005). Clients with OCD may find Veale and Willson (2009) helpful.

THIRTEEN Michael: A Case Study of Post-traumatic Stress Disorder

Kerry Young and Nick Grey

Learning objectives

After reading this chapter and completing the activities at the end of it you should be able to:

- Recognize post-traumatic stress disorder (PTSD) and distinguish it from other related disorders.
- Understand Ehlers and Clark's (2000) Cognitive Model of PTSD and the advantages of using it as a guide to formulation and therapy.
- Feel confident about the information you need to gather at assessment.
- Plan an evidence-based cognitive behavioural intervention for PTSD.

Introduction

There is a range of outcomes following life-threatening or horrific traumatic experiences. Most people will experience some intrusive thoughts and images of the event(s) in the days and weeks that follow. In time, for most people these symptoms subside. For a proportion of people these intrusions and other associated symptoms persist and become chronic, and they may formally meet diagnostic criteria for post-traumatic stress disorder (PTSD).

This chapter will first outline the formal diagnostic criteria and provide a cognitive model to understand chronic adult PTSD. It aims to address: (1) clinical guidance for assessment and diagnosis of PTSD; and (2) individualized formulations, or 'personal models' of PTSD.

We will also briefly describe how these models translate into treatment approaches, give an outline example of such a treatment, and consider how the formulation and treatment may be 'flexed' in more complicated cases.

Theoretical and research basis for therapy

Diagnosis, phenomenology and epidemiology of PTSD

Lifetime prevalence rates of PTSD in Western community samples are about 5–10 per cent (Kessler et al., 1995). Interpersonal events such as rape and torture have higher rates of PTSD than accidents or natural disasters (Kessler et al., 1995). Co-morbidity is the rule rather than exception, with the most common co-morbid diagnoses being affective disorders (e.g. depression), substance-use disorders, and other anxiety disorders (e.g. panic disorder).

The two diagnostic systems, DSM and ICD, differ slightly in their diagnostic criteria for PTSD and both have recently been refined (APA, 2013). The proposed diagnosis of PTSD for ICD-11 looks like it will probably be the more parsimonious and clinically useful (World Health Organization, in preparation). This states that PTSD follows exposure to an extremely threatening or horrific event or series of events and consists of three elements:

1. **Re-experiencing**: vivid intrusive memories, flashbacks or nightmares that involve re-experiencing of the traumatic event in the present, accompanied by fear or horror.
2. **Avoidance**: marked internal avoidance of thoughts and memories or external avoidance of activities or situations reminiscent of the traumatic event(s).
3. **Hyperarousal**: a state of perceived current threat in the form of hypervigilance or an enhanced startle reaction.

The symptoms must also last for several weeks and interfere with normal functioning. More severe presentations within ICD-11 are likely to be accounted for with a new diagnosis of 'Complex PTSD'.

A cognitive model of PTSD

Ehlers and Clark's (2000) model offers clear guidelines for therapy and has increasing empirical support with adults in efficacy studies/randomized controlled trials (Ehlers et al., 2003; Ehlers et al., 2005; Ehlers et al., in press) and effectiveness studies in routine care (Gillespie et al., 2002; Duffy et al., 2007; Ehlers et al., 2013).

Ehlers and Clark (2000) noted that people with PTSD typically experience high levels of anxiety. Anxiety is generally associated with *future* threat in other disorders. However, in PTSD, people experience high levels of anxiety in response to unwanted memories of the *past*. Accordingly, they proposed that PTSD becomes persistent when traumatic information is processed in a way that leads to a sense of serious *current* threat. This can be a physical threat (e.g. 'I'm going to die') and/or a psychological threat to one's view of oneself (e.g. 'I've let myself down', 'Nobody cares'.) Due to high levels of arousal at the time of the trauma, the trauma memory is poorly elaborated, fragmented, and not well integrated with other autobiographical memories. Because of this, it can be unintentionally triggered by a wide range of low-level cues. In particular, there is no 'time-code' on the memory that tells the individual that the event occurred in the past. Thus, when the memory intrudes, it feels as if the event is actually happening again to some degree.

The persistence of the sense of current threat, and hence PTSD, arises from not only the nature of the trauma memory but also from the negative interpretations of the symptoms experienced (e.g. 'I'm going mad'), the event itself (e.g. 'It's my fault'), and the sequelae (e.g. 'I should have got over it by now'). Change in these appraisals and the nature of the trauma memory is prevented by a variety of cognitive and behavioural strategies. These are: avoiding thoughts and feelings, places or other reminders of the event; suppression of intrusive memories; rumination about certain aspects of the event or its sequelae; and other avoidant/numbing strategies such as alcohol and drug use (see Figure 13.1).

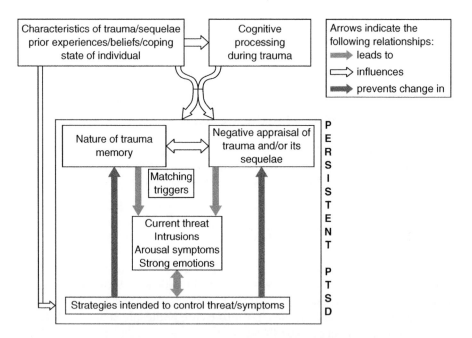

Figure 13.1   Cognitive model of PTSD (Ehlers and Clark, 2000)

Reprinted from Ehlers and Clark (2000) with permission from Elsevier

Cognitive therapy for PTSD

The aim of treatment derived from Ehlers and Clark (2000) is therefore threefold:

1. To reduce re-experiencing by elaboration of the trauma memory, discrimination of triggers, and integration of the memory within existing autobiographical memory.
2. To address the negative appraisals of the event and its sequelae.
3. To change the avoidant/numbing strategies that prevent processing of the memory and reassessment of appraisals.

A wide range of both general and PTSD-specific cognitive behavioural interventions can be used to achieve such changes (Ehlers and Clark, 2000; Ehlers et al., 2005, in press).

To help address the nature of the trauma memory, the most commonly used strategy is that of 'reliving' the event; imagining and describing the event in full detail with eyes closed, speaking in the present tense. This is not used in order to allow habituation to any fear associated with the trauma memory, but in order to identify the main cognitive themes activated during and after the event(s). These are typically accessed at the most emotional, 'worst', moments of the traumatic experience ('hotspots'; Foa and Rothbaum, 1998). The cognitive themes in these hotspots are as likely to be related to psychological threat as they are to physical threat (Holmes et al., 2005; Grey and Holmes, 2008). These cognitive themes can then be addressed with many cognitive therapy strategies. Guided discovery leads to 'new' information or syntheses such as, 'It wasn't my fault', which can then be brought to mind while reliving again each hotspot in order to 'update' the traumatic memory (Ehlers and Clark, 2000; Grey et al., 2002; Ehlers et al., in press). This updating can be achieved by inserting words or phrases or by using mental imagery. Thus, there is a direct interweaving of reliving and cognitive restructuring rather than their being applied purely sequentially. Other strategies used to address the nature of the trauma memory include using written narratives, and behavioural experiments with stimuli that trigger the trauma memory. These experiments allow stimulus discrimination of neutral stimuli that have become sensory triggers for the memory, such as a particular smell or sound that was present at the time of the trauma. Further experiments will also typically include revisiting the site of the trauma if it is possible and safe to do so.

For changes in the nature of the trauma memory to occur, treatment must provide a safe environment for the client. Therapists should allow up to 90 minutes for sessions so that there is enough time for clients to engage fully with the traumatic material. Ehlers and Clark's studies typically allow 12 sessions on a weekly basis, followed by three 'booster' sessions on a monthly basis. The total amount of reliving across all sessions is about

90 minutes. Compared to other published treatment trials there are very low (<5 per cent) dropout rates in the treatment studies from Ehlers and Clark's group. For full detailed descriptions of these treatment strategies see Ehlers et al. (in press), and for a single chapter introduction see Grey (2007).

Case summary and main presenting problem

Michael was a 24-year-old student studying for a postgraduate qualification in engineering. Six months prior to the referral, he was mugged at knifepoint and assaulted by a group of teenage boys. Michael's details are provided in the box below:

Michael's current circumstances and relevant background

Current circumstances

- Walking home from a party late at night, moderately drunk.
- Afterwards, too scared to leave student house but, under pressure to attend college, forced himself to go to lectures.
- Trouble sleeping and concentrating and fell behind with his work.
- After meeting student counsellor, arranged to suspend his studies for the rest of the academic year.
- Returned home to live with parents.
- GP referred him to your service.
- Michael not comfortable living back with his parents.

Background

- Youngest of three boys, mother is a teacher, father retired from the police.
- Brothers live with partners in different parts of the country.
- No past psychiatric history – happy and uneventful childhood.
- Got on well with brothers but felt that he was trying to live up to their success at school and university.
- Closer to his mother than father but family not one in which people talked 'about feelings and stuff'.
- Father always drank heavily – when drunk, was liable to become verbally abusive. Whole family scared of father.
- No history of substance misuse but had started drinking heavily at night to help him sleep.
- Michael has a group of good friends at university and several school friends lived near his parents.

Case assessment

It is sensible to allow at least 90 minutes for an assessment of PTSD as it is uncertain in how much detail the person will be able to describe the traumatic event(s) and how distressing it will be. Thus, it may be necessary to have more than one assessment session.

The therapist needs to acknowledge the unpleasantness of emotional memories entering the person's mind during assessment and to be able to empathize with the person, while still managing the assessment process. In particular, it can be reassuring for people to know that they will not have to go into details any more than they feel comfortable with in the first appointment.

Key assessment issues

Establishing the diagnosis of PTSD

In establishing the diagnosis of PTSD, there are two key questions clinicians must address:

1. What actually is the traumatic event?
2. Is there a match between the re-experiencing symptoms and the event?

A structured clinical interview is probably the nearest thing that there is to a 'gold standard' for assessment. In this respect, the Clinician Administered PTSD Scale (CAPS; Blake et al., 1990), which is used extensively in current PTSD research, is recommended. The CAPS covers the diagnostic criteria, with helpful follow-up questions and qualifiers to establish both frequency and severity of symptoms, and further associated features such as guilt and dissociation. This can be obtained free of charge from the US Department of Veteran Affairs (www.ptsd.va.gov; www.ptsd.va.gov/professional/assessment/adult-int/caps.asp).

1. What actually is the traumatic event?

People talk colloquially about events in their life being 'traumatic', such as a relationship break-up and losing employment. However, we should not assume that the casual use of this term means that the event could possibly lead to PTSD. Good questions to ask about the traumatic event are, 'What was the worst event that occurred? How did you feel during it? Did you fear that you or someone else might die?'

2. Is there a match between the re-experiencing symptoms and the event?

A core feature of PTSD is the presence of re-experiencing symptoms of the event(s). A helpful way to think about these symptoms is to imagine that a multi-sensory recording has been made during the traumatic event. When any part of this 'recording' currently intrudes into the person's mind, either during the day or at night, then it is a re-experiencing symptom. Typically these intrusions are in the form of visual mental images but can also occur in other sensory modalities (e.g. the sound of screeching brakes, the physical impact of an assault, the smell of an assailant, the taste of blood) (Hackmann et al., 2004). The re-experiencing symptoms that occur during the day take two forms – vivid intrusive memories of the trauma and flash-backs to the trauma. Both represent 'clips' (varying in length from a split second moment to a minute or more) of the aforementioned 'recording' of the traumatic event. Both also disrupt ongoing mental/physical activity while they intrude. However, one feature that distinguishes flashbacks from other autobiographical memories is that they are experienced as happening 'now' rather than as a memory in the past (Ehlers and Clark, 2000; Hackmann et al., 2004). The degree of 'nowness' of intrusive memories is a good predictor of chronic PTSD (Michael et al., 2005).

Clinically there is also a need to differentiate intrusions of (aspects of) the traumatic memory itself from rumination about the event(s) or the sequelae of the event(s). Also, clinicians should not assume that intrusions indicate PTSD, as intrusive memories occur in other disorders such as depression (Reynolds and Brewin, 1999) and across many, if not all, disorders. Finally, there is a need to clarify that the trauma memories are qualitatively different to normal everyday memories – that they constitute intrusive 'reliving' or 're-experiencing' rather than 'remembering'.

Good questions to ask about re-experiencing symptoms include, 'What is it that comes back into your mind? What memories/images do you have? Do they feel different to your normal everyday memories? If so, in what way? Do they feel more real or "now"?' and 'From what part of the event do these memories/images come?'

Establishing that a trauma-focused therapy is indicated

Even if the person has PTSD, this may not be their main problem and they may not be best helped with a trauma-focused therapy. Some indicators of when not to provide a trauma-focused therapy as a first step are:

1. When there are issues of immediate risk that need addressing, such as the risk of self-harm or suicide, or when the person is still at risk of further trauma (as might be the case in domestic violence).

2. If the person has impaired information processing: CBT in general, and trauma-focused CBT (TF-CBT) in particular, requires people to be able to process information and be able to attend and to concentrate in a session. If the person attends sessions intoxicated and/or is misusing alcohol or other substances between sessions then this will be impaired. Similarly people who are very depressed may be unable to engage in trauma-focused work and would be better helped initially by focusing on the low mood.

3. If the main preoccupation is with ongoing social or physical problems. If the person's main goals are to address their housing problems, asylum status, physical health concerns, legal proceedings or other similar issues, then these should be addressed prior to TF-CBT, in many cases by other professionals. For legal guidance, a discussion with the solicitor involved may be important and the CPS Practice Guidance for the provision of therapy for adult witnesses (Crown Prosecution Service 2001) can also be consulted.

Establishing a personal model of PTSD

We are focusing here on the *problem formulation* of PTSD rather than the wider *case formulation* in which it is embedded. The case formulation will hold greater detail about the wider context, other problems, and historical information. The focus is also on PTSD-specific questions rather than the generic CBT assessment questions you would ask in order to establish level of risk, the impact on the person's life more widely, a problem list, or goals.

The questions below fit with the boxes in the Ehlers and Clark (2000) model in Figure 13.1. We have included the information gathered from Michael in each case.

a) Nature of the trauma memory

You will already have gathered information about the nature of the trauma memory to be confident about the diagnosis – i.e. that the memory does not feel like normal everyday memories, that it feels more real and has a sense of 'nowness' as if it is happening in the present day rather than the past.

> Michael told you that his trauma memory does feel as if it is happening again, 'Like a video'.

b) Cognitive processing during the trauma

Good questions to ask about this include: 'Had you been using alcohol or any other drugs at the time of the event? Did you experience any blows to the head during the event? Did you lose consciousness? If so, for how long do you think? What bits can't you remember? Did you have a scan at the hospital? What did they tell you at the hospital? Did anyone mention a head injury?'

> Michael's processing during the trauma was likely to be affected by the fact that he was drunk. In addition, he describes how his body 'froze' during the attack. This suggests that he dissociated which, again, will prevent him from processing events normally.

c) Prior trauma and stressful circumstances, and coping

Good questions to ask about this include: 'Have you ever experienced similar events before? Have you ever experienced other types of traumatic, life-threatening or very frightening events before? How about when you were a child? How did you cope with them then? Did you ever have intrusive memories or bad dreams following these events? How did you cope with that? How well did that work? How have you coped with other stressful times in your life? What sort of things do you usually do to cope with stress?'

> Michael had no major traumatic events as a child but often felt afraid of his father when he was drunk. He tells you that he coped with this fear by suppressing it and not talking about it.

d) Assessment of cognitive themes

Good questions to ask about this area are:

(i) For intrusions: 'What are the main intrusive memories you have? Which come most often? Which are the most emotional? What emotions? What is the "main" intrusive memory? What were you thinking at that moment during the event?'

> Michael experiences severe nightmares every night and visual, somatosensory and olfactory flashbacks. In the nightmares, he sees the whole mugging unfold but tends to wake up at the moment he was attacked, coated in sweat. The flashbacks vary – sometimes he sees the whole event, 'just like a video' and can 'feel' the blade of the knife against his throat and 'smell' the breath of the teenagers. At other times, he sees just one moment. The emotions he experiences during the flashbacks are a mixture of fear, shame and helplessness.

(ii) For the worst moments during the trauma ('hotspots'): hotspots are identified during treatment, after reliving, and remind us of the ongoing role of assessment throughout treatment (see Grey et al., 2002). Useful questions include: 'What were the "worst" moments during the event itself? What were you feeling and thinking at that moment?'

> Michael tells you that the worst moment was when they held a knife against his neck and he thought they would kill him. He felt very afraid and his body 'froze'.

(iii) For post- and pre-trauma beliefs: 'How has this event changed how you see: yourself as a person; other people; the world; the future?'

> Michael tells you that he believes you need to be strong to be a man and that, because he is so afraid, he has let himself down.

(iv) For misinterpretation of symptoms: 'What do you make of these symptoms that you are experiencing? Do you have any particular concerns about what these symptoms mean? Do you ever think that these symptoms mean you are going mad or "losing it"?'

> Michael is very concerned about his symptoms and about how he coped during the trauma. His cognitions include: 'I should be over this by now'; 'There must be something wrong with me because I can't get over this'; 'I can't tell anyone the details, as they will judge me for not fighting back'; 'I will never be able to get back to studying and will have to drop out – I will let the family down'.

e) Assessment of possible maintaining factors

Good questions to ask about each possible area are:

(i) For rumination: 'Do you ever dwell on what happened? What aspects? Do you ever think about how it could have been avoided, or of things that you could have done differently? How long do you dwell for? Does dwelling on it get in the way of you doing other things?'

> Michael does not ruminate about what happened.

(ii) For avoidance: 'Are there things you avoid now, such as people, places, reminders, thoughts, feelings? Why is that? What do you think would happen if you didn't avoid these things?'

> Michael tries to avoid thinking about the mugging, he avoids going out alone anywhere where there might be teenagers, and he avoids going out at night. Michael also avoids talking to others about what happened, fearing they will judge him.

(iii) For thought suppression: 'When you have intrusive memories or thoughts about what happened what do you do? Do you ever push these out of your mind? Do you try to suppress thoughts and feelings related to the trauma? Why do you do that? What do you think would happen if you didn't do that?'

> When Michael has intrusive memories and thoughts about what happened, he tries hard to push them out of his mind. He is scared that if he doesn't, the memories and thoughts will take over his mind completely.

(iv) For safety behaviours: 'Do you ever take extra precautions now? Are there particular things that you do to try to keep yourself safe? Are there things you always make sure you have with you when you go out?'

> On the rare occasions that Michael does go out, he walks only on main streets and looks behind himself constantly. He crosses the road if he sees teenage boys.

(v) For numbing: 'Do you ever feel like you have no feelings at all? Do you ever do anything to try to make this happen or take unpleasant feelings away? Do you try to numb out? Do you use alcohol and/or drugs to take these feelings away?'

> Michael is using alcohol to help numb his emotions.

Using self-report questionnaires

Self-report questionnaires are very useful for efficiently obtaining a lot of information both at assessment and during the course of treatment. Commonly used questionnaires for traumatic stress symptoms are the

Revised Impact of Events Scale (IES-R; Weiss, 1997) and the Posttraumatic Diagnostic Scale (PDS; Foa et al., 1997).

In order to assess for particular cognitive themes, a commonly used questionnaire is the Posttraumatic Cognitions Inventory (PTCI: Foa et al., 1999). This has three factors, negative cognitions about the self, negative cognitions about the world, and self-blame. Used clinically, individual cognitions can be focused on in treatment and outcome tracked over time.

Case formulation

Figure 13.2 shows a diagrammatic version of a preliminary formulation of Michael's difficulties.

Michael has processed the assault in way that has led to a sense of current threat. There are three main sources of this current threat:

1. Due to his extreme fear at the time of the mugging, as well as his intense shame at freezing and not fighting off his assailants, the trauma memory was poorly elaborated into autobiographical memory. The fact that Michael was also drunk and briefly dissociated when assaulted will have affected how the memory was processed. As a consequence, it can be triggered by lots of different reminders (e.g. knives, teenagers). When it comes into his mind, it has no 'time-code' and feels as if it is happening again. He feels afraid for his life again and helpless and ashamed.
2. The appraisals he has made, particularly since the trauma, all contain a sense of current threat. In Michael's case there is a great deal of current intrapersonal threat (to his view of himself and his future). We can hypothesize that these appraisals have their roots in his prior beliefs about the need to be strong to be a man and to suppress/ignore emotions. They may also have been informed by his experience of being afraid of his father and feeling that he needed to keep up with his brothers. There is also current interpersonal threat: 'It's not safe to go out alone'.
3. Changes in the nature of the trauma memory are prevented by Michael not talking and thinking about what happened, avoiding places that remind him of the assault and by his excessive use of alcohol. Changes in his unhelpful appraisals are prevented by his avoidance of telling others about what happened and how he is feeling (thus making it impossible for him to find out whether or not they would judge him) and his avoidance of going out alone (thus making it impossible for him to check out whether or not it is safe).

Therapist details and supervisory arrangements

Given that PTSD is about a sense of serious current threat, the therapist's main job is to help make the person feel safe. To this end, it is important

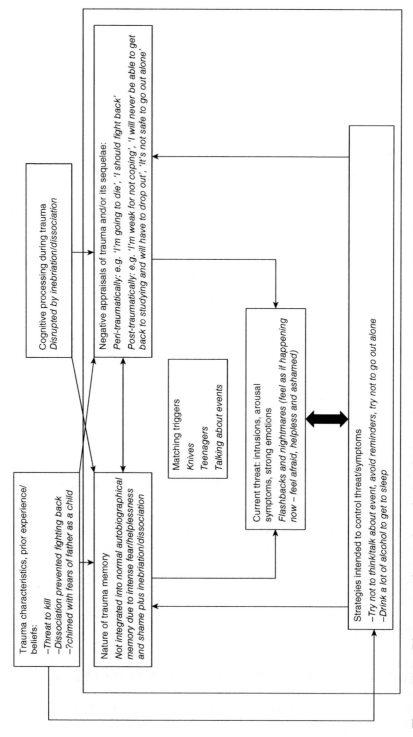

Figure 13.2 Diagrammatic version of a preliminary formulation of Michael's difficulties

to spend time developing rapport and demonstrating empathy. In addition, therapists can often get into an unhelpful conflict with PTSD clients as they try to encourage them to talk through what happened during the traumatic event(s). Unsurprisingly, clients are not keen to do this. In our experience, it is worth spending time explaining the model of PTSD, and its treatment efficacy, so that the client knows why the therapist is suggesting the counter-intuitive idea of revisiting this frightening memory. You may also need to elicit and explore any unhelpful thoughts they might have about what will happen if they think again about what happened (e.g. 'I will go mad'). Finally, one item in the therapist's own supervision agenda should be their emotional reaction both to hearing the traumatic stories and to witnessing the often extremely high levels of distress present during reliving.

Course of therapy

As outlined above, the treatment derived from Ehlers and Clark (2000) aims to address the sense of current threat attached to Michael's memory of trauma. The treatment plan is outlined in Table 13.1.

Table 13.1   Outline of Michael's TF-CBT treatment

Session	Activity
#1	• **Outline of event** • **Normalize** • **Reclaim life** • **Rationale for reliving**
#2	• **Reliving** • **Identify hotspots and meanings** • **Michael had four hotspots:** (1) fear as he realized they were about to attack him; (2) fear as they held a knife to his neck and he smelt their breath; (3) helplessness at his 'frozen' body; (4) shame for not fighting back as the assailants left.
#3	• **Address meanings of hotspots outside of reliving:** bring in updating information for fear hotspots, education about dissociation for helplessness and shame hotspots.
#4	• **Reliving with restructuring/updating hotspots**
#5	• **Continued to address cognitive themes and update memory**
#6	• **In vivo exposure** (work on going out alone in the day then at night); • **Discriminating triggers** (then vs. now work while looking at groups of young men and knives).
#7	• **Continue to work on cognitive themes** (safety and masculinity/strength)
#9	• **Michael returned to site of mugging**
#10	• **Made a blueprint**

Reclaiming life is a strand that runs through every session, although time spent on it varies (in some instances it may only be five minutes). Not all techniques are used with everybody or exactly in this order. There is a technical flexibility based on each client's personal model of PTSD, while the treatment remains based conceptually on the same theoretical foundations.

Complications

Michael represents a fairly straightforward PTSD presentation. There are various common complications, which we will run through in brief, with reference to the Ehlers and Clark model. In our view, the model can incorporate more complex presentations and flexing it in this way provides a helpful 'road map' when faced with assessing and formulating less straightforward PTSD.

Complications to do with the nature of the trauma memory

What if the client is very dissociative?

Probably the most useful recent explanatory model for dissociation in PTSD is that of Schauer and Elbert (2010). They suggest that dissociation is a biologically adaptive response to being in an inescapable traumatic situation (e.g. when trapped or restrained, imprisoned or penetrated by another or by a weapon).

Recent evidence (Hagenaas et al., 2010; Halvorsen et al., 2014) suggests that clients who dissociate when they discuss their trauma respond just as well to reliving as those who do not dissociate, so clinicians should not avoid assessing and treating such clients. Rather, they should anticipate some dissociation in any client who was trapped, raped, assaulted with a weapon or imprisoned. Simple grounding techniques, using materials to reinforce the present (see Table 13.2), can be introduced to such clients early on in the assessment process who are then encouraged to use them at any early sign of dissociation. Clients may also want to use these techniques to control flashbacks at other times (see Schauer and Elbert, 2010, and Kennedy et al., 2013, for more information about managing dissociation).

What if the client experienced more than one trauma?

When a client has been involved in multiple traumatic events, your assessment should focus on which events are being re-experienced – these provide you with the 'clues' to which parts of their history have been processed in a

Table 13.2   Useful grounding materials by sense

Sense	Grounding material
Smell	• Smelling salts • Decongestant sprays/sticks • Essential oils • Air fresheners • Citrus fruits
Taste	• Strong mints • Chilli gum • Cough sweets • Breath sweets
Sight	• Notices stating the location, year etc. • Decoration/lighting that discriminates between current location and the traumatic event e.g. Union Jack bunting for clients traumatized abroad, bright lights for those involved in night-time trauma • Pictures of loved ones • Night-lights to ensure clients can see these materials if they dissociate at night
Touch	• Stress balls • Elastic bands on wrists • Stones/objects with interesting textures • Hot or cold compresses • Applied tension • Being in postures that were not possible during the trauma
Sound	• Music/noises that distinguish the current situation from the traumatic event • A loud ticking clock to focus on

(NB: for most clients, the more senses you address at once, the better)

way that led to a sense of current threat. It is these events in particular on which you will need to focus in a problem formulation. However, if many events were experienced and are now re-experienced, Narrative Exposure Therapy (NET; Schauer et al., 2011) can also be considered as the evidence for its efficacy is encouraging (Robjant and Fazel, 2010; Stenmark et al., 2013; Morkved et al., 2014).

Complications to do with appraisals of the trauma or sequelae

What if the client has significant pre-existing difficulties?

If a client has long-standing difficulties with their self-esteem, they may experience intense shame, guilt or anger during the traumatic event.

In such instances, a longitudinal case formulation (rather than a PTSD-specific problem formulation) will be needed. If indicated by this formulation, for shame and anger in particular, compassion-focused approaches may be of value (see Lee, 2012).

Complications to do with coping strategies

What if the client self-harms either prior to, or in response to, your treatment?

If a client has an extremely limited repertoire of strategies to cope with distress, they may need to work on this before TF-CBT. Cloitre et al. (2010) has developed STAIR (Skills Training in Affect and Interpersonal Regulation) which is an eight-session package to be deployed before a trauma-focused intervention and teaches distress tolerance and emotion management to good effect.

Outcome and follow-up

Michael made good progress in therapy. His score on the IES-R reduced from 72 (pre-treatment) to 15. Similarly his PHQ-9 score reduced from 22 to 7. Crucially, he reported that, although he still felt a little nervous of going out alone and of groups of young men, he was sure that this would continue to improve and he now felt ready to return to college.

Recommendations to therapists

There are several things that you should bear in mind when assessing and formulating and treating a PTSD case. See Tables 13.3 and 13.4 below.

Table 13.3 Recommendations to therapists for assessing and formulating PTSD

1. Establish the diagnosis of PTSD:

   a) Clearly identify the traumatic event(s) and ensure that it/they would be considered as 'traumatic' diagnostically.
   b) Clearly identify the re-experiencing symptoms. Make sure there is a match between these and the traumatic event(s).
   c) Take care to distinguish intrusions (re-experiencing/'nowness') from rumination (which could be depression).

2. Make sure PTSD is the main problem and that the person is able to work on it:

   a) Ensure the person is not in imminent danger or at risk.
   b) Ensure that they have the information processing capacity to work with you on the trauma memory.
   c) Ensure that as far as possible the person's situation is stable/they are not excessively preoccupied with any instability and that TF-CBT is not contra-indicated.

3. Make sure you have information for all aspects of the cognitive model:

   a) Identify key appraisals/meanings associated with symptoms, the trauma, and sequelae.
   b) Identify the nature of the trauma memory ('nowness'/reliving nature) and likely triggers.
   c) Identify ways of coping that are maintaining the problem.

Table 13.4   Recommendations to therapists for treating PTSD

There are also several things you should bear in mind when treating a PTSD case:

1. Make sure you set things up properly:

   a) Leave enough time for sessions.
   b) Have a way to monitor progress.

2. Make sure your treatment is trauma-focused (i.e. memory-focused).
3. Make sure you tackle the key meanings/appraisals of the event(s)/sequelae of the trauma.
4. Make sure you help the person overcome problematic ways of coping in the real world.
5. Make sure you look after yourself.
6. 'Flex' the model (be driven by an individualized formulation, not techniques).

Activities

Complete a blank model for a client of your own to see where you have enough information and where it is missing. Think about what questions you might need to ask to complete a personal model of PTSD.

Further reading

Grey, N. (ed.) (2009) *A Casebook of Cognitive Therapy for Traumatic Stress Reactions*. Hove, East Sussex: Brunner-Routledge.
This state of the art text includes descriptions and case studies of clinical cases of cognitive behavioural treatments involving people who have experi-enced a wide range of traumatic events. It is written by experts in the field and considers what may be learned from such cases.

FOURTEEN Greg: A Case Study of Chronic Pain

Helen Macdonald and Dzintra Stalmeisters

Learning objectives

After reading this chapter and completing the activities at the end of it you should be able to:

- Understand and appreciate the complexity and the extent of detail necessary when conducting a cognitive behavioural assessment with clients who have chronic pain, in order to produce a workable formulation.
- Understand how biopsychosocial elements can affect the experience of pain.
- Understand the impact of having chronic pain on all areas of lifestyle and functioning.
- Reflect upon the importance of the therapeutic relationship and therapist creativity and flexibility when working with a client who has chronic pain.

Introduction

The number of people experiencing chronic pain is startling. The Chief Medical Officer's Report in 2009 indicated that in the UK, 7.8 million people live with chronic pain, 25 per cent of these people lose their jobs, and 16 per cent experience such bad pain that they sometimes feel as if they want to end their life (Donaldson, 2009). It is frequently debilitating and can clearly have a significant negative impact on the sufferer's quality of life (Jensen and Turk, 2014). Chronic pain is a long-term health condition, which is described as 'pain that is often (but not always) elicited by an injury but worsened by factors removed from the original cause, and is not explained by underlying pathology' (Thorn, 2004: 7). The original cause may also not be identified, and the condition may not have a recognized diagnosis. According to the British Pain Society (2014) the pain cannot be resolved by available medical or other treatment. Indeed, it is this group of people that psychotherapists are likely to encounter within the therapeutic setting, rather than those at the inception of an acute pain related episode (Fetter and Fetter, 2009).

The biopsychosocial approach

The 'biopsychosocial' approach is considered as the most heuristic approach to chronic pain (Gatchel et al., 2007). From this perspective, focusing solely on the injury or tissue damage is viewed as inadequate in the assessment and treatment of chronic pain. Rather, the dynamic and complex interaction of biological, psychological and social factors is perceived as significant (Theodore et al., 2008). The relationship of these factors is viewed as affecting the meaning and maintenance of chronic pain, and hence what is experienced. Research supports this approach (Stalnacke, 2011). Moreover, it is consistent with an array of cognitive behavioural conceptual models that acknowledge the reciprocal nature and the complex interrelatedness of processes and systems (Teasdale, 1996; Wells, 1997; Power and Dalgeish, 2008).

The Chronic Illness Coping Model

A biopsychosocial approach, together with predisposing, precipitating and perpetuating factors, underpins the Chronic Illness Coping Model (CICM). The CICM is a diagrammatic representation of the interaction of these elements that can help illustrate how an adverse illness experience might be maintained. It enables an idiosyncratic understanding of the client's experience of chronic pain, helping both the client and therapist to make sense of the client's experience, progressing to the development of a formulation. Once this is completed a relevant and collaboratively agreed treatment plan can be considered. This not only allows for interventions based on areas where change is possible and that are a priority to the client, but also promotes opportunities to accept and grieve for losses. When employed with the client, it is advisable to seek to obtain succinct information on the CICM, in order to reduce the likelihood of the client feeling overwhelmed.

We will now look at aspects of the CICM and then demonstrate its employment with a client who experienced chronic pain.

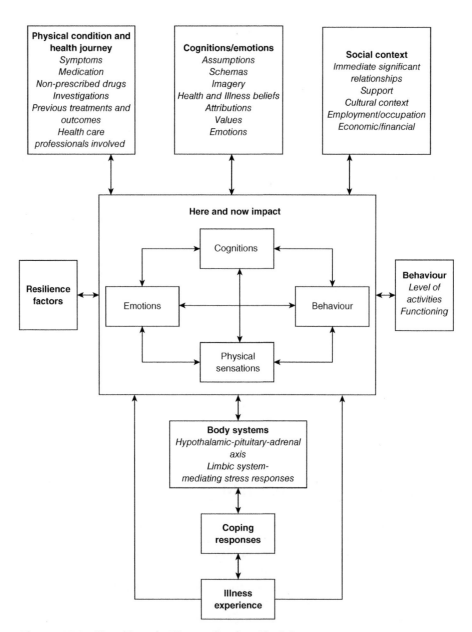

Figure 14.1 The Chronic Illness Coping Model

Biological and physiological factors

In the CICM biological and physiological aspects are collated under the heading 'Physical condition and health journey'. The knowledge from this section forms a foundation for the other areas to be built upon. Detailed information about previous treatment, medication and outcomes, variations in pain levels, plus involvement of health care professionals, helps to build a picture of the client's pain journey. This will help determine whether the necessary investigations have been conducted to exclude a physical disease that could be treated medically.

The CICM can be used as a collaborative tool to formulate the problem with the client; the section on Body Systems helps reinforce understanding of the complex nature of pain, and the association between mind, social and physiological factors for the client. This is particularly important as many people who have experienced pain for some time can feel rebuffed or failed by the medical system or believe that they are being blamed, or are to blame for their pain (Gatchel et al., 2007).

Under the heading 'Body systems', the hypothalamic-pituitary-adrenal axis (HPA) is evident. Clinical studies have suggested that persons with chronic widespread pain display altered HPA function (McBeth et al., 2005), also sizeable evidence suggests that the HPA axis is implicated in various aspects of pain appraisal (Blackburn-Munro, 2004). As a minimum, corti-sol and other 'stress' hormones are controlled by the HPA axis. In chronic pain conditions, elevated levels of stress can be experienced which disturb homeostasis, intensifying the pain experience. It is suggested that pro-longed secretion of cortisol can result in adverse reactions within the body, such as impairment of tissue growth and immune suppression (Gatchel et al., 2007). Within the CICM body systems are positioned as mediating the relationship between biopsychosocial factors and coping responses; ultimately the illness experience.

Psychological aspects

Psychological aspects are pooled under the heading of 'Cognitions/emotions'. As well as collecting information about negative automatic thought, assumptions, schemas, and images that are related to the pain, it is ben-eficial to gather information about health and illness beliefs/attributions. Clients who attribute their pain to purely biological factors, and hence have an external locus of control, are more likely to have greater levels of pain and psychological distress (Toomey et al., 1996). Such clients experience lit-tle control over their pain. Similarly, clients who experience 'mental defeat' may experience diminished control as their perception of autonomy can be adversely affected. Mental defeat, a cognitive phenomenon that involves a form of catastrophizing whereby chronic pain is perceived as an assault on the individual's identity and humanity, can lead to a negative self-evalua-tion in relation to the pain (Tang et al., 2007). It is feasible that a reduced sense of autonomy can affect engagement in treatment, particularly as it is theorized that people with an external locus of control find it challenging to employ self-management coping skills (Toomey et al., 1996), a fundamental aspect of CBT for chronic pain. This said, an extreme internal locus of control can contribute to difficulties in acceptance and adjustment to long-term health problems (Macdonald, 2001). Nevertheless, increasing self-efficacy and reduced catastrophizing concerning the harmful effects of pain encourages self-management of pain (Turner et al., 2007).

As Dima et al. point out, pain 'is simultaneously a sensory and emotional experience' (2013: 185). Indeed, emotions are perceived as both a cause and a consequence of pain (Hawthorne and Redmond, 2004). Irrespective, pain grabs attention, and can elicit an array of negative emotions. Research suggests that people experiencing chronic pain with greater acceptance of their situation experience less fearful thoughts about the pain (Crombez et al., 2013), potentially moderating the negative emotions experienced. Given this, together with research suggesting that people with chronic pain can find it difficult to process their emotions (Esteves et al., 2013), it is important to investigate how the client experiences and manages emotions. Looking at links between pain experience and emotional experience will allow more depth of information, and increased understanding.

Social context

The heading 'Social context' provides an opportunity to collate information that relates to the individual's relationship within their life circumstances and people within their environment. Research indicates that culture (Edwards et al., 2001) and significant others can influence how pain is perceived, expressed and experienced. Kostova et al. (2014) found that doctors and the external social context can either hinder or assist acceptance of the condition and development of a new narrative, whilst research conducted by Brook et al. (2013) highlighted the importance of significant others as a source of support. However, they also discovered that significant others reinforced unhelpful self-limiting behaviours and beliefs, notably of those that were not employed. In view of this, it is necessary to find out about the level of support received and how this contributes to autonomy or reinforcement of unhelpful behaviours. It is important to facilitate effective responding from family members and friends. Additionally, their occupational and economic situation should be considered. Overall, the impact on the person's life situation gives the context for their individual experience.

Behaviour

As part of the assessment process information about the client's behaviour will be collected. Research indicates a close relationship between cognitions and behaviours in chronic pain. A study conducted by Snelgrove et al. (2013), for instance, found that participants who adopted a biomedical understanding of their pain, centring on the physical aspects of their pain, engaged in a restricted range of behaviour-focused coping strategies. Furthermore, loss remained an enduring theme. By comparison, relief from pain was experienced by participants who were able to adopt self-management strategies with an emphasis on mind and body. These participants were also more future orientated.

Behaviourally, the person's activity level is important. There is often a tendency to be over- or under-active in relation to the pain. In the long term, this reduces functioning and participation in meaningful activities and therefore pacing, which involves balancing rest and activity, is encouraged (Cole et al., 2005). Looking at activity levels, including what is done, what is avoided, and pain behaviours, is included in the assessment process. Behaviours which are designed to relieve pain need consideration which may include drinking alcohol and substance use. Risky behaviours should be taken into account as part of a whole picture. Additionally, the impact of chronic pain on functioning, sleep and appetite can be examined. Detailed information about levels of activity and functioning will enable appropriate targets to be set. Such targets will include valued occupational activities, possibly employment, balancing activity and rest, and working towards optimizing behavioural functioning in the context of physical difficulties.

Engagement

The purpose of the assessment is to establish sufficient information in order to create a formulation of the problem, and subsequently an appropriate treatment plan. However, engaging the client in the process is imperative. Many people who experience chronic pain will have had a great deal of contact with various medical and other health care professionals. Often they are passed from one to another, in the hope of finding a diagnosis and cure for their pain. In these interactions, it is possible that they have not experienced being treated as 'whole persons', and that aspects of the impact on them have been missed. It may be that they have had repeated experiences of 'failing' to get better as a result of these investigations and interventions.

Ensuring that this is not repeated in the CBT assessment and therapy sessions enables the therapist to relate to the whole person with an openness to understanding the client's experience, genuinely listening to them, whilst empathizing and being non-judgemental. Adopting a person-centred approach, seeing the whole person (Gatchel et al., 2007) and not just a set of symptoms, will facilitate the client's engagement in the therapeutic process. Finally, acknowledging the client's strengths, featured under the heading 'Resilience factors' on the CICM, is important. Dudley et al. (2011) remind us that a strengths-focused approach can increase engagement in the therapeutic process, plus develop further resilience to enhance lasting recovery. Collaboratively, the therapist and the client can utilize these strengths and resources to progress goals.

Case introduction: Greg

This is a case example of a person presenting with long-term pain problems following a workplace injury. The case will be used to demonstrate the style of assessment and then a working formulation using the CICM.

Greg was 34 years old. He lived with his partner. They had no children. Prior to the assessment, Greg had experienced an accident at work. He had a job in a restaurant, and was cleaning the kitchen at the end of the shift where he slipped on some spilled vegetable oil, and fell. He hurt his back and knee and had experienced severe pain in his back and his leg ever since. He had some exploratory surgery on his knee and had been told that further surgery would not help. He had also had some physiotherapy. Greg had been referred for CBT to help him to manage his pain.

On assessment, Greg expressed frustration that the doctors would not 'sort out his knee', believing that they were not helping because of cuts in funding.

Presenting complaints

Greg described pain which was present all the time, and rated this as 9/10 on a scale of 0–10 at its worst (where 0 is no pain at all, and 10 is the worst possible pain), and 6/10 on 'good days' which happened 2–3 days per week. About every three months he experienced a 'flare up' in the pain, when it would be severe for a couple of weeks without a break. He said that he had really tried the exercises from the physiotherapist, but that these seemed to make the pain worse.

Observations made by the therapist during assessment were that Greg held his knee stiffly and did not bend it fully when sitting. After about 15 minutes, he began moving around in his chair, and wincing, rubbing the side of his leg and frowning.

Impact of pain for the formulation of Greg's difficulties

This is how Greg described his current experiences.

Physical

'The pain is excruciating, it takes all my attention when it's bad. The pain in my knee is worst, sometimes 9/10 at night, and it's never better than 6/10 on a good day. My back aches a lot, especially if I have been on my feet. I get headaches at least three times a week, and nothing seems to relieve them. I can't sleep properly, and I wake often in the night. I am tired all the time. The painkillers help a bit, but I get drowsy and feel sick and constipated and have stomach aches. I can only stand for a few minutes at a time, and when I am walking it gets worse after 10–15 minutes. I have put on weight, but seem to be eating about the same. My appetite is about the same as before.'

Emotional

'I get very angry, irritable and frustrated. At times it's like I have a "short fuse" whereas I always used to be more patient. I get moody and down in myself, feel sad a lot. I worry about the future, and notice I am easily upset. I get scared and anxious sometimes, too.'

Cognitive

'I spend lots of time thinking about the pain and how it has ruined my life. I am old before my time. I think I might as well give up sometimes, but I would never hurt myself. I get to thinking it just isn't fair, and if only I had seen that spilled oil on the floor I would be fine. I go over in my mind what happened, and think it could all be so different. I think about needing a walking stick when I'm older, and people laughing at me because I have a limp. It's only going to get worse. I worry about keeping my job. I often think they are only keeping me on because I got hurt at work. I think that my partner is getting fed up with me, and wonder why she stays with me when I am so grumpy. I end up feeling guilty when I have been irritable with her. People will think I am weak, and my friends will be losing interest in me because I don't go and do stuff with them anymore.'

Behavioural

'I carry on as much as I can, and keep going until the pain is unbearable. I try to get as much as possible done before the pain gets too bad. Then I have to sit with my leg up on the settee for the rest of the day. I have stopped seeing my friends as often as I used to. I can't do the five-a-side football with them anymore. There's no way I could ride a bike, never mind go mountain biking at the weekends with them like I used to. They say I could come with them to the pub afterwards, but I usually tell them I am busy or out with my partner. I don't really take her out anymore; just sometimes we do go to see a film. I avoid talking about how difficult it is with my partner, but then I avoid her when I am irritable and don't explain that the pain is bad. I have stopped going to see bands with my brother like we used to. I can't stand for long, and I am worried about people bumping into me and causing a flare up. I am really careful if I have to lift anything, and try not to have to bend too much.'

Life situation

'I am still working in the restaurant, but feeling 'stuck' and unable to move into a management position or another job because I have needed time off sick with the bad leg. Financially, we're not well off but are managing because my partner is working. I am concerned that the relationship is suffering, but my partner is supportive and caring, and rarely complains unless I shout a lot. We wanted to have children, but can't really afford it unless I get a better paid job. I am losing contact with friends and becoming more isolated. My big brother comes to see me every week, and he really cares about me, too.'

Working hypothesis

Greg's perceived difficult pain journey, together with his negative self-evaluation and his negative perception of others' attitudes toward him, is compounded by low mood and increased anxiety with his challenging work and financial situation. These factors combine to contribute to his fear and stress in relation to the pain by lowering his tolerance, increasing its significance and reducing his sense of control and self-efficacy. This combination of biopsychosocial factors interacts with his withdrawal and avoidance producing a subtle cycle that is maintaining his uncontrolled experience of pain.

Measures

Greg's PHQ-9 score at the first session was 14 indicating 'moderately severe' depression. As he scored 1 ('several days') on the item 'Thoughts that you would be better off dead or hurting yourself in some way', this was investigated further. Greg reported only fleeting thoughts that it might be better if he never woke up but was very sure he would never act on such thoughts or deliberately hurt himself, and had never done so in the past.

The GAD-7 score of 8 indicated 'moderate' anxiety. On the Pain Catastrophizing Scale (PCS), his score of 28 was below the range for clinically significant levels of catastrophizing, although it fell within the range of scores where people are more at risk of developing chronicity and reduced chances of remaining in employment. On the Pain Self-Efficacy Questionnaire (Nicholas, 2007), his score of 45/60 indicated a lack of confidence in successful management of the pain, which is in the clinical range. An Impact of Event Scale (revised) was also administered, as an initial screening for symptoms of post-traumatic stress. Greg's score of 25 fell below the clinical range, and was consistent with his description of experiences at interview.

Working together, Greg's current experiences could be summarized as shown in Figure 14.2.

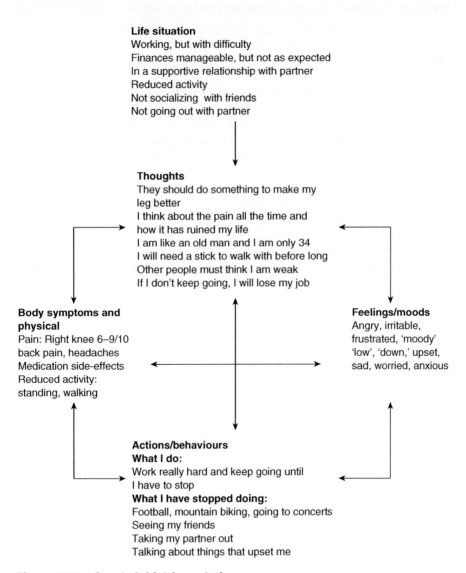

Life situation
Working, but with difficulty
Finances manageable, but not as expected
In a supportive relationship with partner
Reduced activity
Not socializing with friends
Not going out with partner

Thoughts
They should do something to make my leg better
I think about the pain all the time and how it has ruined my life
I am like an old man and I am only 34
I will need a stick to walk with before long
Other people must think I am weak
If I don't keep going, I will lose my job

Body symptoms and physical
Pain: Right knee 6–9/10
back pain, headaches
Medication side-effects
Reduced activity:
standing, walking

Feelings/moods
Angry, irritable,
frustrated, 'moody'
'low', 'down,' upset,
sad, worried, anxious

Actions/behaviours
What I do:
Work really hard and keep going until I have to stop
What I have stopped doing:
Football, mountain biking, going to concerts
Seeing my friends
Taking my partner out
Talking about things that upset me

Figure 14.2   Greg's initial formulation

Developing the formulation

Working together, the therapist and Greg looked in more detail at the impact of his long-term pain and its context, taking into account previous learning and thinking styles, the history of his current difficulties and a theoretical view of what can happen for people living with long-term pain. Valuing the client's current coping strategies and including these with short- and long-term effects is an opportunity to identify the impact of unhelpful approaches to coping and consider alternatives. Using the CICM, Figure 14.3 shows a diagram of the agreed formulation.

Setting goals

Once the initial formulation had been agreed, there was an opportunity to look at how the impact could be changed so that the goals for intervention could be agreed using realistic targets. Since there are often many areas where change is possible, it is important to agree some initial priorities.

Aiming for a manageable number of realistic, achievable goals reduces the likelihood of the client feeling overwhelmed. Deciding what to prioritize might include looking at what is the most easy to change; what would make the biggest impact on quality of life, or what is the most important in terms of the individual's values (Cole et al., 2005). Educational input contributes to developing a comprehensive formulation and can help establish what can, and cannot, be changed (Butler and Lorimer-Moseley, 2003). Motivational interventions can help enhance engagement in the process of change and increase self-efficacy (Rollnick et al., 1999; Macdonald, 2001; Rollnick et al., 2008).

For the areas where change is not currently within the control of the person, or where 'mental defeat' is having a significant impact on coping style and responses (Tang et al., 2007) then therapy may also include work on identifying the resulting losses and allowing space and time to grieve for and come to an acceptance of those losses (McCracken and Vowles, 2014).

Interventions

Increasing understanding of pain and pain systems, including education about acute and chronic pain, can help reframe the meaning of the pain experience; for example, using a brief and easily understood description of the main principles of 'gate control' theory (Melzack and Wall, 1982). The gate control theory proposes that there are 'gates' in the nerve junctions of the spinal cord and central nervous system. Messages encounter these 'gates', both to and from the central nervous system. If they are

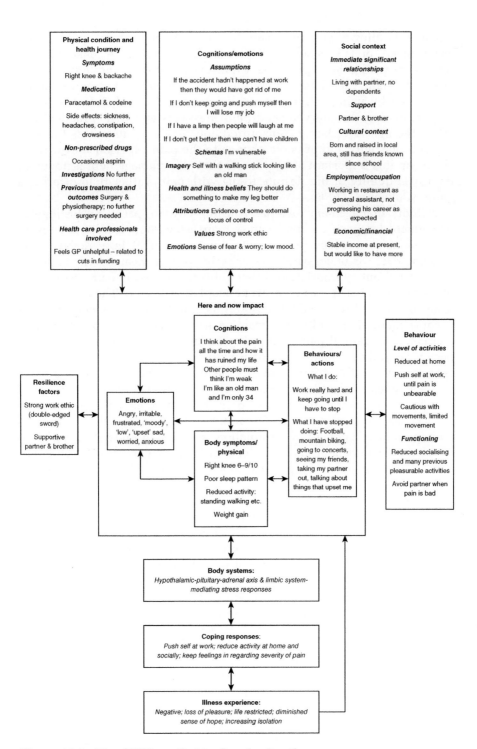

Figure 14.3   The CICM applied to Greg's situation

'open' this allows pain messages through; if they 'close', pain is not experienced, or is less severe. This may help a client to make connections concerning how previous experiences, moods and tension can affect the pain experience, including information on how pain can be influenced by using activity or medicines can also enhance outcomes. Understanding that nerves send pain messages and that 'practice' can affect the messages being transmitted and received introduces the idea of neuroplasticity and possible change to the pain experience over time. However, it is important to emphasize that pain management is about an improved quality of life despite living with pain, rather than offering a 'cure' (Cole et al., 2005).

Activity management includes learning how to 'pace', by testing out how much of a specific activity can be managed without leading to a severe increase in pain. Many people with pain are caught in a vicious cycle of being over- or under-active. Over-active pacing means doing so much activity without appropriate rest that a severe increase in pain results. It is often based on beliefs which prevent adaptation to pain. The over-activity leads to enforced rest, and because of this, muscles become weaker, joints become increasingly stiff, and stamina is reduced over time. The main alternative unhelpful pattern is being under-active. In this situation, the person is afraid of making the pain worse and the main coping strategy is to rest and avoid activity. This also leads to a situation where muscles become weaker, joints become increasingly stiff, and stamina is reduced over time. The overall outcome of both these extreme styles of pacing is reduced activity, and increased discomfort. The person's style of activity is an important component of formulation, assisting in understanding more about the development and maintenance of their current difficulties. In order to address unhelpful patterns of activity, pacing is used to gradually reach an optimum level.

Here is a simplified example, using the activity of walking. The individual records how long they can walk on three consecutive days, without causing a severe increase in pain. This might be 10 minutes on day one; 12 minutes on day two, and eight minutes on day three. The mean of the three is calculated and in this case it is 10 minutes. This is then reduced by 20 per cent, resulting in eight minutes, which becomes the daily walking goal (that is, the person walks for eight minutes every day). After two weeks, an attempt is made to increase this by approximately 10 per cent, leading to nine minutes. If nine minutes can be achieved without a severe increase in pain, this becomes the daily walking goal for the next two weeks. This process continues until a point of no increase is reached or the person is able to walk as far as they wish without a severe increase in pain. If the person is unable to increase their walking time, they keep the current daily walking goal, and test whether an increase is possible every couple of weeks as an ongoing approach. This method can be used to address most activities affected by persistent pain.

Management of the impact of chronic pain

Figure 14.4 gives a summary of possible interventions using the same modified 'five areas' model. The CBT therapist may not be the person who delivers all of these interventions but key areas for CBT are marked in bold.

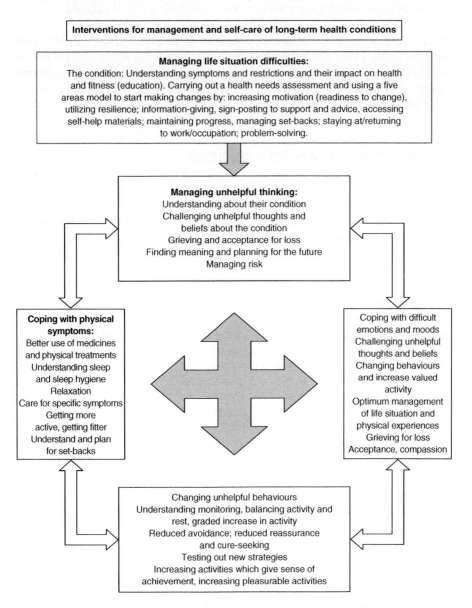

Interventions for management and self-care of long-term health conditions

Managing life situation difficulties:
The condition: Understanding symptoms and restrictions and their impact on health and fitness (education). Carrying out a health needs assessment and using a five areas model to start making changes by: increasing motivation (readiness to change), utilizing resilience; information-giving, sign-posting to support and advice, accessing self-help materials; maintaining progress, managing set-backs; staying at/returning to work/occupation; problem-solving.

Managing unhelpful thinking:
Understanding about their condition
Challenging unhelpful thoughts and beliefs about the condition
Grieving and acceptance for loss
Finding meaning and planning for the future
Managing risk

Coping with physical symptoms:
Better use of medicines and physical treatments
Understanding sleep and sleep hygiene
Relaxation
Care for specific symptoms
Getting more active, getting fitter
Understand and plan for set-backs

Coping with difficult emotions and moods
Challenging unhelpful thoughts and beliefs
Changing behaviours and increase valued activity
Optimum management of life situation and physical experiences
Grieving for loss
Acceptance, compassion

Changing unhelpful behaviours
Understanding monitoring, balancing activity and rest, graded increase in activity
Reduced avoidance; reduced reassurance and cure-seeking
Testing out new strategies
Increasing activities which give sense of achievement, increasing pleasurable activities

Figure 14.4   Interventions for management and self-care of long-term health conditions

Case conceptualization: complicating factors

Clients with an external locus of control are likely to require a greater degree of psycho-education to enable them to engage actively in a CBT approach (Macdonald, 2001). Engagement may also be affected by prior experiences of health care interventions and their level of success.

In longer-term health conditions, people may be affected by the provision (or lack) of disability-related welfare benefits, care from significant others, or withdrawal of (or from) sources of support, which means that a significant change in functioning can have an impact on role identity. Potential for factors maintaining difficulties such as 'secondary gains' should be considered.

Further implications for clinicians

Prior to the initial meeting, it is important to consider factors such as accessibility, both of the clinic location and within the consulting room. Thinking about choice of seating; inviting and modelling standing up or moving around during session; and offering alternative formats for delivery such as telephone or video-conferencing may all enhance the individual's ability to take part meaningfully in a process of change.

Summary

Although chronic pain can be difficult to treat, research suggests that psychological approaches, specifically CBT, are more helpful for long-term outcomes than medical management (Morley et al., 1999; Turk, 1996). CBT has been demonstrated to be effective for managing certain types of chronic pain, for instance, chronic back pain (Lamb et al., 2010; Morley et al., 1999; Nielson and Weir, 2001). However, a recent Cochrane review into the efficacy of CBT for general chronic pain revealed inconclusive results (Williams et al., 2012). Nevertheless, the process of formulation can help clients make sense of their experience and develop collaboratively realistic goals to manage the pain. Utilizing the CICM can help ensure full details are collated to develop a picture of the client's pain journey.

Activities

1. Apply pacing to yourself as an experiment in order to develop an understanding of the potentially challenging nature of pacing.
2. Reflect upon the daily challenges faced by someone with chronic pain.
3. Experiment with collecting information using the CICM to develop a more complete picture of the client's experience with chronic illness.
4. Consider what changes in practice you might make as a result of this chapter.

Further reading

Cole, F., Macdonald, H., Carus, C. and Howden-Leach, H. (2005) *Overcoming Chronic Pain: A Self-help Guide Using Cognitive Behavioural Techniques.* London: Robinson.

Kabat-Zinn, J. (1990) *Full Catastrophe Living: Using the Wisdom of Your Body and Mind to Face Stress, Pain and Illness.* London: Random House Publishing.

Owen, R. (2013) *Living with the Enemy: Coping with the Stress of Chronic Illness using CBT, Mindfulness and Acceptance.* London: Taylor and Francis Ltd.

FIFTEEN Sophie: A Case Study of Borderline Personality Disorder

Michael Townend and Kate Davidson

Learning objectives

After reading this chapter and completing the activities at the end of it you should be able to:

- Appreciate the epidemiological significance of personality disorder.
- Recognize the important advantages of underpinning the therapy relationship and formulation from a variety of perspectives.
- Understand the importance of a client's history and background in the onset, formation and subsequent maintenance of borderline personality disorder.
- Understand and appreciate the key elements of assessment and formulation as it applies to personality disorder.
- Recognize the importance of linking formulation to empirically validated interventions.

Personality disorder

In the last three decades CBT has developed theory and techniques, traditionally applied to depression and anxiety disorders, to help clinicians in their work with individuals described as having 'personality disorders' (Beck et al., 1990; Young, 1990; Young et al., 2003). Within this literature, cognitive approaches have been articulated which focus on personality disorder (Layden et al., 1993; Morse, 2002; Young et al., 2003; Mills et al., 2004, Davidson, 2007). Personality disorder is a common problem with community estimates of prevalence ranging from four to 20 per cent of the population with a significant burden on the individuals themselves, those around them, health care resources and society in general (Coid et al., 2006).

Theoretical and research base

Personality disorder is defined within DSM-5 (APA, 2013) according to four criteria followed by three more specific clusters of symptoms. The broad criteria are shown in Table 15.1.

Table 15.1 DSM-5 summary of diagnostic criteria for personality disorder (APA, 2013)

1. An enduring pattern of psychological experience and behaviour that differs prominently from cultural expectations, as shown in two or more features in the areas of cognitive (i.e. perceiving and interpreting the self, other people or events); affect (i.e. the range, intensity, ability and appropriateness of emotional response); interpersonal functioning; or impulse control.
2. The pattern must appear inflexible and pervasive across a wide range of situations, and lead to clinically significant distress or impairment in important areas of functioning.
3. The pattern must be stable and long-lasting, have started early or at least in adolescence or early adulthood.
4. The pattern must not be better accounted for as a manifestation of another mental disorder, or be due to the direct physiological effects of a substance (i.e. drug or medication) or a general medical condition (i.e. head injury).

Diagnostically three clusters of features are currently recognized. Cluster A is defined under 'Odd and Eccentric'; cluster B as 'Dramatic, Emotional and Erratic' with cluster C being 'Anxious or Fearful.' Borderline personality disorder (BPD) is classified within cluster B (APA, 2013). Individuals within this cluster are described as sharing impulsivity, mood instability, antisocial behaviour and disturbed thinking. BPD clients are further sub-categorized in terms of an extended set of criteria including efforts to avoid real or imagined abandonment; unstable and intense interpersonal relationships; identity disturbance; impulsivity; affective instability and chronic feelings of emptiness (APA, 2013).

In this chapter the term BPD is used simply for reasons of consistency and ease of communication. In contrast to psychiatric diagnosis, a relation-based, formulation-driven approach provides a more compassionate approach to understanding BPD. This, in turn, can foster greater awareness of the person in need, and as deserving of help, rather than a quasi-medical representation of a 'disordered' individual with an intractable problem.

A formulation-based approach offers a further advantage: at the individual level, people with a diagnosis of BPD can be understood in the face of their disadvantaged developmental backgrounds and also from a variety of schema, cognitive, behavioural, social and attachment theoretical perspectives (Mills et al., 2004; Davidson et al., 2010). Although those with BPD may have never experienced an ability to function optimally, they can recognize that the emotional and social aspects of their lives are unsatisfactory. This can help motivate the client to change or at least aspire to a different way of living. The structure, direction and consistent accepting compassionate approach that therapy provides can harness this and a positive outcome can be achieved.

In keeping with the view of BPD as a developmental problem, Young et al. (2003) propose a clinical theory of 'early maladaptive schemas' (EMS) which, along with related rules for living, are proposed as developing in response to early toxic experiences. Thus in a circular way, individuals living with BPD may engage in behavioural strategies, information- and emotional-processing or avoidance in ways which confirm the apparent 'truth' of their EMS (known as schema maintenance). They may equally engage in cognitive and emotional avoidance of their EMS (schema avoidance), or adopt cognitive and behavioural styles which seem contrary to what might have been predicted from knowledge of their EMS (schema compensation) (Young, 1990). Examples of these will be given later in this chapter.

Attachment theory has also been influential in psychological accounts of personality disorder. Attachment theory proposes that children and young people develop internal representations of relationships through their interactions with their early caregivers and others with whom they have regular contact (Bowlby, 2005). These internal representations, or working models of relationships, influence how personality develops, how individuals interact with others, how they view the world and other people and the strategies they use to regulate their emotions (Davidson, 2007). An insecure attachment combined with genetic, other biological and environmental risk factors (for example, physical abuse or consistent neglect) may thus lead to the development of a personality disorder.

The problems associated with BPD (including behaviours such as self-harming or sexualized behaviours) can wax and wane as individuals age and as a function of life events triggering 'flare-ups'. Co-morbid problems such as depression, anxiety and PTSD are also common with a history of sexual abuse being prevalent, although abuse is not believed to exert a causal influence (Zanarini et al., 1989).

Evidence for psychological therapies for borderline personality disorder

Psychological therapy is considered the main treatment for BPD, largely because the evidence for pharmacotherapy is limited (Stoffers et al., 2010).

There are approximately 30 randomized controlled trials of psychological therapies for BPD. These have involved a variety of therapeutic traditions including psychodynamic psychotherapy, CBT and therapies designed to be adjunctive to usual care (e.g. STEPPS; Blum et al., 2008). With the exception of nidotherapy that aims to change the environment to fit with the person's problems or find an environment where the patient's problems will have less of an impact (Tyrer et al., 2005), the approaches investigated tend to assume that it is the individual who wants to change.

Almost all psychological therapies have been shown to be effective in reducing borderline psychopathology, although no single therapy is seen as being superior to another. Even dialectical behaviour therapy, which has been more thoroughly investigated than other therapies, produces similar outcomes to structured clinical care or general psychiatric management (McMain et al., 2012). However, it should be noted that structured clinical care differs from usual clinical care in that clinicians have to be knowledgeable about personality disorders and take a consistent and compassionate approach (Chanen et al., 2008; McMain et al., 2012).

Overall it would appear that severity of borderline pathology or having an additional co-morbid mental state disorder is not a determinant of outcome as may often be assumed (Black et al., 2009; Barnicot et al., 2012). Indeed studies on the course of the disorder have indicated that clients do get better and that the majority remain better. However, up to one third may have symptomatic recurrence, and loss of recovery over time and some social dysfunction may persist (Gunderson et al., 2011; Zanarini et al., 2012).

Outcome measures

There is a wide choice of measures to support the assessment of personality disorders. This reflects in part the diverse range of impacts that these disorders can have on the individual, others and society. The range of outcomes that can be measured is, therefore, very wide.

Unfortunately, there is no standard set of measures of either global outcomes for personality disorder or for specific problems that may be present in a specific personality disorder such as BPD. Affective disturbance is a key problem in BPD. Studies have utilized measures of depression, anxiety and distress to try to capture change in affect over time with therapy. However, changes in specific symptoms such as affect may be a result of changes in mental state, not changes in personality disorder status per se.

In the absence of definitive measures, a theoretical, best evidence and idiosyncratic approach is suggested. Idiographic measures can include Problem and Target statements (Marks, 1986), a form of individualized goal attainment scaling, and the Work and Social Adjustment Scale (WSAS; Marks, 1986) to assess and measure the effect of the problems on the client's wider life. In addition, the Young Schema Questionnaire (Young, 1988) can be used if the therapy is based on schema theory, whilst the Relationship Questionnaire (Bartholomew and Horowitz, 1991) can be useful if the therapy is underpinned by attachment theory.

Case study

Assessment

Sophie's assessment took place over four interlinked and overlapping stages. The first stage consisted of a cognitive behavioural analysis of the main presenting problem (guidelines for cognitive behavioural analysis can be found in Part 1 of this book). A cognitive behavioural analysis was carried out in order to develop an idiographic understanding of the cognitive, attentional, emotional, behavioural and physical factors maintaining Sophie's difficulties, as well as the interplay between them. Motivation and mental state were also assessed – the former to identify any potential challenges with therapeutic engagement and the latter to rule out any contraindications to a psychological approach. It was also important to assess for suicidal risk, risk of self-injurious behaviour and risk to others.

The final stage of the assessment process consisted of developing an understanding of Sophie's psychiatric, developmental and personal history in order to identify early learning experiences, stability or otherwise of early relationships and in order to understand belief formation and changes over time. Baseline measures were also used.

Sophie: A brief biography

Sophie was a 20-year-old social science undergraduate at a UK University. She had recently taken a break from her course on the grounds of psychological difficulties and was actively negotiating a return to her studies. Prior to her self-referral for CBT she was regularly self-harming and reported feeling depressed and worthless. She had a few friends and a boyfriend who was abusive towards her by shouting and being continuously critical.

Sophie had managed to maintain some of her hobbies. She had coped at university through isolating herself in her room, although this behaviour had stopped when she returned home. Nonetheless, despite doing some voluntary work, Sophie was underactive and significantly overweight. She habitually stayed in bed until late morning and occasionally spent time with a friend in the evenings or with her father (her parents were separated).

Sophie's formative experiences were of emotional invalidation from both parents. They were reported as lacking in warmth and empathy and very critical, both parents giving the message that 'success is everything'. Her mother used to repeatedly stress to Sophie how exceptionally clever she was, and that she must succeed academically. Sophie internalized those messages at an early age, judging her early and subsequent performance accordingly. This resulted in harsh self-criticism and self-defeating behaviour (such as procrastination) in case she performed 'second best' or below. Her romantic relationships and friendships became increasingly problematic, any form of criticism was experienced as a threat, and she found it difficult to manage her emotions with increased anxiety and low mood. During late adolescence Sophie began to cope with her intense affect through increased isolation and self-injury (cutting her arms and legs with knives and razors).

Sophie was brought up within a religious household and attended a faith school. Given this background, and her later interest in social science, her own personal moral position became a crucial life issue for her, as represented in the cognitive aspects of the case formulation shown in Figure 15.1.

What happened in therapy

A key feature of CBT for BPD is that therapy is 'chunked up' into linked and overlapping phases with agreed explicit goals for each phase. This is because therapy is typically longer than is the case for axis 1 problems (that is, clinical disorders) and can at times feel overwhelming for both client and therapist. Incremental changes can be achieved and priority areas targeted in a systematic and focused way.

Sessions 1–6

Sophie had had difficulties with coping and relationships since early adolescence. Although she had previously been offered therapy and supportive case management, she had never received CBT. Throughout this initial phase of assessment and formulation a further focus was on engagement in a process which by its very nature was likely to activate the schema and relationship difficulties for which she was seeking help. In relation to this point, Young (1990; Young et al., 2003) highlights the relevance of a limited re-parenting role for the therapist in order to provide a therapeutic relationship that counteracts EMS in personality disordered clients:

> As the therapist becomes the (limited) substitute parent, the patient is no longer so dependent on the real parent and is more willing to blame and get angry at the parent. By becoming a stable, nurturing base, the therapist gives the patient the stability to let go of or stand up to a dysfunctional parent... Once patients understand the parent's reasons for mistreating them, they are more able to break the emotional tie between their parent's treatment of them and their self-esteem. They learn that, even though their parent mistreated them, they were worthy of love and respect. (Young et al., 2003; p. 346)

Sophie's statement of her main problems

I find it hard to be compassionate with myself. I experience strong emotions that feel out of control and I think and behave in extremes such as harming myself regularly.

Core beliefs

Self
I am worthless and stupid
I'm more important than anyone else
I'm very clever
I'm special

Others and relationships
Others are better than me
Men are out to abuse me
Other women are inferior

World and future
The world is dangerous
I will be like this forever

Underlying assumptions

Self
If I am seen not to be as clever as others, then I'm worthless
I must be the best or I am a failure
I must be in control all of the time or I won't be able to cope
If I don't try, then I won't have to cope with the uncertainty of how well I've done
If it's all going to go wrong, then I shouldn't try in the first place
If I have to work at understanding things, then I'm not clever
Emotions
If I show emotions, then it means that I have failed and I am weak
If I feel strong and distressing emotions, then I must do something to get rid of them
I have stronger emotions than other people and I can't therefore
control them, nobody could
Moral
I should always be humble, self-effacing and put others before myself
I along with everyone else should always be doing worthwhile activity in the
eyes of their God
If I don't engage in worthwhile activity, then I'm a bad person
Others
If people try to get close to me it's because they want something
If I keep away from people I will be safe and they can't harm me
All men are abusive and will use me for sex, so I must protect myself
When people try to accept and understand my emotions they are a fraud and are not to
be trusted; when people ignore or don't behave as I expect they don't care for me
General
Other people have far more serious problems than me and I am therefore wasting
everyone's time
I can't be helped therefore there is no point even trying as I am beyond help

---

Figure 15.1 Sophie's cognitive case formulation

An integration of Beck's model of personality disorder and behavioural models was used at this stage. This was chosen as it is relatively easy to understand and explain. The model is shown in Figure 15.2.

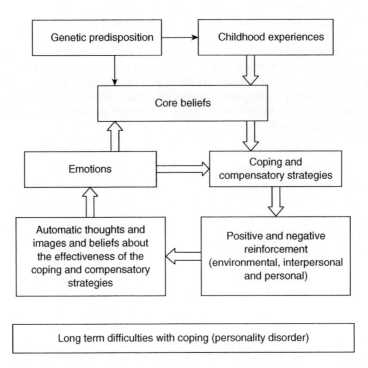

Figure 15.2   Overarching framework for formulation for personality disorders

One of the initial aims was to make the structure and process of therapy understandable to Sophie and to help her understand the interpersonal and behavioural challenges that we would be facing together. In part this was achieved through psycho-education, with the areas covered shown in Table 15.2.

It was also carefully explained that CBT encourages people to learn to understand themselves better and use various strategies to facilitate coping and relationship development. CBT for personality problems, whilst using similar structures, processes and techniques as for the treatment of anxiety and depression, does have some differences of emphasis that address specific issues.

Therapeutic relationship and supervision

From early on in working with Sophie, it became apparent that she had great difficulty in trusting people. This was understandable in the context

Table 15.2   Summary of areas to be covered in psycho-education

1. Educate the client about unmet childhood needs for safety and a stable base, for love, empathy and nurturing, attention, acceptance and praise, consistent and appropriate limits and the recognition and validation of emotions.
2. The process whereby if core needs are unmet or disrupted, unhelpful schema can develop. The aim of therapy is to create a safe and secure environment and process to help the client get their unmet needs met in a helpful and consistent way, and to nurture the development of new, and more helpful schemas.
3. Mid-way in therapy, map out with the client the links between schemas and personal life history making use of assessment tools (that assess schema and attachment) with current difficulties in the client's life and also within the therapeutic relationship.

of her developmental history. The 'limited re-parenting' advocated by Young and his colleagues was an interpersonal focus of attention and was achieved through ensuring clear boundaries and addressing her concerns through guided discovery.

It became equally important to make explicit the automatic thoughts that the therapist and client had about each other. This was because the likelihood emerged in clinical supervision that the automatic thoughts Sophie and the therapist were experiencing were a manifestation of mutual schema activation with potential to impede progress in therapy (Miranda and Andersen, 2007). The working hypothesis considered in supervision was that Sophie, as a person with an insecure attachment, would probably begin to feel strong emotions and perceive the therapist as stronger and wiser. In this context, Sophie's attachment system would be activated, and she would feel increasingly vulnerable. The therapist, because of their own schema and attachment system, might then begin to feel increasingly protective towards the client. Any such responses not only have to be noted by the therapist but also to be managed within professional boundaries and ethical frameworks (Grant et al., 2010).

Grounding and coping skills

From the outset, it was evident that therapy would need to focus on helping Sophie manage episodes of dissociation (a common issue for clients with BPD), as well as fluctuations in her mood. The management of dissociation was achieved through using grounding techniques. Sophie used self-monitoring to identify high risk situations and physical and psychological indicators that she was about to dissociate. An initial grounding technique involved wearing an elastic band that she would 'ping' when an episode began. This approach has ethical concerns as it involves self-inflicted pain and could be interpreted as the therapist seeking to inflict pain or control over the client. However, following discussion, we agreed that it was acceptable on the grounds that it was less harmful for Sophie than cutting herself. We also agreed that it would be an interim strategy.

With practice Sophie learned how, on noticing the first signs of dissociation, to switch her attention to her external world and tune into what was going on around her. At the same time, she engaged in what she termed 'self-dialogue', with self-statements that she was at risk of dissociation but that she could cope. During the latter part of this initial phase mood and stress management was also introduced and continued into the next phase. The standard cognitive and behaviour strategies used were self-monitoring of her mood and activity scheduling, graded tasks to increase her range of activities, training in breathing control and applied relaxation (Öst, 1987), distraction and coping-focused self-talk facilitated through the use of flash cards.

Sessions 7–15

Initially in this stage of therapy, the focus was on the development and consolidation of new, more helpful behaviours. The assessment and formulation can also help identify areas of strength and competence in behaviours that can be encouraged. Sophie's belief that she had to demonstrate how clever she was led to constant striving and at times an exclusive focus on her academic work and social isolation. Her beliefs about being unable to cope with strong emotions resulted in avoidance of situations that had historically triggered an emotional response, and self-regulation through harmful behaviours such as cutting herself. The formulation helped to establish short- and longer-term goals. It also enabled her to determine that a more balanced approach to studying might actually improve her grades through greater focus and quality whilst at the same time enabling her to work on building relationships with her peers. Sophie chose to work on these issues by creating the 'laboratory situation' of joining the university debating society and a political society, using her grades as a benchmark. It was hypothesized that this would ultimately promote changes in her unhelpful beliefs.

The approach of schema therapy differs slightly from standard cognitive therapy in that it emphasizes past to present. The historical focus enables the client to learn about themselves, their beliefs and behaviour in a reflective context and to reconceptualize these as understandable given their learning history and experiences. It also gives a rationale for the difficult schema change work that will be needed. The overall principles of the approach in this phase of therapy are shown in Table 15.3.

Using the information from the assessment and formulation, increased focus was on linking the new experiences and new behaviour testing to the development of new alternative schema. The therapeutic strategy was for the new schema to replace the old ones and then be continually reinforced by the new behaviours.

Table 15.3   Overall principles for schema-focused CBT

1. All interventions are formulation-guided to ensure that a clear rationale is in place and that the client is fully involved.
2. The emphasis is on working together with strengths highlighted, reinforced, maintained, or strengthened further (Kuyken et al., 2009)
3. Psycho-education ensures that the client has an understanding of the cognitive model of schema using metaphors (Stott et al., 2010) where appropriate and supporting hand-outs.
4. Therapy follows the important classical cognitive behavioural philosophy of collaborative empiricism.
5. Begin therapy with coping enhancement and ensure sufficient stability is achieved before commencing schema-focused work.
6. Emphasize building new schemas rather than challenging old ones. In some cases, learning to recognize and ignore schema, acting against the schema or engaging in schema camouflage (where the client hides from others that their schema has been activated) also need to be deployed.
7. Close attention to ongoing evaluation, monitoring for relational fractures and addressing these as they occur is usually required.
8. In the process of developing more helpful schema, it is highly likely that experiential methods will be used to create new experiences and ways of relating to self and others. This includes strategies such as imagery, metaphor, role-play, behavioural experiments, as well as creative approaches for some clients such as art or psychodrama.

Session 16 to the end of therapy

During this phase of therapy, beliefs and behaviours were targeted further as Sophie's competence and confidence increased. Within cognitive therapy, a number of cognitive and emotional strategies can be utilized to target specific schema and behaviour change. The rationale is included in Table 15.4 and demonstrates how, in the case of Sophie, these were derived from the assessment and formulation.

Preparation for the end of therapy, maintenance and relapse prevention

Preparation for the end of therapy had begun at the initial assessment stage. Sophie had expressed anxieties about further rejection as symbolized and enacted through being discharged. The formulation was very helpful in this regard; it was predictable that the ending of therapy would be difficult and so the formulation provided an opportunity to plan for this and prepare Sophie. This phase can signal a change in protocol from standard CBT where therapy sessions might become more spaced. For Sophie the strategy

Table 15.4 Summary of cognitive, behavioural and emotional change strategies used with personality disorder

Cognitive change strategy	Description of the strategy	Rationale for the strategy
Guided discovery (Socratic questioning)	Using a combination of automatic thought records and within-session work, specific examples of therapy-interfering beliefs and behaviours were identified with alternatives generated within session and tested across the sessions and in real-life situations.	This strategy is at the heart of CBT and increases self-awareness, recognition of automatic processing and direct change of unhelpful thoughts and beliefs.
Emotional regulation	Self-monitoring of emotions through diary keeping and labelling emotions.	The self-monitoring increased awareness of the situations that were triggering strong emotions and avoided experiences that were later targeted though behavioural experiments and exposure. The labelling of emotions helped with decentring and recognition of the normality of the experience for Sophie. This was often combined with guided discovery to identify beliefs about emotions and decrease unhelpful meaning-making and processing.
Continuum	This strategy involves the identification of unhelpful negative core beliefs and working with the client to generate an equal but opposite belief. This creates the two ends of the pole of dichotomous beliefs. Guided discovery is then used to challenge the rigidity and polarization.	This was an important approach for Sophie as it helped her address her automatic reaction to situations where schema were activated, and supported the initial stages of identifying more helpful beliefs. It was also found to be a 'cold' and detached strategy. Whilst this helped her be objective it needed linking to behavioural experiments to achieve the actual belief change.

(Continued)

Table 15.4 (Continued)

Cognitive change strategy	Description of the strategy	Rationale for the strategy
Historical test of schemas	This involves identifying the origins of schema and the surrounding circumstances.	This was another strategy that Sophie found helpful and involved her seeking supporting and disconfirming evidence for beliefs about herself and her own and others' responsibilities throughout her lifetime. It was especially helpful for Sophie to understand her belief changes and understandable consequential behaviours as they had developed over time.
Positive data log	This is a structured notebook that lists positive situations and responses.	Again Sophie found it helpful when schema were targeted for change, helping her recognize positive situations that were not being acknowledged. It began the process of adding a balance to her perceptions of herself and others. Later in the therapy this intervention was used to gather data to support the development of new, more adaptive schema.
Schema flashcard	This is a card designed to help the client focus on the here and now and the reality of a situation, rather than their own unhelpful schematic response. The schema flashcard headings were: Acknowledge current situation... Right now I feel... The schema is... This makes me feel... And I want to do... This schema exaggerates...	Sophie quickly internalized what was needed in order to remind herself of what she needed to do.

was to plan in weekly sessions in order to address her anxieties. Care was taken from the initial stages to stress that the aim of therapy was to enable Sophie to cope as her own therapist. It was emphasized that rather than being a rejection, agreed reductions in the frequency of sessions were a sign of increased autonomy, self-determination and important milestones of progress. Sophie's thoughts, feelings and behaviours were checked carefully every two to three sessions in respect to progress and discharge in order to identify any activated schema. Sophie developed flashcards to help her challenge her old schema and to remind her of helpful behaviours if she felt out of control or began to dissociate. In the final few sessions a written summary of the therapy process was developed, as well as a formulation-driven blueprint of predicted difficulties and how she might address them.

Outcome of therapy

Sophie was engaged in CBT for 20 sessions. At the last session, she reported that she had noticed a number of changes in her experience which suggested that sufficient progress towards achieving her goals had been made. Sophie reported these changes as shown in Table 15.5.

Table 15.5   Sophie's description and reflection on the outcome and process of therapy

---

I am less fearful of how I feel, although this is still very difficult for me at times and I still get the urge to hurt myself but I can now understand that I can cope, that I will only feel this way for a short time and that feeling this way is normal and that it is OK. I can now recognize some of the triggers for feeling out of control and detached. I try not to avoid these but notice how I think and feel without getting over involved in them.

I try to be more myself with people and project being confident and happy. This is still difficult for me because knowing who I am is in many ways new to me. I now recognize that there is no 'standard me' and that this will also change over time.

Every few weeks I sit down and review my own progress by working through my relapse prevention plan. This helps to remind me of how far I have come. It also reminds me that I have a long way still to go and that can be scary at times.

I have also realized that it is not just the strategies I have learned that have helped me. I now realize how important the therapy relationship can be. This is because at times I did not believe in some of the therapy techniques or the vicious circle models that my therapist drew for me. I felt doubtful and scared. With help I took some risks – that then became my mantra: 'take the risk.' Through this I learned to rely on the trust I felt and that helped me to trust myself and to give it a fair try. Also, it was important to me early on to feel that my therapist could understand me. My therapist was a lot older than me and I desperately wanted to be liked. They had a terribly dry sense of humour that I somehow liked. It was important that we connected and got along well fairly quickly.

Follow-up

After completion of therapy, a follow-up period was initiated as part of Sophie's relapse prevention plan. This consisted of the client being seen at one month, three months, six months and 12 months after discharge. At each of these sessions the outcome measures were completed to check progress against baseline measures, and a review and problem-solving of any difficulties was carried out.

Therapy, formulation and supervision implications of the case

Sophie's experience of BPD and the therapy illustrate a number of important issues for schema-focused cognitive therapy. CBT has been shown to be at least as effective as other therapies but also that complete recovery is unlikely. Sophie was fairly typical in this sense. This has to be acknowledged with the client from the early stages of therapy.

Attention to the therapeutic relationship and the co-constructed experience of the processes within the relationship also have to be at the forefront of practice and addressed in supervision. The assessment and formulation helps greatly with making sense of, and dealing with, problems as they arise and can be useful in predicting likely issues that will need to be addressed. In addition therapy has phases, organized around specific goals, to break down the overwhelming nature of the problems and complex issues being addressed. In Sophie's case testing and ending the relationship were particular issues that were predicted and addressed.

Supervision

One of the aims of this chapter is to illustrate in simple terms the situational formulation for the therapist's and Sophie's relational roadblocks. It is difficult to both attempt to focus on the processes and content of therapy and for the therapist to attend to their own internal processes. This has the potential to be disorientating. Thus Sophie was discussed in clinical supervision and a formulation developed, as shown in Figure 15.3, alongside the principles for supervision (Table 15.6) as a road map to guide the supervisor and the therapist through the process. This way, it proved possible to ensure that boundaries were maintained and that the goals of each session and phases of therapy were clear and adhered to in the face of strong emotions and Sophie's challenging interpersonal behaviours.

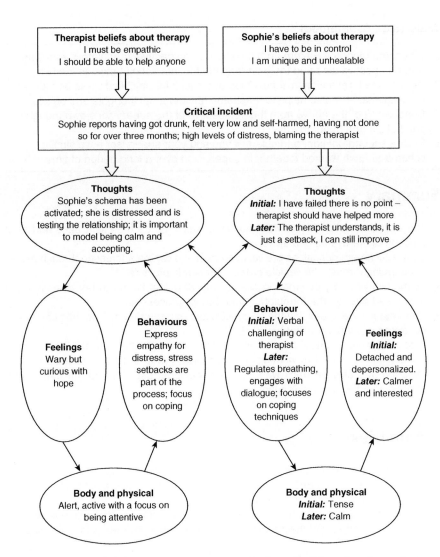

Figure 15.3   Cognitive behavioural formulation showing the therapist's and client's responses to a client's self-harming behaviour

Table 15.6   Principles for the use of supervision for CBT with personality disorders

1. When experiencing an alliance rupture or other interpersonal issues in the therapy process, try to stay calm and remain true to the model by understanding what is taking place through drawing on the formulation. These moments are often the most useful parts of therapy, offering an opportunity to work with affect in the 'here and now'.

(Continued)

Table 15.6   (Continued)

2. When formulating a rupture from the client's perspective, formulate it from your own perspective also and try to understand the interaction between the two.
3. Discuss the formulation in supervision and check for any blind spots or alternative formulations. This also helps to de-shame any personal thoughts and beliefs.
4. Consider all of the above from the perspective of the supervisor's own thoughts and beliefs and about therapy.
5. Seek a second opinion, particularly if you and your supervisor have similar schema or have worked together in supervision over a long period of time.

Summary

✓ The symptoms of BPD can wax and wane over time as the client ages and as a function of life events and stressors.
✓ Early attachment difficulties are very common and can be addressed through partial re-parenting through the vehicle of the therapeutic process.
✓ Co-morbidity is very common in clients with BPD and needs to be assessed and addressed through the formulation and therapy processes.
✓ Understanding and utilising the co-constructed nature of the therapeutic process is central to working with clients with BPD.
✓ A lot of the work is done in session and is intensive for both the client and the therapist.
✓ Supervision is crucial to working with this client group to help to develop the formulation and stay on track with both the relational aspects and the therapeutic strategy in a flexible and responsive way.

Activities

1. Try to apply the methods of case formulation outlined in this chapter to one of your clients with BPD. In particular focus on how you address the relational and co-morbid aspects of the person.
2. Take the above formulation to supervision and develop it further with reflection on your practice and theoretical strengths and areas you may wish to develop.

Further reading

Beck, A.T., Davis, D.D. and Freeman, A. (2014) *Cognitive Therapy of Personality Disorders*. 3rd edn. New York: Guilford Press.
This book has been recently updated with extensive reviews of research, new conceptualizations and techniques, and is illustrated with theorists' and clinicians' knowledge of the therapeutic relationship, therapy practice and techniques and how to address roadblocks to change.

Davidson, K. (2007) *Cognitive Therapy for Personality Disorders: A Guide for Clinicians*. 2nd edn. Hove, East Sussex: Routledge.
This book focuses on the key aspects of working collaboratively with borderline personality disorder and is the ideal follow-up reading to this chapter.

SIXTEEN   Janine: A Case Study of Psychosis

Sandra Bucci and Gillian Haddock

Learning objectives

After reading this chapter and completing the activities at the end of it, you should be able to:

- Be aware of the theoretical base and most recent evidence and innovations for CBT for psychosis.
- Understand the impact of early adverse experiences on current cognitive, emotional and behavioural experiences in psychosis.
- Understand and appreciate the key elements of assessment and formulation as they apply to psychosis.
- Apply the formulation to empirically validated interventions.

Introduction

Psychosis is a term used to describe a broad range of experiences such as hallucinations, delusions and confused thinking. Schizophrenia is a form of psychosis that affects 1 in 100 people worldwide, often below the age of 35, and is typically underpinned by an apparent distortion or confusion of reality. Common symptoms include hallucinations (in all sensory domains), delusions (e.g. paranoid beliefs) and 'negative' symptoms (e.g. cognitive dysfunction, avolition, anhedonia). The onset of psychosis varies but typically occurs between the ages of 15 and 35 years, particularly in males. For women, onset tends to be more varied across the lifespan. It has been shown that the early phase of psychosis is a critical period influencing the long-term course and outcome. First line treatment is often anti-psychotic medication, case management and social care. Psychological interventions (including cognitive behavioural individual and family interventions) are also a recommended treatment for schizophrenia in the UK (NICE, 2014).

Although neurobiological elements regarding the onset of psychosis have been widely explored in the literature, the cause of psychosis is still largely debated. There is evidence that psychosocial determinants, such as childhood adversities, life events and family environment may increase the risk of psychosis and/or contribute to the maintenance or worsening of symptoms and effect recovery (Varese et al., 2012). Recovery from psychosis has been greatly debated and evidence is mixed depending on the definition of recovery that is used. Many researchers first conceptualized recovery in terms of a total absence of symptoms; however, some researchers argue that whilst the biomedical approach to defining recovery from physical illness might be acceptable, the same paradigm is not necessarily applicable when defining recovery from mental health problems (Law et al., 2014). In support of this view, a significant body of research has emerged looking at how service users themselves define recovery. This has led to a widening of the concept of recovery to include other factors such as social functioning, rebuilding one's life and oneself following an experience of psychosis, and acquiring hope for achieving a better future (Pitt et al., 2007). In light of the service user movement, psychological treatments such as CBT have more recently been directed towards a wide range of outcomes for people with a diagnosis of schizophrenia, which may include psychotic symptoms, distress, anxiety, depression, social and role functioning, and self-esteem, to name a few.

Theoretical and research base

Whilst psychological treatments for psychosis have received less attention in the literature than some other mental health problems, a case study by Beck (1952) reported on the treatment of a man with paranoid delusions using a form of cognitive therapy. Since that early case study, there has been a wealth of descriptions of interventions, usually focused on the remediation of particular psychotic symptoms. Whilst case study research showed successful reduction in the occurrence of specific target behaviours, there was little evaluation of this type of approach in larger controlled trials and little evidence that the approaches generalized across situations or people. These approaches also highlighted an emphasis on the removal or reduction of psychotic symptoms rather than focusing on the broader concepts of recovery highlighted above. Nevertheless, these early approaches led to a growing body of well conducted controlled research trials evaluating psychological treatments for psychosis resulting in government bodies (NICE, 2014) endorsing the use of psychological approaches in the management of psychosis.

There are a number of reviews evaluating the effectiveness of CBT interventions for psychosis. Wykes and colleagues (2008) conducted a robust meta-analysis of 34 CBT trials for schizophrenia across various countries. There were overall beneficial effects for the target symptom in 33 studies (effect size = 0.400; 95% CI = 0.25, 0.55) as well as significant effects for positive symptoms (32 studies), negative symptoms (23 studies), functioning (15 studies) and social anxiety (two studies), with effects ranging from 0.35 to 0.44. There was no effect on hopelessness. Overall, results from this meta-analysis indicate a modest effect size in improving positive symptoms compared to standard psychiatric care (TAU). Jauhar et al. (2014) recently updated the Wykes et al. (2008) systematic review and meta-analysis of CBT for schizophrenia. The review examined the effect of CBT on the core symptoms of schizophrenia. Fifty-two studies from various countries were included in the meta-analysis. Pooled effect sizes were −0.33 (95% CI = −0.47 to −0.19) in 34 studies of overall symptoms, −0.25 (95% CI = −0.37 to −0.13) in 33 studies of positive symptoms and −0.13 (95% CI = −0.25 to −0.01) in 34 studies of negative symptoms. Masking significantly moderated effect size in the meta-analyses of overall symptoms and positive symptoms, but not for negative symptoms. The authors concluded that CBT has a small therapeutic effect on core schizophrenia symptoms.

In summary, meta-analyses demonstrate small to moderate effects for CBT for psychosis. There is also encouraging evidence that CBT can help those choosing not to take antipsychotic medication (Morrison et al., 2012a), as well as in reducing transition in those at ultra high risk for developing psychosis (Morrison et al., 2012b). Furthermore, CBT for psychosis seems to show some significant promise in treating sub-groups of people with co-occurring symptoms or diagnoses; for example, for people with co-morbid problems of violence and aggression (Haddock et al., 2009), substance use (Baker et al., 2006; Barrowclough et al., 2010), learning difficulty (Haddock et al., 2004) and for those with specific symptoms, such as command hallucinations (Birchwood et al., 2014).

Case summary

Janine was a 35-year-old White British woman who lives with her mother in a socially deprived area of Manchester, UK. She was seen by the therapist at a secondary care mental health service after her psychiatrist referred her for treatment targeting voices and anxiety. Janine has had a history of psychosis since her late teens.

At initial screening, Janine was concerned that the therapist would share the information she disclosed during sessions with the other members of the multi-disciplinary team and thought it was a 'waste of time' attending therapy. Her view was, 'What's happened in the past should stay in the past'. She explained that the only reason she attended the screening session was because her doctor told her that he thought therapy would be of benefit. Despite her reservations, Janine engaged with the therapist in the screening session: she responded well to Socratic questions around voice-hearing experiences in particular, expressed willingness to understand her voice-hearing experiences and the causes of these (although vehemently stated that she would not answer questions about her childhood), and agreed that between-session tasks would be a helpful way to test out unhelpful beliefs. As such, she was deemed to be an appropriate candidate for CBT.

Presenting problems

Janine's presenting problems were feeling anxious and significant distress associated with hearing a male voice that persistently called her name, 'Janine. Janine'. The voice was both derogatory ('You are useless', 'Nobody cares about you') and commanding in nature ('Cut yourself'; 'Run into the road'). During the assessment, it transpired that Janine also ruminated about past childhood sexual abuse and witnessed extreme domestic violence growing up. She used cannabis (daily) to avoid unwanted intrusions related to past abuse and events, but did not consider her cannabis use to be problematic. Whilst Janine made it clear initially that she did not wish to talk about past abuse, at the end of the assessment phase she felt that continuing to avoid acknowledging past abuse might be maintaining her current presentation. Therefore, at the end of the assessment, her goals for treatment were: (1) to talk about past abuse; and (2) to reduce the distress associated with the male voice she heard.

Janine's history

Janine was an only child whose parents divorced when she was 10 years of age. Up until this time, she described her parents as having a 'loveless' relationship and she often witnessed domestic violence. Janine recalled that her mother required hospitalizing on a couple of occasions following assaults. Janine was incontinent as a child and was often made to sit on a plastic covered chair in the home. She described feeling 'different' to others, including her peers, and described frequent episodes of bullying at school. She struggled academically, often failing to attend school, and left when she was 16 years old. After this time, Janine worked as a retail assistant in a local grocery store until she experienced her first episode of psychosis aged 23 years. She had experienced two further episodes of psychosis since then; both episodes resulted in a six month hospital admission. She had received the disability support pension since her first admission and had always lived with her mother in the family home. Janine described her mother as both hostile and critical but despite this, said that her mother was her main source of support and someone she could not live without.

During the course of the assessment, Janine described being sexually abused by her maternal uncle between the ages of 13 and 15 years. Her uncle would visit the family home two nights a week and on weekends. It was around the time the abuse started that she began experimenting with cannabis, but it was after her first hospital admission that she started using daily. At the time of assessment, she smoked six joints (skunk) per day. Some time after the abuse stopped Janine began hearing a male, malevolent voice which she attributed to the devil punishing her for doing 'bad things in the past'. The voice was of a commanding nature, and often instructed her to take a knife and cut her arms or to walk into a road of oncoming traffic. Janine appeased the voice by carrying a knife in her handbag and by telling the voice that she would walk alongside the road in front of her house. She stepped out in front of oncoming traffic on one occasion and shortly after this incident was hospitalized. Janine recalled a suicide attempt when she was 14 years of age; she took an overdose of painkillers and was taken to hospital, but was discharged a few hours later.

Janine had been compliant with anti-psychotic medication since her first hospital admission in her early twenties. Whilst she attended medication review appointments with her treating psychiatrist on a six-monthly basis, her medication regime had not changed since her first admission. Following her first hospital admission, a referral was made for CBT sessions. Janine attended the first two appointments, but stopped attending after her voice told her that the therapist was putting 'dirty thoughts' in her head and that 'he is just another man who will take advantage of you'. Furthermore, her mother insisted that there was no need for her to see a health professional and air the family problems. Her mother endorsed the view 'what's happened in the past stays in the past'. As such, Janine had never fully attended psychological therapy in relation to past life events and psychosis-related experiences.

Assessment

As with all clinical work, it is important to develop a collaborative, empathic, trusting and warm relationship at the outset. A strong therapeutic relationship is an essential element in gathering information and promoting engagement in the model of therapy being delivered. Normalizing experiences and distress during the assessment phase, as well as the difficulties of entering into a new relationship with a health professional, can assist clients in feeling understood and diffuse any fears associated with therapy.

The assessment with Janine took place over four 45-minute weekly sessions. In order to assess for suitability to a CBT for psychosis intervention, we recommend using some of the assessment measures described in the 'measures' section of this chapter. These measures help elicit many of the defining features of psychotic experiences. Furthermore, using a range of measures can assist the therapist in gathering information about possible co-morbid factors, such as substance misuse, trauma, hopes for recovery and overall functioning.

First, the assessment with Janine was guided by a general clinical model of psychosis (Haddock and Siddle, 2003), which focused on developmental factors that contributed to Janine's psychotic experiences and general psychosis-related factors contributing to the onset and maintenance of her voices (see Figure 16.1).

Second, using some of the measures described below and drawing on the cognitive model of voices, a more specific cognitive behavioural assessment was carried out. The therapist explored the nature and severity of

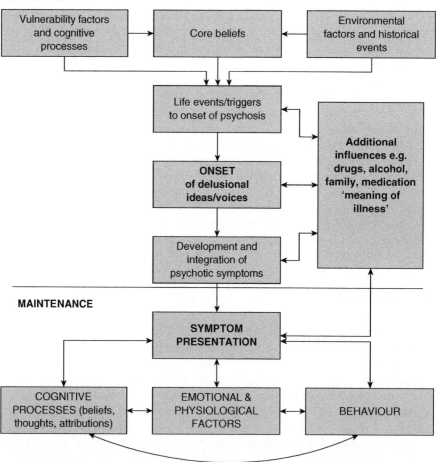

Figure 16.1 Haddock and Siddle's (2003) model of psychosis

the distressing voice, Janine's beliefs about the voice's power and omniscience, resistance and compliance strategies she engaged in in response to voice-hearing, and the level of distress experienced as a consequence of the voice. Using the Beliefs About Voices Questionnaire-Revised (BAVQ-R; Chadwick et al., 2000), the therapist discovered that Janine experienced her voice as extremely powerful because it seemed to know things about her past she had not disclosed to anyone. She further believed that the voice was 100 per cent uncontrollable. When she heard the voice, she described feeling out of breath, nervous, frightened, ashamed and was often fearful of leaving the house. As such, she experienced the voice as extremely distressing. Given her history of trauma, the childhood trauma questionnaire (CTQ; Bernstein and Fink, 1998) was administered in an attempt to elicit further information about the nature and severity of past abuse experienced. The Alcohol Use Disorders Identification Test (AUDIT; Babor et al., 2001) and the Drug Abuse Screening Test (DAST; Skinner, 1982) were also administered to gather more information about the frequency and severity of cannabis use. In addition, the therapist asked about Janine's reasons for using cannabis, which included: to 'take the edge off the voices', to 'relax' and to 'not think about things'.

It was also important to assess Janine's mood given the strong link between affect and the maintenance of psychosis. A thorough risk assessment was carried out in light of her past suicide attempt and the content of the voice commands; it was important to ensure that Janine had appropriate supports and strategies in place to keep her safe. Confidentiality and its limits were openly discussed at the outset of the assessment.

Finally, given the important association between psychosocial determinants (e.g. interpersonal trauma, loss, bullying and abuse) and development of later psychosis, a more general clinical history was taken in addition to administering cognitive behavioural specific assessment measures. The therapist gathered information about Janine's developmental, personal, family and social background. This was with a view to developing a greater understanding of any important adverse life experiences that might be considered in the formulation and the development of core beliefs, unhelpful appraisals and in developing alternative causal explanations for psychotic experiences.

Measures

In order to assess suitability for CBT for psychosis and to gather baseline scores from which to measure progress in therapy and build a CBT formulation, we often use a set of measures or tools to understand the defining features of client's beliefs about, and experiences of, psychotic experiences and associated co-morbidities. There are a range of measures which can be used, including those which aim to elicit symptoms and assess their severity (e.g. Positive and Negative Syndrome Schedule; Kay et al., 1989), those which assess and measure dimensions of symptoms (e.g. Psychotic Symptom Rating Scales (PSYRATS); Haddock et al., 1999), those which allow an in-depth CBT exploration of psychosis (e.g. Maudsley Assessment of Delusions; Wessely et al., 1993; Beliefs About Voices Questionnaire-Revised (BAVQ-R); Cognitive Assessment of Voices Schedule (CAV); Chadwick et al., 2000) and also self-report symptom measures which have been developed in collaboration with services users, such as the Subjective Experiences of Psychosis Scale (Haddock et al., 2011), the Questionnaire about the Process of Recovery (QPR; Neil et al., 2009) and the Choice of Outcome in CBT for Psychoses Scale (Greenwood et al., 2010).

In addition, traditional measures used to assess other mental health problems such as depression (Calgary Depression Scale for Schizophrenia (CDSS); Addington et al., 1993), anxiety (Beck Anxiety Interview (BAI); Beck et al., 1988), self-esteem (Self-Esteem Rating Scale; Lecomte et al., 2006), substance misuse (Alcohol Use Disorders Identification Test (AUDIT); Babor et al., 2001; The Drug Abuse Screening Test (DAST); Skinner, 1982; Readiness to Change Questionnaire; Rollnick et al., 1992) and trauma (Childhood Trauma Questionnaire (CTQ); Bernstein et al., 1994) are commonly used in assessing the overall presentation of someone with psychosis.

Case formulation

CBT for psychosis, although following a common theme and set of principles, has been informed by a number of theoretical and conceptual influences with a number of different models proposed (e.g. Garety et al., 2001; Morrison, 2001; Tarrier and Haddock, 2001; Meaden et al., 2013). Some of these models have been developed to help to conceptualize the overall experiences of an individual with psychosis whilst others are specifically directed at attempting to explain a key symptom or presentation. Regarding Janine, different aspects of her presentation can be formulated by incorporating both an overall model of her experiences and by focusing specifically on her voice-hearing experience. As such, we focus on two models in this chapter: (a) an over-arching formulation model of Janine's problems (see Figure 16.1), which was used to guide the initial assessment and; and (b) a model specifically focused on command hallucinations given that one of Janine's treatment goals was to reduce voice-related distress.

Cognitive model of command hallucinations

The cognitive therapy for command hallucinations model (CTCH) was developed by Birchwood and colleagues in the UK and is described in detail by Meaden et al. (2013). The CTCH model is grounded in both cognitive and social rank theory. CTCH aims to reduce voice-related distress through altering the power balance between voice-hearer and voice. This is achieved by raising the power of the individual and viewing the relationship between voice and voice-hearer as an interpersonal one. In the CTCH model for commanding voices, voice activity is appraised within a dominant-subordinate schema. This gives rise to power beliefs, which in turn have a set of emotional and behavioural consequences. Appraisals concerning omniscience (the sense that the voice is all-knowing), omnipotence (the voice is all-powerful), control, compliance, identity, and the meaning and purpose of the voice elicit emotional distress and safety behaviours. These safety behaviours serve to maintain power beliefs by preventing their disconfirmation (see Figure 16.2).

Initially, a traditional ABC model of formulation with Janine was developed in order to distil the important aspects of the voice and to socialize her to the cognitive model of psychosis. A discussion ensued, encouraging Janine to distinguish between facts and beliefs, and to see how viewing the two as different meant that thoughts were amenable to change (and thus indirectly increasing Janine's sense of control). Applying this to the cognitive model, the therapist can highlight how power beliefs ('the voices are very powerful') in general impact the distress Janine experienced (fear, anxiety) and consequently her behavioural responses to the voices (appeasing the voice by carrying a knife in her handbag and walking alongside the road). This simpler formulation was then fed into the fuller CTCH formulation, and as sessions progressed, beliefs about control compliance, omniscience and so on, were formulated. For Janine, hearing a male voice that repeatedly said her name reminded her of her abuser, thus reinforcing her fear and beliefs about powerlessness and uncontrollability. Other statements, such as 'nobody cares about you' reinforced her core beliefs about being unlovable and undeserving of care and protection. In the latter stages of therapy, reformulating the voice as de-contextualized memories from past abuse dispelled Janine's fears that she was 'going mad' and allowed her to develop alternative causal explanations of psychotic experiences, which ultimately resulted in a significant reduction in the level of distress she experienced in response to voice activity.

Formulating diverse aspects of Janine's case, and sharing aspects of the cognitive model at different points in therapy, serves to avoid overwhelming clients with personally relevant and often highly distressing information, which in turn keeps clients engaged in therapy. In this way, formulation when working with complex cases is better viewed as a process rather than a discrete event.

Engagement in therapy

When working with individuals with psychosis, it is important to address any engagement beliefs that clients might hold. Due to the distressing

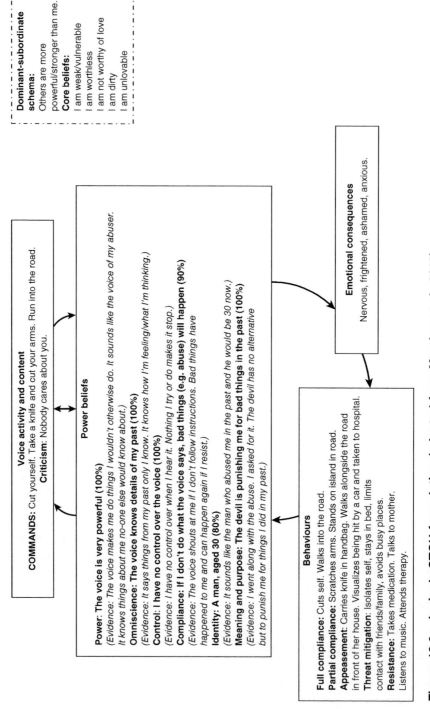

Dominant-subordinate schema:
Others are more powerful/stronger than me.
Core beliefs:
I am weak/vulnerable
I am worthless
I am not worthy of love
I am dirty
I am unlovable

Voice activity and content
COMMANDS: Cut yourself. Take a knife and cut your arms. Run into the road.
Criticism: Nobody cares about you.

Power beliefs

Power: The voice is very powerful (100%)
(Evidence: The voice makes me do things I wouldn't otherwise do. It sounds like the voice of my abuser. It knows things about me no-one else would know about.)
Omniscience: The voice knows details of my past (100%)
(Evidence: It says things from my past only I know. It knows how I'm feeling/what I'm thinking.)
Control: I have no control over the voice (100%)
(Evidence: I have no control over when I hear it. Nothing I try or do makes it stop.)
Compliance: If I don't do what the voice says, bad things (e.g. abuse) will happen (90%)
(Evidence: The voice shouts at me if I don't follow instructions. Bad things have happened to me and can happen again if I resist.)
Identity: A man, aged 30 (80%)
(Evidence: It sounds like the man who abused me in the past and he would be 30 now.)
Meaning and purpose: The devil is punishing me for bad things in the past (100%)
(Evidence: I went along with the abuse. I asked for it. The devil has no alternative but to punish me for things I did in my past.)

Emotional consequences
Nervous, frightened, ashamed, anxious.

Behaviours

Full compliance: Cuts self. Walks into the road.
Partial compliance: Scratches arms. Stands on island in road.
Appeasement: Carries knife in handbag. Walks alongside the road in front of her house. Visualizes being hit by a car and taken to hospital.
Threat mitigation: Isolates self, stays in bed, limits contact with friends/family, avoids busy places.
Resistance: Takes medication. Talks to mother. Listens to music. Attends therapy.

Figure 16.2 Janine's CTCH formulation (adapted from Meaden et al., 2013)

nature of Janine's voices the early sessions were shorter than the average CBT session, lasting around 25–30 minutes in length. Janine also did not attend some of the early sessions. Therapists may need to be persistent and flexible when arranging appointments with individuals who have complex presentations. Engaging Janine's mother was also an important factor in facilitating Janine's attendance to sessions. Openly discussing difficulties in entering a new relationship, particularly in light of the fact that Janine found it difficult to trust important people in her life and often found herself in subordinate positions developmentally (e.g. being bullied at school, being abused by her uncle, powerless over the domestic violence she witnessed) can allay clients' fears and help them feel understood. In addition, anticipating problems in engagement, such as anticipating that the voices might comment on the therapist (which may reflect the client's own anxiety about the trustworthiness of the therapist) and fears that therapy might not help, can dispel concerns and help build trust in the therapeutic process. It is important not to dispute or argue with clients, particularly when they may not be convinced that there is any benefit to be gained from treatment. If clinicians notice that a client has become guarded or suspicious, exploring this shift is vital. Simply stating, 'I wonder if I have I said or done something that has upset you?' can often diffuse the situation and allows the therapist to nip problems in the bud.

Despite these recommendations, given the complexity of individuals' experiences and in keeping with a CBT model of psychosis, it is important to balance persistence with giving individuals the space to consider the pros and cons of therapy to ensure that clients experience a sense of control over therapy sessions (Meaden et al., 2013). Where clients are difficult to engage, and/or do not necessarily see the benefits of engaging in change, rapid engagement using motivational interviewing approaches can be useful (Miller and Rollnick, 2003) to help identify what is important from the individual's perspective and how their current situation is interfering with achieving their goals. This can build engagement and help people identify how changes made in therapy can lead to recovery.

Innovations in therapy

There has been a general growth of therapeutic approaches that extend beyond original cognitive theory to include an eclectic combination of theoretical and philosophical influences (e.g. mindfulness, Acceptance and Commitment Therapy, meta-cognitive therapy, compassion-focused therapy). However, whilst evidence-based psychosocial interventions have been developed in recent years to help clients with psychosis manage symptoms and well-being, they are rarely available; a shortage of trained clinicians and pressure on resources mean that of people who could benefit, only fewer than 10 per cent have access to evidence-based

CBT interventions (Haddock et al., 2014a). Health information technologies (HIT), such as telephone therapy, smartphones and software applications (apps) hold enormous promise in expanding the reach of health care in serious mental health problems (Clarke and Yarborough, 2013) as they are unconstrained by the limitations of existing mental health services. Telephone therapy, for example, can increase access to services for those people who find it difficult to engage in traditional face-to-face therapy, and for some, these offer a viable alternative without any loss of therapeutic alliance (Haddock et al., 2014b). Efforts to develop mobile technologies in monitoring early warning signs of schizophrenia and treating psychosis-related symptoms are also showing much promise (Granholm et al., 2011; Ben-Zeev et al., 2014; Bucci et al., 2015).

Key clinical and case management considerations

Lifetime prevalence of suicide for those with a diagnosis of schizophrenia is higher than other populations (around 4.9–10 per cent; Palmer et al., 2005), and even higher in those with persistent psychotic symptoms. A substantial number of individuals will attempt suicide, and suicidal ideation is common in many more. Risk factors for suicide in psychosis are similar to those in the general population but other factors are also associated with high suicide risk in schizophrenia, including a higher level of education, fear of further psychological deterioration, having a co-morbid chronic physical illness, active hallucinations and delusions, the presence of insight, experiencing feelings of hopelessness in association with depression and poor treatment adherence (Hor and Taylor, 2010). As such, the presence of suicidal ideation needs to be assessed, as does whether any specific plans have been made or actions have been taken.

Co-morbid substance use in people with a diagnosis of schizophrenia is higher compared with other mental health groups. Estimates of prevalence vary depending on the location and type of participants included. For example, Regier et al. (1990) identified 47 per cent of participants with a diagnosis of schizophrenia to have a lifetime prevalence of some form of substance use. The presence of substance misuse is associated with a range of negative outcomes, such as higher rates of violent and aggressive behaviour, more frequent relapse rates, higher suicide rates, and poorer engagement and adherence with services (Maslin, 2003). The reasons for the inflated rates are not clearly elucidated; research suggests a number of contributory factors that vary amongst individuals, such as to control unpleasant symptoms, to manage side effects, to cope with unpleasant affect and to increase social confidence (Gregg et al., 2007) many of which are similar among non-psychosis populations. People with psychosis may not always recognize that their substance misuse is contributing to poor outcomes. In fact, many clients may consider their substance use to be the only good thing in their lives. As a result, it can be difficult to engage individuals in strategies to overcome substance misuse problems and psychosis. Motivational interviewing can be used to help explore the negative consequences of substance use and may be used as a precursor to CBT for some people (Baker et al., 2006; Barrowclough et al., 2010).

Psychosis is in many cases a relapsing problem. Around 80 per cent of those treated for a first episode of psychosis relapse within five years, with cumulative relapse rates of 78 per cent and 86 per cent for second and third relapses during this period (Robinson et al., 1999). Given the prevalence and considerable negative consequences of relapse, an important part of any psychological intervention for psychosis is to plan for the future. The aim of any relapse prevention or 'keeping well' intervention is to minimize the impact or likelihood of a relapse rather than to avoid the possibility of further relapses occurring. Monitoring early warning signs (EWS) involves not only assisting the client in identifying and monitoring early signs of relapse, but also developing concrete action plans for dealing with them (e.g. stress reduction techniques, intensive psychological support). Early signs commonly reported to emerge in the weeks before a relapse include: anxiety, dysphoria, insomnia, poor concentration and attenuated psychotic symptoms (Early Signs Scale (ESS); Birchwood et al., 1989), although no one single trigger or symptom will result in a relapse. Rather, identifying clients' EWS can reduce the time it takes for clients to access necessary treatment. Information gathered from family members/carers can help patients identify EWS and potential triggers of further relapse. Often, towards the end of therapy a detailed 'keeping well' or relapse prevention plan is produced to prepare an individual for dealing with future stressors, which might contribute to relapse.

Follow-up

After therapy was completed, follow-up sessions were arranged at one month and three months post-therapy in order to review Janine's relapse prevention plan as well as symptoms, mood and functioning. At each follow-up session, outcome measures were completed to compare follow-up scores against baseline scores. The relapse prevention plan was reviewed and updated accordingly and discussions were held with Janine's mother and her clinical care team to facilitate gains made in therapy.

Therapy implications of the case

Janine's presentation, alongside adverse early experiences, substance misuse and current symptoms, are fairly typical of clients presenting to therapy with a psychosis-related diagnosis. In many cases, trauma and substance misuse are the rule rather than the exception. Taking time to engage Janine fostered rapport and facilitated trust in the therapist. Focusing on the issues on Janine's problem list, rather than exploring the issues the therapist believed were important, empowered Janine, enabling her to take control of therapy. This was important given her history of disempowerment and her beliefs about powerlessness. Developing alternative explanations for her psychotic symptoms meant Janine developed a personal model for understanding psychotic experiences, in contrast to her previous beliefs and fears of 'going mad'.

Recommendations to therapists

Conducting assessments and delivering CBT interventions for psychosis share the same principles of CBT as for other mental health problems described elsewhere in this book. However, the nature of the symptoms and the challenges with psychosis mean that therapy may be modified depending on the needs of the individual. For example, engagement may take longer as psychotic symptoms and the distress surrounding them can interfere with an individual's ability to spend time talking about their experiences. Increased agitation or drowsiness from medication may also interfere with therapy engagement. Therapists should, therefore, be flexible with the length, timing and place of delivery of therapy. In addition, psychosis is a multidimensional phenomenon and individuals may present with many different problems, making it difficult to prioritize problems and decide on a focus for therapy. As a result, assessment and formulation may be lengthy and therapists are challenged to ensure that a formulation can be reached collaboratively in a way that the client can easily understand.

Summary

✓ Good outcomes can be achieved using psychological approaches for people with psychosis.
✓ The cognitive behavioural model for psychosis is a useful framework that can help clients understand, assess and formulate psychotic experiences and adverse life events that might have impacted on symptom development.
✓ A positive outcome was achieved by carefully engaging Janine in therapy, giving her a sense of control over sessions, and sharing pieces of the formulation throughout the therapy process so as to avoid sharing an overwhelming amount of potentially distressing information all at once.
✓ Keeping well and focusing on long-term goals relating to well-being, minimizing distress and improving overall functioning is just as important as reducing symptoms.

Activities

1. Consider what techniques you use to engage complex clients with psychosis. What are your own beliefs and attitudes about engaging such clients? How do they influence your practice?
2. Review the measures you currently use to assess complex clients with psychosis. How do these measures influence your formulation and subsequent intervention strategies developed to treat complex cases?

Further reading

Haddock, G. and Spaulding, W. (2011) 'Psychological treatment of psychosis', in D. Weinberger and P. Harrison (eds), *Schizophrenia*. 3rd edn. London: Wiley. pp. 666–86.
This book chapter provides an overview of psychological treatments for psychosis and uses clinical examples to support the use of different psychological approaches. The implications of applying the approaches with complex cases are described.

Meaden, A., Keen, N., Aston, R., Barton, K. and Bucci, S. (2013) *Cognitive Therapy for Command Hallucinations*. Hove, East Sussex: Routledge.
This book provides a formulation model and specific intervention strategies to treat complex clients with command hallucinations.

Tai, S. and Turkington, D. (2009) 'The evolution of cognitive behavior therapy for schizophrenia: Current practice and recent developments', *Schizophrenia Bulletin*, 35(5): 865–73.
This article describes the development of CBT for psychosis, the key elements of CBT strategies for psychosis and the evidence for this approach.

PART 3

Concluding Reflections and Future Directions

SEVENTEEN

Looking to the Future: CBT Assessment and Case Formulation in a Changing World

Sarah Corrie, Michael Townend and Adrian Cockx

Learning objectives

After reading this chapter and using the reflective tool provided you should be able to:

- Consider how you locate yourself within some of the emergent trends in the field of CBT.
- Appreciate how your professional context shapes the therapy you provide.
- Reflect on your current level of knowledge and skill having read the different chapters in this book.
- Identify your learning and development needs as a scholar and practitioner of CBT in order to enhance the quality of your practice.

Introduction

In this book we have aimed to provide a contemporary understanding of CBT assessment and case formulation, offer principles and methods that you can use to inform your approach, and share illustrations of how these principles and methods can be applied across different clinical presentations and service settings. As described in Chapter 1, we have not sought to present a 'uniform' view of CBT and how it 'should' be delivered; the intention has been to offer guidelines rather than prescriptions and by doing so, to initiate a process of self-guided discovery into your own learning and development needs.

Competence cannot be acquired in isolation from the broader range of priorities, values and expectations in which CBT is nested. In this final chapter, therefore, we turn our attention to a wider range of influences on our work as CBT therapists, focusing specifically on the three distinct but overlapping areas of:

1. Emergent trends within the field of CBT itself.
2. The enabling and constraining conditions imposed by contextual factors.
3. The implications of the above for how we understand the development of the professional and the need to construe ourselves as lifelong learners.

These are considered in turn.

1. Emergent trends within the field of CBT

The field of CBT evolves as demand increases and as theoretically-informed research and evidence of outcomes pinpoint novel domains of application. Although certain fundamental assumptions may remain (for example that cognition plays an important role in distress and is amenable to change), approaches to assessment and formulation will also be driven by the particular 'school' of CBT that the therapist embraces or is required to practice.

As the field expands its conceptual, clinical and even philosophical horizons, the meaning of the term 'CBT' becomes increasingly ambiguous. Some scholars (e.g. Hayes, 2004) have argued that what is occurring constitutes a paradigm shift in which distinct 'generations' of CBT are evident. Thus, there exists a first (traditional behavioural approaches) and second (the cognitive tradition) generation of cognitive behaviour therapies. A more recent 'third wave' of cognitive behavioural therapies (encompassing approaches such as Acceptance and Commitment Therapy and Mindfulness-Based Cognitive Therapy, as well as the compassion paradigm) seeks to bring about change by raising awareness of how language processes can unhelpfully dominate experience, and through 'unhooking' from difficult cognitive content rather than aiming to restructure it. Although others have challenged the notion of a paradigm shift and argue for the existence of one CBT model but many CBT therapies (see Hofmann and Asmundsen, 2008), the idea of different 'waves' may be intuitively appealing to therapists who seek to expand their armoury of interventions to meet the needs of a broader range of clients. Nonetheless, the technical and procedural requirements of these different generations of CBT spring from different, and potentially incompatible, philosophical perspectives. If therapists are to offer a technically coherent approach to their clients it is, therefore, important to have an understanding of the different philosophical positions that underlie the range of methods now on offer.

A second development that has implications for how CBT therapists practice has been the introduction of transdiagnostic approaches. As discussed in Chapter 5, disorders share many core features, co-morbidity is common and the therapeutic principles and strategies for different disorders often overlap substantially (e.g. exposure to feared internal and external events; the necessity of reducing safety behaviours and compulsions; and the use of cognitive problem-solving skills). While transdiagnostic approaches enable the development of interventions for presentations that do not fall into neat categories (e.g. perfectionism), and may have a degree of intuitive appeal to therapists who, confronted with clients with multiple problems, need to find ways to combine models and methods of working, the evidence-base is limited. Moreover, whilst there is a growing body of research evidence that demonstrates the efficacy of transdiagnostic approaches compared to control conditions within randomized trials (Norton, 2012), to our knowledge there is no research comparing transdiagnostic approaches to disorder-specific protocols that might guide understanding of which disorders respond best to a transdiagnostic approach.

An additional trend worthy of reflection is the growing emphasis on incorporating client strengths into mainstream CBT (e.g. Bannink, 2012). As noted in Chapter 4, although the notion of building on client strengths has been present from its inception, CBT has historically been a problem-focused treatment and it is only more recently that working with strengths has become a specific area of focus. This development is in part a reflection of the influence of positive psychology, a discipline emerging at the turn of the last century which has sought to counter-balance psychology's focus on deficits by investigating those circumstances, resources, methods and techniques that enable individuals to flourish (see Snyder and Lopez, 2005, for a comprehensive introduction to this field).

Although a laudable development, there are a number of questions that arise from this stance. For example, there appears to be a widely held assumption that the strengths movement can be automatically combined with our existing models of assessment and case formulation in CBT. But is this necessarily the case? The existing disorder-specific models are not theoretically 'primed' to focus on client strengths. Should CBT therapists, then, become more fully informed about the current range of models and methods aimed specifically at uncovering and enhancing client strengths? Should teaching on positive psychology make its way into CBT training courses, with specific modules devoted to the various assessment and measurement tools emanating from this field? How should the data they provide be synthesized with those obtained from measures geared towards understanding psychopathology? Although working with client strengths is appealing it is not yet clear how CBT therapists can most effectively assess for client strengths, devise formulations around them, or integrate them with problem-specific formulations that are by their very nature deficit-based.

Of course, this is not to make the claim that the developments which characterize the field of CBT currently are unwelcome. Rather, it is a call to consider in greater depth the rationale for our reasoning, how practice-based innovations are supported by the evidence and the implications of this evidence for the training and development of CBT therapists. New paradigms and novel strategies do not necessarily translate into better outcomes for clients. Moreover, for the novice therapist in particular, they can feel burdensome in that they merely increase the amount of material to be learnt. We may feel some sympathy for the supervisee of one of us (Corrie) who, as a novice CBT therapist attempting to navigate the proliferating concepts, models and techniques protested, 'Why can't they all agree on one model? It would make life so much easier!' Multiple and fresh perspectives, while indicative of a thriving discipline, can also represent a challenge to our knowledge management.

2. The enabling and constraining conditions imposed by contextual influences

The ways in which CBT is evolving and the debates to which these developments give rise are couched within a broader political, social and economic agenda. Drawing on original work by Mohan (1996), Corrie and Lane (see Corrie and Lane, 2010; 2015) propose that therapists are immersed in overlapping local, national and global levels of influence. Local level influences refer to the belief systems, expectations and priorities internal to the contexts that directly impact a practitioner's work, such as training programmes, employing organizations and professional and accrediting bodies. National level influences are concerned with the broader, dominant belief systems which inform government policy and shape how CBT therapists practice and understand that practice. Finally, global level influences concern international trends in welfare and the delivery of health and social care, the need for cost-containment and the growing trend of appealing to science to justify our choices.

One particularly noteworthy global influence that has filtered through to both national priorities and local level influences is the emphasis on the use of evidence to inform practice-related decisions. As Corrie and Lane (2015) observe, amongst the psychological therapies, its commitment to empirical demonstrations of efficacy ensures that CBT is likely to remain an attractive choice to those commissioning psychological therapies. In the first edition of this book, however, Grant et al. (2008) warned of the dangers of an 'overly rational' interpretation of evidence-based practice. In a similar vein, Drake (2008) alerts us to the fact that professionals are increasingly operating in 'a culture of pragmatism'. In reflecting on the era in which we live and work, he highlights how swift outcomes are prized over 'journeys' that enhance self-awareness and personal insight. Working in such an environment, practitioners can find that their own thinking starts to become unhelpfully organized around seeking prescriptive answers on what to do and when.

The promise of concrete procedures that can obtain predictable results holds an understandable allure for the practitioner confronted with large amounts of clinical information and caseload pressures. Nonetheless, many of the challenges encountered in practice do not lend themselves to protocol-based interventions as Meyer long ago argued (Bruch and Bond, 1998). It is also important to remain aware that the evidence-base for the active ingredients of specific interventions and the mechanisms by which change is achieved remain topics of debate. Moreover, CBT therapists need to be able to work with diversity and difference. Chapters 2 and 3 considered some of these issues as they relate to the assessment and case formulation of clients' idiosyncratic needs. However, there is a broader debate about the extent to which our psychological theories and models of practice equip us to respond to the needs of different societal groups.

Milioni (2007) has argued that certain ways of defining health (medical, psychological and pathological) and practices that signify 'otherness' (clinical settings, appointments and note-taking) reinforce positions that compromise clients' egalitarian status, leaving them disempowered. Along similar lines, Mpofu (2014) claims that mainstream therapy services often fail to recognize the different ways in which communities conceptualize health and illness, and ignore the sources of support that such communities trust. He advocates the creation of CBT services which are accessed via community leaders as the first line of referral, rather than the medicalized settings in which many therapeutic interventions continue to be delivered.

As access to psychological therapies has become a UK government priority, so the matter of poor service uptake by minority communities has come to the fore (Glover et al., 2010). Approaches include that offered by Anderson and Goolishian (1992) who advocate a way of working where the client is seen as the expert on their own culturally-informed experience. The CBT practitioner retains expertise in their way of working which is then offered to the client to assist their process of change.

Kelly (2006) has proposed that the collaborative and non-judgemental nature of CBT offers value to marginalized groups. Its contribution as an anti-oppressive framework (to challenge oppressive internal dialogues) has been explored by Ross et al. (2008), with Watts (2004) examining CBT and social justice. Indeed, Corrie and Lane (2015) observed how Radical Black Behaviourism (Hayes, 1991) was an early call in the 1970s to behaviourists to engage in approaches that challenged power relationships in society. For therapists operating at the local level, acquiring multicultural competence raises many questions relating to education and training. How, for example, does the field best equip therapists with the ability to access, interpret and incorporate culturally-specific knowledge (including, as we saw in Chapter 2, culturally derived meanings and interpretations of distress, disorder and symptomatology) for the purposes of client engagement, assessment, case formulation and ultimately the delivery of an optimally effective intervention?

The need to consider how CBT therapists deliver their services cannot be considered apart from the broader issue of how we involve our clients in planning, organizing and delivering the services that are being offered to support their well-being (see Grant and Townend, 2010, for an overview of key issues). Although a neglected area in psychotherapy process research (Rennie, 1994), the underlying value of collaboration means that the experience of the service user is critical to all stages of CBT ranging from planning the agenda for a specific session through to service design and policy development.

Lowe and Murray (2014) observe that a growing number of studies have examined service user experiences of CBT. Using predominantly qualitative research methods, these studies allow for a richer, more contextualized understanding of those aspects of therapy contributing to change than quantitative methods can provide. They note studies that seek this type of understanding from clients who have received CBT for psychosis (McGowan et al., 2005), depression (Clarke et al., 2004) and eating disorders (Laberg et al., 2001). Lowe and Murray (2014) contribute data on trauma-focused CBT to this emerging literature in order to better understand those factors that play a central role in facilitating therapeutic change from the client perspective. However, this is a starting point.

As noted in Part 1 of this book, the client groups for whom CBT is now recommended or offered are highly diverse. In addition to being provided to those receiving a first line intervention for common mental health problems (Department of Health, 2008b), CBT has been adapted for in-patient settings (Curran et al., 2007), developed for couples (Epstein and Baucom, 2002) and families (Dummett, 2006), is being applied to the needs of children (e.g. Stallard, 2005) and older people (Laidlaw et al., 2003) and for individuals with intellectual disabilities (see Kroese, 2014). Moreover, although this book has focused exclusively on therapeutic practice, cognitive and behavioural principles are also being adopted by related disciplines such as coaching psychology (Williams et al., 2010). Identifying how to adapt the core principles of CBT to the needs of diverse service users will test CBT therapists' skills in innovation and design to the full. There is no protocol that can eliminate the need for professional judgement, but our 'culture of pragmatism' may not necessarily support the development of these kinds of decision-making skills in optimum ways.

3. Developing the professional in an age of complexity: The need to facilitate the lifelong learner

Based on analysis of outcomes in routine services, Clark (2014) reports that therapy services need to deliver in two areas: (1) improved treatments; and (2) ensuring that the treatments available and empirically demonstrated as effective, are delivered as competently as possible. This is echoed by Roth (2014: xvii) who comments on the importance of '...not only doing the right thing, but also doing the right thing in the right way'.

The ability for '...making explicit and being able to implement in action the procedural rules of therapy adaptation' (Whittington and Grey, 2014: 4) (also known as 'meta-competence') provides a further lens on the skills needed for effective CBT assessments and case formulations. As Lane and Corrie (2012) note, to be a therapist is to work in a place of ambiguity. The advancements in both the technical and theoretical knowledge that have characterized the field of CBT since its inception are impressive, and provide important understandings that can assist us in working more effectively with clients. Nonetheless, therapeutic work will continue to immerse us in often high levels of uncertainty and can at times confront us with questions for which there is no easy answer (Corrie and Lane, 2010).

To become proficient in CBT requires, therefore, more than subject matter expertise. It also requires the synthesizing of a range of cognitive operations that span curiosity, an openness to new ideas, critical thinking, creativity and innovation, and a genuine commitment to personal learning and self-knowledge. It also requires a willingness to expose our beliefs and actions to a process of scrutiny, testing and revision, in much the same way that we request of our clients when they work with us in therapy. As Bandura and Schunk note:

> Competence in dealing with one's environment is not a fixed act or simply knowing what to do. Rather, it involves a generative capability in which component skills must be selected and organized into courses of action to manage changing task demands. Operative competence thus requires flexible orchestration of multiple subskills. (1981: 587)

Paul (1993) asserts that in order to become effective critical thinkers, the task is one of unhooking from the content of our decisions in order to critically examine the process by which we arrive at them. It is the integrity of the process which is essential, regardless of the form of CBT we are practising and the context in which we are working.

There is currently a paucity of guidance on how CBT therapists should develop their skills in assessment and formulation and how those involved in training and supervising can optimize these specific capabilities amongst their trainees. However, in aiming for a systematic approach, the work by Bennett-Levy and colleagues (see Bennett-Levy, 2006; Bennett-Levy et al., 2009) provides important insights into why different domains of skill develop at different speeds, and why diverse methods of instruction are required for the enhancement of specific skills.

Although an extensive review of this model and its implications for practice is beyond the scope of this chapter (see Thwaites et al., 2014, for a review), in brief, it identifies and differentiates declarative (factual information), procedural (rules of application) and reflective systems, proposing that the reflective system is critical to the other two as well as helping link them. In their recent work on CBT supervision, Corrie and Lane (2015) draw upon and add to models for supporting the delivery of CBT knowledge and skills suggesting that the use of self-practice/self-reflection might provide an integrative approach to both training and supervision practice. There does, however, remain an urgent need for trainers to come together to examine this issue more broadly, with scholastic endeavours focused on determining what enables novice CBT therapists to acquire these skills most efficiently.

Supporting your development as a CBT therapist

No curriculum, however carefully devised, can address the complexities of practice in any enduring way. Increasingly, then, it falls to each of us to take responsibility for our own learning and development to ensure that our knowledge and skill remains fit for purpose for the benefit of our clients and other stakeholders in a knowledge-driven labour market (Lane and Corrie, 2006).

Watts (2014) proposes that '...all learning starts with questions'. The power of questions to uncover new insights and possibilities for action was noted in Chapter 2 and indeed, lies at the heart of guided discovery. In the spirit of this, and by way of concluding this book, we offer you a 'reflective tool' to help you consolidate your learning and plan your next steps. The value of using reflective tools as a basis for learning and development has been described and developed elsewhere (Lane and Corrie, 2006; Corrie and Lane, 2010; Lane and Corrie, 2012). Essentially, they take the form of a series of questions that relate to the different ideas covered in this book as well as the debates drawn from the wider literature. We recommend that you use these questions creatively and repeatedly and that you share your ideas with colleagues, peers, supervisors and trainers to turn them into a form that has implications for your future practice.

Your reflective tool

1. Spend some time reflecting on the journey that has led you to become a CBT therapist. What are the factors from your personal and professional history that have shaped your understanding of CBT therapy and your beliefs about how this approach helps clients make meaningful changes in their lives. Use the following questions to guide you.

a) What (or who) has been most influential in shaping your practice as a CBT therapist?

b) What do you consider to be your most significant achievements as a CBT therapist? What resources did you bring to bear to achieve these ends and what can you learn from your successes?

c) What have been the major challenges you have faced in your work as a CBT therapist? How have you attempted to manage these and what have you learned from them?

d) In terms of assessing and formulating your clients' needs, what learning have you gained from formal training?

e) In terms of assessing and formulating your clients' needs, what learning have you gained from experience?

List any insights below:

2a. Reflect on your usual approach to conducting CBT assessments (recap on Chapters 2 and 3 if you need to refresh your memory on any of the points discussed). Having done so consider your responses to the following questions:

a) What is your usual approach to CBT assessment?

   o To what extent is your thinking organized around nomothetic approaches? To what extent is your thinking organized around idiographic approaches? What factors (including local, national and global influences) are informing your approach?

b) Review the suggested information-gathering areas referred to in Table 2.1 (p.18). Which areas do you routinely assess? Are there any areas that it would be useful to assess more fully?

c) How do you determine whether an individual is 'suitable' for the type of CBT you are offering? Which criteria do you use?

d) Which clinical presentations do you think you are most and least effective in assessing? What might be influencing your level of competence in each case?

e) What informs your decisions about what type of information to gather for each client? To what extent can you be confident that your decision-making is based on the judicious use of the available data (both in relation to the individual case and the evidence-base of the discipline) or is it likely that your thinking is being unduly influenced by familiarity (habit), personal preference or the current service protocol?

f) How effective are you in working effectively with the process and relational aspects of assessment? (You may wish to self-rate on a scale of 0–10 and then to reflect upon what has informed this rating.)

List any insights below:

2b. Having responded to the questions in 2a above, and having reflected on the content of the different chapters, what do you now know about your current level of capability and skill in the area of CBT assessment?

a) What are your strengths/areas where you do best?

b) What are your current limitations/areas where you are least effective?

c) Which specific areas would it make most sense to work on for the immediate future?

List your responses below:

3a. Reflect upon your usual approach to co-constructing case formulations (recap on Chapter 4 if you need to refresh your memory on any of the points discussed). Having done so consider your responses to the following questions:

a) How do you use formulation in your practice? How many and which of the identified functions are relevant to the formulations you devise?

b) What are any typical problems, challenges or dilemmas that you encounter when attempting to construct formulations of your clients' needs?

c) Which types (generic, disorder-specific or idiosyncratic) and levels (case, problem, situation) of formulation are typical of your work? Why is this? If you are currently receiving CBT training, or involved in delivering training, which approaches to formulation are emphasized and for what reasons?

d) Reflecting on your own practice how often do you include: (1) developing problem lists; (2) diagnostic criteria; (3) measures; and (4) a working hypothesis? If so, why? How does this help you? If not, how might your practice change if you were to incorporate these elements more often?

e) Reflecting on your own practice how often do you work to elicit client strengths and build these into your case formulations? If you do, how do these inform your intervention planning? If you do not, what implications might there be of working more explicitly with client strengths?

f) How effective are you in working effectively with the process and relational aspects of case formulation? (You may wish to self-rate on a scale of 0–10 and then to reflect upon what has informed this rating.)

List any insights below:

3b. Having responded to the questions in 3a above, and having reflected on the content of the different chapters, what do you now know about your current level of capability and skill in the area of CBT case formulation?

a) What are your strengths/areas where you do best?
b) What are your current limitations/areas where you are least effective?
c) Which specific areas would it make most sense to work on for the immediate future?

List your responses below:

----

4. Having read this book, what do you now know about how effective you are at linking your assessment and case formulation procedures to intervention planning and delivery?

a) What are your strengths/areas where you do best?
b) What are your current limitations/areas where you are least effective?
c) Which specific areas would it make most sense to work on for the immediate future?

List your responses below:

Spend some time reflecting on your responses so you can fully appreciate their implications for your work and professional learning. Is there anything you would like to change in your CBT practice for the immediate future? Are there any learning needs which reading this book or engaging with these questions have alerted you to, that you need to follow up on (e.g. with your supervisor, line manager, etc.)?

5. Based on all of the above, what future direction do you wish your CBT-related professional development to take and what resources do you need to help you get there?

a) What supervision arrangements might need to be in place to help you take these next steps?
b) What type of supervision interventions might support you? (e.g. doing more role-play, presenting more written formulations, playing segments of sessions where you were conducting assessment or co-constructing formulations with a client – see Corrie and Lane, 2015, for a useful overview of the different types of supervision intervention that can be used).
c) What training courses or workshops might be needed to top up your knowledge and skills?
d) What further reading is necessary?
e) Are there other forms of self-directed learning that might be beneficial? (Bennett-Levy et al., 2015, provide a useful resource on how to approach using CBT principles and methods as a vehicle for therapist development in the context of self-practice/self-reflection.)

List your responses below:

A final word

The purpose of this book has been to help you become more successful at undertaking the tasks of CBT assessment and case formulation in the settings in which you deliver your professional services. In doing so, we believe not only that this will benefit your clients and other stakeholders who have an invest-ment in the outcomes of your work, but also that it will afford greater levels of satisfaction and enjoyment; our work as therapists is typically closely tied to a sense of vocation and a desire to offer service grounded in making a substantive contribution to the well-being of others. Any resource that enables us to achieve this sense of purpose in a more systematic way greatly enhances our prospects of gaining a greater sense of reward from the work we undertake.

This is perhaps particularly important in the current professional, eco-nomic and social climate. In Chapter 1, we noted how we are living and working in times of unprecedented complexity. Professionals offer their services in contexts that are increasingly challenging, uncertain and tur-bulent. Even a cursory knowledge of some of the dilemmas confronting our CBT professional and credentialing bodies illustrates all too clearly how rapidly the CBT community is evolving, and indeed needs to evolve in order to keep pace with the changing demands and expectations of what CBT can offer. This state of affairs permeates our decision-making and the ways in which we are expected to undertake CBT assessments and formu-lations in complex ways. As Lane and Corrie observe,

> We cannot assume that the technical knowledge and evidence of today will prove fit for purpose for the needs of tomorrow. However, we can ready ourselves for the challenges ahead by committing ourselves to the lifelong discipline of critical thinking. (2012: 173)

We hope that by reading this book you feel better equipped to reflect upon, critique and refine your practice in the areas of CBT assessment and case formulation and that as lifelong learners, you will have discovered some principles, concepts, methods and tools that can aid you in your continuing professional development. We wish you well in your endeavours to bet-ter understand the extraordinary and at times, wonderful, unsettling and bewildering stories with which our clients present us and with which we, as therapists, are privileged to work.

References

Abramson, L.Y., Alloy, L.B., Hankin, B.L., Haeffel, G.J., Gibb, B.E. and MacCoon, D.G. (2002) 'Cognitive vulnerability – stress models of depression in a self-regulatory and psychobiological context', in I.H. Gotlib and C.L. Hammen (eds), *Handbook of Depression*. New York: Guilford Press. pp. 268–94.

Abudabbeh, N. and Hayes, P.A. (2006) 'Cognitive behavioural therapy with people of Arabic heritage', in P.A. Hayes and G.Y. Iwamasa (eds), *Culturally Responsive Cognitive-Behavioural Therapy: Assessment, Practice, and Supervision*. Washington, DC: The American Psychological Association. pp. 141–59.

Addington, D., Addington, J. and Maticka-Tyndale, E. (1993) 'Assessing depression in schizophrenia: The Calgary Depression Scale', *British Journal of Psychiatry*, 163 (suppl. 22), 39–44.

Addis, M.E. and Mahalik, J. R. (2003) 'Men, masculinity, and the contexts of help seeking', *American Psychologist*, 58: 5–14.

American Psychiatric Association (2000) *Diagnostic and Statistical Manual of Mental Disorders*. 4th edn. Arlington, VA: American Psychiatric Publishing.

American Psychiatric Association (2013) *Diagnostic and Statistical Manual of Mental Disorders*. 5th edn. Arlington, VA: American Psychiatric Publishing.

Anderson, H. and Goolishian, H. (1992) 'The client is the expert: A not-knowing approach to therapy', in S. McNamee and K.J. Gergen (eds), *Constructing Therapy: Social Construction and the Therapeutic Process*. London: Sage. pp. 25–39.

Antony, M. and Barlow, D.H. (2002) *Handbook of Assessment and Treatment Planning for Psychological Disorders*. New York: Guildford Press.

Arntz, A. and van den Hout, M. (1996) 'Psychological treatments of panic disorder without agoraphobia: Cognitive therapy versus applied relaxation', *Behaviour Research and Therapy*, 34: 113–21.

Augoustinos, M., Walker, I. and Donaghue, N. (2006) *Social Cognition: An Integrated Introduction*. 2nd edn. London: Sage.

Babor, T.F., Higgins-Biddle, J.C., Saunders, J.B. and Monteiro, M.G. (2001) *The Alcohol Use Disorders Identification Test: Guidelines for Use in Primary Care*. Geneva: Department of Mental Health and Substance Dependence, World Health Organization.

Baker, A., Bucci, S., Lewin, T.J., Kay-Lambkin, F., Constable, P.M. and Carr, V.J. (2006) 'Cognitive-behavioural therapy for substance use disorders in people with psychotic disorders: Randomised controlled trial', *The British Journal of Psychiatry*, 188(5): 439–48.

Bandura, A. (2004) 'Model of causality in social learning theory', in A. Freeman, M.J. Mahoney, P. Devito and D. Martin (eds), *Cognition and Psychotherapy*. 2nd edn. New York: Springer Publishing Company. pp. 24–44.

Bandura, A. and Schunk, D.H. (1981) 'Cultivating competence, self-efficacy, and intrinsic interest through proximal self-motivation', *Journal of Personality and Social Psychology*, 41: 586–98.

Bannink, F. (2012) *Practicing Positive CBT: From Reducing Distress to Building Success.* Chichester, West Sussex: Wiley-Blackwell.

Barkham, M., Stiles, W.B., Connell, J., Twigg, E., Leach, C., Lucock, M., Mellor-Clark, J., Bower, P., King, M., Shapiro, D.A., Hardy, G.E., Greenberg, L. and Angus, L. (2008) 'Effects of psychological therapies in randomized trials and practice-based studies', *British Journal of Clinical Psychology*, 47(4): 397–415.

Barlow, D.H., Farchione, T.J., Fairholme, C.P., Ellard, K.K., Boisseau, C.I., Allen, L.B. and Ehrenreich-May, J.T. (2011) *Unified Protocol for Transdiagnostic Treatment of Emotional Disorders (Therapist Guide).* New York: Oxford University Press.

Barnard, P. (2004) 'Bridging between basic theory and clinical practice', *Behaviour Research and Therapy*, 42: 977–1000.

Barnard, P. and Teasdale, J. (1991) 'Interacting cognitive subsystems: A systemic approach to cognitive-affective interaction and change', *Cognition and Emotion*, 5: 1–39.

Barnicot, K., Katsakou, C., Bhatti, N., Savill, M., Fearns, N. and Priebe, S. (2012) 'Factors predicting the outcome of psychotherapy for borderline personality disorder: A systematic review', *Clinical Psychology Review*, 32: 400–12.

Barrowclough, C., Haddock, G., Wykes, T., Beardmore, R., Conrod, P., Craig, T. and Tarrier, N. (2010) 'Integrated motivational interviewing and cognitive behavioural therapy for people with psychosis and comorbid substance misuse: Randomised controlled trial', *British Medical Journal*, 341. doi: 10.1136/bmj.c6325.

Bartholomew, K. and Horowitz, L.M. (1991) 'Attachment styles among young adults: A test of a four-category model', *Journal of Personality and Social Psychology*, 61: 226–44.

Bass, C. (1990) *Somatization: Physical Symptoms and Psychological Illness.* London: Blackwell Science.

Beck, A.T. (1952) 'Successful outpatient psychotherapy of a chronic schizophrenic with a delusion based on borrowed guilt', *Psychiatry*, 15: 305–12.

Beck, A.T. and Steer, R.A. (1993) *Beck Hopelessness Scale.* San Antonio, TX: The Psychological Corporation.

Beck, A.T., Emery, G. and Greenberg, R.L. (1985) *Anxiety Disorders and Phobias: A Cognitive Perspective.* New York: Basic Books.

Beck, A.T., Epstein, N., Brown, G. and Steer, R.A. (1988) 'An inventory for measuring clinical anxiety: The Beck Anxiety Inventory', *Journal of Consulting and Clinical Psychology*, 56: 893–7.

Beck, A.T, Freeman, A., Pretzer, J., Davis, D.D., Fleming, B., Ottaviani, R., Beck, J., Simon, K.M., Padesky, C., Meyer J. and Trexler, L. (1990) *Cognitive Therapy of Personality Disorders.* New York: Guilford Press.

Beck, A.T., Rush, A.J., Shaw, B.F. and Emery, G. (1979) *Cognitive Therapy for Depression.* New York: Guilford Press.

Beck, A.T., Steer, R.A. and Brown, G.K. (1996) *Beck Depression Inventory II.* San Antonio, TX: The Psychological Corporation.

Beck, J.S. (1995) *Cognitive Therapy: Basics and Beyond.* New York: Guilford Press.

Behar E., DiMarco I.D., Hekler E.B., Mohlman J. and Staples A.M. (2009) 'Current theoretical models of generalized anxiety disorder (GAD): Conceptual review and treatment implications', *Journal of Anxiety Disorders*, 23: 1011–23.

Ben-Zeev, D., Brenner, C.J., Begale, M., Duffecy, J., Mohr, D.C. and Mueser, K.T. (2014) 'Feasibility, acceptability, and preliminary efficacy of a smartphone intervention for schizophrenia', *Schizophrenia Bulletin*. doi: 10.1093/schbul/sbu033.

Bennett-Levy, J. (2006) 'Therapist skills: A cognitive model of their acquisition and refinement', *Behavioural and Cognitive Psychotherapy*, 34: 57–78.

Bennett-Levy, J., Butler, G., Fennell, M., Hackmann, A., Mueller, M. and Westbrook, D. (2004) *Oxford Guide to Behavioural Experiments in Cognitive Therapy*. Oxford: Oxford University Press.

Bennett-Levy, J., McManus, F., Westling, B.E. and Fennell, M. (2009) 'Acquiring and refining CBT skills and competencies: Which training methods are perceived to be most effective?', *Behavioural and Cognitive Psychotherapy*, 37: 571–83.

Bennett-Levy, J., Turner, F., Beaty, T., Smith, M., Paterson, B. and Farmer, S. (2001) 'The value of self-practice of cognitive therapy techniques and self-reflection in the training of cognitive therapists', *Behavioural and Cognitive Psychotherapy*, 29: 203–20.

Bennett-Levy, J., Thwaites, R., Haarhoff, B. and Perry, H. (2015) *Experiencing CBT from the Inside Out: A Self-Practice/Self-Reflection Workbook for Therapists*. New York: Guilford Press.

Bernstein, D. and Fink, L. (1998) *Manual for the Childhood Trauma Questionnaire*. New York: The Psychological Corporation.

Bernstein, D.P., Fink, L., Handelsman, L., Foote, J., Lovejoy, M., Wenzel, K., Sapareto, E. and Ruggiero, J. (1994) 'Initial reliability and validity of a new retrospective measure of child abuse and neglect', *The American Journal of Psychiatry*, 151(8): 1132–36.

Bieling, P. and Kuyken, W. (2003) 'Is cognitive case formulation science or science fiction?', *Clinical Psychology: Science and Practice*, 10(1): 52–69.

Birchwood, M., Michail, M., Meaden, A., Tarrier, N. Lewis, S., Wykes, T., Davies, L. and Peters, E. (2014) 'Cognitive behaviour therapy to prevent harmful compliance with command hallucinations (COMMAND): A randomised controlled trial', *The Lancet Psychiatry*, 1: 23–33.

Birchwood, M., Smith, J., Macmillan, F., Hogg, B., Prasad, R., Harvey, C. and Bering, S. (1989) 'Predicting relapse in schizophrenia: The development and implementation of an early signs monitoring system using patients and families as observers, a preliminary investigation', *Psychological Medicine*, 19(3): 649–56.

Black, D.W., Allen, J., St. John, D., Pfhol, B., McCormick, B. and Blum, N. (2009) 'Predictors of response to systems training for emotional predictability and problem solving (STEPPS) for borderline personality disorder: An exploratory model', *Acta Psychiatrica Scandinavica*, 120: 53–61.

Blackburn, I.M., James, I.A., Milne, D.L., Baker, C., Standart, S., Garland, A. and Reichelt, K. (2001) 'The revised cognitive therapy scale (CTS-R): Psychometric properties', *Behavioural and Cognitive Psychotherapy*, 29: 431–46.

Blackburn-Munro, G. (2004) 'Hypothalamo-pituitary-adrenal axis dysfunction as a contributory factor to chronic pain and depression', *Current Pain and Headache Reports*, 8: 116–24.

Blake, D., Weathers, F., Nagy, L., Kaloupek, D., Klauminzer, G., Charney, D. and Keane, T. (1990) *Clinician Administered PTSD Scale (CAPS)*. Boston, MA: National Center for PTSD, Behavioural Sciences Division.

Blum, N., St. John, D., Pfohl, B., Scott, S., McCormick, B., Allen, J., Arndt, S. and Black, D.W. (2008) 'Systems training for emotional predictability and problem solving (STEPPS) for outpatients with borderline personality disorder: A randomized controlled trial and 1-year follow-up', *American Journal of Psychiatry*, 165: 468–78.

Borkovec, T.D. (1994) 'The nature, functions, and origins of worry', in G. Davey and F. Tallis (eds), *Worrying: Perspectives on Theory Assessment and Treatment*. Chichester, West Sussex: Wiley. pp. 5–33.

Bowlby, R.J.M. (2005) *A Secure Base: Clinical Applications of Attachment Theory*. Abingdon: Routledge.

Brewin, C.R., Dalgleish, T. and Joseph, S. (1996) 'A dual representation theory of posttraumatic stress disorder', *Psychological Review*, 103: 670–86.

British Association for Behavioural & Cognitive Psychotherapies (2012) BABCP Minimum Training Standards for the Practice of Cognitive Behavioural Therapy (CBT), 2012. Available at: www.babcp.com/files/Minimum-Training-Standards-V6-0413.pdf.

British Pain Society (2014). Available at: www.britishpainsociety.org.

Brook, J., McCluskey, S., King, N. and Burton, K. (2013) *BMC Musculoskeletal Disorders*, 14: 48. doi: 10.1186/1471-2474-14-48.

Brown, R.J. (2006) 'Medically unexplained symptoms', in N. Tarrier (ed.), *Case Formulation in Cognitive Behaviour Therapy: The Treatment of Challenging and Complex Cases*. Hove, East Sussex: Routledge. pp. 263–92.

Brown, T.A. and Cash, T.F. (1990) 'The phenomenon of non-clinical panic: Parameters of panic, fear, and avoidance', *Journal of Anxiety Disorders*, 4: 15–29.

Brown, T.A., Di Nardo, P.A., Lehman, C.L. and Campbell, L.A. (2001) 'Reliability of DSM-IV anxiety and mood disorders: Implications for classification of emotional disorders', *Journal of Abnormal Psychology*, 110: 49–58.

Brown, T.A., Marten, P.A. and Barlow, D.H. (1995) 'Discriminant validity of the symptoms constituting the DSM-III-R and DSM-IV associated symptom criterion of generalized anxiety disorder', *Journal of Anxiety Disorders*, 9: 317–28.

Bruch, M. (2015) *Beyond Diagnosis. Case Formulation in Cognitive Behavioural Therapy*. Chichester, West Sussex: Wiley.

Bruch, M. and Bond, F.W. (1998) *Beyond Diagnosis. Case Formulation Approaches in CBT*. Chichester, West Sussex: Wiley.

Bucci, S., Barrowclough, C., Ainsworth, J., Morris, R., Berry, K., Machin, M., Emsley, R., Lewis, S., Edge, D., Buchan, I. and Haddock, G. (2015) 'Using mobile technology to deliver a cognitive behaviour therapy-informed intervention in early psychosis (Actissist): Study protocol for a randomised control trial', *Trials*, 16(1): 404.

Buhr, K. and Dugas, M.J. (2002) 'The intolerance of uncertainty scale: Psychometric properties of the English version', *Behaviour Research and Therapy*, 40: 931–45.

Burns, D.D. (1980) *Feeling Good*. New York: Avon Books.

Butler, D. and Lorimer-Moseley, G. (2003) *Explain Pain*. Adelaide, South Australia: Noi Group Publications.

Butler, G. (1998) 'Clinical formulation', in A.S. Bellack and M. Hersen (eds), *Comprehensive Clinical Psychology, Volume 6*. Oxford: Pergamon. pp. 1–24.

Butler, G., Fennell, M. and Hackmann, A. (2008) *Cognitive Therapy for Anxiety Disorders: Mastering Clinical Challenges*. New York: Guilford Press.

Buwalda, F.M. and Bouman, T.K. (2009) 'Cognitive-behavioural bibliotherapy for hypochondriasis: A pilot study', *Behavioural and Cognitive Psychotherapy*, 37(3): 335–40.

Carey, T.A. and Mullan, R.J. (2004) 'What is Socratic Questioning?', *Psychotherapy: Theory, Research, Practice, Training*, 41: 217–26.

Chadwick, P., Lees, S. and Birchwood, M. (2000) 'The revised beliefs about voices questionnaire (BAVQ-R)', *The British Journal of Psychiatry*, 177(3): 229–32.

Chadwick, P., Williams, C. and Mackenzie, J. (2003) 'Impact of case formulation in cognitive behaviour therapy for psychosis', *Behaviour Research and Therapy*, 41: 671–80.

Chambless, D.L., Caputo, G.C., Bright, P. and Gallagher, R. (1984) 'Assessment for fear of fear in agoraphobics: The Body Sensations Questionnaire and the Agoraphobia Cognitions Questionnaire', *Journal of Consulting and Clinical Psychology*, 52: 1090–7.

Chambless, D.L., Caputo, G.C., Jasin, S.E., Gracely, E. and Williams, C. (1985) 'The Mobility Inventory for Agoraphobia', *Behaviour Research and Therapy*, 23: 35–44.

Chanen, A.M., Jackson, H.J., McCutcheon, L.K., Jovev, M., Dudgeon, P., Yuen, H.P., Germano, D., Nistico, H., McDougall, E., Weinsten, C., Clarkson, V. and McGorry, P.D. (2008) 'Early intervention for adolescents with borderline personality disorder using cognitive analytic therapy: Randomised controlled trial', *British Journal of Psychiatry*, 193: 477–84.

Clark, D.A. and Beck, A.T. (2010) *Cognitive Therapy of Anxiety Disorders: Science and Practice*. New York: Guilford Press.

Clark, D.M. (1986) 'A cognitive approach to panic', *Behaviour Research and Therapy*, 24: 461–70.

Clark, D.M. (1988) 'A cognitive model of panic attacks', in S. Rachman and J.D. Maser (eds), *Panic: Psychological Perspectives*. Hillsdale, NJ: Erlbaum. pp. 71–90.

Clark, D.M. (1996) 'Panic disorder: from theory to therapy', in P.M. Salkovskis (ed.), *Frontiers of Cognitive Therapy*. New York: Guilford Press. pp. 318–44.

Clark, D.M. (2001) 'A cognitive perspective on social phobia', in W.R. Crozier and L.E. Alden (eds), *International Handbook of Social Anxiety: Concepts, Research and Interventions Relating to the Self and Shyness*. Chichester, West Sussex: Wiley. pp. 405–30.

Clark, D.M. (2014) 'Foreword', in A. Whittington and N. Grey (eds), *How to become a More Effective CBT Therapist: Mastering Metacompetence in Clinical Practice*. Chichester, West Sussex: Wiley. pp. xv–xvi.

Clark, D.M. and Fairburn, C.G. (2005) *Science and Practice of Cognitive Behaviour Therapy*. Oxford: Oxford University Press.

Clark, D.M. and Salkovskis, P.M. (2009) 'Panic disorder', Unpublished cognitive therapy manual for IAPT high intensity therapists. Oxford: Department of Experimental Psychology, University of Oxford (available on request from first author).

Clark, D.M., Salkovskis, P.M., Hackmann, A., Middleton, H., Anastasiades, P. and Gelder, M.G. (1994) 'A comparison of cognitive therapy, applied relaxation and imipramine in the treatment of panic disorder', *British Journal of Psychiatry*, 164: 759–69.

Clark, D.M, Salkovskis, P.M, Hackmann, A., Wells, A., Fennell, M., Ludgate, J., Ahmad, S., Richards, H.C and Gelder M. (1998) 'Two psychological treatments for hypochondriasis: A randomised controlled trial', *British Journal of Psychiatry*, 173: 218–25.

Clark, D.M. and Wells, A. (1995) 'A cognitive model of social phobia', in R.G. Heimberg, M.R. Liebowitz, D.A. Hope and F.R. Schneier (eds), *Social Phobia: Diagnosis, Assessment and Treatment*. New York: Guilford Press. pp. 63–93.

Clark, L.A. and Watson, D. (1991) 'A tripartite model of anxiety and depression: Psychometric evidence and taxonomic implications', *Journal of Abnormal Psychology*, 100: 316–36.

Clarke, G. and Yarborough, B.J. (2013) 'Evaluating the promise of health IT to enhance/expand the reach of mental health services', *General Hospital Psychiatry*, 35: 339–44.

Clarke, H., Rees, A. and Hardy, G. (2004) 'The big idea: Clients' perspectives of change processes in cognitive therapy', *Psychology and Psychotherapy; Theory, Research and Practice*, 77: 67–89.

Cloitre, M., Chase Stovall-McClough, K., Nooner, K., Zorbas, P., Cherry, S., Jackson, C.L., Gan, W. and Petkova, E. (2010) Treatment for PTSD related to childhood abuse: A randomized controlled trial. *American Journal of Psychiatry*, 167: 915–24.

Coid, J., Yang, M., Tyrer, P., Roberts, A. and Ullrich, S. (2006) 'Prevalence and correlates of personality disorder in Great Britain', *British Journal of Psychiatry*, 188: 423–32.

Cole, F., Macdonald, H., Carus, C. and Howden-Leach, H. (2005) *Overcoming Chronic Pain: A Self-help Guide Using Cognitive Behavioural Techniques.* London: Robinson.

Connor, K.M., Davidson, J.R., Churchill, L.E., Sherwood, A., Foa, E., Weisler, R.H. (2000) 'Psychometric properties of the Social Phobia Inventory (SPIN): new self-rating scale', *British Journal of Psychiatry*, 176: 379–86.

Corrie, S. and Lane, D.A. (2010) *Constructing Stories, Telling Tales: A Guide to Formulation in Applied Psychology.* London: Karnac.

Corrie, S. and Lane, D.A. (2015) *CBT Supervision.* London: Sage.

Covin, R., Ouimet, A.J., Seeds, P.M. and Dozois, D.J. (2008) 'A meta-analysis of CBT for pathological worry among clients with GAD', *Journal of Anxiety Disorders*, 22: 108–16.

Craske, M.G. and Barlow, D.H. (2008) 'Panic disorder and agoraphobia', in D.H. Barlow (ed.), *Clinical Handbook of Psychological Disorders.* 4th edn. New York: Guilford Press. pp. 1–64.

Crombez, G., Viane, I., Eccleston, C., Devulder, J. and Goubert, L. (2013) 'Attention to pain and fear of pain in patients with chronic pain', *Journal of Behaviour Medicine*, 36: 371–78.

Crown Prosecution Service (2001) *Provision of therapy for vulnerable or intimidated witnesses prior to a criminal trial: practice guidance.* Available at: www.cps.gov.uk.

Cuijpers, P., van Straten, A. and Warmerdam, L. (2007) 'Behavioural activation treatments of depression: A meta-analysis', *Clinical Psychology Review*, 27: 318–26.

Curran, J., Gournay, K., Houghton, S. and Lawson, P. (2007) 'Implementing behavioural activation in inpatient psychiatric wards', *Journal of Mental Health Education, Training and Practice*, 2(2): 28–35.

Dalgleish, T. (2004) 'Cognitive approaches to Posttraumatic Stress Disorder: The evolution of multi-representational theorizing', *Psychological Bulletin*, 130(2): 228–60.

Dalrymple, K.L. and Zimmerman, M. (2011) 'Treatment-seeking for social anxiety disorder in a general outpatient psychiatry setting', *Psychiatry Research*, 187(3): 375–81.

Davidson, K. (2007) *Cognitive Therapy for Personality Disorders: A Guide for Clinicians.* 2nd edn. Hove, East Sussex: Routledge.

Davidson, K., Sharp, M. and Halford, J. (2010) 'Antisocial and borderline personality disorder', in A. Grant, M. Townend, R. Mulhern and N. Short (eds), *Cognitive Behavioural Therapy in Mental Health Care.* London: Sage. pp 95–118.

de Bono, E. (1995) *Parallel Thinking*. London: Penguin.

Department of Health (2008a) *Improving Access to Psychological Therapies (IAPT, 2008) Outcomes toolkit 2008/2009*. Available at: http://ipnosis.postle.net/PDFS/iaptoutcomes-toolkit-2008-november(2).pdf.

Department of Health (2008b) *IAPT Implementation Plan: National Guidelines for Regional Delivery*. Available at: www.iapt.nhs.uk.

DeRubeis, R.J., Hollon, S.D., Amsterdam, J.D., Shelton, R.C., Young, P.R., Salomon, R.M. and Gallop, R. (2005) 'Cognitive therapy vs medications in the treatment of moderate to severe depression', *Archives of General Psychiatry*, 62(4): 409–16.

Dima, A., Gillanders, D. and Power, M. (2013) 'Dynamic pain-emotion relations in chronic pain: A theoretical review of moderation studies', *Health Psychology Review*, 1: S185-S252.

Donaldson, L. (2009) *Annual Report of the Chief Medical Officer for 2008*. London: Department of Health. pp. 33–9.

Double, D.B. (2002) 'The overemphasis on biomedical diagnosis in psychiatry', *Journal of Critical Psychology, Counselling and Psychotherapy*, 2: 40–7.

Drake, D.B. (2008) 'Finding our way home: Coaching's search for identity in a new era', *Coaching: An International Journal of Theory, Research and Practice*, 1(1): 15–26.

Dudley, R., Kuyken, W. and Padesky, C. (2011) 'Disorder specific and trans-diagnostic case conceptualisation', *Clinical Psychology Review*, 31(2): 213–24.

Duffy, M., Gillespie, K. and Clark, D.M. (2007) 'Posttraumatic stress disorder in the context of terrorism and other civil conflict in Northern Ireland: Randomized controlled trial', *British Medical Journal*, 334: 1147–50.

Dugas, M.J., Gagnon, F., Ladouceur, R. and Freeston, H. (1998) 'Generalized anxiety disorder: a preliminary test of a conceptual model', *Behaviour Research and Therapy*, 36: 215–26.

Dummett, N. (2006) 'Processes for systemic cognitive-behavioural therapy with children, young people and families', *Behavioural and Cognitive Psychotherapy*, 34: 179–89.

D'Zurilla, T.J. and Nezu, A.M. (1999) *Problem-Solving Therapy: A Social Competence Approach to Clinical Intervention*. New York: Springer.

Edwards, R., Doleys, D. Filligim, R. and Lowery, D. (2001) 'Ethnic differences in pain tolerance: Clinical implications in a chronic pain population', *Psychometric Medicine*, 63(2): 316–23.

Eells, T.D. (1997) 'Psychotherapy case formulation: History and current status', in T.D. Eells (ed.), *Handbook of Psychotherapy Case Formulation*. London: Guilford Press. pp. 1–32.

Ehlers, A. and Clark, D.M. (2000) 'A cognitive model of posttraumatic stress disorder', *Behaviour Research and Therapy*, 38: 319–45.

Ehlers, A., Clark, D.M., Hackmann, A., McManus, F., Fennell, M., Herbert, C. and Mayou, R. (2003) 'A randomized controlled trial of cognitive therapy, self-help booklet, and repeated early assessment as early interventions for PTSD', *Archives of General Psychiatry*, 60: 1024–32.

Ehlers, A., Clark, D.M., Hackmann, A., McManus, F. and Fennell, M. (2005) 'Cognitive therapy for posttraumatic stress disorder: Development and evaluation', *Behaviour Research and Therapy*, 43: 413–31.

Ehlers, A., Grey, N, Wild, J., Stott, R., Liness, S., Deale, A., Handley, R., Albert, I., Cullen, D., Hackmann, A., Manley, J., McManus, F., Brady, F., Salkovskis, P. and Clark, D.M. (2013) 'Implementation of Cognitive Therapy for PTSD in routine clinical care: Effectiveness and moderators of outcome in a consecutive sample', *Behaviour Research and Therapy*. doi: 10.1016/j.brat.2013.08.006

Ehlers, A., Hackmann, A., Grey, N., Wild, J., Liness, S., Albert, I., Deale, A., Stott, R. and Clark, D.M. (2014) 'A randomized controlled trial of 7-day intensive and standard weekly cognitive therapy for PTSD and emotion-focused supportive therapy', *American Journal of Psychiatry*, 171: 294–304.

Ehlers, A., Clark, D.M., Hackmann, A., McManus, F., Fennell, M. and Grey, N. (in press) *Cognitive Therapy for PTSD: A Therapist's Guide*. Oxford: Oxford University Press.

Epstein, S. (1994) 'Integration of the cognitive and psychodynamic unconscious', *American Psychologist*, 49(8): 709–24.

Epstein, N, and Baucom, D.H. (2002) *Enhanced Cognitive-Behavioural Therapy for Couples: A Contextual Approach*. Washington, DC: American Psychological Association.

Esteves, J.E. Wheatley, L., Mayall, C. and Abbey, H. (2013) 'Emotional processing and its relationship to chronic low back pain: Results from a case-control study', *Manual Therapy*, 18(6): 541–6.

Fairburn, C.G., Cooper, Z. and Shafran R (2003) 'Cognitive behaviour therapy for eating disorders: a "transdiagnostic" theory and treatment', *Behaviour Research Therapy*, 41, 509–28.

Fairburn, C.G, Cooper, Z., Doll, H.A., O'Connor, M.E., Bohn, K., Hawker, D.M., Wales, J.A. and Palmer, R.L. (2009) 'Transdiagnostic cognitive-behavioral therapy for patients with eating disorders: A two-site trial with 60-week follow-up', *American Journal of Psychiatry*, 166(3): 311–9.

Fetter, D. and Fetter, H. (2009) 'Chronic pain: Biological understanding and treatment suggestions for mental health counselors', *Journal of Mental Health Counseling*, 31(3): 189–200.

Fisher, P.L. (2006) 'The efficacy of psychological treatments for generalized anxiety disorder', in G.C.L. Davey and A. Wells (eds), *Worry and its Psychological Disorders: Theory, Assessment and Treatment*. Chichester, West Sussex: Wiley. pp. 359–78.

Foa, E.B. (2010) 'Cognitive behavioural therapy of obsessive-compulsive disorder', *Dialogues in Clinical Neuroscience*, 12(2): 199–207.

Foa, E.B. and Rothbaum, B.O. (1998) *Treating the Trauma of Rape: Cognitive-Behavior Therapy for PTSD*. New York: Guilford Press.

Foa, E.B., Cashman, L., Jaycox, L. and Perry, K. (1997) 'The validation of a self-report measure of posttraumatic stress disorder: The posttraumatic diagnostic scale', *Psychological Assessment*, 9: 445–51.

Foa, E.B., Ehlers, A., Clark, D.M., Tolin, D.F. and Orsillo, S.M. (1999) 'The Post Traumatic Cognitions Inventory (PTCI): Development and validation', *Psychological Assessment*, 11: 303–14.

Foa, E.B., Kozak, M.J., Salkovskis, P.M., Coles, M.E. and Amir, N. (1998) 'The validation of a new obsessive compulsive disorder scale: The Obsessive Compulsive Inventory (OCI)', *Psychological Assessment*, 10: 206–14.

Freeman, A. and Martin, D.M. (2004) 'A psychosocial approach for conceptualizing schematic development', in A. Freeman, M.J. Mahoney, P. Devito and D. Martin (eds), *Cognition and Psychotherapy*. 2nd edn. New York: Springer Publishing Company. pp. 221–56.

Freeman, A., Pretzer, J., Fleming, B. and Simon, K.M. (2004) *Clinical Applications of Cognitive Therapy*. New York: Kluwer Academic/Plenum Publishers.

Garety, P.A., Kuipers, E., Fowler, D., Freeman, D. and Bebbington, P.E. (2001) 'A cognitive model of the positive symptoms of psychosis', *Psychological Medicine*, 31(2): 189–95.

Gatchel, R., Peng, Y., Peters, M., Fuchs, P. and Turk, D. (2007) 'The biopsychosocial approach to chronic pain: Scientific advances and future directions', *Psychological Bulletin*, 133(4): 581–624.

George, E., Iveson, C. and Ratner, H. (1990) *Problem to Solution Brief Therapy with Individuals and Families*. London: BT Press.

Gilbert, P. (2005) *Compassion: Conceptualisations, Research and Use in Psychotherapy*. Hove, East Sussex: Routledge.

Gilbert, P. (2006) 'Biosocial and evolutionary approach to formulation with a special focus on shame', in N. Tarrier (ed.), *Case Formulation in Cognitive Behaviour Therapy*. Hove, East Sussex: Routledge. pp. 81–112.

Gilbert, P. (2008) 'Foreword', in A. Grant, M. Townend, J. Mills and A. Cockx (eds), *Assessment and Case Formulation in Cognitive Behvioural Therapy*. 1st edn. London: Sage.

Gillespie, K., Duffy, M., Hackmann, A. and Clark, D.M. (2002) 'Community based cognitive therapy in the treatment of post-traumatic stress disorder following the Omagh bomb', *Behaviour Research and Therapy*, 40: 345–57.

Glover, G., Webb, M. and Evison, F. (2010) *Improving Access to Psychological Therapies: A Review of the Progress made by Sites in the First Roll-Out Year*. Available at: www.iapt.nhs.uk/silo/files/iapt-a-review-of-the-progress-made-by-sites-in-the-first-roll8208-out-year.pdf.

Goffman E. (1969) *The Presentation of Self in Everyday Life*. Reading: Pelican.

Goleman D. (1996) *Emotional Intelligence: Why it can Matter more than IQ*. London: Bloomsbury.

Goodman, W.K., Price, L.H., Rasmussen, S.A., Mazure, C., Fleischmann, R.L., Hill, C.L., Heninger, G.R. and Charney, D.S. (1989) 'The Yale-Brown Obsessive Compulsive Scale: I. Development, Use, and Reliability', *Archives of General Psychiatry*, 46(11): 1006–11.

Gortner, E.T., Gollan, J.K., Dobson, K.S. and Jacobson, N.S. (1998) 'Cognitive-behavioural treatment for depression: Relapse prevention', *Journal of Consulting and Clinical Psychology*, 66: 377–84.

Granholm, E., Ben-Zeev, D., Link, P.C., Bradshaw, K.R., and Holden, J.L. (2011) 'Mobile assessment and treatment for schizophrenia (MATS): A pilot trial of an interactive text messaging intervention for medication adherence, socialization and auditory hallucinations', *Schizophrenia Bulletin*, 38: 414–25.

Grant, A. and Townend, M. (2008) 'The fundamentals of case formulation', in A. Grant, M. Townend, J. Mills and A. Cockx (eds), *Assessment and Case Formulation in Cognitive Behavioural Therapy*. 1st edn. London: Sage. pp. 45–61.

Grant, A. and Townend, M. (2010) 'The service user perspective in CBT', in A. Grant, M. Townend, R. Mulhern and N. Short (eds), *Cognitive Behavioural Therapy in Mental Health Care*. London: Sage. pp. 225–325.

Grant, A., Mills, J., Mulhern, R. and Short, N. (2004) *Cognitive Behavioural Therapy in Mental Health Care*. London: Sage.

Grant, A., Townend, M., Mills, J. and Cockx, A. (2008) *Assessment and Case Formulation in Cognitive Behavioural Therapy*. 1st edn. London: Sage.

Grant, A., Townend, M., Mulhern, R. and Short, N. (2010) *Cognitive Behavioural Therapy in Mental Health Care*. 2nd edn. London. Sage.

Greenberger, D. and Padesky, C.A. (1995) *Mind over Mood: Change how you Feel by Changing the Way you Think*. New York: Guilford Press.

Greenwood, K.E., Sweeney, A., Williams, S., Garety, P., Kuipers, E., Scott, J. and Peters, E. (2010) 'CHoice of Outcome In Cbt for psychosEs (CHOICE): The development of a new service user–led outcome measure of CBT for psychosis', *Schizophrenia Bulletin*, 36(1): 126–35.

Greeven, A., van Balkom, A.J.L.M., Visser, S., Merkelbach, J.W., van Rood, Y.R., van Dyck, R., Van der Does, A.J.W, Zitman, F.G. and Spinhoven, P. (2007) 'Cognitive behavior therapy and paroxetine in the treatment of hypochondriasis: A randomized controlled trial', *American Journal of Psychiatry*, 164(1): 91–9.

Gregg, L., Barrowclough, C., and Haddock, G. (2007) 'Reasons for increased substance use in psychosis', *Clinical Psychology Review*, 27(4): 494–510.

Grey, N. (2007) 'Posttraumatic stress disorder: Treatment', in S. Lindsay and G. Powell (eds), *The Handbook of Clinical Adult Psychology*. 3rd edn. Hove, East Sussex: Routledge. pp. 185–205.

Grey, N. and Holmes, E.A. (2008) '"Hotspots" in trauma memories in the treatment of posttraumatic stress disorder: A replication', *Memory*, 16: 788–96.

Grey, N., Young, K. and Holmes, E. (2002) 'Cognitive restructuring within reliving: a treatment for peritraumatic emotional "hotspots" in post-traumatic stress disorder', *Behavioural and Cognitive Psychotherapy*, 30: 37–56.

Gumley, A. and Power, K.G. (2000) 'Is targeting cognitive therapy during relapse in psychosis feasible?' *Behavioural and Cognitive Psychotherapy*, 28(2): 161–74.

Guest, G. (2000) 'Coaching and mentoring in learning organizations'. Paper presented at TEND Conference, United Arab Emirates, April.

Gunderson, J.G., Stout, R.L., McGlashan, T.H., Shea, M.T., Morey, L.C., Grilo, C.M., Zanarini, M.C., Yen, S., Markowitz, J.C., Sanislow, C.A., Ansell, E.B., Pinto, A. and Skodol, A.E. (2011) 'Ten-year course of borderline personality disorder: Psychopathology and function from the collaborative longitudinal personality study', *Archives of General Psychiatry*, 68: 827–37.

Hackmann, A., Ehlers, A., Speckens, A. and Clark, D.M. (2004) 'Characteristics and content of intrusive memories in PTSD and their changes with treatment', *Journal of Traumatic Stress*, 17(3): 231–40.

Haddock, G. and Siddle, R. (2003) 'Psychosis', in Leahy, R. (ed.), *Roadblocks in Cognitive-Behavioral Therapy*. New York: Guilford Press. pp. 135–52.

Haddock, G., Barrowclough, C., Shaw, J.J., Dunn, G., Novaco, R.W., and Tarrier, N. (2009) 'Cognitive-behavioural therapy v. social activity therapy for people with psychosis and a history of violence: Randomised controlled trial', *The British Journal of Psychiatry*, 194(2): 152–7.

Haddock, G., Berry, K., Davies, G., Dunn, G., Hartley, S., Kelly, J., Law, H., Morrison, A.P. Mulligan, J., Neil, S., Pitt, L., Price, J., Rivers, Z., Taylor, C.D.J., Watts, R., Welford, M., Woodward, S. and Barrowclough, C. (2014b). Delivery preferences for cognitive behaviour therapy for psychosis *(submitted for publication)*.

Haddock, G., Devane, S., Bradshaw, T., McGovern, J., Tarrier, N., Kinderman, P., Baguley, I., Lancashire, S. and Harris, N. (2001) 'An investigation into the psychometric properties of the Cognitive Therapy Scale for Psychosis (CTS-Psy)', *Behavioural and Cognitive Psychotherapy*, 29(2): 221–33.

Haddock, G., Eisner, E., Boone, C., Davies, G., Coogan, C. and Barrowclough, C. (2014a) 'An investigation of the implementation of NICE-recommended CBT interventions for people with schizophrenia', *Journal of Mental Health*, 23(4): 162–5.

Haddock, G., Lobban, F., Hatton, C., and Carson, R. (2004) 'Cognitive-behaviour therapy for people with psychosis and mild intellectual disabilities: A case series', *Clinical Psychology and Psychotherapy*, 11(4): 282–98.

Haddock, G., McCarron, J., Tarrier, N. and Faragher, E.B. (1999) 'Scales to measure dimensions of hallucinations and delusions: The psychotic symptom rating scales (PSYRATS)', *Psychological Medicine*, 29(4): 879–89.

Haddock, G., Wood, L., Watts, R., Dunn, G., Morrison, A.P. and Price, J. (2011) 'The Subjective Experiences of Psychosis Scale (SEPS): Psychometric evaluation of a scale to assess outcome in psychosis', *Schizophrenia Research*, 133(1): 244–9.

Hagenaas, M.A., van Minnen, A. and Hoogduin, K.A.L. (2010) 'The impact of dissociation and depression on the efficacy of prolonged exposure treatment for PTSD', *Behaviour Research and Therapy*, 48: 19–27.

Halvorsen, J.O., Stenmark, H., Neuner, F. and Nordahl, H.M. (2014) 'Does dissociation moderate treatment outcomes of narrative exposure therapy for PTSD? A secondary analysis from a randomized controlled clinical trial', *Behaviour Research and Therapy*, 57: 21–8.

Harvey, A., Watkins, E., Mansell, W. and Shafran, R. (2004) *Cognitive Behavioural Processes across Psychological Disorders*. Oxford: Oxford University Press.

Hawton, K., Salkovskis, P.M., Kirk, J. and Clark, D.M. (1989) *Cognitive Behaviour Therapy for Psychiatric Problems: A Practical Guide*. Oxford: Oxford University Press.

Hawthorne, J. and Redmond, K. (2004) *Pain Causes and Management*. Oxford: Blackwell.

Hayes, S.C. (2004) 'Acceptance and commitment therapy, relational frame theory, and the third wave of behavioural and cognitive therapies', *Behavior Therapy*, 35: 639–65.

Hayes, W.A. (1991) Radical black psychology, in R.L. Jones (ed.), *Black Psychology*. 3rd edn. New York: Harper Row. pp. 65–78.

Hays, P.A. and Iwamasa, G.Y. (2006) *Culturally responsive cognitive-behavioral therapy: Assessment, practice, and supervision*. Washington, DC: American Psychological Association.

Hebblethwaite P. (2002) Helping People Change Part 2. *Accord*, (Summer) pp. 20–2.

Hodgson, R. and Rachman, S. (1974) 'Desynchrony in measures of fear', *Behaviour Research and Therapy*, 2: 319–26.

Hofmann, S.G. and Asmundsen, G.J. (2008) 'Acceptance and mindfulness-based therapy: New wave or old-hat?', *Clinical Psychology Review*, 28: 1–12.

Hofmann, S.G., Asnaani, A., Vonk, J.J., Sawyer, A.T. and Fang, A. (2012) 'The efficacy of cognitive behavioral therapy: A review of meta-analyses', *Cognitive Therapy and Research*, 36, 427–40.

Hollon, S.D., Stewart, M.O. and Strunk, D. (2006) 'Enduring effects for cognitive behaviour therapy in the treatment of depression and anxiety', *Annual Review of Psychology*, 57: 285–315.

Hollon, S.D., Thase, M.E. and Markowitz, J.C. (2002) 'Treatment and prevention of depression', *Psychological Science in the Public Interest*, 3: 39–77.

Holmes, E., Grey, N. and Young, K.A.D. (2005) 'Intrusive images and "hotspots" of trauma memories in posttraumatic stress disorder: An exploratory investigation of emotions and cognitive themes', *Journal of Behaviour Therapy and Experimental Psychiatry*, 36: 3–17.

Holowka, D.W., Dugas, M.J., Francis, K. and Laugesen, N. (2000) 'Measuring beliefs about worry: A psychometric evaluation of the Why Worry-II questionnaire'. Poster presented at the 34th Annual Convention of the Association for Advancement of Behavior Therapy, New Orleans, LA, November.

Hor, K. and Taylor, M. (2010) 'Suicide and schizophrenia: A systematic review of rates and risk factors', *Journal of Psychopharmacology*, 24: 81–90.

Hugdahl, K. (1981) 'The three-systems-model of fear and emotion: A critical examination', *Behaviour Research and Therapy*, 19: 75–85.

IAPT (2011) National Curriculum for High Intensity Cognitive Behaviour Therapy Courses. Available at: www.iapt.nhs.uk/silo/files/national-curriculum-for-high-intensity-cognitive-behavioural-therapy-courses.pdf. Accessed 15 July 2014.

Jacobson, N.S., Dobson, K.T., Traux, P.T., Addis, M.E., Koerner, K., Gollan, J.K., Gortner, E. and Prince, S.E. (1996) 'A component analysis of cognitive behaviour treatment of depression', *Journal of Consulting and Clinical Psychology*, 64: 295–304.

James I.A. (2001) 'Schema therapy: The next generation, but should it carry a health warning?', *Behavioural and Cognitive Psychotherapy*, 29: 401–7.

James, I.A., Morse, R. and Howarth, A. (2010) 'The science and art of asking questions in cognitive therapy', *Behavioural and Cognitive Psychotherapy*, 38: 83–93.

Jauhar, S., McKenna, P.J., Radua, J., Fung, E., Salvador, R. and Laws, K.R. (2014) 'Cognitive-behavioural therapy for the symptoms of schizophrenia: Systematic review and meta-analysis with examination of potential bias', *The British Journal of Psychiatry*, 204(1): 20–9.

Jensen, M. and Turk, D. (2014) 'Contributions of psychology to the understanding and treatment of people with chronic pain: Why it matters to ALL psychologists', *American Psychologist*, 69(2): 105–18.

Jones, C., Hacker, D., Cormac, I., Meaden, A. and Irving, C.B. (2012) *Cognitive Behaviour Therapy versus other Psychosocial Treatments for Schizophrenia*. Cochrane Database of Systematic Reviews. Available at: www.cochrane.org/CD008712/SCHIZ_cognitive-behaviour-therapy-versus-other-psychosocial-treatments-schizophrenia. Accessed September 2015.

Kay, S.R., Opler, L.A., and Lindenmayer, J.P. (1989) 'The Positive and Negative Syndrome Scale (PANSS): Rationale and standardisation', *The British Journal of Psychiatry*, 155(7): 59–65.

Keijsers, G.P., Schaap, C.P., Hoogduin, C.A. and Lammers, M.W. (1995) 'Patient-therapist interaction in the behavioural treatment of panic disorder with agoraphobia', *Behavior Modification*, 19: 491–517.

Kelly, S. (2006) 'Cognitive-behavioral therapy with African Americans', in P.A. Hays and G.Y. Iwamasa (eds), *Culturally Responsive Cognitive-Behavioral Therapy: Assessment, Practice, and Supervision*. Washington, DC: American Psychological Association. pp. 97–116.

Kennedy, F., Kennerley, H. and Pearson, D. (2013) *Cognitive Behavioural Approaches to the Understanding and the Treatment of Dissociation*. Hove, East Sussex: Routledge.

Kennerley, H., Mueller, M.M. and Fennell, M.J. (2010) 'Looking after yourself', in M. Mueller, H. Kennerley, F. McManus and D. Westbrook (eds), *The Oxford Guide to Surviving as a CBT Therapist*. Oxford: Oxford University Press. pp. 57–82.

Kessler, R.C., Sonnega, A., Bromet, E., Hughes, M. and Nelson, C.B. (1995) 'Post-traumatic stress disorder in the National Comorbidity Survey', *Archives of General Psychiatry*, 52: 1048–60.

Kline, N. (1999) *Time to Think: Listening to Ignite the Human Mind*. London: Ward Lock.

Kostova, Z., Caiata-Zufferey, M. and Schulz, P. (2014) 'The impact of social support on the acceptance process among RA patients: A qualitative study', *Psychology and Health*, 29(11): 1283–303.

Kroenke, K. (2007) 'Efficacy of treatment for somatoform disorders: a review of randomized controlled trials', *Psychosomatic Medicine*, 69: 881–8.

Kroenke, K. and Spitzer, R.L. (2002) 'The PHQ-9: A new depression diagnostic and severity measure', *Psychiatric Annals*, 32: 509–21.

Kroenke, K., Spitzer, R. and Williams, W. (2010) 'The PHQ-9: Validity of a brief description severity measure', *Journal of General Internal Medicine*, 16: 606–16.

Kroese, B.S. (2014) 'CBT with people with learning disabilities', in A. Whittington and N. Grey (eds), *How to become a More Effective CBT Therapist: Mastering Metacompetence in Clinical Practice*. Chichester, West Sussex: Wiley. pp. 225–38.

Kumar, N. (2007) 'Challenges faced within the emergent Indian Economy in the delivery of evidence based psychological therapy'. Paper delivered at the World Congress of Behavioural and Cognitive Therapies. Barcelona, July.

Kuyken, W. (2006) 'Evidence-based case formulation: Is the emperor clothed?', in N. Tarrier (ed.), *Case Formulation in Cognitive Behaviour Therapy: The Treatment of Challenging and Complex Cases*. Hove, East Sussex: Routledge. pp. 12–35.

Kuyken, W., Fothergill, C.D., Musa, M. and Chadwick, P. (2005) 'The reliability and quality of cognitive case formulation', *Behaviour Research and Therapy*, 43: 1187–201.

Kuyken, W., Padesky, C.A. and Dudley, R. (2009) *Collaborative Case Conceptualization: Working Effectively with Clients in Cognitive-Behavioral Therapy*. New York: Guilford Press.

Kuyken, W., Watkins, E. and Beck, A.T. (2003) 'Cognitive behaviour therapy for mood disorders', in G.O. Gabbard, J.S. Beck, and J. Holmes (eds), *Oxford Textbook of Psychotherapy*. Oxford: Oxford University Press. pp. 111–26.

Laberg, S., Tornkvist, A. and Anderson, G. (2001) 'Experiences of patients in cognitive behavioural group therapy: A qualitative study of eating disorders', *Scandinavian Journal of Behaviour Therapy*, 30(4): 161–78.

Laidlaw, K., Thompson, L.W., Dick-Siskin, L. and Gallagher-Thompson, D. (2003) *Cognitive Behaviour Therapy with Older People*. Chichester: West Sussex: Wiley.

Lamb, S., Hansen, Z., Lall, R., Castelnuovo, E., Withers, E., Nicholas, Y., Potter, R. and Underwood, M. (2010) 'Group cognitive behaviour treatment for low back pain in primary care: A randomised controlled trial and cost effectiveness analysis', *The Lancet*, 375(18): 916–23.

Lambert, M.J. and Barley, D.E. (2002) 'Research summary on the therapeutic relationship and psychotherapy outcome', in J.C. Norcross (ed.), *Psychotherapy Relationships that Work: Therapist Contributions and Responsiveness to Patients*. Oxford: Oxford University Press. pp 17–32.

Landsman, K., Rupertus, K. and Pedrick, C. (2005) *Loving Someone with OCD: Help for you and your Family*. Oakland, CA: New Harbinger Publications.

Lane, D.A. and Corrie, S. (2006) *The Modern Scientist-Practitioner: A Guide to Practice in Psychology*. Hove, East Sussex: Routledge.

Lane, D.A. and Corrie, S. (2012) *Making Successful Decisions in Counselling and Psychotherapy*. Maidenhead, Berkshire: Open University Press.

Lang, P.J. (1968) 'Fear reduction and fear behaviour: Problems in treating a construct', in J.M. Shilen (ed.), *Research in Psychotherapy, Vol III*. Washington DC: American Psychological Association. pp. 90–102.

LaTaillade, J. (2006) 'Consideration of treatment of African American couple relationships', *Journal of Cognitive Psychotherapy: An International Quarterly*, 20(4): 341–58.

Law, H., Neil, S.T., Dunn, G. and Morrison, A.P. (2014) 'Psychometric properties of the Questionnaire about the Process of Recovery (QPR)', *Schizophrenia Research*. doi: 10.1016/j.schres.2014.04.011.

Layden, M.A, Newman, C., Freeman, A. and Morse, S. (1993) *Cognitive Therapy of Borderline Personality Disorder*. Boston, MA: Allyn and Bacon.

Leahy, R.L. (2001) *Overcoming Resistance in Cognitive Therapy*. New York. Guilford Press.

Leahy, R.L. (2005) *The Worry Cure: Stop Worrying and Start Living*. London: Piatkus.

Leahy, R.L. (2007) 'Schematic mismatch in the therapeutic relationship', in P. Gilbert and R.L. Leahy (eds), *The Therapeutic Relationship in the Cognitive Behavioural Psychotherapies*. Hove, East Sussex: Routledge. pp. 229–54.

Lecomte, T., Corbiere, M., Laisne, F. (2006) 'Investigating self-esteem in individuals with schizophrenia: Relevance of the Self-Esteem Rating Scale-Short Form', *Psychiatry Research*, 143(1): 99–108.

Lee, D (2012) *Recovering from Trauma using Compassion Focused Therapy*. London: Robinson.

Lewinsohn, P.M. (1974) 'A behavioural approach to depression', in R.J. Friedman and M.M. Katz (eds), *The Psychology of Depression: Contemporary Theory and Research*. New York: Wiley, pp.157–78.

Lo, M.-C.M. (2005) 'Professions: Prodigal daughter of modernity', in J. Adams, E.S. Clemens and A.S. Orloff (eds), *Remaking Modernity: Politics, Processes and History in Sociology*. Durham, NC: Duke University Press. pp. 381–406.

Longmore, R.J. and Worrell, M. (2007) 'Do we need to challenge thoughts in cognitive behaviour therapy?', *Clinical Psychology Review*, 27(2): 173–87.

Lowe, C. and Murray, C. (2014) 'Adult service-users' experiences of trauma-focused cognitive behavioural therapy', *Journal of Contemporary Psychotherapy*, 44: 223–31.

Löwe, B., Decker, O., Müller, S., Brähler, E., Schellberg, D., Herzog, W. and Herzberg, P.Y. (2008) 'Validation and standardization of the Generalized Anxiety Disorder Screener (GAD-7) in the general population', *Medical Care*, 46: 266–74.

Lunt, I. (2006) 'Foreword', in D.A. Lane and S. Corrie (eds), *The Modern Scientist-Practitioner: A Guide to Practice in Psychology*. Hove, East Sussex: Routledge. pp. xiii-xiv.

Macdonald, H. (2001) *Cognitive-Behavioural Psychotherapy for Chronic Pain: Development and Pilot of an Assisted Self-help Manual*. University of Derby: Masters' degree thesis. Unpublished manuscript.

Mahoney, M.J. (1988) 'The cognitive sciences and psychotherapy: Patterns in a developing relationship', in K. Dobson (ed.), *Handbook of Cognitive-Behavior Therapies*. New York: Guilford Press. pp. 357–86.

Mahoney, M.J. and Gabriel, T.J. (2002) 'Psychotherapy and the cognitive science: An evolving alliance', in R.L. Leahy and E.T. Dowd (eds), *Clinical Advances in Cognitive Psychotherapy: Theory and Application*. New York: Springer. pp. 127–147.

Maier, W., Gansicke, M., Freyberger, H.J., Linz, M., Heun, R. and Lecrubier, Y. (2000) 'Generalized anxiety disorder (ICD–10) in primary care from a cross-cultural perspective: A valid diagnostic entity?', *Acta Psychiatrica Scandinavica*, 101: 29–36.

Marks, I.M. (1986) *Maudsley Pocket Book of Clinical Management*. Bristol: Bristol Wright.

Martell, C.R., Dimidjian, S. and Herman-Dunn, R. (2013) *Behavioural Activation for Depression: A Clinician's Guide*. New York: Guilford Press.

Martell, C.R., Safren, S.A. and Prince, S.E (2004) *Cognitive-Behavioral Therapies with Lesbian, Gay, and Bisexual Clients*. New York: Guildford Press.

Maslin, J. (2003) 'Substance misuse in psychosis: Contextual issues', in H.L. Graham, A. Copello, M.J. Birchwood and K.T. Mueser (eds), *Substance Misuse in Psychosis: Approaches to Treatment and Service Delivery*. Chichester, West Sussex: Wiley. pp. 3–23.

Mazzucchelli, T., Kane, R. and Rees, C. (2009) 'Behavioural activation treatments for depression in adults: A meta-analysis and review', *Clinical Psychology: Science and Practice*, 16: 383–411.

McBeth, J., Chui, Y., Silman, A., Ray, D., Morriss, R., Dickens, C., Gupta, A. and Macfarlane, G. (2005) 'Hypothalamic-pituitary-adrenal stress axis function and the relationship with chronic widespread pain and its antecedents', *Arthritis Research and Therapy*, 7(5): 992–1000.

McCracken, L. and Vowles, K. (2014) 'Acceptance and commitment therapy and mindfulness for chronic pain: Model process and progress', *American Psychologist*, 69(2): 178–87.

McGowan, J. and Hill, R. (2009) 'The role of psychological therapies in acute psychiatric care', *Clinical Psychology Forum*, 196: 14–17.

McGowan, J., Lavender, T. and Garety, P. (2005) 'Factors in outcome of cognitive-behavioural therapy for psychosis: Users' and clinicians' views', *Psychology and Psychotherapy: Theory, Research and Practice*, 78: 513–29.

McHugh, R.K. and Barlow, D.H. (2010) 'The dissemination and implementation of evidence-based psychological treatments: A review of current efforts', *American Psychologist*, 65(2): 73–84.

McMain, S.F., Guimond, T., Streiner, D.L., Cardish, R.J. and Links, P.S. (2012) 'Dialectical behavior therapy compared with general psychiatric management for borderline personality disorder: Clinical outcomes and functioning over a 2-year follow-up', *American Journal of Psychiatry*, 169: 650–61.

Meaden, A., Keen, N., Aston, R., Barton, K. and Bucci, S. (2013) *Cognitive Therapy for Command Hallucinations*. Hove, East Sussex: Routledge.

Melzack, R. and Wall, P. (1982) *The Challenge of Pain*. Harmondsworth: Penguin Books.

Mennin, D.S., Heimberg, R.G., Turk, C.L. and Fresco, D.M. (2002) 'Applying an emotion regulation framework to integrative approaches to generalized anxiety disorder', *Clinical Psychology: Science and Practice*, 9: 85–90.

Meyer, T.J., Miller, M.L., Metzger, R.L. and Borkovec, T.D. (1990) 'Development and validation of the Penn State Worry Questionnaire', *Behaviour Research and Therapy*, 28: 487–95.

Michael, T., Ehlers, A., Halligan, S. and Clark, D.M. (2005) 'Unwanted memories of assault: What intrusion characteristics predict PTSD?', *Behaviour Research and Therapy*, 43: 613–28.

Milioni, D. (2007) '"Oh, Jo! You can't see that real life is not like riding a horse!": Clients' constructions of power and metaphor in therapy', *Radical Psychology*, 6(1). Available at: www.radicalpsychology.org/vol6-1/milioni.htm.

Miller, W.R. and Rollnick, S. (2003) *Motivational Interviewing: Preparing people for change*. 2nd edn. New York: Guilford Press.

Mills, J., Grant, A., Mulhern, R. and Short, N. (2004) 'Working with people who have complex emotional and relationship difficulties (borderlines or people?)', in

A. Grant, J. Mills, R. Mulhern and N. Short (eds), *Cognitive Behavioural Therapy in Mental Health Care*. London: Sage. pp. 82–99.

Miranda, R. and Andersen, S.M. (2007) 'The therapeutic relationship: Implications from social cognition and transference', in P. Gilbert and R.L. Leahy (eds), *The Therapeutic Relationship in the Cognitive Behavioural Psychotherapies*. Hove, East Sussex: Routledge. pp. 63–89.

Mitte, K. (2005) 'Meta-analysis of cognitive-behavioral treatment for generalized anxiety disorder: A comparison with pharmacotherapy', *Psychological Bulletin*, 131: 785–95.

Mohan, J. (1996) 'Accounts of the NHS reforms: Macro- meso- and micro-level perspectives', *Sociology of Health and Illness*, 18: 675–98.

Mooney, K.A. and Padesky, C.A. (2000) 'Applying client creativity to recurrent problems: Constructing possibilities and tolerating doubt', *Journal of Cognitive Psychotherapy*, 4(2): 149–61.

Mooney, K.A. and Padesky, C.A. (2002) 'Cognitive Therapy to Build Resilience'. Workshop presented at BABCP Conference, Warwick, UK, July.

Moore, R. and Garland, A. (2003) *Cognitive Therapy for Chronic and Persistent Depression*. Chichester, West Sussex: Wiley.

Moorey, S. (2010) 'The six cycles maintenance model: Growing a "vicious flower" for depression', *Behavioural and Cognitive Psychotherapy*, 38: 173–84.

Morkved, N., Hartmann, K., Aarsheim, L.M., Holen, D., Milde, A.M., Bomyea, J. and Thorp, S.R. (2014) 'A comparison of narrative exposure therapy and prolonged exposure therapy for PTSD', *Clinical Psychology Review*, 34: 453–67.

Morley, S., Eccleston, C. and Williams, A. (1999) 'Systematic review and meta-analysis of randomized controlled trials of cognitive behaviour therapy and behaviour therapy for chronic pain in adults, excluding headache', *Pain*, 80: 1–13.

Morrison, A.P. (2001) 'The interpretation of intrusions in psychosis: An integrative cognitive approach to hallucinations and delusions', *Behavioural and Cognitive Psychotherapy*, 29: 257–76.

Morrison, A.P., French, P., Stewart, S.L.K., Birchwood, M., Fowler, D., Gumley, A., Jones, P.B., Bentall, R.P., Lewis, S.W., Murray, G.K., Patterson, P., Brunet, K., Conroy, J., Parker, S., Reilly, T., Byrne, R., Davies, L.M. and Dunn, G. (2012b) 'Early detection and intervention evaluation for people at risk of psychosis: Multisite randomised controlled trial', *British Medical Journal*, 344. doi: http://dx.doi.org/10.1136/bmj.e2233.

Morrison, A.P., Hutton, P., Wardle, M., Spencer, H., Barratt, S., Brabban, A., Callcott, P., Christodoulides, T., Dudley, R., French, P., Lumley, V., Tai, S.J. and Turkington, D. (2012a) 'Cognitive therapy for people with a schizophrenia spectrum diagnosis not taking antipsychotic medication: An exploratory trial', *Psychological Medicine*, 42: 1049–56.

Morse, S.B. (2002) 'Letting it go: Using cognitive therapy to treat borderline personality disorder', in G. Simos (ed.), *Cognitive Behaviour Therapy: A Guide for the Practising Clinician*. Hove, East Sussex: Brunner-Routledge. pp 223–241.

Mpofu, M. (2014) Change2Choose: Summary report on the pilot programme on undiagnosed posttraumatic stress distress in inner city youth exposed to street and domestic violence in Birmingham, England 2014. Unpublished document.

Mundt, J.C., Marks, I.M., Shear, M.K. and Griest, J.H. (2002) 'The work and social adjustment scale: A simple measure of impairment in functioning', *British Journal of Psychiatry*, 180: 461–4.

Muse, K. and McManus, F. (2013) 'A systematic review of methods for assessing competence in cognitive-behavioural therapy', *Clinical Psychology Review*, 33: 484–99.

Needleman, L.D. (1999) *Cognitive Case Conceptualization: A Guidebook for Practitioners.* Hillsdale, NJ: Erlbaum.

Neil, S.T., Kilbride, M., Pitt, L., Nothard, S., Welford, M., Sellwood, W. and Morrison, A.P. (2009) 'The questionnaire about the process of recovery (QPR): A measurement tool developed in collaboration with service users', *Psychosis*, 1(2): 145–55.

Nelson, H.E. (1997) *Cognitive Behavioural Therapy with Schizophrenia: A Practice Manual.* Cheltenham, Gloucestershire: Stanley Thornes Ltd.

Newman, C.F. (2007) 'The therapeutic relationship in cognitive therapy with difficult-to-engage clients', in P. Gilbert and R.L. Leahy (eds), *The Therapeutic Relationship in the Cognitive Behavioural Psychotherapies.* Hove, East Sussex: Routledge. pp. 165–84.

NICE (2005) 'Obsessive-compulsive disorder: Core interventions in the treatment of obsessive-compulsive disorder and body dysmorphic disorder'. CG31. London: National Institute for Health and Care Excellence.

NICE (2009) 'Depression in adults: The treatment and management of depression in adults' CG90. Available at: www.nice.org.uk/guidance/CG90. Accessed 14 August 2014.

NICE (2011) 'Generalised anxiety disorder and panic disorder (with or without agoraphobia) in adults: Management in primary, secondary and community care'. CG113. Available at www.nice.org.uk/guidance/cg113/chapter/4-research-recommendations.

NICE (2013) 'Social Anxiety Disorder: Recognition, Assessment and Treatment'. CG159. Available at www.nice.org.uk/guidance/cg159.

NICE (2014) *Schizophrenia: Core Interventions in the Treatment and Management of Schizophrenia in Primary and Secondary Care.* London: National Institute for Clinical Excellence.

Nicholas, M.K. (2007) 'The pain self-efficacy questionnaire: Taking pain into account', *European Journal of Pain*, 11(2): 153–63.

Nielson, W. and Weir, R. (2001) 'Biopsychosocial approaches to the treatment of chronic pain', *The Clinical Journal of Pain*, 17(4): 114–27.

Nolen-Hoeksema, S. (1991) 'Responses to depression and their effects on the duration of depressive episodes', *Journal of Abnormal Psychology*, 100: 569–82.

Norton, P.J. (2012) 'A randomized clinical trial of transdiagnostic cognitive-behavioral treatments for anxiety disorder by comparison to relaxation training', *Behavior Therapy*, 43(3): 506–17.

Ohman, A. and Soares, J.J.F. (1994) 'Unconscious anxiety: Phobic responses to masked stimuli', *Journal of Abnormal Psychology.* 103: 231–40.

Okazaki, S. and Tanaka-Matsumi, J. (2006) 'Cultural considerations in cognitive-behavioral assessment', in P.A Hays and G.Y. Iwamasa (eds), *Culturally Responsive Cognitive-Behavioral Therapy: Assessment, Practice, and Supervision.* Washington, DC: American Psychological Association. pp. 247–66.

Öst, L.G. (1987) 'Applied relaxation: Description of a coping technique and review of controlled studies', *Behaviour Research and Therapy*, 25(5): 397–409.

Öst, L.G. and Breitholtz, E. (2000) 'Applied relaxation vs cognitive therapy in the treatment of generalized anxiety disorder', *Behaviour Research and Therapy*, 38: 770–90.

Otto, M.W. and Deveney, C. (2005) 'Cognitive-behavioral therapy and the treatment of panic disorder: Efficacy and strategies', *Journal of Clinical Psychiatry*, 66: 28–32.

Overholser, J.C. (1993) 'Elements of the Socratic method: 1. Systematic questioning', *Psychotherapy*, 30: 67–74.

Padesky, C.A. (1989) 'Attaining and maintaining positive lesbian self-identity: A cognitive therapy approach', *Women & Therapy*, 8(1, 2): 145–56.

Padesky, C.A. (1993) 'Socratic questioning: Changing minds or guiding discovery?' Invited keynote address presented at the 1993 European Congress of Behaviour and Cognitive Therapies, London, September. Available at: http://padesky.com/clinical_corner.htm.

Padesky, C.A. (1996a) 'Developing cognitive therapist competency: Teaching and supervision models', in P.M. Salkovskis (ed.), *Frontiers of Cognitive Therapy*. New York: Guilford Press. pp. 266–92.

Padesky, C.A. (1996b) *Guided Discovery Using Socratic Dialogue* [DVD]. Huntington Beach, CA: Center for Cognitive Therapy. Available at: http://store.padesky.com.

Padesky, C.A. (1997) 'A more effective treatment focus for social phobia', *International Cognitive Therapy Newsletter*, 11(1): 1–3.

Padesky, C.A. (1998) 'When there's not enough time: Innovation in cognitive therapy'. Workshop handout, London: Imperial College, 2–3 October.

Padesky, C.A. (1999) *Therapist Beliefs: Protocols, Personalities and Guided Exercises* [Audio recording]. Huntington Beach, CA: Center for Cognitive Therapy. Available at: http://store.padesky.com.

Padesky, C.A. (2003) 'Cognitive therapy unplugged: fine-tuning essential therapist skills'. Workshop delivered by Cognitive Workshops. Institute of Education, London: 17–18 June.

Padesky, C.A. (2008a) *CBT for Social Anxiety* [DVD]. Huntington Beach, CA: Center for Cognitive Therapy. Available at: http://store.padesky.com//vsa.htm. Accessed 8 April 2015.

Padesky, C.A. (2008b) *CBT for Social Anxiety* [Audio CD]. Huntington Beach, CA: Center for Cognitive Therapy. Available at: http://store.padesky.com/sanx.htm. Accessed 8 April 2015.

Padesky, C.A. (2012) Anxiety traps: CBT antidotes. Cognitive Workshop. Centre for Cognitive Therapy; London, 21–22 May 2012.

Padesky, C.A. and Mooney, K.A. (1990) 'Clinical tip: Presenting the cognitive model to clients', *International Cognitive Therapy Newsletter*, 6: 13–14. Available at: http://padesky.com/clinical-corner.

Padesky, C.A. and Mooney, K.A. (2005) 'Winter Workshop in Cognitive Therapy' [Workshop handouts]. Palm Desert, CA.

Palmer, B.A., Pankratz, V.S. and Bostwick, J.M. (2005) 'The lifetime risk of suicide in schizophrenia: A reexamination', *Archives of General Psychiatry*, 62(3): 247–53.

Paniagua, F.A. (2014) *Assessing and Treating Culturally Diverse Clients: A Practical Guide*. 4th edn. London: Sage.

Paul, R.W. (1993) *Critical Thinking: What Every Person Needs to Survive in a Rapidly Changing World*. Santa Rosa, CA: Foundation for Critical Thinking.

Paykel, E.S., Scott, J., Teasdale, J.D., Johnson, A.L., Garland, A., Moore, R. and Pope, M. (1999) 'Prevention of relapse in residual depression by cognitive therapy: A controlled trial', *Archives of General Psychiatry*, 56: 829–35.

Persons, J.B. (1989) *Cognitive Therapy in Practice: A Case Formulation Approach*. New York: Norton.

Persons, J.B. and Davidson, J. (2010) 'Cognitive-behavioral case formulation', in K.S. Dobson (ed.), *Handbook of Cognitive Behavioral Therapies*. 3rd edn. New York: Guilford Press. pp. 172–95.

Persons, J.B. and Tompkins, M.A. (1997) 'Cognitive-behavioral case formulation', in T.D. Eells (ed.), *Handbook of Psychotherapy Case Formulation*. New York: Guilford Press. pp. 314–39.

Pitt, L., Kilbride, M., Nothard, S., Welford, M. and Morrison, A.P. (2007) 'Researching recovery from psychosis: A user-led project', *Psychiatric Bulletin*, 31(2): 55–60.

Power, M.J. and Dalgleish, T. (1997) *Cognition and Emotion: From Order to Disorder*. Hove, East Sussex: Psychology Press.

Power, M. and Dalgeish, T. (2008) *Cognition and Emotion: From Order to Disorder*. 2nd edn. New York: Psychology Press.

Regier, D.A., Farmer, M.E., Rae, D.S., Locke, B.Z., Keith, S.J., Judd, L.L. and Goodwin, F.K. (1990) 'Comorbidity of mental disorders with alcohol and other drug abuse: Results from the Epidemiologic Catchment Area (ECA) study', *Jama*, 264(19): 2511–18.

Rennie, D.L. (1994) 'Clients' deference in psychotherapy: Special section; Qualitative research in counselling process and outcome', *Journal of Counselling Psychology*, 41(4): 427–37.

Reynolds, M. and Brewin, C.R. (1999) 'Intrusive memories in depression and post-traumatic stress disorder', *Behaviour Research and Therapy*, 37: 201–15.

Rief, W. and Hiller, W. (2003) 'A new approach for the assessment of the treatment effects of somatoform disorders', *Psychosomatics*, 44: 492–8.

Robichaud, M. and Dugas, M.J. (2005a) 'Negative problem orientation (part I): Psychometric properties of a new measure', *Behaviour Research and Therapy*, 43: 391–401.

Robichaud, M. and Dugas, M.J. (2005b) 'Negative problem orientation (part II): construct validity and specificity to worry', *Behaviour Research and Therapy*, 43: 403–12.

Robinson, D., Woerner, M.G., Alvir, J.M.J., Bilder, R., Goldman, R., Geisler, S. and Lieberman, J.A. (1999) 'Predictors of relapse following response from a first episode of schizophrenia or schizoaffective disorder', *Archives of General Psychiatry*, 56(3): 241–7.

Robjant, K. and Fazel, M. (2010) 'The emerging evidence for Narrative Exposure Therapy: A review', *Clinical Psychology Review*, 30: 1030–9.

Roemer, L. and Orsillo, S.M. (2005) 'An acceptance-based behavior therapy for generalized anxiety disorder', in S.M. Orsillo and L. Roemer (eds), *Acceptance and Mindfulness-Based Approaches to Anxiety: Conceptualization and Treatment*. New York: Springer. pp. 213–40.

Rollnick, S., Heather, N., Gold, R. and Hall, W. (1992) 'Development of a short Readiness to Change Questionnaire for use in brief opportunistic interventions', *British Journal of Addiction*, 87: 743–54.

Rollnick, S., Mason, P. and Butler, C. (1999) *Health Behaviour Change: A Practitioner's Guide*. Oxford: Churchill Livingston.

Rollnick, S., Miller, W. and Butler, C. (2008) *Motivational Interviewing in Health Care: Helping Patients Change Behaviour*. London: Guilford Press.

Ross, L.E., Doctor, F., Dimito, A., Kueli, D. and Armstrong, M.S. (2008) 'Can talking about oppression reduce depression?', *Journal of Gay & Lesbian Social Services*, 19(1): 1–15.

Roth, A.D. and Fonagy, P. (1996) *What Works for Whom? A Critical Review of Psychotherapy Research*. New York: Guilford Press.

Roth, A.D. and Pilling, S. (2007) *The Competences Required to Deliver Effective Cognitive and Behavioural Therapy for People with Depression and with Anxiety Disorders*. London: Department of Health.

Roth, T. (2014) 'Foreword', in A. Whittington and N. Grey (eds), *How to Become a More Effective CBT Therapist: Mastering Metacompetence in Clinical Practice*. Chichester, West Sussex: Wiley. pp. xvii–xviii.

Roth, W.T., Doberenz, S., Dietel, A., Conrad, A., Mueller, A., Wollburg, E., Meuret, A.E., Taylor B.C. and Kim, S. (2008) 'Sympathetic activation in broadly defined generalized anxiety disorder', *Journal of Psychiatric Research*, 42(3): 205–12.

Safran, J.D. and Muran, J.C. (2000) *Negotiating the Therapeutic Alliance: A Relational Treatment Guide*. New York: Guilford Press.

Safran, J.D. and Segal, Z.V. (1990) *Interpersonal Processes in Cognitive Therapy*. New York: Basic Books.

Safran, J.D. and Segal, Z.V. (1996) *Interpersonal Process in Cognitive Therapy*. Northvale, NJ: Aronson.

Safran, J.D., Segal, Z.V., Vallils, T.M., Shaw, B.F. and Samstag, L.W. (1993) 'Assessing patient suitability for short-term cognitive therapy with an interpersonal focus', *Cognitive Therapy & Research*, 17: 23–38.

Salkovskis, P.M. (1988) 'Phenomenology, assessment and the cognitive model of panic', in S. Rachman and J.D. Maser (eds), *Panic: Psychological Perspectives*. Hillsdale, NJ: Erlbaum. pp. 111–36.

Salkovskis, P.M. (1991) 'The importance of behaviour in the maintenance of anxiety and panic: A cognitive account', *Behavioural Psychotherapy*, 19: 6–19.

Salkovskis, P.M. (1999) 'Understanding and treating obsessive-compulsive disorder', *Behaviour Research and Therapy*, 37(1): S29-S52.

Salkovskis, P. (2002) 'Empirically grounded clinical interventions: Cognitive-behavioural therapy progresses through a multi-dimensional approach to clinical science', *Behavioural and Cognitive Psychotherapy*, 30(1): 3–9.

Salkovskis, P.M and Warwick, H.M. (1986) 'Morbid preoccupations, health anxiety and reassurance: A cognitive-behavioural approach to hypochondriasis', *Behaviour Research and Therapy*, 24: 597–602.

Salkovskis, P.M., Clark, D.M., Hackmann, A., Wells, A. and Gelder, M. (1999) 'An experimental investigation of the role of safety-seeking behaviours in the maintenance of panic disorder with agoraphobia', *Behaviour Research and Therapy*, 37: 559–74.

Salkovskis, P., Forrester, E., Richards, C., and Morrison, N. (1998) 'The devil is in the detail: Conceptualising and treating obsessional problems', in N. Tarrier, A. Wells, and G. Haddock (eds), *Treating Complex Cases: The Cognitive Behavioural Therapy Approach*. Chichester, West Sussex: Wiley. pp. 46–80.

Salkovskis, P.M, Warwick, H.M. and Deale, A.C. (2003) 'Cognitive-behavioural treatment for severe and persistent health anxiety (hypochondriasis)', *Brief Treatment and Crisis Intervention*, 3: 353–67.

Sanders, D. and Wills, F. (2005) *Cognitive Therapy: An Introduction*. 2nd edn. London: Sage.

Sanovio, E. (1988) 'Obsessions and compulsions: The Padua Inventory', *Behaviour Research and Therapy*, 26: 169–77.

Sayer, J. and Townend, M. (1992) 'A very personal problem: A case study of hypochondriasis', *Nursing Times*. January 1–7(1): 44–6.

Schaap, C., Bennun, A., Schindler, L. and Hoogduin, K. (1993) *The Therapeutic Relationship in Behavioural Psychotherapy*. Chichester, West Sussex: Wiley.

Schauer, M. and Elbert, T. (2010) 'Dissociation following traumatic events', *Journal of Psychology*, 218: 109–27.

Schauer, M., Neuner, F. and Elbert, T. (2011) *Narrative Exposure Therapy: A Short Term Treatment for Traumatic Stress Disorders*. Gottingen: Hogrefe. 2nd edn.

Sexton, K.A. and Dugas, M.J. (2008) 'The Cognitive Avoidance Questionnaire: Validation of the English translation', *Journal of Anxiety Disorders*, 22: 355–70.

Sierra Hernandez, C.A., Han, C., Oliffe, J.L. and Ogrodniczuk, J.S. (2014) 'Understanding help-seeking among depressed men', *Psychology of Men and Masculinity*, 15(3): 346–54.

Skinner, H.A. (1982) 'The drug abuse screening test', *Addictive Behaviors*, 7: 363–71.

Snelgrove, S., Edwards, S. and Liossi, C. (2013) 'A longitudinal study of patients' experience of chronic low back pain using interpretative phenomenological analysis: Changes and consistencies', *Psychology and Health*, 28(2): 121–38.

Snyder, C.R. and Lopez, S.J. (2005) *Handbook of Positive Psychology*. Oxford: Oxford University Press.

Solomon, D.A., Keller, M.B., Leon, A.C., Mueller, T.I., Lavori, P.W., Shea, M.T., Corywell, W., Warshaw, M., Turvey, C., Maser, J.D. and Endicott, J. (2000) 'Multiple recurrences of major depressive disorder', *American Journal of Psychiatry*, 157(2): 229–33.

Spitzer, R.L., Kroenke, K., Williams, J.B.W. and Löwe, B. (2006) 'A brief measure for assessing generalized anxiety disorder: The GAD-7', *Archives of Internal Medicine*, 166: 1092–7.

Stallard, P. (2005) *A Clinician's Guide to Think Good Feel Good: Using CBT with Children and Young People*. Chichester, West Sussex: Wiley.

Stalnacke, B. (2011) 'Life satisfaction in patients with chronic pain – relation to pain intensity, disability and psychological factors', *Neuropsychiatric Disease and Treatment*, 7(1): 683–9.

Stenmark, H., Catani, C., Neuner, F., Elbert, T. and Holen, A. (2013) 'Treating PTSD in refugees and asylum seekers within the general health care system: A randomized controlled multicenter study', *Behaviour Research and Therapy*, 51: 641–7.

Stobie, B., Taylor, T., Quigley, A., Ewing, S. and Salkovskis, P.M. (2007) 'Contents may vary: A pilot study of treatment histories of OCD patients', *Behavioural and Cognitive Psychotherapy*, 35(3): 273–82.

Stoffers, J., Vollmer, B.A., Rucker, G., Timmer, A., Husband, N. and Lieb, K. (2010) *Pharmacological Interventions for Borderline Personality Disorder (Review)*. The Cochrane Collaboration. Chichester, West Sussex: Wiley.

Stott, R., Mansell, W., Salkovskis, P.M., Lavender, A. and Cartwright-Hatton, S. (2010) *Oxford Guide to Metaphors in CBT: Building Cognitive Bridges*. Oxford: Oxford Medical Publications.

Tallis, F., Eysenck, M. and Mathews, A. (1991) 'Elevated evidence requirements and worry', *Personality and Individual Differences*, 12: 21–7.

Tang, N., Salkovskis, P. and Hanna, M. (2007) 'Mental defeat in chronic pain: Initial exploration of the concept', *Clinical Journal of Pain*, 23(3): 222–32.

Tarrier, N. and Haddock, G. (2001) 'Cognitive-behavioural therapy for schizophrenia: A case formulation approach', in Hofmann, S.G. and Tompson, M.C. (eds), *Treating Chronic and Severe Mental Disorders: A Handbook of Empirically Supported Interventions*. New York: Guilford Press. pp. 69–95.

Tarrier, N., Wells, A. and Haddock, G. (1998) *Treating Complex Cases: The Cognitive Behavioural Therapy Approach*. Chichester, West Sussex: Wiley.

Taylor, S. and Asmundson, G.J.G. (2004) *Treating Health Anxiety: A Cognitive Behavioural Approach*. New York: Guilford.

Teasdale, J.D. (1996) 'Clinically relevant theory: Integrating clinical insight with cognitive science', in P.M. Salkovskis (ed.), *Frontiers of Cognitive Therapy*. New York: Guilford. pp. 26–47.

Teasdale, J.D. (1997) 'The relationship between cognition and emotion: The mind-in-place in mood disorders', in D.M. Clark and C.G. Fairburn (eds), *Science and Practice of Cognitive Behaviour Therapy*. Oxford: Oxford University Press. pp. 67–93.

Teasdale, J.D. and Barnard, P. (1993) *Affect Cognition and Change: Re-modelling Depressive Thought*. London: Lawrence Erlbaum Associates.

Teasdale, J.D. and Cox, S.G. (2001) 'Dysphoria: Self-evaluative and affective components in recovered depressed patients and never depressed controls', *Psychological Medicine*, 31: 1311–16.

Teasdale, J.D., Moore, R.G., Hayhurst, H., Pope, M., Williams, S. and Segal, Z. (2002) 'Metacognitive awareness and prevention of relapse in depression: Empirical evidence', *Journal of Consulting and Clinical Psychology*, 70: 275–87.

Theodore, B., Kishino, N., and Gatchel, R. (2008) 'Biopsychosocial factors that perpetuate chronic pain, impairment and disability', *Psychology, Injury and Law*, 1: 182–90.

Thorn, B.E. (2004) *Cognitive Therapy for Chronic Pain: A Step-by-Step Approach*. New York: Guilford Press.

Thwaites, R., Bennett-Levy, J., Davis, M. and Chaddock, A. (2014) 'Using self-practice and self-reflection (SP/SR) to enhance CBT competence and metacompetence', in A. Whittington and N. Grey (eds), *How to become a More Effective CBT Therapist: Mastering Metacompetence in Clinical Practice*. Chichester, West Sussex: Wiley. pp. 241–54.

Titov, N., Dear, B.F., Johnston, L., Lorian, C., Zou, J., Wootton, B., Spence. J., McEvoy, P. and Rapee, R.M. (2013) 'Improving adherence and clinical outcomes in self-guided internet treatment for anxiety and depression: Randomised controlled trial', *PLoS ONE*, 8(7): e62873.

Tolman, J.B. and Dugard, P. (2001) *Single-case and Small-N Experimental Designs: A Practical Guide to Randomization Tests*. Mahwah, NJ: Lawrence Erlbaum Associates.

Toomey, T., Seville, J. and Mann, J. (1996) 'The pain locus of control scale: Relationship to pain description, self-control skills and psychological symptoms', *Pain Clinic*, 8(4): 315–22.

Townend, M. and Grant, A. (2008) 'Process and related issues in cognitive behavioural assessment', in A. Grant, M. Townend, J. Mills and A. Cockx (eds), *Assessment and Case Formulation in Cognitive Behavioural Therapy*. London: Sage. pp. 22–44.

Townend, M., Iannetta, L., and Freeston, M.H. (2002) 'UK study of the supervision practices of behavioural, cognitive and rational emotive behavioural psychotherapists', *Behavioural and Cognitive Psychotherapy*, 30: 485–500.

Turk, D. (1996) *Cognitive Factors in Chronic Pain and Disability. Advances in Cognitive Behavioural Therapy*. London: Sage.

Turner, J., Holtzmann, S. and Mancl, L. (2007) 'Mediators, moderators, and predictors of therapeutic change in cognitive-behavioural therapy for chronic pain', *Pain*, 127: 276–86.

Tyrer, P. and Bajaj, P. (2005) 'Nidotherapy: Making the environment do the therapeutic work', *Advances in Psychiatric Treatment*, 11: 232–328.

Varese, F., Smeets, F., Drukker, M., Lieverse, R., Lataster, T., Viechtbauer, W., Read, J., van Os, J. and Bentall, R.P. (2012) 'Childhood adversities increase the risk of psychosis: A meta-analysis of patient-control, prospective and cross-sectional cohort studies', *Schizophrenia Bulletin*, 38(4): 661–71.

Veale, D. (2003) 'Treatment of social phobia', *Advances in Psychiatric Treatment*, 9: 258–64.

Veale, D. and Willson, R. (2009) *Overcoming Obsessive Compulsive Disorder*. London: Constable & Robinson.

Veale, D., Freeston, F., Krebs, G., Heyman, I. and Salkovskis, P. (2009) 'Risk assessment and management in obsessive-compulsive disorder', *Advances in Psychiatric Treatment*, 15: 332–43.

Waite, P. and Williams, T. (2009) *Obsessive Compulsive Disorder: Cognitive Behaviour Therapy with Children and Young People*. Hove, East Sussex: Routledge.

Waller, G. (2009) 'Evidence-based treatment and therapist drift', *Behaviour Research and Therapy*, 47: 119–27.

Warwick, H.M.C. and Marks, I.M. (1988) 'Behavioural treatment of illness phobia and hypochondriasis: A pilot study of 17 cases', *British Journal of Psychiatry*, 152: 239–41.

Warwick, H.M.C. and Salkovskis, P.M. (1990) 'Hypochondriasis', *Behaviour Research and Therapy*, 28: 105–18.

Warwick, H.M., Clark, D.M., Cobb, A.M. and Salkovskis, P.M. (1996) 'A controlled trial of cognitive-behavioural treatment of hypochondriasis', *British Journal of Psychiatry*, 169: 189–95.

Watkins, E. (2011) 'Targeting rumination by changing processing style: Experiential and imagery exercises'. Paper presented at BABCP Conference, Exeter, UK, July.

Watts, R.J. (2004) 'Integrating social justice and psychology', *The Counseling Psychologist*, 32(6): 855–65. doi: 10.1177/0011000004269274.

Watts, M. (2014) Opening Address, 4th International Congress of Coaching Psychology. London, December.

Weiss, D.S. (1997) 'The Impact of Event Scale – revised', in J.P. Wilson and T.M. Keane (eds), *Assessing Psychological Trauma and PTSD: A Handbook for Practitioners*. New York: Guilford Press. pp. 168–89.

Weiss, J.A. (2014) 'Transdiagnostic case conceptualization of emotional problems in youth with ASD: An emotion regulation approach', *Clinical Psychology Science and Practice*, 21(4): 331–50.

Wells, A. (1995) 'Meta-cognition and worry: A cognitive model of generalized anxiety disorder', *Behavioural and Cognitive Psychotherapy*, 23: 301–20.

Wells, A. (1997) *Cognitive Therapy of Anxiety Disorders: A Practice Manual and Conceptual Guide*. Chichester, West Sussex: Wiley.

Wells, A. (2006) 'Metacognitive therapy for worry and generalized anxiety disorder', in G.C.L. Davey and A. Wells (eds), *Worry and Psychological Disorders: Theory, Assessment and Treatment*. Chichester, West Sussex: Wiley. pp. 259–72.

Wen-Shing, T. (2006) 'Peculiar psychiatric disorders through culture-bound syndromes to culture-related specific syndromes', *Transcultural Psychiatry*, 43(4): 554–76.

Wessely, S., Buchanan, A., Reed, A., Cutting, J., Everitt, B., Garety, P. and Taylor, P.J. (1993) 'Acting on delusions. I: Prevalence', *The British Journal of Psychiatry*, 163(1): 69–76.

Westbrook, D., Kennerley, H. and Kirk, J. (2011) *An Introduction to Cognitive Behaviour Therapy*. London: Sage.

Whittington, A. and Grey, N. (2014) *How to become a More Effective CBT Therapist: Mastering Metacompetence in Clinical Practice*. Chichester, West Sussex: Wiley.

Wiles, N., Thomas, L., Abel, A., Ridgway, N., Turner, N., Campbell, J., Garland, A., Hollinghurst, S., Jerrom, B., Kessler, D., Kuyken, W., Morrison, J., Turner, K., Williams, C., Peters, T., Lewis, G. (2013) 'Cognitive behavioural therapy as an adjunct to pharmacotherapy for primary care based patients with treatment resistant depression: Results of the CoBalT randomised controlled trial', *Lancet*, 381: 375–84.

Wilhelm, S. and Steketee, G.S. (2006) *Cognitive Therapy for Obsessive Compulsive Disorder: A Guide for Professionals*. Oakland, CA: New Harbinger Publications.

Williams, A., Eccleston, C. and Morley, S. (2012) *Psychological Therapies for the Management of Chronic Pain (excluding headaches) in Adults. Cochrane Database of Systematic Reviews*. Issue 11.

Williams, C.J. and Garland, A. (2002) 'A cognitive-behavioural therapy assessment model for use in everyday clinical practice', *Advances in Psychiatric Treatment*, 8: 172–9.

Williams, H., Edgerton, N. and Palmer, S. (2010) 'Cognitive behavioural coaching', in E. Cox, T. Bachkirova and D. Clutterbuck (eds), *The Complete Handbook of Coaching*. London: Sage. pp. 37–53.

Williams, J.M.G., Teasdale, J.D., Segal, Z.V. and Soulsby, J. (2000) 'Mindfulness-based cognitive therapy reduces overgeneral autobiographical memory in formerly depressed patients', *Journal of Abnormal Psychology*, 109: 150–5.

Williams, K.E. and Chambless, D.L. (1990) 'The relationship between therapist characteristics and outcome of *in vivo* exposure treatment for agoraphobia', *Behavior Therapy*, 21: 111–16.

Wolfgang, G.J. (2001) 'Cultural factors in psychiatric disorders'. Paper presented at the 26th World Congress of the World Federation for Mental Health, July.

World Health Organization (1993) *The ICD-10 Classification of Mental and Behavioural Disorders: Clinical Descriptions and Diagnostic Guidelines*. Geneva, Switzerland: World Health Organization.

World Health Organization (2002) *International Classification of Disease, Mental and Behavioural Problems Version 10*. Geneva, Switzerland: World Health Organization.

World Health Organization (2006) *WHOSIS*. Available at: www3.who.int/icd/currentversion/fr-icd.htm/. Accessed 18 September 2006.

World Health Organization (in preparation) *The International Classification of Diseases (11th revision)*. Geneva, Switzerland: World Health Organization.

Wykes, T., Steel, C., Everitt, B., and Tarrier, N. (2008) 'Cognitive behavior therapy for schizophrenia: Effect sizes, clinical models, and methodological rigor', *Schizophrenia Bulletin*, 34(3): 523–37.

Young, J.E. (1988) *Young Schema-Questionnaire Short Form*. New York: Cognitive Therapy Centre.

Young, J.E. (1990) *Cognitive Therapy for Personality Disorders: A Schema-Focused Approach*. 3rd edn. Saraosta, FL: Professional Resource Exchange.

Young J.E., Klosko J.S. and Weishaar, M.E. (2003) *Schema Therapy: A Practitioner's Guide*. New York: Guilford Press.

Zanarini M.C., Gunderson, J.G., Marino, M.F., Schwartz, E.O. and Frankenburg, F.R. (1989) 'Childhood experiences of borderline patients', *Comprehensive Psychiatry*, 30(1): 18–25.

Zanarini, M.C., Frankenburg, F.R., Reich, D.B. and Fitzmaurice, G. (2012) 'Attainment and stability of sustained symptomatic remission and recovery among patients with Borderline Personality Disorder and Axis II Comparison Subjects: a 16-year prospective follow-up study', *American Journal of Psychiatry*, 169: 476–83.

Zigmond, A.S. and Snaith, R.P. (1983) 'The hospital anxiety and depression scale', *Acta Psychiatrica Scandinavica*, 67: 361–70.

Zivor, M., Salkovskis, P.M. and Oldfield, V.B. (2013) 'If formulation is the heart of cognitive behavioural therapy, does this heart rule the head of CBT therapists?', *The Cognitive Behaviour Therapist*, 6(e6): 1–11.

Index

Note: Page numbers in *italics* indicate figures and tables.